Ethics from a Theocentric Perspective

James M. Gustafson

Ethics from a Theocentric Perspective

VOLUME TWO
Ethics and Theology

The University of Chicago Press

Chicago and London

The University of Chicago Press, Chicago 60637
The University of Chicago Press, Ltd., London

Paperback edition 1992
Printed in the United States of America
93 92 5432

Library of Congress Cataloging in Publication Data
Gustafson, James M.
Ethics from a theocentric perspective.

Includes bibliographical references and indexes. Contents: v.
1. Theology and ethics–v. 2. Ethics and theology.
1. Christian ethics. 2. Ethics. I. Title.
BJ1251.G876 241 81-11603
ISBN 0-226-31112-0 (cloth)
ISBN 0-226-31113-9 (paper)

∞ The paper used in this publication meets the minimum requirements of the American National Standard for Information Sciences–Permanence of Paper for Printed Library Materials, ANSI Z39.48–1984

For Elmer W. Johnson

Contents

Preface

A number of reviews of volume 1 of this work appeared before I completed the manuscript for volume 2. I have not responded to them here, nor have they deterred me from following the course I have taken.

Among the persons and institutions that have given me special reasons for gratitude are the following.

Elmer W. Johnson, now an executive in a major American corporation, who again provided ideal conditions in which to work and showed great interest in the development of my work.

Mary Ann Minelli, Joyce Yurko, Lola Kaduskiewicz, and Heather Stanford, each of whom typed portions of the manuscript. To Joyce Yurko I give special thanks for pleasant and efficient facilitation of various phases of the production of this volume.

The following institutions which invited me to prepare papers and lectures that contributed to the arguments of this volume:

The University of Nebraska, Lincoln: an Atkinson Lecture, "The Place of Man in the Universe: A Critique of Theology and Ethics."

The University of Santa Clara, Department of Philosophy: a paper, "Nature: Its Status in Theological Ethics."

The Smithsonian Institution: an essay, "Ethical Issues in the Human Future," for its seventh international symposium, "How Humans Adapt: A Biocultural Odyssey."

The Community of Atonement Friars and the Catholic University of America: a Paul Wattson Lecture, "Ecumenism and Ethical Methodology: The Theological Choice."

The University of Chicago: the eighth annual Ryerson Lecture, "'Say Something Theological!'"

Knox College, Toronto: Laidlaw Lectures derived from a draft of this volume.

The theological faculties of the University of Aarhus and the University of Copenhagen in Denmark, the University of Lund and the University of Uppsala in Sweden, and the Åbo Academy and the University of Helsinki in Finland: lectures and seminars which enabled me to get some European responses to my work. Lars and Anne-Marie Thunberg of Ebeltoft, Denmark, friends and intellectual comrades for many years, arranged the Nordic trip and extended especially warm hospitality.

Union Theological Seminary, Richmond, Virginia: the James Sprunt Lectures. The invitation of its faculty in 1978 to deliver these lectures in 1983 provided the major impetus to undertake this project at this point in my career. President T. Hartley Hall, the faculty (especially Charles Swezey), and the assembled auditors did not disappoint me. The hospitality was marvelous and the discussions were lively.

On all of these occasions, and on others less formal, my ideas were respectfully heard and taken seriously by audiences that were not disposed to agree with many of them.

The University of Chicago, for granting me another research leave of absence.

Stephen S. Bowen, for the most persistent, helpful, and detailed critical responses I received from manuscript readers during the course of writing, for very careful reading of it upon completion, and for steadfast personal friendship.

Margaret Farley, R.S.M., for intensive and extensive comments on the manuscript and for correspondence which led to some important clarifications and also to greater precision about our agreements and differences.

David Tracy, for comments which might lead to subsequent writing based on both volumes.

Charles Reynolds and Lisa S. Cahill, for their reviews of the manuscript. Cahill's extensive response proves that one's former student can be a very penetrating critic. My rejection of Reynolds's proposal that I write a third volume should relieve my readers.

Dr. Clifford W. Gurney, for reading and commenting on chapter 8.

I have carefully attended to all the comments, though I have not accepted many of the suggestions made.

Robin W. Lovin, for again relieving me of some of my academic responsibilities, and Lois Daly for attentive proofreading and editorial comments.

Louise, who, as always, provided sustaining companionship.

1

Theocentric Ethics in Profile

In the first volume of this work the principle concern was theological. The dominant concepts and most of the crucial literature used were theological. A theocentric perspective was developed in its course. In this volume the principal concern is ethical. Concepts and terms of ethical thought replace those of theology as dominant. Ethical literature is used primarily. It is the task of this volume to develop a coherent view of morality that follows from the theocentric perspective. The basic question can be put quite simply: What difference does a theocentric perspective make in the interpretation of morality? How does it affect the choice and use of ethical concepts? In the first volume I analyzed how different theological concepts arose to primacy from different theological perspectives, and how the ordering of the importance of concepts varied as a result of the perspective. In this volume I shall show how some reordering of values and ethical concepts is required in comparison with some other perspectives in both philosophy and theology. The reordering is grounded in an understanding of human experience from a theocentric perspective; it is not simply an enterprise of theoretical reason, drawing logical deductions from a different set of premises.

I pursue the objective of this volume by drawing a profile of the distinctive features of theocentric ethics and then using ethical writings of some theologians and philosophers as benchmarks to show how and why theocentric ethics is dissimilar or similar to their work. Subsequently I address four areas of moral activity to see what conclusions about some specific moral and social issues can be drawn from theocentric ethics, how general or precise those conclusions are, and how one proceeds to arrive at a choice, or at a a judgment about a choice made by others. (Recall the last chapter of volume 1, on discernment.) I have deliberately chosen not to deal with a large number of issues; rather I have selected four which I am more competent to explore in some depth and breadth. These, I believe, can function as analogues for the reader; one can see how other issues can be addressed in similar ways.

The theocentric perspective requires that the practical moral question be asked as follows: What is God enabling and requiring us to be and to do? God: the ultimate ordering power in the universe, the divine governance. Enabling: this term is important for recognizing that the occasions for activity and the capacities for action arise "prior" to human interventions and choices. The conditions for possibilities are given by the divine governance. It also opens the door to ethics of "aspiration" as well as "obligation." Requiring: this term is used not simply because ethics is a prescriptive enterprise, involving obligations and duties. The divine governance "demands" some conformity to it; failure to consent to these demands is perilous both to human well-being and to "nature." The "content" of what we are to be and to do is grounded in part in requisites of the divine governance. Us: moral activity is engaged in not only by individuals facing choices in a restricted set of circumstances but by communities collectively making choices and engaging in actions. To be: the divine governance enables us *to be* certain kinds of persons and certain kinds of communities; it requires qualities of our being as individuals and collectivities. This is so not only because "doing" follows from "being" in important respects but also because certain qualities of individual life and states of affairs in communities display an appropriate ordering of life. To do: life is activity; it is the exercise of powers and capacities. Morality pertains to actions, individual and collective, as well as to qualities of individuals and states of affairs.

The general answer to the moral question from a theocentric perspective is: we are to relate ourselves and all things in a manner (or in ways) appropriate to their relations to God. We are enabled to do this; we are required to do this. The basic "substance" or "content" of morality from a theocentric perspective must be derived from our most adequate perception and conception of the relations that are appropriate for ourselves and for other things to the ultimate power and orderer of life. As was made clear in volume 1, the practical intellectual task is not to develop ethics in the light of anthropocentric concerns, and then find theological principles that justify those concerns. Rather a major portion of the task is to discern the proper relations of things to each other, of parts to various wholes, in the light of what we understand the divine governance to be in the various conditions set by human finitude. This involves the relations of human activity to the wider realm of nature of which it is a part, as well as interhuman relations and activity.

Although I am more concerned with our "being" than are some ethicians, both theological and philosophical, it is important to establish a basic description of human action that is assumed throughout this volume. That description is relatively noncontroversial; what distinguishes my use of it is the conviction that there are seldom actions that are "purely" moral; rather, the moral is an aspect or a dimension of actions that can be denominated by other adjectives: political, economic, medical, sexual, military, and so forth. My description of action is as follows: Agents (individually and/or collectively) exercise capacities or powers (or deliberately refrain from exercising them) in accordance with purposes (principles, rules, aspirations, goals, and values) in order to alter (or restrain alteration of) a course of events or a state of affairs.

All the aspects of this description are qualified from a theocentric perspective, though some of the qualifications are more ethically significant than others. An interpretation of man in relation to God and the world is spelled out in chapter 6 of volume 1. Other aspects are also interpreted from a theocentric perspective in that volume, though not precisely according to this description. For example, our capacities and the powers available to us were shown to be dependent upon "forces" we do not create or fully control.

It is with reference to purposes that a theocentric perspective makes the greatest difference to moral activity; this aspect is developed much more fully in this volume. The agenda of this volume requires more specific attention to interpretations of courses of events and states of affairs than was developed in volume 1.

At many places in the first volume there were indications of qualifications that a theocentric perspective makes of moral life and ethical thought. In chapter 2 I specifically raised the question whether theocentric ethics was ethics at all in the terms that dominate both the theological and philosophical traditions in the West. In chapter 7 various indications of the theocentric qualification were drawn together in the development of the idea of discernment. Ethics, as I indicated in the introduction, is the primary focus of concentration of this volume; the entire volume seeks to fulfill a general purpose by answering a single general question: How does the theocentric perspective qualify ethics? This question requires elaboration and some distinctions that are not apparent in its most general form. It includes both a concern for the life, the being, of the moral agent and the action-guides that direct conduct. It includes a concern both for individuals and for communities, and thus does not separate ethics and "politics" as sharply as most philosophical literature does.[1] Thus one form that the general question takes is: How does the piety evoked by the powers that bear down upon us and sustain us qualify moral life? Included in "moral life" are our basic postures toward the world of which we are a part, our dispositions toward the others with whom we interact, as well as our reflections on what we should do and our actions that seek to fulfill purposes. I am concerned to develop how theocentric piety qualifies the life of moral agents and communities.

I am also concerned to show the qualifications that theology makes of ethical thought. Ethical thought and moral life, obviously, are related. The distinction is a practical one, but the general question is meant to include the relations of the theology developed in volume 1 to ethics as a pattern of ideas. And ethics includes both a descriptive-analytical aspect and a normative, or prescriptive, aspect. Thus the general question can take this form: How do the ideas about God and God's relations to the arenas in which we live and act qualify our valuations of things? What values, principles of conduct, ideals and aspirations, and rules are grounded in, backed by, or based upon our understanding of God and God's relation to the world?

This chapter draws a *profile* of the ethics that follow from volume 1 to make clear some of its distinctive features. This should give the reader his or her bearings by indicating some of the issues about which I have made

1. See, for example, Henry Sidgwick, *The Methods of Ethics*, 7th ed. (reprint, Indianapolis: Hackett Publishing Co., 1981), p. 15. "Ethics aims at determining what ought to be done by individuals, while Politics aims at determining what the government of a state or political society ought to do."

critical judgments. In this chapter I do not develop those judgments as fully as I do in the following chapters.

Chapters 2 and 3 consist of further elaboration and justification of some of the distinctive features of theocentric ethics. This is done by relating the argument more explicitly and comprehensively to some important positions in both Christian theological ethics and in moral philosophy. In this way the profile is fleshed out in more detail, and readers can make more specific assessments. Chapter 4 is a brief transition to the remaining chapters in which I address the areas of marriage and family, suicide, population and nutrition, the allocation of biomedical research funding, and then draw the whole project to some conclusions. The conclusions do not have the tight logical consistency of, for examples, the admirable works of my colleagues Alan Gewirth and Alan Donagan.[2] Indeed, there are important reasons that follow from the theocentric perspective which do not warrant the same formal logical consistency of these and similar works in moral philosophy. I am certain that my project would be developed more rigorously if I were a better philosopher, but I am equally certain that some fundamental assumptions made and defended by many moral philosophers cannot be sustained on the basis of the theology I have delineated.

The Profile

The most critical difference between ethics as I develop it and most Western ethics is the theocentric focus as such. Man—individual human beings, human communities, and the human species—is not the ultimate center of value. This moral difference follows from the redescription of the place of man in the universe, and of man in relation to the divine powers and ordering that is given in volume 1.

I believe that every ethical theory rests in part on some implied or explicit descriptive premises if it establishes any substantive moral norms. These premises affect both the form and the content of any ethics. If the theory prescribes only formal consistency, such as the principle of universalizability, without making judgments about specific ends, the "is-ought" or "fact-value" problem can be avoided. Perhaps, however, even the formalistic theories of ethics make some assumptions about how certain things "really are." What the theologian or philosopher chooses to be the adequate descriptive premises for the development of a moral theory is critical.

Alan Gewirth, for example, develops with exceedingly great care the *generic* features of human action; these are "voluntariness or freedom and purposiveness or intentionality."[3] These features are the necessary condi-

2. Alan Gewirth, *Reason and Morality* (Chicago: University of Chicago Press, 1978), and Alan Donagan, *The Theory of Morality* (Chicago: University of Chicago Press, 1977).

3. Gewirth, *Reason and Morality*, p. 27.

tions for moral action. On the basis of this description it follows necessarily, for him, that every agent

> [n]egatively, . . . ought to refrain from coercing and harming his recipients; positively, he ought to assist them to have freedom and well-being whenever they cannot otherwise have these necessary goods and he can help them at no comparable cost to himself. The general principle of these obligations and rights may be expressed as the following precept addressed to every agent: *Act in accord with the generic rights of your recipients as well as of yourself.*[4]

The description of the generic features of action grounds certain rights—to freedom and to pursuing one's well-being. To fail to acknowledge these rights in oneself and in others is to be self-contradictory. Utilitarians obviously have a different description which grounds different principles and ends of action. Augustine is like the utilitarians in that his description of man is one of a creature with desires for happiness or fulfillment, but the context in which he describes the ends of human aspiration and desires is very different.[5] My basic point is that the descriptive premises are critical to how prescriptive, or normative, ethics are developed.

The description is not selected and developed arbitrarily. Insofar as the description can be called a "belief," the argument among moralists, philosophical and theological, concerns what constitutes true, or at least adequate, beliefs. If the description is incorrect, i.e., if the beliefs are false, the prescriptive ethics are also wrong. If, for example, Freud's beliefs about the proper explanation of human activity are correct, Kant's prescriptive ethics are wrong.

Another reasoned choice that is made in rendering a description concerns what constitutes the moral, as distinguished from the nonmoral. If the generic features of action isolate the moral, then other features such as a person's roles in society, while they have to be taken into account in the application of the supreme moral principle, are not of equal significance. Roles do not describe generic features of action, and thus their relevance to the moral is qualified.

Part of the argument of volume 1 is that in the Western moral tradition there are descriptions of man which, because of the distinctive features of human life, place man at the center of all valuation, or as the ultimate value, and see all things in the service of man. The theological construal of the world that I have proposed fundamentally alters this view. It follows from that construal that there are occasions or circumstances in which a course of action that is apparently beneficial to the well-being of individuals or communities is not necessarily the right thing to be done.

4. Ibid., p. 135.

5. James M. Gustafson, *Ethics from a Theocentric Perspective* 2 vols. (Chicago: University of Chicago Press, 1981), 1:171–72.

As I made clear in volume 1, chapter 2, to interpret human life in theocentric terms is not necessarily to affirm that the well-being of some "whole" of which individuals, communities, or the species is a part always takes precedence over the individual, a community, or the human species. The theocentric perspective does not on every occasion for human activity subvert the common morality as we know it in Western culture, though frequently its presses us to raise the question of the place of man with greater force. As I pointed out in that chapter, I am cognizant of the perils to cherished and defensible human values that the theocentric construal might create.

Thus, while man is interpreted in the context of larger patterns of interdependence, the value of the human is not necessarily subordinated to some judgment about the well-being of the wider natural order, nor is the individual necessarily subordinated to the group. The value, however, may be altered or qualified in the light of the theocentric construal, and obligations to restrain and even "sacrifice" human interests and ends are more likely to be defended.

Certainly man is the focus of attention in the ethical enterprise, even when man is not the only or highest value to be considered. I cannot think of a definition of ethics that would not be in substantial agreement with Henry Sidgwick's. "I prefer to consider Ethics as the science or study of what is right or what ought to be, so far as this depends upon the voluntary action of individuals."[6] My own qualification of this, as I noted earlier, would not differentiate corporate activity from individual activity as sharply, though the distinction is warranted. Sidgwick also believed that ethics ought to deal with what is good for man: "the primary subject of ethical investigation is all that is included under the notion of what is ultimately good or desirable for man."[7] What is nicely unspecified by the first quotation, however, is: "Right" in relation to whom and what? and "Ought to be" for whom and for what? We write ethics for human beings and not for animals and trees and not for God. To alter the place of value that the human has had in much of ethical thought and in human activity is not to say that ethics is not addressed to human beings as those creatures who have the capacity to act. To say that human beings are part of a whole that is governed by the divine ordering, since that divine ordering is not interpreted to mean the rigid metaphysical determinism of some classic theological and philosophical traditions, is not to demean the importance of human activity, and thus the practical importance of ethics. The task, however, is to serve God; human values are set in the context of more inclusive divine purposes.

The patterns of interdependence and development within which hu-

6. Sidgwick, *Methods*, p. 4.

7. Henry Sidgwick, *Outlines of the History of Ethics for English Readers* 6th ed. (reprint, London: Macmillan, 1949), p. 2.

man activity and life occur become a basis, ground, or foundation for ethics from a theocentric perspective. This is the second feature. In volume 1 I indicated some of the difficulties involved in discerning what that ordering is, and what human activities are proper in relation to it. Indeed, the "will of God," and "nature" as a basis for ethics have been widely discredited in moral philosophy. To argue that the divine ordering is known by revelation is to appeal to a "private" source of knowledge the authorization of which is dependent upon uncritical subjective or historically relative factors. If it is to be known by "reason," a host of epistemological and metaphysical issues are raised that are, to put it mildly, quite disputed. The concept of nature and its status are not matters on which philosophers of science, theologians, and others are in agreement. The theocentric perspective rests on grounds developed in volume 1, and functions in its more specifically theological statements as beliefs about the ultimate power and powers that created, sustain, order, and make possible the conditions for life. The argument was not made to establish a necessary basis for ethics, but rather because it has merit in itself. Thus given its (controversial, to be sure) status as an adequate belief about God and God's relations to the world, which is to say a belief about some the most important features of life as they really are, the ethics necessarily must be based upon, grounded in, authorized, or backed by those beliefs.

The enterprise is fraught with theological and philosophical difficulties. The religious convictions that underlie the claim for the importance of theology per se, and especially for the theology I developed, make confrontation of these difficulties necessary. Kant, in the precritical ethics, makes some very cogent remarks that are pertinent here, though his constructive response to them is different from my own. "The purposes of the Godhead must be determined by God."[8] It is hard to conceive how any theologian would argue against that, though many Christians act as if the purposes of God should be determined by human beings. But can they be known?

> The ways of God are the divine intentions which determine the government of the world. We should not seek to define these in detail; we must be content to judge *generaliter* that therein holiness and righteousness bear rule. It is presumptuous to attempt to particularize the ways of God, to try to define His intentions.[9]

It is presumptuous, indeed, and as I argued in volume 1 theologians have often erred in saying too much about the ways of God with excessive certainty, and now in reaction to that error frequently do not say enough.[10]

8. Immanuel Kant, *Lectures on Ethics*, trans. Louis Infield (New York and Evanston: Harper and Row, 1963), p. 96.
9. Ibid., p. 94.
10. Gustafson, *Ethics*, 1:31–62.

But part of the experience that leads to the theological conviction of an ultimately sovereign God is our human dependence upon, interdependence with, and participation in an ordering of nature and other aspects of human life which are beyond ultimate human control. Those patterns of dependence and interdependence can, at least provisionally, be described on the basis of evidences from various sciences, and from human experience. Such a belief is warranted, and thus proper human ends and right relations have to be determined in part by these patterns. Indications are given by these patterns of interrelationship of the right ordering of the human beings and actions to the wider natural world, of society, culture, and history, and even of aspects of our individual persons. The "ways" of "nature" are indicators of the ways of God, and inferences are drawn from them to aid human beings to discern how they and all things are to be related to each other in a manner appropriate to their relations to God.

Not only are there the perennial difficulties in justifying those indications, particularly as indications of the divine ordering. Account must also be taken of modern theories of how nature is developing, and particularly of how modern science and technology enlarge the scope and effects of human participation in that ordering. But if the theocentric perspective is defensible, and if the interpretations of the divine ordering in and through patterns of dependence and interdependence are adequate, ethical thought has to be based upon, grounded in, and authorized or backed by critically established descriptions of that ordering. The determination of right action, proper ends, and fitting aspirations for human activity—the subject matter of ethics, that is—has objective referents in this objective ordering of all life. The second feature of the profile, then, is that moral values, principles, ends, and duties are grounded in an objective "reality" of which human life is a part.

The third feature of the profile is related to the second. Rather than perceiving the moral primarily to stand over against the natural and the historical, as an alien force, moral thinking gives direction to our natural impulses and desires as individuals within the context of the arenas of life in which we act.[11] Similarly, in dealing with institutions and policies, moral reasoning attempts to give guidance to the exercise of various forms of power that are occurring. Mary Midgley is correct to point out that the exercise of reason in morality has often been understood to be basically opposed to natural inclinations, to feelings and desires.[12] Moral action involves the ordering and directing of existing powers in accordance with moral principles, values, ends, and ideals. It gives direction to our natural drives for sustenance and sexuality, for example. This does not imply that

11. See ibid., pp. 284–87, for a discussion of man as a valuing animal.
12. Mary Midgley, *Beast and Man* (Ithaca: Cornell University Press, 1978), pp. 256ff.

we do not use reason in some circumstances to restrain our natural drives, but even when we do it is nature that is being ordered and directed by rational activity.

Similarly in matters of social morality and policy, we are not privileged to begin *de novo* except as an exercise in ideal moral thinking or in abstract reflection on concepts, their uses, and their relations to each other. Rather, social ethics is a matter of addressing existing institutions and policies, which have various degrees of intransigence or pliability, so that the events that they affect take a morally approvable course. Social moral action directs powers that already exist, or it seeks powers in the name of some social and moral ends in order to affect future events now dominated by others. Even utopian thought, if it is to be more than a literary exercise, must evoke the sentiments and powers of persons in order to affect social change. And when it does so, it is injected into an already existing course of events with the suppressions and injustices that occur in present arrangements. If it is of a revolutionary sort, it appeals to the sentiments and unrest that are present in portions of a given population. To be sure, prophets and utopians can make us conscious of the evils of the world as it is, but even that is to reshape existing social forces and desires.

This feature best distinguishes theocentric ethics from the most rationalistic moral philosophies. It marks its kinship in the Christian tradition with classic natural-law theories which begin with perceptions and interpretations of human inclinations toward what persons grasp as ends that serve good purposes. It marks its kinship with the theological anthropology of those who see great continuity between desires, affections, volition, and rational activity. Care must be taken in developing this feature, since it can too readily fall into a rationalization for desires and interests of both individuals and human communities. It might seem to deny the prophetic impulses in the religious tradition to take a stand over against a whole way of life, or a whole system of social ordering. The prophetic distancing of the moralist from persons and institutions is not impossible within theocentric ethics, but theocentric ethics always takes more cognizance of the need to affect presently existing personal valuations and social institutions, and how they can be redirected toward more appropriate ends. The temptation is to lapse into tunnel vision, but that is a temptation and not a necessity.

The fourth feature of the profile is the consequences of piety for moral life. The experience of the ultimate power and of powers bearing down upon, sustaining, and creating possibilities for action induces or evokes piety.[13] Ethics from a theocentric perspective is religious ethics not only in the sense that ethical thought is grounded in beliefs about God and God's relations to the world, but also in the sense that the human community lives

13. See Gustafson, *Ethics*, 1:201–4 and elsewhere.

in part by those senses of dependence, gratitude, obligation, remorse and repentance, direction, and hope that are fundamental religious affections.[14]

Biblical morality and the morality of Judaism and Christianity have been fundamentally correct in their interpretations of the importance of the human disposition or posture toward God for proper attitudes or dispositions toward other persons, toward human communities, and toward the natural world of which we are part. This aspect of moral life is consistently underrated in its importance by moral philosophers who develop more rationalistic models for the conduct of human life.

It is, for example, one thing to judge moral failures in the light of a universalizable principle that persons are not to be treated simply as means to ends. Actions which violate the principle can be described, and a moral indictment can be made of their failure to conform to the principle. It is, however, another thing to see that treating persons simply as means to ends is a matter of a flawed disposition, or of what is often described in modern literature as a technical mentality: a lack of an aura of respect for others. The solution to the first diagnosis is almost purely rational; the solution to the second requires that attention be given to deeply affective aspects of moral agents. Of course, a more proper disposition is not sufficient to issue in proper relations to other persons; to argue for the import of affectivity and dispositions is not to leave out of account rational activity in the determination of conduct. And, to be sure, there have been philosophers who have accented the importance of feelings, of moral sense, and other designations of affective dimensions in their accounts of morality. But the theocentric perspective, as it arises out of the religious dimensions of experience, profoundly affects the more "subjective" aspects of human agency. Morality has profoundly religious dimensions.[15]

Piety and the attitudes and dispositions that it evokes and sustains are important features of morality in a theocentric perspective. To use ancient religious symbols, morality is a matter of the heart as well as the mind. The

14. Ibid., pp. 129–36.

15. How these dimensions are to be symbolized or articulated is a matter on which various writers have commented. Gibson Winter, working from different theological and philosophical materials than I, has recently proposed a very worthy metaphor, namely, an "artistic" one that views humanity as "dwelling" in the world. The more aesthetic features of Winter's religious moral response have great affinity with some of my proposals. His argument identifies two root metaphors that dominate our culture, the organic and the technical. He proposes no simple discarding of either of these in his symbolization of what modern culture needs as a more adequate root metaphor. Working, however, from a carefully developed framework of phenomenology and hermeneutics, he proposes that the symbol of dwelling best accounts for human sociality, temporality, and historicity, and for the religious dimensions of social ethics. The more adequate analogy for proper human living and activity is not that of the organism or of the machine, but that of artistic life. The merit of Winter's proposal is considerable, for it does capture a great deal of the religious dimension of moral experience, and also leads to some proposals about the general lines of ethics that follow from it. Gibson Winter, *Liberating Creation: Foundations of Religious Social Ethics* (New York: Crossroad, 1981).

consequences for moral activity are several, and they will depend in part on how the powers that evoke piety are construed. From my perspective, one consequence that has some distinctiveness from some current ethics is the importance of humility as an attitude. Another is the readiness to deny one's own interests for the sake of the well-being of others, or of particular "wholes" of which individuals and communities are a part. While there is a proper respect for self and duties to oneself that are necessary conditions for acting on behalf of others, to view human life in the service of God may mean that agents are both enabled and required to act for the well-being of others at great cost to themselves.[16] Because historic theocentric interpretations of the moral life have viewed human activity in the service of the large purposes of the divine ordering, they have not been able to draw the line between acts of obligation and acts of supererogation in the way that many moral philosophers have done.[17] It is a distinctive feature of theocentric ethics to hold piety and morality together; it is a perversion when piety becomes separated from morality as if God were concerned primarily for the salvation of the individual and not the ordering of the creation, and when morality gets separated from piety, as if moral activity were independent of the wellsprings of the human spirit in both their commendable and perverse forms.

A fifth feature of the profile is that ethics from a theocentric perspective requires a description of individuals, communities, events, the species, and other things in the context of large wholes. In volume 1 I made the point that one of the critical choices made by writers of ethics was that of the evaluative description or descriptive evaluation of the context of human life and activity.[18] Here I shall show how a larger descriptive context distinguishes my work from some others.

What is the "unit" that is judged to be the sufficient focus of attention in ethical thinking? If we embellish this question, some of the options will become clear. Does the individual agent act upon a discrete "recipient"?[19] If the focus of attention is on a discrete individual agent engaged in a particular

16. Compare Gewirth's statements, "[The agent] ought to assist [his recipients] whenever they cannot have these necessary goals *and he can help them at no comparable cost to himself.*" *Reason and Morality*, p. 135 et passim. Italics are mine.

17. The recent Anglo-American philosophical discussion has been stimulated by J. O. Ursom, "Saints and Heroes," reprinted in A. I. Melden, ed., *Essays in Moral Philosophy* (Seattle: Washington University Press, 1958), pp. 198–216, and Joel Feinberg, "Supererogation and Rules," reprinted in Feinberg, *Doing and Deserving* (Princeton: Princeton University Press, 1980), pp. 3–24. For extended discussions, see Millard Schumaker, *Supererogation: An Analysis and a Bibliography*, (Edmonton, Alberta: St. Stephen's College, 1977), and William R. St. John, "Supererogation: Some Theological Perspectives" (Ph.D. diss., University of Chicago, 1983).

18. Gustafson, *Ethics*, 1:333–37, and elsewhere.

19. See Gewirth, *Reason and Morality*, pp. 129–31. Gewirth uses the plural, recipients. "Both the agent and his recipients *participate* in transactions, although the former does so actively and the latter passively . . . " (p. 129). His preference for the term "transaction" rather than "interaction" is carefully justified.

act, there are two possible explanations for that choice. Either the determination of what constitutes the moral, something argued for and not arbitrary, determines in turn the scope of the "whole" to be taken into account as relevant, or a descriptive anthropology expresses the understanding and belief that a more individualistic interpretation of social reality is correct. I have argued that an interactional model for interpreting human life and activity is more adequate than either the individualistically oriented contractarian model or a more literal use of the organic model.[20] Interaction of persons and communities with each other, and (at least metaphorically) of humans with the natural world of which they are a part is the more adequate term. Alan Gewirth is correct, of course, to claim that individual "transactions" do occur, and that any larger pattern of interactions consists of particular transactions that can be described. The focus of attention on a larger whole, however, makes a difference in how ethics is developed.

One effect is to enlarge the considerations that are relevant for moral life and particular moral choices and judgment. H. Richard Niebuhr was correct to emphasize the importance of interpretation of the context of action in the development of his model of response and responsibility.[21] While the immediate focus of attention is very specific and discrete, how one understands the specific and discrete individual or the event in which one is acting is qualified if it is seen in a larger pattern of interactions or of causal relationships. As Niebuhr argues, the interpretation involves an anticipation of possible responses and long-range consequences to any initiative that the agent takes. Certainly, in most circumstances, the interpreting agent can assess only the *probability* of anticipated responses and consequences, but he or she does attempt to see beyond the immediate relationships and events and to anticipate the kinds of actions the immediate "recipients" will take in response to the initiative.

The interactional model follows from the theology developed in volume 1. If the divine power and powers are, in some sense, providing the conditions of possibility of human action and the ultimate ordering of the creation, the larger context in which individual acts and events take place must be taken into account in morality. Not only do the patterns of relationships ascend in importance as indications of what relationships are right or wrong and what ends of action are good or bad, but also the importance of assessing probable wider and longer-range responses and consequences becomes greater in the determination of particular initiatives. Individuals (including social collectives as "individuals") are the agents, but when they are viewed in the context of interactions in larger wholes there is a qualification of their discrete acts.

20. Gustafson, *Ethics*, 1:292–93.

21. H. Richard Niebuhr, *The Responsible Self: An Essay in Christian Moral Philosophy* (New York: Harper and Row, 1963), pp. 61–63, et passim.

I used the term "participant" to refer to human agents in volume 1, but I did not stress it. It does, however, encapsulate better than alternative terms how I believe the human venture is to be understood. The human venture is participation.[22] Agents are participating not only in "transactions" with the immediate "recipients" of their initiatives; they are participants in larger spheres of interaction, and even in the development of the natural world. When we attend to participation in interaction within wholes, we acknowledge the prior reality of the arenas of activity to which persons and institutions respond and exaggerated notions of human creativity (as if we somehow created the worlds of which we are a part *ex nihilo*) are avoided. Participants in interaction, however, are not mere spectators, nor do they simply react to external stimuli as our eyes react to a blazing midday sun. They have capacities for innovation, intervention, and intentional action that do affect courses of events and states of affairs. Thus, to be a participant is to claim far more for human capacities of self-determination and the determination of courses of events and states of affairs than to be a "reactor" or even a "responder." Yet such a claim avoids the language of "creativity" and of man being a co-creator with God, which Karl Rahner seems to suggest.[23] To reiterate the main point here, a proper understanding of ourselves and of our participation requires that we have in view a broader context of interactions than is central to some other versions of ethics, both theological and philosophical. It is congenial to Gibson Winter's proposed metaphor of "dwelling" in the world, if that is not understood in its possible passive interpretations.

The interpretation of individuals and communities as *interacting* and *participating* within the context of larger wholes is not the only significant feature of a reconsideration of the relationships of parts to wholes. It follows from the "objective ethics" implied by the theocentric perspective that the determination of right relationships between entities and of the proper ends of human participation must take into account larger wholes of which individual entities are a part. In volume 1 I indicated my tempered agreement with Mary Midgley's suggestion that the language of part and whole needs to become more central to our thinking.[24] To take this turn, however,

22. See Gustafson, "Ethical Issues in the Human Future," in Donald J. Ortner, ed., *How Humans Adapt: A Biocultural Odyssey* (Washington, D.C.: Smithsonian Press, 1983), pp. 491–504. Stephen Toulmin develops the significance of participation in science. See Toulmin, *The Return of Cosmology: Postmodern Science and the Theology of Nature* (Los Angeles and Berkeley: University of California Press, 1982), pp. 217–74.

23. The kind of language used by Rahner that suggests the notion of co-creator comes in some of his discussions of human freedom. For example, "In contradistinction to 'things' which are always complete and which are moved from one mode of completion to another and thus are at the same time always in a final state and yet never ultimate, man begins his existence as the being who is radically open and incomplete. When his essence *is* complete it is as he himself has freely created it." Karl Rahner, "The Experiment with Man," in *Theological Investigations*, vol. 9, trans. Graham Harrison (New York: Herder and Herder, 1972), p. 213.

24. Gustafson, *Ethics*, 1:342.

is to face difficulties of both thought and practice, as I have taken pains to anticipate.[25]

It is not difficult to defend an argument that in order to explain any particular entity to which we attend we must take account of a larger whole of which the entity is a part. No explanation of why an individual person has certain preferences of value can avoid taking into account not only the biological drives of that individual but also the social and cultural milieus in which he or she lives. Any explanation of a particularly nettlesome international situation, such as the perennial eruptions of violence in the Middle East, must take into account historical factors of political, economic, and religious sorts, as well as the sequence of particular crises such as the Holocaust and the 1948 War. Many of the sciences provide explanations of fundamental importance for the emergence of our planet and the development of life, particularly human life. One does not have to be a genetic determinist to appreciate the importance of genetic bases of particular qualities of human life, both admirable and disruptive from normative points of view. Entities that become foci of attention are parts of larger wholes, and an adequate explanation of their existence and of their activities requires that the relations of the whole to the parts be delineated. To be sure, particular human acts have not yet been explained fully in deterministic terms, but there are no challenges to the proposition that there are necessary conditions not only for human action per se but also for particular actions in particular circumstances. The intentions invoked to explain a particular human act have, at least, necessary conditions that are susceptible to interpretation as a part of some larger whole.

Persons who would generally agree with the above would not necessarily agree on its importance for ethics, that is for the justification of certain states of being and certain actions. For example, if the focal point of value is the maximum of happiness that can be achieved by individuals, the position of egoistic hedonism, any whole within which individuals are a part is purely instrumental to the achievement of that value. The whole is of value, but only as an instrument for individual fulfillment. Alan Gewirth is able to justify quite extensive intervention in what I call wholes on the basis of his Principle of Generic Consistency (PGC) as the logical requirements of maintaining the conditions necessary for the freedom and well-being of both the agent and the recipient. With great intellectual cogency he argues that these duties can be justified on the basis of that principle and can avoid the errors in utilitarianism and other species of moral philosophy. But the ultimate justification always reverts to the necessary conditions for individual voluntariness, or freedom, and purposiveness, or intentionality.[26] These and other ethical theories, one can say, do have implicit and explicit

25. Ibid., pp. 49–108.
26. Gewirth, *Reason and Morality*, chaps. 4 and 5.

concerns for the relations of wholes to a part, but the appropriate relations are always under the governance of what sustains the well-being of the part—the human community or the individual.

There are two questions to which I give different answers than do most other Western moral theorists, though currently there are proposals that move in a direction similar to mine.[27] The first question is: What is the "scope" of the whole that has to be taken into account, both in its spatial and its temporal dimensions? The second is: Both descriptively and normatively, is the whole for the sake of our part, that is, for the sake of humanity and/or of individual persons? My theocentric construal of the world requires that I answer these questions differently than do many others.

I take it as axiomatic that no human being can perceive, conceive, and respond to "*the* whole," that is, to the totality of all things and the interrelationships of each of the differentiable parts. But surely many of the modern sciences are engaged in an expanding consciousness and explanation of larger and larger entities. To be sure, as an intellectual venture this is not new; classic cosmologies and metaphysics as well as modern proposals by philosophers have proposed various theories of "the whole." The various sciences, however, are providing knowledge about and interpretations of causal relationships and patterns of interdependence in nature that enlarge the known wholes within which many particularities exist. In volume 1 I noted the seriousness, for example, with which I think theologians need to take evidences and explanations of the origins and probable end of the universe, and the origins and development of life with particular attention to the human species.[28] Both temporal and spatial dimensions of explanations of particular events and entities are expanded; longer "time frames" and broader "space frames" have to be taken into account. Thus, while *the* whole cannot be perceived, and can be conceptualized only at the highest levels of abstraction about Being, there is still a proper incentive to expand the arenas of relationships and interdependencies within which particular entities are explained and understood.[29]

From such a descriptive enterprise I believe we can discern some indications of the necessary conditions for the preservation and development not only of parts which are the foci of our attention but of designated wholes. This is not a novel proposal, for in quite common discourse we think in these terms. "The economy" of a nation is talked about as if it were an entity, though perhaps no one has satisfactorily defined the referents and limitations of the term for all who use it. Interestingly, we even speak of the

27. See, for example, K. E. Goodpastor, "From Egoism to Environmentalism," and R. and V. Routley, "Against the Inevitability of Human Chauvinism," in K. E. Goodpastor and K. M. Sayre, eds., *Ethics and Problems of the 21st Century* (Notre Dame, Ind.: University of Notre Dame Press, 1979), pp. 21–33, and pp. 36–59.

28. Gustafson, *Ethics*, 1:97–99.

29. See Gustafson, "Ethical Issues in the Human Future."

"health" of the economy, as if it were a biological entity. It is, even if imprecise, a whole in which parts are seen to be interrelated, and in which there are mutual consequences of changes that affect each other and the vitality of the whole. Certain aggregates of data can be used to demonstrate, at least in comparison with other times and places, that the economy is declining or growing; we even have terms to describe the state of the economy, such as recession or depression. But aggregates of particular data are not sufficient to account for the interrelationships between aspects of the economy. Interest rates, consumer income, productivity, exchange rates, and other features are mutually interdependent. Changes in one affect the others and the well-being of the economy as a whole.

We speak in similar ways about social units and about the natural world. When I studied the sociology of the family, for example, my instructor defined the family as "a group of people who live in a given household and share a common economy." (If one desired a good grade in the course, one had to pretend, at least, that this was an adequate definition.) Certainly some aspects of a family are referred to in that definition, but it is hardly adequate. Even the addition of biological relationships would not make it complete. A family is made up of individuals, to be sure, and they are, normally, biologically related. But there are other dimensions to family life. And while the well-being of a particular family, or of family life collectively, is related to and affected by its relations to other communities and institutions, it is possible for purposes of reflection to isolate a given entity. But the well-being of the family is not simply the aggregate of the happiness or well-being of its individual members; their interrelationships affect the well-being of the family as a whole, and the well-being of the family as a whole affects that of the individual members. The pursuit of legitimate ends by individual members often has to be restrained for the good of the whole.

In the past decades we have come to think more frequently of a natural whole called the ecosphere. In it some relationships are defined with greater precision and with greater certainty of cause and effect than in the economy or the family, though the sciences that address ecology are by no means as precise as those that address, for example, the effect of a particular drug on a particular organism. Put very generally, the well-being of the whole has to be taken into account not only for the sake of the parts but for the "system," and the interactions of the parts greatly affect the whole.

The scope of the whole to be taken into account, then, is dependent upon a focus of attention, either in terms of what is to be explained or in terms of what sorts of actions ought to occur and what relationships ought to prevail. Where those relationships are physical and chemical, our understanding is more precise, and the prediction of probable consequences both for parts and for a designated whole (or totality, to use a term from Roman

Catholic moral theology) for any intervention is more accurate. Where human interactions, governed by intentions, are involved we are less certain.

The theocentric construal of reality at least presses us to expand the scope of the wholes that are taken into account in any normative proposal for human action. Such enlargement greatly complicates ethics, and I believe that we have not satisfactorily developed concepts, ways of understanding, and procedures to deal with these complexities.

The answer to the question, Is the whole for the sake of our part? follows from the theology of volume 1. With this interpretation, in which the whole takes greater import, one cannot argue that it is *only* or even *ultimately* for the sake of our part. Just as it is axiomatic for me that no one can perceive, conceive and respond to *the* whole, so it is axiomatic that we cannot give a simple answer to the question: What is the good of *the* whole? While, from a religious perspective, there are grounds for saying that the purpose of the whole is to glorify God—the ultimate power that brings all things into being, sustains them, and determines their ultimate destinies—this theological assertion does not yield precise inferences about all other matters of valuation or (in itself) about precise ends of human activity and principles of conduct. John Passmore is correct to call attention to the fact that there is no preestablished harmony between a number of goods or ends that we can reasonably justify pursuing.[30] To pursue a legitimate end of a particular community, or even what seems to be in the interests of the well-being of a natural whole, is often necessarily costly to other communities or other wholes. Persons have proposed that at the deepest level the good of individual parts and the good of wholes to which they belong are harmonious; but in the conditions of finitude and the need to make particular choices about particular courses of action, this is false. Christian theologians have envisioned some eschatological state of affairs, often similar to the ways in which they construe Edenic experience, when perfectly harmonious relationships will occur. To affirm that there is no preestablished harmony is not to say that there are no principles and procedures for making judgments, and in some cases resolving very satisfactorily conflicting values and claims. But since the good of *the* whole is beyond human ken, there is no way in which particular actions and relationships can be justified as fitting to that whole. There are actions and relationships, however, that can be justified with relation to some more particular totalities; yet even here there are debits as well as credits, costs and well as benefits. One does not have to

30. John Passmore, *Man's Responsibility for Nature: Ecological Problems and Western Traditions* (New York: Scribner's, 1974), p. 135.

construe the whole or any particular whole as a "zero-sum" game to be forced to face seriously the conflicts of legitimate ends.[31]

The feature of the relationship of parts to whole in the profile of theocentric ethics foreshadows, or even necessitates, other features that distinguish this ethics from some other ethical views, namely, a great concern for the common good, and the inevitability of moral ambiguity and some genuinely tragic choices.

A concern for the common good is implicit in some of the above features, but it deserves highlighting. The common good is not a matter about which conceptual clarity is easily achieved, nor is the usage of the concept universally agreed to. As a concept in Western Culture it has been used primarily in the arena of political and social philosophy; few philosophers and theologians have extended its usage to the natural world. Two extreme interpretations of the common good can set the context for our discussion of it as a feature of theocentric ethics in profile. The extremes begin from either a highly individualistic point or a very "organic" or corporatist point. From the individualistic starting point the common good becomes the aggregate of the goods of all the individuals who belong to a designated entity—the family, the state, or by extension the natural world. From the organic point the common good refers to the well-being of a whole, a totality. Just as the well-being of a human body is more than the aggregate of the well-being of its various organs, so the well-being of a community (or some other entity) must be conceived in holistic terms. In political and social philosophy, the first view is generally labeled "radical libertarian," and the second is associated with Plato's *Republic*. In volume 1, chapter 2, I have indicated in general ways that each of these extremes preserves what is valued, and I have pointed out the threats to human well-being that occur when each is pursued without qualification.[32]

Toward which extreme the weight of any given interpretation is located will make a difference to what ends and values are justified over others, and what principles of conduct are defended.[33] The fundamental issue is whether there exists a possible state of affairs in which the good of individual particularities is in perfect harmony with the good of a whole of

31. "A zero-sum game is any game where the losses exactly equal the winnings." Lester C. Thurow, *The Zero-Sum Society: Distribution and the Possibilities for Economic Change* (New York: Penguin Books, 1981), p. 11.

32. For an essay that draws relevant distinctions about "common" and about the "good" that is common, see Alan Gewirth, "Political Justice," in Richard B. Brandt, ed., *Social Justice* (Englewood Cliffs, N.J.: Prentice-Hall, 1962), pp. 154–69.

33. The most consistent individualistic political philosophy in recent decades is that of Robert Nozick, *Anarchy, State, and Utopia* (New York: Basic Books, 1974). The most "organic" thinking is coming from writers who perceive very critical situations in the "ecosystem" and particularly in the pressures of population growth. See, for example, Garrett Hardin, "The Tragedy of the Commons" *Science* 162 (13 December, 1968):1243–48.

which they are a part. The relationship between the good of individual parts and the common good is reciprocal, but it is seldom, if ever, harmonious. Generally the concept of justice is invoked to sustain a fair distribution of benefits and costs among individual members of a human community, not only for their sake as individuals, but also for the sake of the whole. The common good requires a fair distribution of goods among those who are a part of the "common" under attention. Also, to relate to persons in a manner appropriate to their relations to God requires the honoring of their capacities for self-determination. These capacities are part of the nature of human life. In these ways the possible tyrannies of the corporatist and the possible anarchist outcomes of the individualist extremes are avoided. These matters can never be settled at high levels of abstraction; how they are settled requires attention to the empirical realities of the contexts in which judgments and proposals about courses of action and states of affairs must be made. And different theories of justice develop different principles for adjudicating conflicting claims.

My theocentric construal of the world requires that parts be interpreted in relation to relevant wholes, and that the common good of various wholes is the object of proper concern not only for the sake of the parts but also for the sake of those wholes. It follows from this that theocentric ethics will be weighted more readily, in circumstances of conflict between the claims of parts and the whole, on claims for the common good of a whole. This does not resolve other pertinent questions, such as when it is appropriate to use coercive means to achieve what is judged to be in the common good. The answer to this question is also context-bound; voluntary restraint will always sustain individual freedom and be preferable because that freedom is valued, but there are arenas of social policy and interpersonal activity in which the limitations of resources or other factors warrant moral and legal restraints on the pursuit of individual ends. Conscription during wartime is an example. Choices that favor the well-being of a whole at a particular state of development are sometimes required even if the zero-sum analogy breaks down.

The seventh feature of the profile is that it accents the experience of moral ambiguity, and even in some particular circumstances the deeply tragic character of particular choices. A great deal of moral philosophy is dedicated to developing basic principles and their application in such a way that most, if not all, conflicts can be resolved rationally. For some moral philosophers there are no genuine moral dilemmas; fully good reasons can be given for every particular choice. There is, in such views, never an occasion for remorse when the well-reasoned choice is made. Whether it is the application of Gewirth's Principle of Generic Consistency, or an intricate refinement of the Principle of Double Effect in the natural-law tradition, the desired outcome is a clear moral choice for one course of action over another.[34] At the other extreme is a situational ethic of an existentialist sort. Jean-Paul Sartre's often-cited example is perhaps the best instance of this in recent literature. The young male underground agent in the time of war is faced with a large number of conflicting moral and social claims on him—various duties, ends of action, and motives—all of which are admirable. As Sartre construes the circumstances of the young man, there are no decisive reasons for choosing among any of the conflicting claims, not to mention invoking a supreme moral principle that will warrant his final choice. Sartre's answer to the young man's query was: "You're free, choose, that is, invent."[35]

It is quite clear that ambiguities are more readily overcome where there is a single moral principle, formal or substantive or a combination of the two, which has both the specificity and the universal applicability to be brought to bear upon all, or almost all, specific occasions and events. Or there may be a combination of factual judgments with implied moral premises that resolve all ambiguity.

Current debates about induced abortions of human fetuses provide excellent material for analyzing how ambiguities can be resolved. The extreme antiabortion argument is quite simple. The fetus is a person. To take the life of a human being, except when it is an unjust aggressor, is murder. The fetus is not an unjust aggressor. Therefore abortion is murder. There is no ambiguity in part because of the description of the relevant circumstances, a description the limits of which follow from the moral views used to resolve the question. Gewirth's PGC enables him to justify abortions in a very careful way.

> When someone is less than a full-fledged prospective agent, his generic rights are proportional to the degree to which he approaches having the generic abilities constitutive of such agency, and the reason for this proportionality is found in the relation between having the rights and having the generic abilities required for acting with a view to purpose-fulfillment. The fetus, of course, lacks the abilities, except in a remotely potential form.[36]

The issue of abortion comes up when there is a conflict between the rights of the fetus and those of the mother. "The conflict involves that the mother's generic rights to the use of the abilities required for purpose-fulfillment are threatened by the fetus's being carried to full term."[37] Since the fetus does

34. For discussions of the principle of double effect, see Richard A. McCormick, S.J., *Ambiguity in Moral Choice* (Milwaukee: Marquette University Press, 1973), and Richard A. McCormick, S.J., and Paul Ramsey, eds; *Doing Evil to Achieve Good: Moral Choice in Conflict Situations* (Chicago: Loyola University Press, 1978).

35. J. P. Sartre, *Existentialism* (New York: Philosophical Library, 1974), pp. 28–33; the quotation is from p. 33.

36. Gewirth, *Reason and Morality*, p. 142.

37. Ibid., p. 143.

not fully have those abilities yet, there are good reasons under a variety of circumstances to induce abortions. Once one has the reasons, there is no indication that they justify any sense of remorse for the loss to the fetus, which normally would develop the abilities required, and would defend his or her rights. The simple antiabortion argument is equally rational (given its factual premises), and leaves one with no greater sense of remorse since the consequencs for the mother and others that might well be deleterious do not count.

My own conclusions are very close to Gewirth's, though I would give other reasons for them. It follows, however, from the theocentric construal of life, both in its ethics and its piety, that even the best reasons justifying the taking of fetal life involve a tragic choice. Even if the abortion can be defended as a just act, it is a "mournful" act, just as justification for killing in self-defense or in war properly evokes remorse. Someone has suffered the loss of a life for what is a justified moral reason. The tragic character of many actions resides precisely in the fact that the legitimate pursuit of legitimate ends, or action in accordance with reasonable moral principles, entails severe losses to others—not only persons but other living things—and even sometimes diminishes the possibilities for development of future life and future generations of human beings. Therein lie the reasons for anger with God. The task of ethics is to reduce, if not resolve, moral ambiguities. It is to give good reasons for actions and for the state of affairs and course of events that agents seek to shape. Theocentric ethics, as I develop it, however, is less able to resolve all conflicts and ambiguities, and the basic grounds for this inability are theological. But this does not license an existentialist ethics, not to mention the vulgar "If it feels good, do it." And the extent of ambiguity is relative to the complexity of the circumstances and issue under scrutiny and demanding a choice. Later in this volume there are essays on particular issues in which I illustrate how I would resolve, insofar as I can, the ambiguities.

The final feature to be highlighted is that theocentric ethics warrants a strong emphasis on self-denial, and in extreme circumstances on self-sacrifice. This is the case whether the "self" involved is an individual person or a human collectivity. Self-denial follows both from theocentric piety and from the ethics grounded in the sovereign ordering of God.

To a great extent, restraints, if not explicit self-denial, are simply part of the necessary conditions for living together in human communities. They are part of the requisite ordering of life required even for proper individual self-interest, as well as for communities living together in the conditions of finitude. And they come to our attention also in our human dependence upon the natural world of which we are part. A modicum of harmony in the family requires restraints on the actions and aspirations of individual members both for their sake and for the sake of the common good of the family.

The interests of a particular social group in society cannot be pursued without taking into account the interests of other groups both for the sake of each part and for the sake of some social ordering and peace. Human interventions into the ordering of nature, such as the use of certain insecticides, are withdrawn when it is realized that there are deleterious consequences to the health of others and to nonhuman aspects of nature. Restraints and denials of interests, even those that have a considerable justification, are simply part of the ordering of life. That they are matters of prudence does not make them unethical from a theocentric perspective.

A theocentric piety, I believe, motivates and issues in a readiness to restrain particular interests for the sake of other persons, for communities and the larger world. What are from other ethical standpoints acts of supererogation are not only obligations within theocentric ethics but are seen as actions which follow from piety. Something important to theocentric ethics in this regard is seen in the biblical traditions, and particularly in the Christian ethics of discipleship. The apostle Paul, interestingly, in two different contexts makes different statements in this regard. "Let no one seek his own good, but the good of his neighbor," he wrote to the church in Corinth. To the church in Philippi he wrote: "Let each of you look not only to his own interests, but also to the interests of others."[38] At issue is the perennial problem of the proper place of one's own interests.[39] One does not have to be willing to be damned for the glory of God to be moved to forms of self-giving toward others and restraint of individual and corporate interests out of concern for the needs of others and gratitude for all that has been given to (and not earned by) us. Most dramatically, the theocentric piety and fidelity of Jesus make clear that the readiness to be concerned for the well-being of others even at cost to oneself is a part of Christian morality. The cross, and the way of the cross, are revealing symbols of what is enabled and required of persons who seek to serve and glorify God.

In the following two chapters, features of the profile are developed in relation to benchmarks of formidable ethical theories (or positions) grounded in Christian theology and in philosophy.

38. 1 Corinthians 10:24 and Philippians 2:4 (R.S.V.).

39. For a recent novel that powerfully portrays deep ambivalence between self-sacrifice in the service of others and individual self-fulfillment, see Mary Gordon, *Final Payments* (New York: Random House, 1978). See also Stephen G. Post, "Love and Eudaemonism: A Study in the Thought of Jonathan Edwards and Samuel Hopkins" (Ph.D. diss., University of Chicago, 1983). Post is primarily concerned about the relation between love for God and the desire for personal happiness, but the issue of self-denial and self-fulfillment receives a great deal of attention. Post explores historical antecedents to his major figures and proposes a constructive position.

2

Benchmarks from Theology

Theological literature in the Western tradition always has implications for ethics, even if it does not have specifically developed moral theories. How theological beliefs and principles are related to ethical principles and to interpretations of moral life in various theologies is a matter to which I have given considerable attention in previous publications.[1] The will of God has always been conceived in one way or another as, at least in part, a moral will. Thus language that is more distinctively ethical has always been a part of theology, and interpretations of proper human relationships to God have always affected the accounts of moral life.

The variety of moral language in the Western religious tradition has been great. In the Bible itself there are many forms of moral discourse, many types of morally relevant language. One finds legal terminology, historical analogies, aphorisms, indictments, parables, moral ideals, narratives, prudential reasoning, use of paradigmatic individuals as examples, and others. The ethics in the Bible is not, in any philosophical sense, systematic. In the history of Christian theology there is a considerable variation in the degree to which theologians have been ethical theorists, and the influences of various philosophical traditions on different theologians is palpable. Stoicism, Neoplatonism, Aristotelianism, nominalism, Kantianism, idealism, existentialism, analytical philosophy, phenomenology, and others are detectable. There have been virtue- and disposition-oriented ethics and act-oriented ethics. And in the works of those few very comprehensive and systematic theologians one finds well-developed arguments for the adaptations of various ethical theories to the particular theological choices and methods that are used.

Obviously it is not possible in this chapter to take into account all the contributors to the theological ethical tradition. And, in this volume, it is important to focus attention on the more distinctively ethical (rather than theological) features of patterns of thought. Thus I do not provide fully adequate accounts of the ethics of even those theologians whom I have selected as benchmarks for the further development and detailing of the profile provided in the previous chapter. Their works function in this chapter primarily as points of indication for defending and developing my own argument, and I select from them to show further the distinguishing features of it. In my judgment Thomas Aquinas has provided the most comprehensive account of theological ethics in the Roman Catholic tradition, and the most systematically developed account in the history of Christian thought. The most coherent and comprehensive account of theological ethics in the Protestant tradition comes from the twentieth century, and is found in the

1. James M. Gustafson, *Christ and the Moral Life* (New York: Harper and Row, 1963; reprint, Chicago: University of Chicago Press, 1976), *Can Ethics Be Christian?* (Chicago: University of Chicago Press, 1975); *Protestant and Roman Catholic Ethics: Prospects for Rapprochement* (Chicago: University of Chicago Press, 1978).

works of Karl Barth. This warrants the choice of these figures as critical benchmarks. I shall also use relevant works from two contemporary authors, Karl Rahner and Paul Ramsey. With each of these authors my work has some affinities and some significant differences both theologically and ethically; each has been important as a "conversation partner" through the years as I have delineated my own constructive position. Other thinkers have been equally important in some respects, but these provide useful benchmarks for further development of my theocentric ethics.

Karl Barth

No pages in my personal theological library show as much wear as Karl Barth's *Church Dogmatics*, II/2, chapter 8, entitled "The Command of God."[2] What is so instructive and stimulating about this section is that here Barth comprehensively develops both his basic theological ethical method and the main lines of the substance or content of his theological ethics. Much more is developed in subsequent volumes, and while all that is stated later is generally coherent with this section from *The Doctrine of God*, there are strains in the system as ethics gets elaborated under other of the major headings of his work. Students of Barth know that the reader moves back and forth through the many volumes, and that both great repetition and brilliant nuances occur as his fertile and voluble mind expounds both theological principles and their significance for interpreting almost everything under the sun. It is not my intention to expound and formulate a thoroughgoing critical analysis of Barth's theology and ethics. Rather, his formidable account provides powerful alternatives to my own work, and yet has some significant affinities with it.[3] Indeed I am convinced that Barth has stated the complete agenda for theological ethics, has made judgments about all the crucial issues, and defended them well from his point of view. To come to grips with Barth's agenda is one of the best ways to formulate a comprehensive and coherent theological ethics. Key judgments and positions taken by him must be considered in defending and elaborating any alternative to his work.

The first major subheading under "The Command of God" is "Ethics as a Task of the Doctrine of God." This makes very clear that ethics for Barth is and must be theological. Ethics is not merely applying biblical teachings to various moral problems; it is not finding moral positions and then developing a theology that backs them. The critical question is the

2. Karl Barth, *Church Dogmatics*, II/2, trans. G. W. Bromiley, J. C. Campbell, et al. (Edinburgh: T. and T. Clark, 1957), pp. 509–781.

3. The major study of Barth's ethics in English is Robert E. Willis, *The Ethics of Karl Barth* (Leiden: E. J. Brill, 1971). See Eberhard Busch, *Karl Barth: His Life from Letters and Autobiographical Texts*, trans. John Bowden (Philadelphia: Fortress, 1976), for an informative and interesting biography.

theological question in the most precise and restricted sense: What is the proper doctrine of God? There are writers of "Christian ethics" who are not theological ethicians; they can accept various bases of authorization from the Bible, from the narratives of the community, and from other sources without confronting as fully as Barth does the question of God.

Here the primary affinity of my work with Barth's is very clear. The first task of a theological ethician is to develop a coherent interpretation of God. It is not that this provides a sufficient basis for deducing ethical conclusions about all particular matters. Indeed, when one examines Barth's own "practical casuistry" dealing with both matters of political and social significance and questions of taking life, one finds that he necessarily draws upon quite a rich and varied learning to point the direction in which he believes one will hear the command of God. But a careful study of Barth shows that how one conceives and states beliefs about God and God's relations to the world decisively forms the proper procedures for coming to particular moral judgments and gives content to the judgments that are made. Ethics is shaped by the account one renders of God and God's relations to the world. How God is construed, and how the world is construed in the light of one's convictions about the ultimate power and the powers that bring life into being, sustain it, and bear down upon it is the most critical choice made in theological ethics. On this basic, but quite formal, point I fully agree with Karl Barth.

From this point onward, however, judgments I have made and defended in volume 1 lead to quite a different view of ethics. These differences follow from differences in how God and God's relations to the world are construed. To show the differences in ethics requires a brief indication of crucially different theological judgments as well.

One such judgment is about the source or sources of our knowledge of God, and thus how we adduce evidences for our beliefs about God. Karl Barth would clearly reject the use made of human experiences of dependence, gratitude, remorse, and others as bases for coming to the acknowledgment of God. Those terms that I developed in volume 1 do, interestingly, appear in Barth's theological ethics, but their location in the argument and thus how they are warranted is very different. Just as clearly Barth would reject those indications from our understanding of the natural world on which I have relied so heavily—the patterns of interdependence which provide the conditions for life and also set limitations upon it, for example. This rejection follows from Barth's arguments against natural knowledge of God. It is interesting to note that some of the descriptions of life in the world that I have made are and can be incorporated into Barth's theology, but they are "annexed" only after one has made the critical turn, namely, after one has admitted that the knowledge of God comes through the revelation of God in the Bible as interpreted Christologically.

For Barth, we have knowledge of God only because God has chosen to reveal himself to man. And God has chosen to reveal himself in the life and events of a particular people, and in Jesus Christ. Thus the biblical record and materials are the source of God's revelation and of any reliable knowledge of God. I deliberately refrained from using the term "revelation" to characterize how humans become informed about God on the grounds that what is called revelation is reflection on human experiences in the face of the ultimate power and powers. The biblical records, in such a view, are an account of great importance but not the exclusive source of our understanding of God. The term "revelation" could be used within the framework of my discussion only in a very weak sense, if at all. If our understanding of God comes through human experience and through our interpretations of nature, it could be said that God reveals himself through these means. But this is to use a stronger interpretation of God in the image of man, that is, as a person, than I believe is sustainable. The personal and interpersonal language that Barth uses to construe God and God's relations to the world is one of the most critical differences between his theology and mine. And for Barth, the use of that language is grounded in the authority of the Bible as the source of our knowledge of God. Its implications for ethical thought are deep and broad, and to these I shall return.

Jesus Christ is the center of Barth's theology, both in terms of how human beings know God, and what it is about God that is known. It is through the biblical exposition of Christ that God is known as a gracious God, as God who is for man. It is through the Christological developments in the Johannine literature and the Epistles to the Ephesians and the Colossians that Barth builds his classic Christological and trinitarian theology. There one comes to know that the sovereign God is gracious and good and that his graciousness and goodness are for man in a special way. Thus while, from one perspective, Barth's theology contains a theocentric ethics (it is the ruling and commanding sovereign grace of God that orders life), from another perspective his theology sustains the excessive focus on the salvation of persons that was the burden of much criticism in volume 1. God's power is sovereign, but it is graciously ordered to the salvation of humanity. The differences in Christology between Barth and what I briefly developed in volume 1 are not only great but crucial to the differences in our theological ethics both for their methods and their substance.

Before I examine these differences, I shall attend further to the ways in which Barth's fundamental theological judgments affect the methods of his theological ethics, and show how and why I agree and disagree with those methods. One crucial outcome of his theology is the dominance of the language of interpersonal relationships and social metaphors in his construal of God and God's relations to the world and to man. The fundamental model is not one of powers that are impersonally ordering the world of which human activity is a part, but one of God personally relating to human beings as persons in the spheres of their moral activity. The authorization and the source of this model are biblical. For Barth, God speaks and man is to hear; God acts and man is to conform to the prior action of God; God commands and man is to obey. The idea of a covenant between God and man is central to Barth's ethics; covenants are basically social documents, ordering relationships voluntarily entered into by both parties and holding both parties responsible for the agreement. All of these terms, and others such as that of an encounter between God and man, are based and built upon what Barth adduces as the biblical understanding of God and the correlative understanding of man. The point is that human beings are not to discern what is morally right and good by their assessment of the natural and social patterns of dependence and interdependence in life in the world, but are to hear and obey the command of God, to witness to God's gracious action in the world by conforming their actions to his actions, to testify in their lives and in the ordering of human activity to the prior gracious covenant of God with man. The gulf between Barth and traditional Roman Catholic theology becomes clear at this point; analogies are drawn from relationships between persons rather than from an order of being.

The implications of this fundamental model for ethics are thoroughgoing. It shapes Barth's "objective" ethics. The determination of what is right and good is made by God and not by man. To be sure, because God is for man, what is determined is finally to the benefit of the human; the point to be stressed here, however, is not only that God ought to be the determiner of what is right and good but that God does in every particular occasion do so. Barth's strongest statement of this is as follows.

> The divine decision, in which the sovereign judgment of God is expressed on our decisions, is a very definite decision. . . . [I]n the demand and judgment of His command God always confronts us with a specific meaning and intention, with a will which has foreseen everything and each thing in particular, which has not left the smallest thing to chance or our caprice. The command of God as it is given to us at each moment is always and only one possibility in every conceivable particularity of its inner and outer modality. It is always a single decision, including all the thoughts and words and movements in which we execute it. We encounter it in such a way that absolutely nothing either outward or inward, either in the relative secret of our intention or in the unambiguously observable fulfillment of our actions, is left to chance or to ourselves, or rather in such a way that even in every visible or invisible detail He wills us precisely the one thing and nothing else, and measures and judges us precisely by whether we do or do not do with the same precision the one thing that He so precisely wills.[4]

4. Barth, *Church Dogmatics*, II/2, pp. 663–64.

God, and no human being, is the decisive determiner of proper human activity. The image of man is not the self-legislating moral agent exercising reason in the determination of what is right according to some moral principles or action guides. It is not Sartre's young man being told that he is free to invent in the particular circumstances. It is not the calculator of costs and benefits. It is not the biblical ethician applying the analogies or the laws given in the Bible to decide what Christians are to do. It is not the moral idealist seeking to approximate some vision of the Kingdom of God or the human good. Man is the hearer of this very precise and objective command of God. To be sure, for Barth human beings have explosive encounters with God; their obedience is not predetermined by an overriding power and will. They can fail to hear the command, and they can disobey it when they do hear it. But, again, what is right and good is determined objectively (in relation to human impulses, dispositions, and reasoning) by God; it is not determined by human beings.

Barth's "objective" ethics clearly is quite different from that of traditional natural-law theory. In the latter view the norms are objective to our human desires and willing; they are, so to speak, there in the moral ordering of the universe, and in the proper relations of things to each other in that moral order. Laws can be inferred from that order, and moral activity is proper when it is in conformity to those laws. But the role of human agents is very different from that in Barth's ethics; they are the practical reasoners and the judges of what is to be done. They can err, and are accountable for their errors, but the principles and laws that are the measures of their rectitude or error are mediated through "nature."

Clearly the profile delineated in the previous chapter is closer to the natural-law tradition than it is to Barth in its conception of where the objectivity of ethics lies. Like Barth, I wish to defend a form of objective ethics; the form I defend is different in large measure because of differences in how God and God's relations to the world are construed. Barth's interpersonal model of transcendence supports a different view of the objective character of moral norms.[5] To use distinctions employed in moral philosophy, Barth's objective ethics are basically deontic in character, rather than teleological as in the natural-law tradition. They can be labeled "act-deontic" in the sense that what is to be conformed to is not a universal moral principle but a particular command of God to act in a particular way in very particular circumstances. It is God's command, not a rule or principle, that is to be obeyed.

A further implication of Barth's view is that the gravest human error is to usurp the place of God by determining what is right and good on the basis

5. See Gordon D. Kaufman, "Two Models of Transcendence," in *God, The Problem* (Cambridge, Mass.: Harvard University Press, 1972), pp. 72–81, for a study that illuminates this section and the following one on Thomas Aquinas.

of purely human judgments. It is in this sense that ethics itself can become a grave sin, since the forms of ethics given in the philosophical and much of the Christian tradition make the final point of reliance in moral life the reasonable judgments of persons, or make rules and principles (including those derived from biblical sources) the ultimate basis of decision. Thus, Barth's critical response to a human moral choice is not to provide an alternative, distinctly moral argument, but to make a religious and theological judgment. This can be seen in the way in which he writes about issues of taking human life. For example, his response to the question of euthanasia, a response in which he seems certain of the divine command as an "unequivocal No" because a gracious God has said "Thou mayest live," is that mercy killing "can be regarded only as murder, i.e., as a wicked usurpation of God's sovereign right over life and death."[6] The person who chooses to have an induced abortion "desires to discharge a divine office"; the legitimation of capital punishment by the state also is based on "usurped divinity" because the state "destroys life instead of maintaining it."[7] It is the case that Barth equivocates on the questions of abortion and capital punishment, and raises the question about artificially prolonging life as itself human arrogance, but the most decisive error is always the religious one of assuming the prerogatives of God on the basis of some human ethical determination of what is right. The issue is more distinctively religious than it is moral; the response is more a theological one than a distinctively ethical one. This turns us back to the fundamental model again; the interpersonal model as Barth uses it seems to undercut the kind of careful moral reasoning that from most other points of view is required to come to judgments in particular cases. There is no "structure of the world" that mediates the divine ordering to which one can recur to make a moral argument for precise guides to action in complex matters. Ethics itself can be "sin"; the question of faith becomes the true ethical question.[8]

Yet the interpersonal model only *seems* to undercut practical moral reasoning. Barth, after attacking the casuistic tradition, and by implication almost any other way of engaging in practical moral reasoning, insists that it has a place but that it cannot be decisive.[9] "If special ethics becomes casuistry, this means that the moralist wishes to set himself on God's throne, to distinguish good and evil."[10] Casuistry, which assumes that the command of God is a "universal rule," is a destruction of Christian freedom.[11] Once these points are made, however, Barth can write about the need for a

6. Karl Barth, *Church Dogmatics*, III/4, trans. A. T. McKay, T. H. L. Parker, et al. (Edinburgh: T. and T. Clark, 1961), p. 423.
7. Ibid., p. 416 and p. 445.
8. Barth, *Church Dogmatics*, II/2, p. 641.
9. Barth, *Church Dogmatics*, III/4, pp. 7–19.
10. Ibid., p. 10.
11. Ibid., p. 11 and p. 13.

"formed reference" within which the command of God is likely to be heard. The function of moral thinking in the formed reference "is not to pronounce an anticipatory judgment on the good or evil of human action in encounter with the command of God, but to give definite instruction with regard to this event."[12] Note the language of event; hearing and obeying the command is always an event, an encounter between a person and God's command. But definite instruction can be given about the event; this is a move that legitimates the kinds of observations about experience, the uses of biblical teachings and analogies, and the grasping of political and social realities that inform Barth's often richly insightful discussions of all sorts of occasions in which moral action is required: marriage, family, politics, tyranny, capital punishment, and many more. The point of all this, however, is not to come to a decision based on the consideration of the relevant circumstances, the biblical warrants, and plain good sense. The point is that this process of practical casuistry prepares one to hear the command of God. God remains free to command what God wills, though it is unlikely that God will command something that is inconsistent with Barth's practical casuistry. And it is sure that God will not command anything contrary to his grace as known in Jesus Christ.

Again we see how a theological judgment is carried out in ethics. The interpersonal model of God's relations to man and the world forecloses appealing to any ordering patterns of life in the world as a basis on which to make moral choices. Yet many patterns and much knowledge can instruct the agents concerned, and one can come to almost certain convictions about what God will command, but finally the determination is God's and not man's.

The patterns and information drawn from many sources make Barth more certain about what the divine command will be in some circumstances than in others; and even where he can announce a divine No, he raises the possibilities of exceptions (as in capital punishment) or that certain sins (as in abortion) are forgivable in the light of his large storehouse of reading and reflection.

These proposals of Barth's are both similar and dissimilar to the line of discussion I offered in chapter 7 of volume 1. The similarity lies in the considerations that I believe are required in the process of discernment of what God is requiring and enabling us to be and to do. That process of discernment, I argued, cannot lead to absolute moral certainty in many complex circumstances; there is always a moment of intuition, though it is sharply focused as a result of practical moral reflection. Barth's own discussions of many issues are highly instructive, though not worked out through a systematic philosophical theory of ethics. I agree with Barth that our human

12. Ibid., p. 18.

moral judgments are fallible, and that the overweaning confidence that some views of ethics have in the certainty of the final judgment is often misplaced. But a different theology provides a different pattern for coming to particular moral choices; the indications given in our perceptions of the ordering of life in the world have greater reliability for me than they do for Barth.

The dissimiliarity with Barth is quite radical; the discernment of the divine will is a human discernment, and any final judgment (whether morally right or not) is always a human judgment. Practical moral reasoning, based on resources Barth cannot legitimately include as well as on the kinds of "instruction" he does include, seeks to discern the will of God according to the maxim that we are to relate ourselves and all things in a manner appropriate to their relations to God. Maybe, from Barth's point of view, when that discernment is accurate, one has "heard" the command of God; his language, however, is ruled out of ethics on the basis of my theological judgments. Discernment is based upon human understanding of proper ordering and relationships, proper ends of human activity. It is not based upon hearing a specific command and obeying it. The error of wrong moral judgments, for example, in issues of taking human life is not that humans have usurped the place of God (though there is an appropriate warning implied in that about accepting the conditions of human finitude). It is that human beings have not exercised their dispositions and their processes of discernment in the most appropriate way. What is correct about Barth's powerful indictment is that it makes clear that human beings are not God, and thus their judgments are fallible. To that judgment I also come. What is not warranted is Barth's confidence in the objectivity of a particular command of God that can be heard, and thus can provide a moral certainty on a different basis. In the end Barth is as sure that there are no genuine moral dilemmas as are some philosophers; moral ambiguity is finally overcome when God's command is heard. He does, however, recognize the costliness to others of engaging in proper moral acts.[13]

It should be clear now that fundamental theological judgments that Barth makes entail, even logically, his methods in ethics. While my account of his work does not do full justice to many nuances, it is sufficient to indicate where crucial theological judgments I have made lead to affinities as well as deep differences with Barth on ethical method.

Theological judgments also make a difference in the substance or content of ethics. It was necessary to introduce some of Barth's points relevant to this in the discussion of method, but more elaboration is required. The Divine Commander is not capricious. God commands in accord with his gracious covenant with man. This gracious covenant is disclosed

13. See his discussion of the slaying of animals, in ibid., pp. 351–56.

both in its central significance and in great detail through Barth's Christological interpretation of the biblical materials. The priority and triumph of grace is the constantly recurring theological theme in his *Church Dogmatics*. It is the basis of the assurance that "God is for man";[14] that Gospel is prior to Law and thus Law is the form of the Gospel;[15] that the word of the Lord is "Thou mayest live";[16] that human beings can be open to the novel in events and history in the assurance that the gracious God is ultimately reigning;[17] that sin is the "impossible possibility" from the perspective of God's grace, though it is humanly actual;[18] that there is a ground for confidence and courage in human life that is deeper than death and despair.[19] The delightful music of Mozart's *The Magic Flute*, of which Barth was very fond and on which he commented, seems to be a fitting aesthetic symbolization of the proper response to the goodness of God.[20]

This divine Yes did not make Barth, either in his writings or his actions, insensitive to the presence of struggle and evil in the world. It did not restrain his polemical powers against his theological opponents. But the deeper theme throughout is the affirmation of life, the perception of possibilities for juster social orders within political conflicts, and the kind of joy that comes through in many passages of his theology. God has said Yes to man; God is for man. His Yes is prior to his No; his grace is prior to his judgment. This is Barth's basic theological point; it is grounded in his interpretation of the Bible and is not based upon observations from the ordering of the natural world, aspects of human experience, or abstractions from various scientific accounts of the world. To be sure, once one knows God to have made his gracious covenant with man these other things are seen to be indications of that covenant.

I need not repeat the criticisms of this deep strand in the Christian tradition that were made in volume 1. Suffice it to say that I believe there are many strands of biblical material that are not so easily brought into Barth's Christological interpretation of a coherent biblical theology. Thus, although I have not supported the assertion in sufficient detail, there are grounds in the biblical material to show that its reflections on the power and powers that sustain and bear down upon us are more varied than Barth's dominant theme elucidates. The insights of the biblical people are more complex and

14. Karl Barth, *Church Dogmatics*, III/2, trans. Harold Knight, G. W. Bromiley, et al. (Edinburgh, T. and T. Clark, 1960), p. 609 and many other places.

15. Barth, *Church Dogmatics*, II/2, pp. 511–12.

16. Barth, *Church Dogmatics*, III/4, pp. 409–10.

17. Barth, *Church Dogmatics*, II/2, pp. 645–59.

18. Karl Barth, *Church Dogmatics*, IV/2, trans. G. W. Bromiley (Edinburgh: T. and T. Clark, 1958), p. 399 and elsewhere.

19. Barth, *Church Dogmatics*, II/2, pp. 598–99.

20. See Barth's essay, "Wolfgang Amadeus Mozart," trans. Walter M. Mosse, in Walter Leibrecht, ed., *Religion and Culture: Essays in Honor of Paul Tillich* (New York: Harper and Row, 1959), pp. 61–78.

varied, in my judgment, and thus even if one uses the Bible as the source of theology in a more singular way than I do, its implications for understanding the content of theological ethics offer more alternatives than Barth does.

My reading of the theology in the Bible confronts a Deity who does many different things, is addressed in many different ways, and is manifest in many different events and places. The Bible tells us of a God who is transcendent and a God who is immanent, a God who acts in history and a God who is nature's God, a God whose kingdom is to come and a God who has been ordering the creation from its inception, a jealous God and a friendly God, a God who creates and redeems and a God who judges and destroys, a God who is a commander and lawgiver and a God who liberates, a God who speaks and a God beyond gods who is mysterious and silent, a profoundly moral God before whom humans are guilty and profoundly compassionate God who creates new possibilities in reconciliation, a God to whom we can cry for comfort and a God who is indifferent to our private ills, a God of justice and war and a God of peace, a God who is feared and a God who is loved and adored, a God who is the ground of security and a God who undercuts most of the grounds of security on which we depend. In the light of such a reading of the Bible I find Barth's singular Christological interpretation to be too simple and neat. The theology of the Bible backs and warrants more diversity in ethics than Barth permits.

Further, in my judgment, although Barth sees God's covenant as present in the Creation, it is a covenant focused on man. While Barth showed greater sensitivity to the human dependence upon nature than did many other theologians, the centrality of man in the covenantal relationship rules out for Barth consideration of the ordering of nature as a source both for theology and for the backing of ethical norms. A basic spatial pattern in his thought is that there is a vertical dimension to man's relationship to God; there is a horizontal relationship between persons, and by extension between persons and nature.

His sensitivity to the large natural world is clear from his discussion of the human use of animals and plants.

> [T]he world of animals and plants forms the indispensable living background to the living-space divinely allotted to man and placed under his control. As they live, so can he. He is not set up as lord over the earth, but as lord on the earth which is already furnished with these creatures. Animals and plants do not belong to him; they and the whole earth can belong only to God. But he takes precedence of them. They are provided for his use.[21]

He goes on to distinguish between human use of plants and animals; the harvesting of plants and fruits is not their annihilation.

21. Barth, *Church Dogmatics*, III/4, pp. 350–51.

> [B]ut the killing of animals presupposes that the peace of creation is at least threatened and itself constitutes a continuation of this threat. And the nearness of the animal to man irrevocably means that when man kills a beast he does something which is at least very similar to homicide.[22] The slaying of animals is really possible only as an appeal to God's reconciling grace, as its representation and proclamation. It undoubtedly means making use of the offering of an alien and innocent victim and claiming its life for ours. Man must have good reasons for seriously making such a claim. . . . The killing of animals in obedience is possible only as a deeply reverential act of repentance, gratitude and praise on the part of the forgiven sinner in the face of the One who is Creator and Lord of man and beast.[23]

There is a kind of piety in these remarks. But here the point to be stressed is that while there is great sensitivity to the natural order as the sustaining environment for human life the focus is on God's relation to man, who is then related to nature, and not on the ordering of the relationships in nature and man's place in it. Barth could never say with Calvin that "nature is God," even if that is said with the reverent heart that Calvin prescribes.[24] That he cannot say this, nor relate God more directly to nature, affects the substance as well as the form and method of his ethics. Substantively it means that our understandings of the interdependencies and orderings of the natural world are not legitimate sources of ethical norms and values. We cannot ground patterns of obligation in those natural interdependencies. For Barth we are to respect nature because it, like man, belongs to God. In God's covenant with man the use of nature is legitimated, but the ordering of nature does not provide the principles for its use. Its use is set immediately in a religious context rather than a moral one. Barth's maxim that would be parallel to my own would be "Use everything as belonging to the gracious God," rather than "Relate to all things in a manner appropriate to their relations to God."

Further implications of Barth's views about nature, broadly conceived, can be seen in his discussions of "real man," of marriage, and of parents and children.

In volume 1, I argued for a view of persons that, while it made a place for self-determination, did not divide as sharply as some others our biological and social natures from our freedom and rational activity. Barth, quite to the contrary, argues expansively for a sharp distinction between the "phe-

22. Ibid., p. 352.

23. Ibid., pp. 354–55.

24. "I confess, of course, that it can be said reverently, provided that it proceeds from a reverent mind, that nature is God. . . ." He goes on to warn that we ought not to confuse God with his inferior works. John Calvin, *Institutes of the Christian Religion*, I, 5, 5; 2 vols., trans. Ford Battles, ed. John T. McNeill (Philadelphia: Westminster, 1955), 1:58.

nomena of the human" on the one hand, and "real man" on the other.[25] His erudition in this section, as in others, is very impressive, for he discusses biological, ethical, existentialist and other interpretations of man that are alternatives to his theological one. It is in principle fitting and proper that studies of the human be undertaken from various scientific and philosophical perspectives. And it is appropriate to make critical assessments of the adequacy of various studies. But none of these studies can tell us who "real man" is.

> For these phenomena as such are neutral, relative and ambiguous. They may point in various directions. They may or may not be symptoms of real man. They are so only for those who know him already and can therefore interpret them correctly. In themselves they convey no knowledge of real man. . . . [T]hey all refer to a human characteristic which is plain to us but which unfortunately is of no significance for understanding the true nature of man.[26] The real man whom we are seeking must obviously be the being which is distinguished as man from all other beings and which in spite of any affinity or relationship of common features that it may have with them is always man and only man, and is not therefore interchangeable with them.[27]

Insofar as this is an affirmation of the distinctiveness of the human it is, of course, correct. And, as Barth so frequently does, he gives back what he has taken away once he has established the correct perspective. Once the correct theological anthropology has been established, "we can now affirm that all scientific knowledge of man is not objectively empty, but that it has a real object."[28] Once "real man" is known, the knowledge of the phenomena of man can disclose symptoms of real man, and such nontheological studies are not only justified but also necessary.[29]

What then is "real man"? The answer is, of course, theological in the mode of the interpersonal model. "To be a man is to be in the particular sphere of the created world in which the Word of God is spoken and sounded." To be human is to be "addressed, called, and summoned" by God. "Man *is* the being which is addressed . . . by God."[30] "When the reality of human nature is in question, the word 'real' is simply equivalent to 'summoned'."[31] "Real man lives with God as His covenant-partner."[32] This

25. Barth, *Church Dogmatics*, III/2, pp. 71–202.
26. Ibid., p. 76.
27. Ibid., p. 78.
28. Ibid., p. 198.
29. Ibid., p. 202.
30. Ibid., p. 149.
31. Ibid., p. 150.
32. Ibid., p. 203.

view affects the content as well as the form of ethics, for the address is that of the gracious God known in Jesus Christ as God for man.

Differences in theology, that is in ways of construing God and God's relations to the world, lead to differences in theological views of man, and thus to different content as well as methods in theological ethics. A perspective different from Barth's leads to a different ethics. If the human body, with its desires and drives and with its necessities and propensities to live in communities and institutions, is part of the ordering activity of God, then what Barth calls the "phenomena" cannot be as sharply separated from the human capacities for self-determination. Those bases for human activity are part of the ordering of the creation, and are related to the Divine not through a personal summons to respond to God's call but as mediations of, and grounds for, norms of relationships. Nature has a different status and therefore a different dignity; it provides indications of what the proper ordering of even physical drives and impulses ought to be. From my perspective one cannot say with Barth that "phenomena" of man "convey no knowledge of real man."

A similar point can be made by observing how Barth treats marriage and family. The covenantal language is central, and thus he explicitly does not develop ideas of marriage and family as orderings of life into which persons enter by choice and by birth. To be sure, in part he is reacting against the static view of the orders of creation, to which marriage and family have traditionally belonged, particularly in Lutheran theology. The language of command of God, of events and of encounters, requires that the importance of persisting institutional forms be different from such a view.[33] What from another perspective requires the development of institutional ethics, seeing in institutions the requisites for the ordering of society and of human relations to nature, from Barth's perspective are "spheres" within which the divine command is heard. To be sure, there is a consistency of the command, and the Bible is the source for instruction about it, but the command is to persons in covenant partnership with each other. Marriage is not an institution, but

> the form of the encounter of male and female in which the free, mutual, harmonious choice of love on the part of a particular man and woman leads to a responsibly undertaken life-union which is lasting, complete and exclusive.[34]

One must agree that each marriage is a "particular occurrence," but the state of marriage can be viewed not merely as the sphere for an encoun-

33. See *Church Dogmatics*, III/4, pp. 19–23, where Barth critically analyzes the writings of Emil Brunner, Dietrich Bonhoeffer, and Niels H. Søe on the issue of how to account for persisting social patterns.

34. Ibid., p. 140.

ter between man and woman. Marriage is a requisite ordering of human relations not only for the benefit of the particular persons but also for the wider ordering of life in the human community. The ethics of marriage are thus not derived from the ordering and relating of the life of a man and women in obedience to the divine command. They are derived in part from the requisite ordering of social relations between particular persons with the duties and obligations that these relations entail. They are also derived from the relationships of the institution of marriage to the wider society, including the legal ordering of life.

To set forth an alternative ethical perspective, consistent with a different theology, is not to claim that Barth's extensive discussions of the encounter between man and woman lack insight. He is, indeed, very perceptive in many respects, but shortsighted in others. And surely all that he has to say is not derived from the biblical sources alone. But Barth's theology, because it systemically rules out patterns of ordering and interdependence as a theological ground for ethics, has difficulty in dealing with institutions per se. Institutions become spheres within which the command is heard and encounters between covenant partners occur.[35]

I have demonstrated that not only the form or method of Barth's ethics but also the content is decisively determined by his basic theological choices. The Bible is the source of knowledge of God; thus it is the central source both for the basic model of God and God's relations to the world and for moral instruction. Of course, Barth does not treat the biblical materials in a literalistic fashion. The Christological interpretation of biblical theology and the use of the interpersonal model back the view that whatever God does and commands is an expression and manifestation of his grace. Thus the goodness of God, for man, is the ultimate moral grounding, and thus there is a very positive note in all that Barth commends. Since man is the one who is covenant partner with God, and God addresses man in ways coherent with the biblical materials, the content of ethics comes to persons, in their encounters with each other in various events and spheres, as a command which is gracious.

I have pointed to the differences that the theology developed in volume 1 make for ethics, in comparison with Barth's. Knowledge, or at least indications of the ordering of the ultimate power and powers, comes through experience and our perceptions and interpretations of the requisites for life together in the world—not only with other individuals, but in

35. In a similar way, Barth deals with the relations of parents and children. "The word and concept of 'family' are deliberately avoided. . . . In the more limited sense particularly the idea of the family is of no interest at all for Christian theology." Ibid., p. 241. The family, like marriage, is a "sphere" in which the command of God is heard, in which God's action (and not God's ordering) is primary, and to which human actions are to attest. To develop this further would be redundant.

institutions and communities. Knowledge of the presence of God in the world also comes through nature and even through the aspirations and tendencies of human nature, and not just through the biblical covenant. Thus the content of ethics is derived heavily from these perceptions and interpretations. And since this is the case, it is not as readily possible to affirm Barth's Christocentric conviction that God is for man. Yes, God is the source of the human good; but God is not its guarantor, as is the case for Barth. Some of the practical implications of this view are given in the illustrations in the second part of this volume.

There is, however, a point of very deep affinity with Barth's theology and ethics that requires attention. That is in the relations between religious life and moral life, between religion and morality—what I have called piety. Different construals of God's relations to the world do not imply totally different affective and sensible responses to the world as ultimately ordered by the sovereign God. In terms of some fundamental attitudes toward God and the world, Barth's views are very similar to my own. Indeed, within the context of his biblical theology he uses in one way or another the same terms I have used for the "senses" that emerge out of human experience and that point to the power of God.

One aspect of this affinity is Barth's prophetic thrust which reminds us that only God is God. Many passages could be cited, but one good example is sufficient. In his very profound discussions of "Respect for Life," Barth writes, "Life is no second God, and therefore the respect due it cannot rival the reverence owed to God."[36] To be sure, the warrants he provides for this statement are stated differently than mine. But what is made clear is that we live in the conditions of finitude, and that biological life or any other aspect of finite world cannot be made of ultimate value for the human community. The worlds of which we are part are to be respected as given, and not as the objects of human creation. Thus there is a fundamental respect for *and* a relativization of all objects of human valuation short of the Diety. Only God is absolute; all things are in relation to God, and are to be valued in that relationship and not as final ends. In Barth's language, "[T]his relativisation never means that man is released from this respect. . . . Indifference, wantonness, arbitrariness or anything else opposed to respect cannot even be considered as a commanded or even a permitted attitude."[37] Sloth, on which Barth wrote in provocative ways, is no more permitted than is pride.[38]

Thus fundamental to Barth's view of human activity is the outlook of stewardship, of man as a participant in and a caretaker of a world that is

36. Ibid., p. 342.
37. Ibid., p. 343.
38. See Karl Barth, *Church Dogmatics*, IV/2, pp. 403–83, for the discussion of sloth; see *Church Dogmatics*, IV/1, trans. G. W. Bromiley (Edinburgh: T. and T. Clark, 1956), pp. 413–78, for the discussion of pride.

given by God. The classic biblical notion of stewardship expresses, in many respects, the idea of participation that I have developed. The world is here as given, and not of our creation. But our capacities are such that it is in our care in ways different from anything else that is known to exist.

Barth develops those "senses" I have described in volume 1.[39] To be sure, he does not stress that they are aspects of natural piety which is a basis both for religion and morality; his interpretation of them is bound to the context of his doctrine of a God who is for man. But they are there, and are powerfully portrayed. Man is a creature of God, as are all other aspects of the worlds of which we are a part. Human being "derives from God. It is a being dependent on God."[40] Gratitude is emphasized; to be sure, for Barth it is grounded in the Word of divine grace. But his statement that "being of man can and must be more precisely defined as a being in gratitude" can be affirmed on other theological bases as well.[41] To respond to what is given in gratitude is not to forget that the powers of God bear down on us and threaten us, but it is to live in the recognition that the ground of possibilities for human life and achievement is given, ultimately, by God. Like dependence, this sustains the attitude of human stewardship in the world. "Gratitude implies obligation towards the benefactor," Barth writes.[42] A response of thankfulness for the possibilities of life calls forth a sense of obligation, again as the caretakers and stewards of life in the world. Human beings, because of their capacities, have a unique responsibility among created things for the sustaining, ordering, and developing of life in the world. But they fail in their responsibilities; they share not only in the necessary conditions of finitude which create limits of foreknowledge and of control of consequences of their interventions, but also share in the human fault, one I have described in terms of the constriction of the soul.[43] Thus a sense of remorse and of repentance is evoked, and an awareness of the need for a turning toward God both for a redirection of life and a consciousness of the possibilities to alter its adverse conditions.

Barth's theology sustains, no doubt, a deeper sense of possibilities, of hope, than does mine, for like all traditional Christian theology it proclaims the salvation of man.[44] But the powers of the Divine, for me as well, do not fate us in ways that block all paths of change in ourselves and in the world; indeed, they are gracious in the sense that they enable human action to be rectified and human beings to develop aspirations, and in the sense that the external conditions are susceptible to human intervention for the possible

39. Gustafson, *Ethics*, 1:130–34.
40. Barth, *Church Dogmatics*, III/2, p. 140.
41. Ibid., p. 166.
42. Ibid., p. 167.
43. Gustafson, *Ethics*, 1:293–306. Barth's discussion of sin can be found, among other places, in *Church Dogmatics*, IV/1 and IV/2.
44. For Barth's discussion of eschatology, see *Church Dogmatics*, III/2, pp. 437–640.

improvement of life in the world. In order to live with a sense of possibilities created and sustained by the ordering of the world by God, one does not have to adhere to the traditional Christian eschatology of the ultimate fulfillment of a gracious will of God for man. Various ends provide direction for human activity, and the possibilities of these ends are grounded in the enabling powers of God.

In all theological ethics piety and morality are part of each other. All that is, including ourselves, is gift; it is given to us in reliance upon powers man does not create and on which all of life continues to rely. This affects our senses and sensibilities, our basic attitudes and dispositions toward other persons, communities, and the natural world. Opportunities for human life are given as well as threats against it; in many respects our rationally directed moral activities are empowered and directed by the recognition of our dependence on and gratitude for what is given. The sustenance of piety is of fundamental importance for morality.

Barth is extensively eloquent in developing the relations of faith to morality in his theology. The central point can be equally sustained on other theological grounds. What his theology does not allow, however, is a legitimate anger toward God as a result of experiences in which the fact that God is the source of human good does not issue in the fulfillment (even in very legitimate senses) of human life. God, the orderer of life, is a threat to human well-being; God is enemy as well as friend. The ultimate assurance of the fulfillment of human salvation, a point central to Barth's Christocentric theology, cannot be sustained, I believe, in the face of what we know both about the probable *finis* of human life and about grave threats to its well-being that result from such human capacities as nuclear destruction.

What my theocentric ethics shares, in spite of the differences, both with Barth and with a biblical vision of life, is a piety that issues in human stewardship (and not domination) of life in the world. It issues in a sense of calling, a vocation, that is both a responsibility and an opportunity, to participate in the developing of life in the world toward those ends that we can judge to be morally worthy. We have become agents, but at best we are only deputies of the divine orderer of the world.

Thomas Aquinas

To use a twentieth-century Protestant theologian and a thirteenth-century theologian as points of reference is fraught with historical difficulties. Both Barth and Thomas Aquinas worked, as all theologians do, within the context of their times and places, and in relation to antecedent works that were for them sources of support as well as points of differentiation. Both of them, however, had complete agendas of questions that a writer of theological ethics must answer, and each defended his answers thoroughly.

Comparative study of these authors, a project in which I periodically engage graduate students, forces any person to become clear about fundamental choices made both about the method or form of theological ethics on the one hand, and its substance or content on the other.

No full-length comparison of the two is made here, and with reference to Thomas, as to Barth, I select aspects of the writings that are most useful to indicate particular features of the profile drawn in chapter 1.[45] There are important affinities and differences between my work and that of Thomas and the Catholic tradition following him.

Karl Barth and Thomas Aquinas are comparable because of certain very general features of their theological ethics. Both wrote ethics that account for God and God's relations to the world, although Thomas's theory of natural law can be removed from its theological context to become a basis for ethics in a way that nothing in Barth's work can. For Thomas all things proceed from God and return to God; the pattern of *exitus et reditus* is essential for a proper grasp of the theological character of his ethics. This is fundamentally different from Barth's biblically backed interpersonal view of God speaking or commanding and man hearing or obeying. Each has objective ethics; the norms are objective to the moral agent, and there are sources of knowledge of these norms that are accessible to human beings. For Thomas, of course, they are to be found in large part in the moral ordering of nature, and particularly human nature; Barth rejects this on theological grounds that are, again, related to his version of a biblical theology. It would be an error to claim that Thomas does not have biblical backing for his ethics; the theological framework is based on his interpretation of revelation, and because of the unity of the moral law he can adduce evidences from the revealed law in the Bible as well as from natural law to sustain particular moral judgments. Since both men are comprehensive in their work, each has a view of human agency and action. Both have accounts of human freedom, but Thomas's, in my judgment, finally retains the unity of the body with human reasoning and choosing in a more integral way than does Barth's sharp distinction between the phenomena of man and real man. The relationships between faith or piety and morality are important for both of them; for Thomas the piety is teleological in its fundamental

45. Among the secondary sources I have studied are M. D. Chenu, O.P., *Toward Understanding St. Thomas*, trans. A. M. Landry, O.P. and Dominic Hughes, O.P. (Chicago: Regnery, 1964); James A. Weisheipl, O.P., *Friar Thomas D'Aquino: His Life, Thought, and Works* (Garden City, N.Y.: Doubleday, 1974); F. C. Copleston, S.J., *Aquinas* (Baltimore: Penguin Books, 1955); F. C. Copleston, S. J., *A History of Philosophy*, 8 vols., (London: Burns Oates and Washbourne, 1946–66), 2:302–434; Thomas Gilby, O.P., *The Political Thought of Thomas Aquinas* (Chicago: University of Chicago Press Midway reprint, 1973); Gerard Gilleman, S.J., *The Primacy of Charity in Moral Theology*, trans. William F. Ryan, S.J., and Andre Vachon, S.J. (Westminster, Md.: Newman Press, 1959); and Frederick Crowe, S.J., "Complacency and Concern in St. Thomas," *Theological Studies* 20 (1959):1–40, 198–231, 343–96.

pattern with human beings oriented toward a supernatural as well as natural end that the work of grace enables them to fulfill. For Barth morality is grounded in faith, in a very Protestant sense. These are the comparable points that are most relevant to my purposes here.

The major affinity of my work with Thomas's is the importance that an interpretation of the ordering of "nature" has for theological ethics. Barth's interpersonal model for understanding the relations of God to the world ruled out the possibility of natural ordering becoming significant in his ethics. For Barth, God is related to nature primarily through man. One can say that for Thomas man is, in very important ways, related to God through the ordering of nature.[46] The theological difference between these two interpretations is vast, and the implications for ethics are decisive. Thomas adduces evidences for his view through his epistemology and metaphysics as well as from revelation. Many features of his ethics are affected by this, including his understanding of the place of man in the universe and the relations of parts to the whole.

While there are grounds in Thomas's ethics for claiming that it is anthropocentrically oriented, a point to which I shall return, this anthropocentrism is qualified by his view of how aspects of the creation are related to each other for the sake of the final end of the whole. He believed and argued that there is a unity of the world. "The very order of things created by God shows the unity of the world. For this world is called one by the unity of order, whereby some things are ordered to others."[47] The unity of the whole can be adduced metaphysically; on the basis of observation of things, and a process of reflection in which abstractions are drawn from the observations, it can be shown that the relations of aspects of the creation to each other serve the end of the whole. But not all things are of "one grade of goodness." Natural things "seem to be arranged in a hierarchy." The divine wisdom is the cause both of the distinction of things from each other and of the inequalities between them; this is "for the sake of the perfection of the universe."[48] This perfection of the universe requires that some things be corruptible, and even that some can fail in goodness. "God and nature and any other agent make what is better in the whole, but not what is better in every single part, except in relation to the whole." And the whole universe of creatures "is all the better and more perfect if there be some things in it

46. Nature is not a univocal term in the writings of Thomas, and one must take care to read the context in which it is used. It is used for the order of creation; the principle of motion; with regard to man, both for reason which distinguishes human activity (the human essence) and the biological laws which man shares with animals; etc. For a discussion of some of these uses in relation to homosexuality, see John Boswell, *Christianity, Social Tolerance, and Homosexuality* (Chicago: University of Chicago Press, 1980), pp. 318–30.

47. Thomas Aquinas, *Summa Theologiae*, 1a, q.47, art.3, in *Basic Writings of Saint Thomas Aquinas*, Anton C. Pegis, ed., 2 vols. (New York: Random House, 1945), 1:462–63.

48. Ibid., q.47, art.2, 1:461.

which can fail in goodness, and which do sometimes fail."[49] I believe that Jonathan Edwards's question about the end for which God created the world is answered by Aquinas in the same terms as it is by Edwards, namely, that God created the world to glorify himself. It is a creation of the fullness of God; human activity plays a proportionate part in it but is related to the whole of the creation, which as a whole glorifies God.

The basic pattern of ethics is the right ordering of things in relation to each other as each is related to the other for the sake of the purpose of the whole. And the source for understanding these relations of things to each other is given in the natural ordering of the creation. To be sure, there is also an end of man, the vision of God and friendship with God, which goes beyond the right ordering of things to each other in nature, but grace corrects, fulfills, and perfects nature as human beings are oriented by it to their true and ultimate end.

Thomas's interpretation of the ordering of all things was, thus, both philosophically grounded and theologically directed. As Frederick Copleston stresses, there is an empirical aspect to Aquinas's epistemology; our knowledge of the metaphysical ordering begins with the observation of very particular things. The reflection is done by human beings, thus as human the intellect "must start from sense, from material being confined to material essences."[50] Immaterial objects are manifested in and through the sensible world, and thus finite and contingent objects can "reveal" their relations to God.

One implication of this is that how human beings perceive and interpret the natural things in the world can make a difference in how they interpret the relations of things to God. Thomas was, of course, dependent upon such knowledge of things as was available to him. Thus if one draws inferences from our contemporary interpretations of nature for the kind of ordering and ends (or absence of knowable ends) that are appropriate, one is engaged in an enterprise similar to his. That he would come to different conclusions in the light of twentieth-century perceptions and interpretations of nature than he did with his thirteenth-century ones is a very distinct possibility. Certainly he saw in nature a tendency of things to achieve their potentialities, and thus simpleminded accusations that he had a totally static conception of nature are not correct. His metaphysical claims were not simply deductions from science, but I believe they were not incongruent with the understandings of nature available to him.

While his metaphysics and theology were related to each other, Thomas makes very clear at the beginning of the *Summa Theologiae* that the knowledge proper to sacred doctrine "comes through revelation, and not

49. Ibid., q.48, art.2, 1:467.
50. Frederick Copleston, S.J., *A History of Philosophy*, 2:393.

through natural reason."[51] God is the subject matter of the science of sacred doctrine; its principles are "the articles of faith, for faith is about God."[52] This seems to lead to two aspects of his theological ethics: one is the understanding of nature which comes from observation, reflection, and abstraction not only about human activity but also about the relations of human activity to the wider order of nature; the second is the revealed knowledge of God pertaining to the final ends of nature and particularly of proper human activity.

Theological choices that Thomas made, very different from Barth's, decisively affect both the form or method and the content or substance of his ethics. One ought never to forget that his interpretation of the ordering of nature is theologically grounded; all things are coming from God and returning to God; all things are naturally ordered to their ends as God has created them; the natural moral law participates in the mind of God, in the eternal law.

A contrast with Barth helps to highlight the importance of this; for him the *words* and *acts* of God given in particular occasions ground the objective ethics theologically, whereas for Thomas it is the *mind* of God in which the natural moral law and the revealed law in the Bible participate that grounds objective ethics theologically. The mediation of the ultimate ground of ethics for Thomas is through continuities and relationships that persist, through laws, and not through the immediacy of a direct command. For Thomas, God on exceedingly rare occasions commanded something that violated the natural moral law; for Barth the form of the individual command is the norm.[53] What gives the commands of God consistency for Barth is that they will always be in accordance with his grace known in Jesus Christ; for Thomas the creation of the natural moral order is an act of grace, but the form and content of the order are given in nature. It is fitting to say that for both men the human responsibility is to conform one's action to God's moral will, but how that will is known is radically different. For Barth, information about the will of God is most likely to be found in the Bible; for Thomas, human experience and observations of things provide knowledge of the moral law, and it is the exercise of human practical reason that draws inferences from the law's first precept relative to particular choices. For Thomas, natural inclinations of persons could be governed and "shaped" into virtues through habituation, and these virtues have some reliability in directing the course of moral activity. For Barth, such reliance tends to

51. Thomas Aquinas, *Summa Theologiae*, 1a, q.1, art.6; Pegis ed., 1:11.

52. Ibid., q.1, art.7, 1:12.

53. One such exception is Samson's "suicide." See Thomas Aquinas, *Summa Theologiae*, 2a, 2ae, q.64, art.6, in St. Thomas Aquinas, *Summa Theologiae*, trans. Fathers of the English Dominican Province, 3 vols. (New York: Benziger Brothers, 1947), 2:1470. Here Thomas quotes from Augustine, *The City of God*, bk. 1, 21. He also excepts Abraham's willingness to kill Isaac and Hosea's "fornication"; see ibid., q.154, art.2, 2:1817.

usurp the place of God. The practical casuistry which for Barth might help one to hear the command of God can lead Thomas to quite secure judgments in many cases, and informed by charity and prudence it is likely, but not certain, to lead to right choices in ambiguous circumstances.

A brief comparison of these authors on comparable questions will make the differences more precise. Both are given to mixed arguments on very particular issues, but the forms of argument and the backing for them are very different. I noted above that for Barth the principal persistent command that protects life is, "Thou mayest live." Sin occurs when humans take the responsibility to determine who is to live and who is to die; they have usurped the divine prerogatives. Yet Barth opens up two possible exceptions to the divine No to the question of capital punishment: taking the life of a person for high treason during wartime and tyrannicide.[54] In the discussion of the exceptions Barth's arguments draw on various sources of insights.

Thomas's article, "Whether It Is Lawful to Kill Sinners?" provides an illuminating contrast to Barth which shows the practical ethical consequences of different theological choices.[55] The objections to an affirmative answer are made by quoting some biblical passages and giving syllogisms based on them, by citing Augustine (and by implication Paul) that one cannot do anything evil in itself for the sake of good, and by citing Aristotle on friendship. The "on the contrary" quotes two biblical passages that sanction death penalties. It must be noted that all the quoted biblical passsages function as laws or rules, as premises for moral syllogisms, if only implied ones. The body of the article, however, is an argument from Thomas's interpretation of nature. One can kill animals for human use "as the imperfect is directed to the perfect." Also, "every part is naturally for the sake of the whole." It is on these bases that surgery is justified; one can remove a decayed or infected member of the body for the sake of the whole. The individual person is to the community as part is to whole—an analogy to the human body is drawn. The conclusion is, "Therefore if a man be dangerous and infectious to the community, on account of some sin, it is praiseworthy and advantageous that he be killed in order to safeguard the common good." A biblical verse is added, "A little leaven corrupteth the whole lump (I Cor. 5:6)."

Two of the replies to objections are of particular interest. The first refers to Jesus' teaching that one ought to forebear uprooting the weeds to spare the good grain.[56] The "principle of double effect" is invoked to

54. Barth, *Church Dogmatics*, III/4, pp. 437–50.

55. Thomas Aquinas, *Summa Theologiae*, 2a, 2ae, q.64, art.2, in Benziger ed., 2: 1466–67.

56. The parable of the wheat and the weeds, Matthew 13:24–30 ("No, lest in gathering the weeds you root up the wheat along with them" [v. 19, R.S.V.]).

explicate this. An analogy to Jesus' teaching occurs when one cannot for some reason kill the wicked without also endangering the good. The conclusion is that Jesus teaches "that we should rather allow the wicked to live, and that vengeance is to be delayed until the last judgment, rather than that the good be put to death together with the wicked." If, however, no danger is incurred to the good and they can be protected by slaying the wicked, it is lawful.

The third reply states the factual premise that a sinner "departs from the order of reason, and consequently falls away from the dignity of his manhood." Indeed, he falls into "the slavish state of the beasts." These are statements based on the nature of the human. Two biblical passages are also quoted to support this. The conclusion is that while it is evil in itself to kill a person who preserves his "dignity," "it may be good to kill a man who has sinned, even as it is to kill a beast." Finally, he cites Aristotle in support of the notion that a bad man is worse than a beast and is more harmful.

By attending further to Thomas's arguments in this illustration we can continue to analyze both the form and the content of his ethics. It is an exercise in practical, and not speculative, reason. Whereas the conclusions of speculative reason lead to universal principles that "contain the truth without fail,"

> [t]he practical reason . . . is concerned with contingent matters, which is the domain of human actions; and consequently although there is necessity in the common principles, the more we descend towards the particular, the more frequently we encounter defects. . . . [I]n matters of action, truth or practical rectitude is not the same for all as to what is particular, but only as to the common principles, and where there is the same rectitude in relation to particulars, it is not equally known to all.[57]

A careful reading of the argument shows that even where it seems to come to decisive conclusions there are still remaining matters of judgment. For example, there is no specification of the conditions under which one can be sure that the infected member of the body is a threat to the health of the whole community. Nor are any criteria offered by which to judge under what conditions a danger would be incurred for the good by uprooting the social weeds. Similarly the criteria for when a human being has lost his or her dignity and thus can be classed as a beast are not indicated. Yet the argument is founded on more basic principles; it assumes that "the good is that which all things seek after," and that the first precept of the law, "that good is to be done and promoted, and evil is to be avoided," is being applied.[58] For Thomas, in addition to the process of practical reason, judg-

57. Thomas Aquinas, *Summa Theologiae*, 1a, 2ae, q.94, art.4, in Pegis ed., 2:777.
58. Ibid., q.94, art.2; Pegis ed., 2:774.

ments about particular cases are informed by prudence and equity; indeed *caritas*, graced love, can inform them. The use of syllogisms is explicit most of the time, and in some places where biblical verses are only quoted the use is implied.

When Barth discusses capital punishment he invokes some points that are similar to Thomas's and others that are different, but these matters are to him "points" which must be "considered" when there is a historical possibility that a command of God might be heard to take the life of a criminal.[59] Barth's strictures against practical causistry would be applied to Thomas's argument, and the most decisive is that the agent making the determination of good and evil is man rather than God. It is, of course, the case that Thomas is making a decision, but it is also the case that the decision is being made on the basis of a larger argument that natural law and the divine revealed law participate in the eternal law in the mind of God, and thus it is God's law that is the ultimate basis for the argument. And it is an order of God's creation in which the imperfect serves the perfect, and the part serves the whole, that is also invoked. Where Thomas does use a biblical analogy (the weeds) he is able to derive from it a moral principle, and uses the procedural principle of the double effect as he works it out. If it can be said that the final choice with reference to a particular case involves a process of discernment, that discernment is in sharp focus as a result of the understanding of law and uses of practical reason. The agent is an authorized human being, not God. The confidence implied is no superficial optimism, but is itself theologically grounded both in Thomas's theory of law and in his understanding of persons as moral agents who can exercise reason in this way.

Both the "Treatise on Law" and the "Treatise on Prudence and Justice," of which the discussion of taking life is a part, belong to the second part of the *Summa Theologiae*. They refer to the path of all things returning to God, and to the kinds of human actions that are in accord with that movement. To be sure, the arguments can be extracted from this context; there are arguments in the articles from the ordering of nature that lead to the same conclusion as those that are based on biblical revelation. But the larger framework of intention should not be lost from view; choices about particular matters are in accord or in disaccord with the final end of all things. While practical reasoning can err, the serious exercise of it (i.e., "ethics" per se) can hardly be sin, for moral actions make a difference to their agents and to the course of events, as both are directed toward man's final end, God. Ethics has a theological dignity that it cannot have in Barth's theology; moral life has a religious import in directing persons and all things

59. "We must now consider what are the points which must decide whether capital punishment is commanded or forbidden in the light of the 'Thou shalt not kill.'" Barth, *Church Dogmatics*, III/4, p. 439.

toward God that it cannot have in Barth's interpretation of the religious life. And Thomas's form or method of ethics is decisively determined by his theology.

If, for purposes of analysis, one distinguishes content from form, there are some significant differences, but also similarities. Thomas has access to the ordering of the created world that Barth denies. The denial is based not only on Barth's deep Protestant suspicion of claims to human self-sufficiency and thus the denial of God as sovereign, but also on his biblical theology. Thus the place that philosophical reflection has in each is different, and Thomas's "naturalism" as a basis for his metaphysics and ethics warrants his use of knowledge derived from "nature" as well as from the bible. Thomas can claim that the imperfect serves the perfect, and that the part serves the common good of the whole on the basis of his interpretation of the natural world, including embodied human souls.

Like all of Barth's discussions of the protection of life, his discussion of capital punishment interestingly brings in "points" to be "considered" which are drawn from society and human experience. And these do not merely specify or describe the particular case to be addressed. The commandment "Thou shalt not kill" is the starting point. This is a command of grace, "Thou mayest live." It is not that every created thing by nature seeks to preserve its life. And it is not an unexceptionable or even general rule to be applied, but a summary of God's gracious particular commands. His discussion of captial punishment initially takes into account various theories of punishment: (1) a common-good theory which justifies removal of a criminal to protect society, (2) the retribution theory, and (3) the "moral, pedagogic, and even pastoral" theory in which punishment is to incite a reformation of the criminal.[60] In these passages Barth draws upon various sources of understanding and insight, and not on biblical materials. Even with regard to the divine No to capital punishment, Barth allows for "the exceptional case," as I have noted. Behind any possible use of the death penalty must "stand" three considerations: a recognition, "not immediately apparent," that it is better for one person to die "than that the whole nation perish," i.e., a common-good condition; a recognition based on "the ultimate depths of the Christian faith" that it is God's will that the victim should be made a companion to the thieves on Golgotha as "a just reward for their deeds," but that Jesus is the expiation of their sin; and a recognition that causing the death is "the only mercy" that can be shown to the victim.[61]

The exceptional cases can be interpreted to meet these considerations. First, treason during a war.

60. Ibid., p. 440.
61. Ibid., p. 447.

> If a man surrenders military secrets to an actual or potential enemy and thus violates his military oath and endangers his own country, the existence of the state, and the lives of possibly thousands of his comrades, he may be said to have forfeited his right to live in this community and therefore be rightly subject to death, assuming that the gravity of his action has been scrupulously weighed and proved.[62]

His life is still in God's hands, and a minister should tell him explicitly that "Christ died for his sins too."

On the other exception, tyrannicide, Barth is more equivocal. He asks good questions.

> May not someone from the lower ranks of the political hierarchy, or even from outside it, take up the obviously abandoned cause of the state on his own responsibility for the salvation of the whole, and, since all others are barred, proceed at the risk of his own life to the elimination, i.e., the killing of this publicly dangerous person? Is this really murder, or is it an act of loyalty commanded *in extremis*, and therefore not murder?[63]

This is followed by an account of efforts to justify the assassination of Hitler, including that of 20 July 1944. The response is most equivocal.

> The only lesson to be learned is that they had no clear and categorical command from God to do it. Otherwise they would have overcome what was not in any case an ethical difficulty. Nor can we seriously blame these men for seriously considering and even deciding upon assassination. In such a situation it might well have been the command of God. For all we know, perhaps it was, and they failed to hear it.[64]

In both of these exceptions it is basically a threat to the common good that warrants the possibility that God might command that a life be taken.

Thomas's arguments on similar cases are found in the question "On Sedition." He argues that "sedition is contrary to the unity of the multitude, viz. the people of a city or kingdom."

> Wherefore it is evident that the unity to which sedition is opposed is the unity of law and common good: whence it follows manifestly that sedition is opposed to justice and the common good. . . . [A]nd its gravity will be all the greater according as the common good which it assails surpasses the private good which is assailed by strife.

62. Ibid., p. 448.
63. Ibid., p. 448–49.
64. Ibid., p. 449.

In a reply to an objection he deals specifically with tyranny.

> A tyrannical government is not just, because it is directed, not to the common good, but to the private good of the ruler. . . . Consequently there is no sedition in disturbing a government of this kind, unless indeed the tyrant's rule be disturbed so inordinately, that his subjects suffer greater harm from the consequent disturbance than from the tyrant's government. Indeed it is the tyrant rather that is guilty of sedition, since he encourages discord and sedition among his subjects.[65]

There is no discussion of capital punishment in this article, but the problems addressed are as similar as are any in the *Summa* to Barth's cases in which capital punishment is licit. Are the conclusions different from Barth's about the severity of treason and tyranny? My judgment is that Thomas's concern for "unity of law and the common good," when coupled with the conclusions of the article on killing sinners, would make him readier to justify capital punishment for sedition than Barth. Barth refers to a very precise case of treason and does not suggest application to generally similar cases. On the question of tyranny, both make general appeals to the common good, and Thomas surely is as concerned to find a way to have legal authorization for resistance to tyranny as Barth's question suggests that he is. But Thomas invokes the consequentialist concern: whether greater harm would be done as a result of disturbing a tyrannical government. And the fact that he does not even suggest the possibility of killing the tyrant can be taken to indicate his greater anxiety over disorder and his greater respect for authority. But the fact that he does not simply ask rhetorical questions and respond to them with a narrative that comes to equivocal conclusions indicates that whatever conclusion he might come to in a particular case would be supported by reasons based on his moral theory.

65. Thomas Aquinas, *Summa Theologiae*, 2a, 2ae, q.42, See particularly art.2, "Whether Sedition Is Always a Mortal Sin," Benziger, ed., 2:1365–66. Quotations from p. 1366. See also, "How Provision Might Be Made That the King May Not Fall into Tyranny," *Of Kingship*, chap. 6, in *The Political Ideas of St. Thomas Aquinas*, ed. Dino Bigongiari (New York: Hafner Press, 1953), pp. 186–92. "If there be not an excess of tyranny it is more expedient to tolerate the milder tyranny for a while than, by acting against the tyrant, to become involved in many perils more grievous than the tyranny itself" (p. 189). Speculation about probable consequences follows. "If the excess of tyranny is unbearable, some have been of the opinion that it would be an act of virtue for strong men to slay the tyrant and to expose themselves to the danger of death in order to set the multitude free" (p. 189). But this opinion is not in accord with apostolic teaching. "For Peter admonishes us to be reverently subject to our masters" (p. 190). "Should private persons attempt on their own presumption to kill the rulers, even though tyrants, this would be dangerous for the multitude as well as for their rulers" (p. 190). "If, on the other hand, it pertains to the right of a higher authority to provide a king for a certain multitude, a remedy against wickedness of a tyrant is to be looked for from him" (p. 191). "Should no human aid whatsoever against a tyrant be forthcoming, recourse must be had to God, the King of all, Who is a helper in due time of tribulation" (p. 191). "But to deserve to secure this benefit from God, the people must desist from sin, for it is by divine permission that wicked men receive power to rule as a punishment for sin" (p. 192).

Some of my responses to Thomas have been noted or alluded to in the course of the comparisons and expositions made thus far. It remains to make more specific references to the differences as well as similarities in order to bring more detail to the profile drawn in chapter 1.

One issue is that of anthropocentrism. We have seen that Thomas argued for the unity of all things, and that the activity of human beings is in a context of dependence on the wider ordering of nature. Thomas developed two ways in which human beings are related to God. One is through the ordering of which they are a part related to the whole. The other is a direct relationship based upon the creation of man in the image and likeness of God. The whole matter is dealt with quite succinctly in the following passage.

> [T]he entire universe is constituted by all creatures, as a whole consists of its parts. Now if we wish to assign an end to any whole, and to the parts of that whole, we shall find first, that each and every part exists for the sake of its proper act, as the eye . . . for seeing; secondly that less honorable parts exist for the more honorable, as the senses for the intellect . . . ; and, thirdly, that all parts are for the perfection of the whole. . . . Furthermore, the whole man is for the sake of an extrinsic end, namely, the fruition of God. . . . [T]hose creatures that are less noble than man exist for the sake of man. Furthermore, each and every creature exists for the perfection of the entire universe. Further still, the entire universe, with all its parts, is ordained towards God as its end, inasmuch as it imitates, as it were, and shows forth the divine goodness to the glory of God. Reasonable creatures, however, have in some special and higher manner God as their end, since they can attain to Him by their own operations, by knowing and loving Him.[66]

Relative to the greatness of God's work of justifying the ungodly in Christ the contrast is made even more dramatically. "The good of the universe is greater than the particular good of one, if we consider both in the same genus. But the good of grace in one is greater than the good of nature in the whole universe."[67]

While man as a part of the ordering of nature is a part of a whole that glorifies God, it is also the case for Thomas that a person as a part has his or her own end, that the less noble creatures serve man, and that with human capacities for reason, the image of God, there is an immediate and special relation to God. And, the salvation of a single person, "grace in one," is greater than the good of nature in the whole universe. While Thomas makes his case for God's concern for man and for individuals in distinctive ways, he is in this regard true to the biblical tradition. In the end it is the salvation of

66. Thomas Aquinas, *Summa Theologiae*, 1a, q.65, art.2, in Pegis ed., 1:612.
67. Ibid., 1a, 2ae, q.113, art.9, in Pegis ed., 2:1035.

individuals that is the chief purpose of God. But unlike many Protestant theologians, particularly modern ones, the creature with the immediate relation to God is also related to God through the rest of nature. The fact that the lower is ordained for the sake of the higher requires for Thomas that the ethical implications of the relations of man to nature take a different direction than those I have proposed and defended.

More in modern than in earlier times we are aware of how man, the "higher," participates in, often exploits for quite dramatic purposes, and to a larger extent controls the natural order. Indeed, if one reflects on the ordering of dependence of the human on the fundamental processes of nature, and on the capacities of humans to intervene in more and more intensive ways into nature, the order of valuation can be reversed; those necessary conditions for life, particularly for human life, are to be guarded even in our participation in them. One need only mention the probable consequences of an all-out nuclear war to see that human capacities to intervene in natural processes (while using them) can drastically affect human life and the conditions necessary for its proper fulfillment, not to mention the affect such intervention would have on the rest of nature and culture. As part of a larger whole in which relations are not merely the "lower" serving man, but interdependence in which human activity has serious consequences for the "lower," the larger whole becomes a proper object of moral concern and attention. Thomas would certainly be concerned about the possibilities of nuclear catastrophe, much as I am also concerned about them, primarily for the sake of human life. But the difference is a weight of emphasis on preserving possibilities for future developments of a larger whole even beyond the concern for human life and its future. That human beings, as a result of our capacities, have a special accountability to God, cannot be gainsaid, but that accountability needs to be developed in terms of our being a distinctive part of an interdependent ordering of the whole world.

The second issue is whether the objectivity of Thomas's ethics depends on some judgments that can be sharply questioned in the light of some modern ways of interpreting nature and its relations to the ultimate power and powers. One aspect of this is whether there is a *telos*, an end, that can be known with the assurance that Thomas has. The argument of volume 1 runs counter to Thomas's theological ethics on this issue. While I offered some reasons for affirming that the end of the creation is the glorification of God, and have noted that Thomas has a similar view, there are critical differences. Thomas's theology rests heavily on the judgment that in the return of all things to God, particularly the return of individual persons to God, there will be a restoration, fulfillment, and perfection of nature. The argument is based upon sacred doctrine, a matter of revelation, as well as on the conviction that all things have a tendency to fulfill the potentialities of their ends. I need only note here that in the light of contemporary interpretations of the future of life in this world and of the universe we know, the fulfillment that Thomas affirms cannot be sustained. The relationship between the world and God is one of *dependence* upon powers beyond our creation and ultimate control, not one of God as the end toward whom all things are moving as their certain perfection and fulfillment. Thomas's interpretation of the personal end of each human being requires that there be an immortal soul which, although it is the form of the body in our temporal existence, continues and can achieve friendship with God and the vision of God. This traditional Christian conviction about human immortality I have also brought into question.[68]

The implications of the differences for ethics are important. Without the assurance of a final purpose for the whole of creation and of human beings, a "naturalistic" basis for ethics must be satisfied with a variety of ends of human activity that are not forged into an ultimate single end.[69] Human aspirations and goals are related to the natural ordering of life within the conditions of our finite existence, and there is no guarantee of a preestablished harmony of proper ends, or of the fulfillment of the human good in individual or in species terms. The need for a "naturalistic" basis for ethics, as one has it in the works of Thomas, is affirmed, but his assurance of the telos is denied. This does not make ethics less theological in principle; we are to discern what we can of the proper ordering of life within the governing order of the powers that bring it into being and sustain it. But for both theological reasons and reasons drawn from contemporary interpretations of nature, Thomas's teleological vision cannot be adhered to.

A second aspect of Thomas's objective ethics is his conviction that there is a human "essence." I believe he comes to a conviction of such an essence on two different grounds. The first is metaphysical. The essence of a particular class of things is determined by a process of observation and reflection. We first apprehend particular objects via our senses—rocks, trees, and human beings, for example. In the process of reflection distinctions are drawn from these observations, the major one being between substance and accidents. A child appears different from a mature person, but both share something that persists through change and distinguishes them as human beings, different from dogs and trees. And different persons at the same stage of life are different, but we recognize the sameness as well. There is a substantial form of the human which gives us knowledge of the essence of the human. This essence is actualized in the existence of particu-

68. See Gustafson, *Ethics*, 1:182–83.
69. Ibid., 1:310–11.

lar human beings; it acts to order and direct the potentialities that are the matter we empirically observe in such a way that we can distinguish a class called human from one, for example, called simian.

Insofar as one identifies the distinctive features of a species, and the distinctive features are called the essence, one has no quarrel with this procedure. The question is whether this essence assumes the absence of development in human evolution. Of course one does not fault Thomas for not having access to twentieth-century knowledge, and as I noted above, there is reason to believe that in his interpretation of the development of potentialities he could have taken into account a modern interpretation. Also, insofar as the "essence" indicates that there are particular potentialities and values to human life, and thus that human beings have an accountability for the ordering of life and a distinctive value within it, there is no quarrel.

But when the large time-frame that I have argued in volume 1 is taken into account, and one attempts to think about the religious and ethical significance of the process of development from the simian to the human, some qualifications are required. While there is disagreement among paleoanthropologists about what the distinctive features of human life are, and when they developed, there is general acceptance of the development of human life from some common stock out of which developed forms of simian life.[70]

Of course, our ethical questions are raised within the context of the present state of development of human life, and we cannot foresee all possible future states of development. But the valuation of the human, relative to other forms of life, is qualified, in my view, by the recognition that there is no timeless essence of man. Further, the recognition of our biological kinship with other animals qualifies, in my judgment, both the significance of the distance between us and the idea that because of this distance the more imperfect are created to be in the service of us who are more perfect.

Thus, insofar as the conviction of an eternal essence in man is a foundation for a valuation of the human that decisively affects certain moral judgments and actions, changes in ethics result from the different interpretation of the human. One does not need to affirm that human life is of supreme value in order to defend the view that it is of distinctive value. The concept of the ensouled body, which gives it supreme value has, in Catholic ethics, had a decisive significance for certain moral choices. The traditional arguments against the induced abortions of human fetuses is only one case in point.

70. See, for example, C. Owen Lovejoy, "The Origin of Man," *Science* 221 (23 Jan. 81):341–50. Subsequent letters to *Science* undertook arguments against some of the particular conclusions of this article, but the general developmental view was not doubted.

The second ground for the conviction that there is a human essence is based on revelation. Man is made in the image and likeness of God. Those human capacities for rational activity which distinguish the human on the basis of comparison with other forms of life are the marks of the image of God in man. Thus the two grounds converge.[71] Religiously, the image of God is related to the final end of each person, namely, the movement toward the beatific vision. Ethically, it establishes the superiority of human life over other forms of life, and thus backs the arguments that the lower serves the higher, the imperfect serves the perfect, and similar convictions. It also establishes the direct relationship between persons and God that coexists with the mediated relationships through the ordering of nature. Insofar as these convictions sustain the same moral conclusions that Thomas's naturalistic delineation of the essence of man serves, they are subject to the same criticism.[72]

A third aspect of Thomas's objective ethics, already alluded to, requires more particular attention. It is the hierarchy of entities with the assumption that in the natural order the lower serves the higher. Granted the possibility for development of potentialities that is present in Thomas's thought, it remains the case that modern achievements in science and technology have altered radically the relations of human activity to the given natural world, something that no one in Thomas's age could have foreseen. Interventions into "nature" are morally approved in Thomas's thought; the excision of diseased parts of the body is one example. And human beings have no doubt intervened into the ordering of nature when it has been beneficial to do so since the dawn of consciousness; indeed, even animals intervene in ways that destroy some aspects of "nature" for the sake of their own needs.

The critical move I have made relative to this is to interpret the relationship as one of *interdependence* rather than simply dependence of man on the ordering of the world around us. Interdependence includes dependence, but takes into account the increasing human capacities to alter in more fundamental ways the nature which sustains and threatens us. Even with regard to human life, the possibilites for genetic surgery and for manipulation of the responses of our neural system are evidences of these new capacities. When one moves beyond the biological individual to recall the capacities to manipulate the ordering of society (though still limited), additional evidence occurs. And the achievements of modern agriculture, as well as those of the controlled use of nuclear energy, point to ways in which what occurs in the "natural" order is subject to very powerful human interventions.

71. I do not elaborate on Thomas's interpretation of the image and likeness of God in man. See Thomas Aquinas, *Summa Theologiae*, 1a, q.93, in Pegis ed., 1:885–901.

72. For my comments of the theme of the *imago dei*, see Gustafson, *Ethics*, 1:100–101.

While Thomas surely affirms human freedom, or the capacities to act in accord or discord with the natural moral order, the capacities of modern technology have enlarged the range of consequences of human choices. It is for this reason that the idea of man as participant becomes important. We participate in patterns of interdependence, and can alter the conditions on which we depend. The ethical implications of this are that the "natural order" is less natural in the sense that it is determined simply by "laws" of nature. We have not dominated nature, even though we have controlled more aspects of it than was possible in previous times. But our capacities to intervene into it mean that "nature" does not provide the kind of blueprint for proper human conduct that is more strongly the case in the ethics of Thomas.

I have argued that we must find our fitting relationships to nature, that we are to relate all things in a manner appropriate to their relations to God. This requires that restraints be taken into account in pursuing human ends which have some moral justification. Ultimate dependence upon what we did not, and cannot, create is always present. But while this ultimate dependence and what we can learn about its ordering are a deep basis for ethics, they are not a sufficient basis in the light of our participation in an interdependent ordering of life. The determination of right conduct and appropriate ends of action becomes more complex and difficult, and the degree of assurance that our activities are right and good that Thomas could provide on the basis of natural law is brought into question.

The relationship of parts to wholes is something that Thomas's interpretation of the world and his ethics takes very seriously. This relationship is to be affirmed. The issue is what constitutes an appropriate larger whole to be taken into account when determining what human actions are right and what ends of action are good. Roman Catholic moral theology has conceived of this in terms of a "totality."[73] In my judgment, both in the writings of Thomas and in subsequent Roman Catholic moral theology, the determination of a morally approvable totality is unduly restricted. Diseased organs can be removed for the benefit of the whole of the human body. Sinners can be killed for the sake of the well-being of the common good of the community. But the supreme value given to human life individually, and the limitation of the common good to human communities, shows the depth of the anthropocentrism in Thomas and in our culture. The issue is whether any larger whole can be morally justified as the totality whose common good is to be taken into account.

One need not go into a detailed analysis of the argument of the controversial encyclical of Pope Paul VI, *Humanae Vitae*, to see how the

73. For a discussion, see Martin Nolan, "The Principle of Totality in Moral Theology," in Charles E. Curran, ed., *Absolutes in Moral Theology?* (Washington: Corpus Books, 1968), pp. 232–48.

question is answered there.[74] Most of the criticisms of the encyclical by Roman Catholic moral theologians are focused on the issue of the encyclical's view of the nature of the person, which is judged rightly to be "physicalist" or "biologistic" in character. The affirmation that every act of sexual intercourse must be open to the possibility of the transmission of life is the key point for this criticism. More germane to my argument here is the fact that, in the encyclical, considerations for the social well-being of even the family, not to mention various nation-states and the human species, are not sufficient to justify artificial means of birth control. That they might justify abortion under certain circumstances is, of course, also ruled out.

If the family is a totality whose common good is to be taken into account, as it is in other encyclicals that back a notion of a just wage based on family need, it can be argued that for the sake of the common good of a particular family with limited means or with already existing interpersonal tensions, the birth of another child is debilitating to the good of the whole.[75] To make such an argument is, no doubt, to get onto the "slippery slope" that is feared by moral rigorists, for it requires that judgments of probable consequences be made on the basis of evidences that cannot assure the accuracy of the prediction. While the use of the refined principle of double-effect provides some more rationally secure basis for making such a judgment, and preserves the maxim that no good end justifies an "evil" act to achieve it, even this is not acceptable to the teaching authority of the church. The intention, so critical to Catholic moral theology, might well be that the common good of the family is served, but the use of contraception as a means is deemed contrary to nature. And if the issue comes up with reference to the abortion of a fetus for the sake of the well-being of the family, even a fetus that is prenatally detected as very radically defective, further arguments are made.

One is a descriptive argument that makes a theological difference: the fetus is described as a person and thus already has a direct relationship to God. Another is more strictly moral: the fetus is not an unjust aggressor, as is the criminal whose life can be taken for the sake of the good of the community. Catholic moral theology, based on Thomas's natural-law ethics, does not argue that there is a harmony of human ends so that all things work together for an apparent temporal human good. There is no

74. Pope Paul VI, *Humanae Vitae*, in Joseph Gremillion, ed., *The Gospel of Peace and Justice: Catholic Social Teaching Since Pope John* (Maryknoll, N.Y.: Orbis Books, 1976), pp. 427–43.

75. For discussion of the just wage, see Leo XIII, *Rerum Novarum*, 44–46, in Etienne Gilson, ed., *The Church Speaks to the Modern World: The Social Teachings of Leo XIII* (Garden City, N.Y.: Doubleday Image Books, 1954), pp. 229–30; and Pius XI, *Quadragesimo Anno*, 63–75, in Terence R. McLaughlin, C.S.B., ed., *The Church and the Reconstruction of the Modern World: The Social Encyclicals of Pius XI* (Garden City, N.Y.: Doubleday Image Books, 1957), pp. 242–46.

assurance that another child, or a defective child, will not severely affect the good in common of the other members of the family, or the common good of the whole family. Nonetheless, the value intrinsic to the person (or potential person) requires that the common good of the family not be used as an argument against the fetus's life.

The issue is similar, for this view, if one argues that the common good of other totalities, such as a nation-state or the human species, can be invoked. "Overpopulation" in a particular country, which threatens even the health of its poor citizens, does not legitimate a voluntary policy of birth control, not to mention incentives that border on coercion, or coercion outright. As a "global" problem, the possibility of threats to the well-being of even large "totalities," including the resources needed to guarantee sufficient nutrition for future generations, is not sufficient to warrant contraception. To be sure, modern capacities to intervene in nature which increase available food and other resources are warranted, but the capacities to intervene to restrict population growth are not.

In chapter 1 I introduced the way in which I think the relations between parts and wholes, and the common good, ought to be pursued. The interpretation of interdependence of human activity with the natural world necessitates the enlargment of the totalities whose common good must be taken into account. It is, after all, the result of our capacities to intervene in nature, drastically to lower death rates for one example, that have created problems human beings now face. This capacity must be taken into account in the formation of what are considered to be proper entities whose good in common, and whose collective good, are morally legitimate concerns. And my theological construal of the world requires that more than the good of the human species must be considered. To argue this is not to say that the morality of the means of achieving defensible ends is irrelevant. But it is to open the possibility that some of the means traditionally considered illicit in moral theology based on Thomas's thought can be defended, and that in some dilemmas or conflicts between justifiable ends there is no avoidance of painful and tragic choices.

Like the work of other Protestants in recent decades my study of the works of Thomas Aquinas and subsequent Catholic moral theology was motiviated in part by growing dissatisfaction with the weakness of moral arguments used not only in ecclesiastical documents but also by Protestant theologians. Different Protestants have gone to different lengths in their prescriptions of how that weakness is to be overcome; some have taken Kant and neo-Kantians as their guides, and some have been satisfied to be the analytical disposers of weakness without proposing substantial alternatives. Many are dissatisfied with Karl Barth's language of "points to be considered"; that formulation in itself is very ambiguous because it does not determine *what* count as "points" and *how* they are to be considered. It can well be argued that the practical reason in Thomas is an illustration of how relevant points are to be considered in coming to a particular moral choice. Barth clearly disagrees on what points are relevant and why they are, and he disagrees on the procedures involved in considering them. I believe that my development of the idea of discernment in volume 1 has significant affinity with the work of Thomas, though the differences are also important.

Some further attention needs to be given to Thomas's interpretation of the person as moral agent and of how moral choices ought to be made. There are many significant distinctions that make for precision in his moral theory which I will ignore for the sake of brevity and the limited purpose of this section. One cannot but be impressed with the comprehensiveness of Thomas's account; there is a thoroughly developed interpretation of human beings as agents, the importance of circumstances, the nature of human acts, the ends of action, and the criteria to be used in making a choice. If one uses the current distinction between agent-oriented and act-oriented ethics, it is clear that Thomas has both, and that any moral theory that attended to one to the exclusion of the other would be, for him, insufficient. Thomas is not a voluntarist in the sense of the Franciscan voluntarists such as Ockham; it is equally an error, however, to interpret him as a rationalist, or even an "intellectualist." "The movement of the will follows the act of the intellect. But the intellect understands some things naturally. Therefore the will, too, wills some things naturally."[76] And while there is self-determination in the will, it is related to the appetites.

This is developed in his argument pertaining to love as a passion of the soul. Love pertains to the appetites; it has good as its object. After distinguishing between the natural appetite (which seeks a good according to its nature), the sensitive appetite (which operates from a mixture of necessity and freedom), and the intellectual or rational appetite (the will, which follows from a free apprehension of an object), Thomas argues that love is the principle of movement towards the end loved in each form of the appetites. There is a natural love which is the subject's "connaturalness with the thing to which it tends." But in the will there is a "complacency in good," a kind of openness to or receptivity of the good; and in the intellectual love there is what might be called a rational choice of the good.[77] For Thomas moral choices stem from rational activity which governs and directs the inclinations of our nature as human beings. Man is a valuing being, i.e., a being directed by "love" in Thomas's sense, and part of moral life is to govern our natural valuations. The general lines of his arguments, then, are similar to those I made about "natural man" in volume 1.[78]

I have argued that moral choices flow, in part, from the sort of persons

76. Thomas Aquinas, *Summa Theologiae*, 1a, 2ae, q.10, art.1, in Pegis ed., 2:259. Qqs. 8–11 discuss the will; ibid., pp. 245–71.

77. Thomas Aquinas, *Summa Theologiae*, 1a, 2ae, q.26, art.1, in Benziger ed., 1:703–4; quotation from p. 704.

78. Gustafson, *Ethics*, 1:281–93.

we have become. On this point as well there are affinities with Aquinas, particularly with his discussion of "habit," for which he relies heavily on Aristotle. Of course, there are differences; one is with Thomas's conviction that there is *a* nature to persons whose powers are perfected by habits. Theologically, one difference is with his argument that God infuses habits in persons, though I can agree that whatever are the works of renewal and redirection of life as a result of a theocentric orientation, they are suitable to our human characteristics. Thomas writes, "[God] does nothing contrary to that which is suitable to nature," even though he can do things that "nature cannot do."[79]

"Habits," he argues, "are dispositions to acts."[80] While the dispositions to act in certain ways are dependent upon our natural inclinations, they are also formed as a result of the choices persons make through their rational activity. For Thomas, the goodness or badness of a habit depends upon whether it is suitable to human nature, i.e., whether it is in accord with reason.[81] His argument about how human nature is precisely conceived is one that I have called into question, at least by implication, above. But insofar as his argument is that dispositions are formed as a result of not only our natural capacities and appetites, or our natural evaluations, but also as a result of sequences of choices and actions, its basic lines can be developed in ways congruent with my understanding of human persons. Our access to saying anything about a person's moral disposition is through our observations of a sequences of actions and the signs of consistency that they indicate. It is on these grounds that we make particular judgments about persons as being "just" or "loving" or "honest." While acts of love might flow with ease and pleasure from a loving disposition, it is also the case that the "readiness" to love is endorsed and even reinforced by loving actions, and that rational activity is required to direct particular acts of love in a morally fitting way. I would argue, however, that the formation of our dispositions stems in part from our loyalties to particular persons and communities, and from our conscious commitments to particular values and ways of life. The norm for good habits is not our "nature" in Thomas's sense, though our habits are grounded in our natural capacities; the normative question is, What convictions, loyalties, and communities are appropriate? If such a question would be included in Thomas's understanding of reason, there would be even deeper affinity.

It is a mistake to charge Thomas with a purely deductive system for coming to particular choices about particular moral acts. To be sure, as indicated in the comparison of Barth with Thomas on the question of capital

79. Thomas Aquinas, *Summa Theologiae*, 1a, 2ae, q. 51, art.4, in Pegis ed., 2:392. The "Treatise on Habits" begins with q.49, Pegis ed., 2:393.

80. Thomas Aquinas, *Summa Theologiae*, 1a, 2ae, q. 54, art.2, in Pegis ed., 2:408.

81. Ibid., art.3, Pegis ed., 2:410.

punishment, there is a first principle, and there is a primary precept derived from the principle. And the discussions of many moral questions in the *Summa Theologiae*, 2a, 2ae, show how both these principles are applied. In contrast with Barth's ambiguous use of practical casuistry, certainly Thomas's brings the range of choices into very sharp focus. And since, on the whole, he is not concerned with the usurpation of the divine prerogatives (though this is adduced in some places), the agent receives quite precise directions about what is right conduct. That many later moral theologians claimed more certainty about the rightness of more particular acts than Thomas could is the case.

But since his ethics is one of virtues, i.e., agent-oriented, as well as one of acts, and since moral choices are by persons of virtue as well as those of vice, more than simply logical deductions from basic and secondary principles is a part of his moral theology. In the classic tradition, Thomas places great importance on the moral virtue of prudence.

> Moral virtue can be without some of the intellectual virtues . . . ; but not without understanding and prudence. Moral virtue cannot be without prudence, because [it] is a habit of choosing, i.e., making us choose well. Now in order that a choice be good, two things are required. First, that the intention be directed to a due end; and this is done by moral virtue, which inclines the appetitive power to the good that is in accord with reason. . . . Secondly, that man choose rightly those things which are means to the end; and this he cannot do unless his reason counsel, judge and command rightly, which is the function of prudence and the virtues annexed to it.[82]

To be sure, prudence is a matter of "right reason about things to be done," but it is a habit, and thus a readiness to think rightly that has developed over time.

More to the point, however, is his discussion, also following Aristotle, of the virtue of *epikeia*, or equity. While the discussion focuses on legislation, it is also applicable to moral "laws." It is not possible to develop rules to apply to every single case.

> [L]aws attend to what commonly happens: although if the law be applied to certain cases it will frustrate the equality of justice and be injurious to the common good. [In such cases] it is good to set aside the letter of the law and to follow the dictates of justice and the common good.[83]

Laws and rules are applied to matters of contingency, and it "belongs to *epikeia* to moderate something, namely, the observance of the letter of the

82. Thomas Aquinas, *Summa Theologiae*, 1a, 2ae, q.58, art.4, in Pegis ed., 2:445–46.
83. Thomas Aquinas, *Summa Theologiae*, 2a, 2ae, q.120, art.1, in Benziger ed., 2:1695.

law."[84] It must be noted that this virtue does not give license to radically intuitive judgments, nor is it a matter of taking into account all the points to be considered and then hearing a command of God. It is a virtue exercised in the application of rules; it applies them to contingent matters and sees exceptional cases to which they do not apply. It sees a larger intent of rules, and in the light of that intent (here justice and the common good) makes judgments in some cases that are not in accord with the rules.

Certainly many manualists in the Catholic moral theology tradition had little or no confidence in the virtue of equity; for every "case of conscience" they seemed to be able to find more and more particularized distinctions and rules to apply.[85] Conscience for Thomas is an act in which habitual knowledge of moral principles is applied to individual cases. It has three functions: it witnesses "insofar as we recognize that we have done or not done something"; it excuses, accuses, or torments us by judging whether we have done something well or not; and it judges "that something should be done or not done, and in this sense conscience is said to incite or to bind."[86] When the conscience judges that something is to be done or not done it not only incites but binds. It is an act of the individual person, and thus cannot be determined by another. Copleston quotes a very powerful passage in this regard. "Every conscience, whether it is right or wrong, whether it concerns things evil in themselves or things morally indifferent, obliges us to act in such a way that he who acts against his conscience sins."[87]

For Thomas there is a process of discernment which moves from the principles and rules that cover a class of cases to their application in particular circumstances. Prudence, equity, and conscience, when shaped and informed by natural inclinations and rational activity, can be relied upon to choose in a way fitting to the contingent factors that are present in many occasions of moral choice. Although I did not develop the process of discernment in Thomas's terms, that discussion is much more in accord with his thought than it is with the thought of Karl Barth and many other Protestant theologians.

Karl Rahner

Contemporary Roman Catholic moral theology has reacted against the rigid "manualist" tradition with some vehemence. To be sure, the

84. Ibid., art. 2, in Benziger ed., 2:1696.

85. Those moral theologians who wrote textbooks for priests and who applied principles and precepts in a rationalistic way to very detailed and precise circumstances are called "manualists." Examples are, among many, Henry Davis, S.J., *Moral and Pastoral Theology*, 4 vols. (New York: Sheed and Ward, 1935); Thomas Slater, S.J., *A Manual of Moral Theology for English-Speaking Countries*, 3d ed., 2 vols. (New York: Benziger, 1908); and Arthur Preuss, *A Handbook of Moral Theology Based on the "Lehrbuch der Moraltheologie" of the Late Antony Koch*, 3d ed., 5 vols. (St. Louis: B. Herder, 1925).

86. Thomas Aquinas, *Summa Theologiae*, 1a, q.79, art.13, Pegis ed., 1:767.

87. Thomas Aquinas, *Quodlibetum*, 3, 27, quoted in F. C. Copleston, *Aquinas*, p. 220.

conservative viewpoint has its defenders, and the reformers are not all alike. It is clear that reformers cannot tamper with particular moral prescriptions and rules that are judged to be in error without looking also at fundamental moral theology, i.e., at basic theological and philosophical theories that underlie particular choices.[88] Karl Rahner, S.J., has attended more to fundamental and dogmatic theology than he has to moral theology, but he has written sufficiently on moral theology to make clear some of the implications of his major work for that field. His thought is also a source for changes made in moral theology by other writers. Rahner's work is highly complex and systematic, and is couched in concepts that are very distinctive. This makes it difficult to respond to briefly. Necessarily, my response to it as a basis for ethics, and to its specifically moral reflections, cannot adequately develop its philosophical anthropology and doctrine of God.[89]

It is fair to say that not only in the work of Rahner, but also in that of many moral theologians, there has been a twofold move from the manualist tradition, and to some extent from the work of Thomas Aquinas. It is also the case that Thomas's theology has been retrieved in certain ways that highlight features which were not adequately attended to in late nineteenth- and early twentieth-century moral theology. One move has been from a more static to a more dynamic interpretation of natural law. This point is sometimes stated as a transition from a classical to a historical world view. This move opens the way to take into account some of the modern interpretations of nature and historical change, and to learn some different things about what is morally required. Universal and persisting principles are at least open to new applications in the light of modern circumstances, and for some theorists the principles, as well as the precepts and rules themselves, are open to revision.[90] This move is clearly congenial to aspects of my ethics from a theocentric perspective.

The other basic move is from a more cosmocentric to a more anthropocentric view of life, and thus of ethics as well. The caption that is often used for this is "the turn toward the subject." This turn is made in part for philosophical reasons, particularly for epistemological ones. It results from taking into account the philosophy of Immanuel Kant, and in Rahner's case it is informed deeply by the thought of Heidegger.

The turn is also made for theological reasons too complex to be developed here. One of them, however, is the retrieval of certain forms of biblical theology with its concern more for historical activity than for cosmic order.[91] Another theological reason is the recovery of the primacy of God's

88. For a fuller development of this statement, see Gustafson, *Protestant and Roman Catholic Ethics*, pp. 46–59, 80–94, and 111–26.

89. For my discussion of Rahner on God, see Gustafson, *Ethics*, 1:34–37.

90. For some examples, see Gustafson, *Protestant and Roman Catholic Ethics*, pp. 50–59.

91. This is seen most dramatically in liberation theology, for example: "Other religions think in terms of cosmos and nature. Christianity, rooted in Biblical sources, thinks in terms of

grace, a matter that Rahner and others share particularly with the theology of Karl Barth. The "subject" is not only an epistemological datum; the subject is also the ultimate focus of the divine purpose. God is very much a God for man, and for all persons, as Rahner has particularly developed the argument. Not only is the centrality of the traditional concern for human salvation clear in this, but because God's grace is, for Rahner, offered to all persons it is possible to respond to it without being explicitly Christian.[92].

Both the theological and the philosophical reasons come to bear on what is at the crux of the matter, namely, a conception of the nature of man as personal. The basic argument of traditional natural law is maintained; from a proper description of "nature" the norms for ethics are developed. Ethics deals with human nature, and thus when human nature is redescribed, a different interpretation of the norm is established. The new description is one of the subject as radically free, and thus the realization and preservation of that freedom is the principal line that particular norms are to follow. This is a point on which my work will be differentiated from Rahner's.

The turn is also taken for moral reasons, and its direction is guided by the philosophical and theological ones. The critique of the received tradition of manualist moral theology is very similar to some of the Protestant criticisms of legalism. It is a cautious criticism; it does not open the door to radical existentialist or situational ethics.[93] Rahner described what he is defining himself against. "According to the common teaching, ethics is syllogistic, deductive ethics." The major premise is an abstract universal one; the minor one asserts that the here and now is the point of application. "The conclusion finally converts the major into a concrete and clear imperative. Conscience, accordingly, is conceived exclusively as the mental-moral function of the person which applies the universal norm to the concrete '*casus*'."[94]

> [I]n so far as man belongs to the material world by his concrete activity, his activity is an instance and fulfilment of something universal which determines his actions as something different from the individual and opposed to it, i.e. as a *law* expressed in universal propositions. In so far as the same man subsists in his own spir-

history." Gustavo Gutierrez, *A Theology of Liberation*, trans. Canidad Inda and John Eagleson (Maryknoll, N.Y.: Orbis Books, 1973), p. 174.

92. See "Anonymous Christians," in Karl Rahner, *Theological Investigations*, vol. 6, trans. Karl-H. and Boniface Kruger (Baltimore: Helicon Press, 1969), pp. 390–98; and "Atheism and Implicit Christianity," in Karl Rahner, *Theological Investigations*, vol. 9, trans. Graham Harrison (New York: Herder and Herder, 1972), pp. 145–64.

93. See "The Appeal to Conscience," in Karl Rahner, *Nature and Grace and Other Essays*, trans. Dinah Wharton (New York: Sheed and Ward, 1963), pp. 84–111.

94. Karl Rahner, "On the Question of Formal Existential Ethics," in *Theological Investigations*, vol. 2, trans. Karl-H. Kruger (Baltimore: Helicon Press, 1963), p. 221.

ituality, his actions are also always more than mere applications of the universal law to the *casus* in space and time; they have a substantial positive property and uniqueness which can no longer be translated into a universal idea and norm expressible in propositions constructed of universal notions.[95]

The spiritual individuality of persons directs their actions "to the concrete as such, as it really is—to the concrete in its positive, and particularly its substantial, material uniqueness."[96]

The two features of Rahner's ethics that have greatest affinity with my project are the developmental view of natural law, and his interpretation of moral choice as being what I have called a process of discernment. The affinity is with his method and his procedures. The major point of differentiation pertains to Rahner's isolation of the essence of man in transcendental freedom, and the normative role that this essence then has in shaping moral ends and principles. The difference, then, is with his content or substance. On all of these matters Rahner is subtle and complex, and I shall attempt to do justice to his views within a brief space.

Rahner's developmental view of natural law is based on his interpretation of several related factors. First there is "something universal" that determines human actions, and that can be expressed in terms of law. Second, there is transcendental freedom, which not only is the ground for particular perceptions in particular cases of moral choice but also for the continued exploration and investigation of the world from which derives human knowledge, including the sciences. It is this latter that points to the third factor, namely, change and development in human knowledge through history. In history, man, because of freedom, learns more and more about "nature," and what is learned about nature and possible interventions into it is important for ethics. And fourth, man also learns from experience; experience can correct itself. Two of his essays, "The Experiment with Man" and "The Problem of Genetic Manipulation," provide excellent resources for a brief account of a developmental view of natural law, i.e., the ways in which new knowledge of nature has to be taken into account in ethics.[97]

The moralist is no longer self-sufficient in knowing the subject matter that is analyzed from a moral point of view, but must rely on knowledge that comes from relevant scientific specialists. Rahner is not naive about reliance on specialists, but emphasizes the requirement for the moralist to take their conclusions into account. A moral conclusion might well be altered by the inclusion or omission of relevant data.

95. Ibid., p. 226.
96. Ibid., p. 228.
97. Rahner, *Theological Investigations*, 9:205–24, and 225–52.

> It is at least possible that the very "detail" of which the theologian is ignorant, or of which he has only a vague notion, might be the decisive factor in his case; it might be the very detail which would alter the whole conclusion. A small example: for a few centuries Catholic moral theology has been convinced that the moment of union of male and female germ cells is also the moment when an individual human being comes into existence. Will today's moral theologian still have the courage to maintain this presupposition as the basis of many of his moral theological statements, when faced with the knowledge that 50 per cent of all fertilised female cells never succeed in becoming attached to the womb? Will he be able to accept that 50 per cent of all "human beings"— real human beings with "immortal" souls and an eternal destiny—will never get beyond this first stage of human existence?[98]

While Rahner does not draw particular moral conclusions from his "small example," the implication that it requires a possible change in arguments about birth control is very clear.

Experience as well as new knowledge has to be taken into account, and sometimes simply is taken into account, in the course of history. Human freedom is "co-determined" by its categorical aspect—our bodily and social characteristics, for examples. Freedom is the norm, but here the basic point is that there are corrections to a violation of the norm that arise out of experience and even conscious experimentation. From the use of human freedom in such "categorical" areas as our biological, psychological, and social natures,

> laws can be apprehended and accepted which, without vitiating the freedom of self-manipulation, *act to a certain extent like regulating systems and in the long run and on the whole stop this self-manipulation from going off the path into an absurdity contrary to man's essence.* As a few crude examples: every lie gradually reduces itself *ad absurdum*; where there are few children they become all of a sudden interesting and desirable again; the man who is too concerned about his own health becomes ill.[99]

> Even aberrant categorical self-manipulation . . . can be an ultimately harmless experiment *on the part of nature*, experimenting and slowly trying to bring forth what the genuine future holds in promise.[100]

These assertions do not license human beings to do whatever they have the capacities to do in the expectation that the self-correcting process will follow. Indeed, Rahner can be quite specific about the moral wrongness of

98. Ibid., pp. 225–26.
99. Ibid., p. 217. Emphasis added.
100. Ibid. Emphasis added. See also ibid., p. 249.

certain "self-manipulations," and he is especially concerned to forbid anything that leads to irreversible evil consequences. Nonetheless, the idea of self-correction backs what James F. Bresnahan, S.J., names the "pragmatic" aspect of Rahner's theory of natural law.[101]

Rahner is also cognizant of new historical developments of human interdependence. By implication he is critical of the individualism that has dominated moral theology, and of a kind of excessive scrupulosity that avoids doing harm in the present regardless of long-range future consequences.

> One ought soberly and courageously to consider, according to a supra-individual morality, what sacrifices could be expected of humanity today on behalf of humanity tomorrow, *without* being too quick to speak of immoral cruelty, of the violation and exploitation of the dignity of man today for the benefit of man tomorrow.[102]

The counsel to sobriety is very sound; so also is the counsel to courage. The quotation clearly assumes opportunities and responsibilities of a present generation for future generations, and opens the door to considering policies and actions that are beneficial to future generations at some cost to the present one. It recognizes that costs are involved, but does not flinch from the implication that they might well be morally licit in the light of long-range ends.

The affinity of these cautiously suggested views with my work is clear; ethics develops in the light of new scientific knowledge, historical experience, the "supraindividual" characteristics of life, and consideration of future generations. In this respect, Rahner's proposals are closer to aspects of my profile of theocentric ethics than are Barth's and Thomas's. The issue on which there is a major difference, however, is that of the scope of considerations to be taken into account.

Extensions of scope that are defensible in the light of my theocentric construal of reality would not be in the light of Rahner's view of the essence of man as individual transcendental freedom. The implications of experience in societies and in the ecosphere, from my perspective, might very well require experimentations that are risky to persons and restraints on human activities for the sake of the interdependencies of life in the world. Inferences drawn from sciences might well open possibilities for novel actions and new forms of restraints about the morally licit character of various human interventions. Manipulation, not only of self, but of the world in which we live, might be justified at deeper levels than Rahner would permit.

101. James F. Bresnahan, S.J., "Rahner's Ethics: Critical Natural Law in Relation to Contemporary Ethical Methodology," *Journal of Religion* 56 (1976):51.

102. Rahner, *Theological Investigations*, 9:224.

Morality is not merely supraindividual in the sense that it must take into account wider human communities; even "suprahuman" realities of our interdependence with and participation in nature have to be seriously considered. Indeed, restraints on the activities of human beings might be required for the good of larger wholes, and not merely for the preservation and expansion of human freedom. If the common good ascends in importance, its implications might well restrict human freedom and also require deeper restraints on our aspirations about the true end of human life which Rahner would not permit. Hard choices sometimes have to be made between legitimately valued ends and consequences.

The second feature of Rahner's ethics that has considerable affinity with my work is his interpretation of what is involved in making particular moral choices. Rahner's discussions of this feature are presented in different places with different degrees of technicality.[103] Whether writing in a pastoral or a technical mode, he has always presupposed his philosophical anthropology, and aspects of his dogmatic theology. I shall not engage in an exposition of these underlying theories. Instead, I shall attempt to state Rahner's case in more accessible terms.

I have argued elsewhere that the contemporary trend of reforms in Roman Catholic moral theology is from the more fixed, static, and immutable principles, rationalistically applied, to a greater openness to change and to the distinctiveness of particular occasions.[104] Rahner not only participates in this trend, but has provided it with substantial theological and philosophical support. The focus on the individual and the particular, both with reference to the agent and with reference to the circumstances in which a choice is to be made, opens the door to existentialist and situationalist possibilities. Rahner was cognizant of this possibility in the face of radical situational ethics espoused in Germany, and he responded to it critically.[105] Yet for theological, philosophical, and moral reasons he does not retreat to the position of the manualists. Another resource to which he turns is Ignatius of Loyola, the founder of Rahner's own order; he retrieves insight into the process of discernment from *The Spiritual Exercises*.[106] The path that Rahner takes seeks to avoid both the rationalism of the moral theology his generation received from its teachers and the situational intuitionism that was one response to that rationalism.

One of the simplest presentations of his argument is in his distinction between principles and prescriptions. Principles ground prescriptions,

103. The critical technical essay is Rahner, "On the Question of a Formal Existential Ethics," in *Theological Investigations*, 2:217–34.

104. Gustafson, *Protestant and Roman Catholic Ethics*, pp. 31–32ff.

105. See Rahner, "The Appeal to Conscience," cited in n. 93 above.

106. See "The Logic of Concrete Individual Knowledge," in Karl Rahner, *The Dynamic Element in the Church*, trans. W. J. O'Hara (New York: Herder and Herder, 1964), pp. 84–170.

which are more particularly directed to concrete occasions. But even prescriptions are not applied rationalistically; they direct but do not necessarily determine an individual choice. In his distinction he is subject to the "naturalistic fallacy" (as is my work) that has been so extensively criticized for decades in Anglo-American moral philosophy.[107] Principles are, in the first place, statements of "what is." They express "the structure of some reality," for example, "that of man."[108] There is also in those principles that pertain to man a normative element or claim.[109] But the moral principles grounded in the descriptive statements "are not intended to defend the idea of man, but the concrete individual man; they do not make a claim on the idea but on an individual here and now in flesh and blood."[110] The realization of the principle is demanded in a particular individual in particular circumstances.

In this argument Rahner is fighting the level of abstraction and the rationalism that I pointed to above. The particular individual agent and the positive content of the circumstances are not merely a limitation of the universal. It follows that "precisely this individual feature can be the object and goal of a moral demand which is not identical with the validity of general principles, but is a concrete, particular, individual obligation."[111] There is a universal principle, but it has an individualized realization. That individual realization is through the person, who is spiritual reality as well as a participant in the determinations of nature. Thus the person makes a genuinely free choice. Because the person is "a spiritual, personal being, he is more than the point of intersection of general truths and maxims, more than the particular instance of a multipliable essence." It follows from this, for Rahner, that "this single human existence can be summoned by an imperative prescription which is different in kind [but not in contradiction to, opposition to, or superiority to general principles] from the moral principles that derive from general characteristics."[112] Love and knowledge, seeing and deciding, are woven into a person's apprehension of a prescription and its application.

Thus even prescriptions cannot be rationalistically applied to cases. There is an *individuum ineffabile* that has to be taken into account. A definite decision takes place not just in a case, but in "what is unique in the

107. For a major essay, see William Frankena, "The Naturalistic Fallacy," In Philippa Foot, ed., *Theories of Ethics* (Oxford: Oxford University Press, 1967), pp. 50–62.

108. Karl Rahner, "Principles and Prescriptions," in *The Dynamic Element in the Church*, pp. 14–15.

109. Rahner uses the following example. "The human person of flesh and blood . . . possesses intrinsic significance and is an end and not a means, and in order to be himself and develop, stands in orderly relation to a surrounding world of material things. This state of affairs can be translated into the general maxim: The human person has a right to private property; such property should exist." Ibid., p. 15.

110. Ibid.

111. Ibid., p. 16.

112. Ibid., p. 18.

case, even if the case viewed precisely as a case is not unique."[113] Not only individual persons, but also social groups have individual ineffability. The prescription is a "pointing gesture" to the unique. Rahner takes recourse to the virtue of prudence to explain and interpret what occurs in the particular choice. Prudence is "a distinct part of the human power of moral decision," and shrewdness and erudition, moral theology and casuistry, cannot take its place.[114] He also suggests that in the rational activity of moral theology a modern "probabilism" is desirable, for that classic distinction recognized the need of practical principles to focus the issues involved in a choice without rationalistically determining what the choice should be.[115]

Rahner is usually frustratingly imprecise about the implications of this process of discernment in individual cases. Below I examine his argument against artificial insemination by a nonhusband donor. In the choice of a vocation, one example that he uses, this process of discernment certainly works easier than it does in a choice to have an abortion when the life of the fetus is a threat to the life of the mother. He is, however, quite certain that an agent does not incur guilt before God in all ambiguous moral circumstances, even though the divine will is for one particular thing. The argument for this is theological rather than experiential.

Following the tradition, Rahner says that there is guilt only when one knowingly sins against God. There are different degrees of guilt relative to the degrees of knowledge and freedom, and there can be, consequentially speaking, wrong actions that are guiltless.

> Insofar as there can be guilt only before the One God and his undivided will . . . , man can also never find himself, objectively speaking, in the tragic situation of being able to choose only between different ways of becoming guilty, so that no matter what alternative he chooses, he necessarily incurs guilt. In certain situations the only choice open to us may lie between two actions, both of which must be regarded as harmful and wrong in a certain respect; yet, objectively speaking, no situation can ever force us into guilt. For this would imply the contradiction that God at the same time imposes and condemns the self-same behaviour.[116]

There are circumstances in which one has to act courageously even though one's actions may harm oneself or others, but such circumstances do not license an imperative to incur guilt courageously.

113. Ibid., p. 22.

114. Ibid., p. 24.

115. Ibid., p. 39. Probabilism represents the idea that certainty is impossible in some moral cases, and thus any course may be followed that is seen to be solidly probable either on the basis of a clear perception of the principle that is involved or on the basis of support from reputable authority. It is one type on a continuum from rigorism to laxism; others include equiprobabilism, and probabiliorism.

116. Karl Rahner, "Guilt and Its Remission: The Borderline Between Theology and Psychotherapy," in *Theological Investigations*, 2:267.

It is not necessary to develop in detail the affinities between Rahner's interpretation of particular moral choices and the process of discernment I developed in volume 1, chapter 7. Both seek a path between the boundaries of rationalism and perceptual intuitionism; both see rational activity about choices to coexist with sensibilities; both affirm that in the particular choice there are elements of unique perception.

I included some of Rahner's remarks on guilt, however, to indicate that, while he clearly observes the ambiguity of many moral choices, he is more concerned than I to offer certitude, and perhaps spiritual comfort, to persons who make them. For Rahner moral ambiguity is a matter of epistemological ambiguity; it is in the agent. Backing his view is, I believe, the central importance of the intention of the agent when judgments are made about moral culpability, a strong point in Roman Catholic moral theology.[117] If one's moral intention is right, one is not subjectively guilty even though the consequences of actions are knowably harmful to others. From the perspective of theocentric ethics, moral ambiguity is "objective" in the circumstances. One necessarily makes a choice in circumstances that are deeply ambiguous; one is still accountable for the foreseeable bad outcomes, and one duly has a sense of remorse, at least, if not guilt.

A brief illustration will make the point. It is argued that when the life of a radically defective newborn child is not to be maintained it is morally better to permit the child to die (even though this might take ten days of minimal care) than to take its life.[118] The death comes by an act of omission rather than commission. The ultimate intention and knowable final outcome will be the same in either case: the death of the infant. The distinction preserves the agents from moral culpability because they do not overtly act to hasten the death. But that preservation of innocence is at cost to the infant. I do not know what Karl Rahner would say about such a case. From my standpoint, however, either choice implies causal and moral accountability for the death of the infant. For either choice, in view both of the intent for the death of child and of those consequences, one is accountable. Remorse, if not guilt, occurs. Either choice is tragic, and knowledge that it is tragic does and ought to bring with it remorse, subjectively, because one has incurred responsibility for a death, objectively.

Rahner is correct to perceive and interpret so clearly the distinctiveness of agents and circumstances, and the ambiguity of extreme choices that persons have to make. He is correct in foreclosing the ambiguity insofar as that is possible. He is correct to perceive that the consequences of actions

117. Rahner's ideas about intentions are most fully developed in "Some Thoughts on 'A Good Intention,'" in *Theological Investigations*, vol. 3, trans. Karl-H. and Boniface Kruger (Baltimore: Helicon Press, 1967), pp. 105–28.

118. For a discussion of the ethics of a case like this, see James M. Gustafson, "Mongolism, Parental Desires, and the Right to Life," *Perspectives in Biology and Medicine* 16 (1973):529–57.

governed by good intentions might be costly to the agent or to others. But the conflict of ends might well be the consequence of the way that the finite world is ordered by the divine governance, and thus there is no single divine will for those circumstances. And agents who act in the face of ambiguity, while their accountability is mitigated by their intentions and their limitations, nonetheless are accountable and duly remorseful even for such conscientious choices. Forced, or even "fated," tragic choices provoke guilt and remorse.

The major dissimilarity between my work and that of Rahner pertains to the understanding of the human essence. In his case it is transcendental freedom, the actualization of which is the principal end of moral and social activity. If the essence of the human for Thomas is reason, for Rahner it is freedom, and the implications of the difference in emphasis for ethics are important. Stated oversimply, for Rahner the ordering of life serves human freedom as its goal; for Thomas one reasons about the proper ordering of life ultimately for the sake of human fulfillment, but the ordering itself requires that more complex ends and purposes be attended to.

I have noted that the "turn to the subject" which involves the accenting of transcendental freedom took place for philosophical, theological, and moral reasons. Its reception by many Roman Catholic "religious" and laity has been enthusiastic. Indeed, it could be argued that a kind of repressive atmosphere had long hung over Roman Catholicism in its intellectual, cultic, and moral life, and that this atmosphere was one of the impulses for the recovery of the importance of the subject and human freedom. Great relief and creativity were impelled by the mitigation of a host of "Thou shalt nots" and the legitimation of many "Thou mayests." The conditions were ripe for both the development of the importance of freedom and for its favorable reception. To some extent the course of some important modern Protestant ethics has been from the acceptance of freedom to stating criteria for its exercise; the course of much of Roman Catholic ethics has been from excessive and restrictive criteria for moral activity to the recovery of freedom and creativity.

Karl Rahner is no dualist who has an essence of man in freedom hovering over human biological, social, and historical embodiment but unconnected with it. The transcendental is always and only present in the categorical, that is in specific realities of human bodies, institutions, and historical events.[119] There are many expositions of freedom in Rahner's

119. In an interesting way, similar issues emerge in Rahner's and in Karl Barth's writings. I discussed above the problems of the relation of Barth's "real man" to the "phenomena of man"; certain parallel problems emerge in Rahner's interpretation of the relation of the essence of man, the transcendental freedom, to the categorical aspects of man. This invites a deeper comparative analysis of the philosophical and theological underpinnings of Rahner's and Barth's systematic thought, but such an excursus would be out of place here.

works, beginning with his early systematic philosophical writings and continuing throughout his career. I shall not attend to these, but rather analyze how those theories are appealed to in some of his more applied moral writings.

If the norms or ends of moral life and activity are grounded in "nature," then the interpretation of nature is critical to both the generation of norms and values and to their actualization. This is axiomatic, and has been discussed above. So far, this does not necessarily entail anthropocentrism and human individualism; how human life is related to the wider ordering of life is critical to the ethical enterprise. If the ordering of the rest of nature is seen to be in the service of man as a species, and finally in the service of individual persons, and if the essence of the person (that is, its "nature") is transcendental freedom, a clear course for the development of ethics follows. To develop these assertions in relation to Rahner's thought I shall move in three steps. First, a brief exposition of his understanding of the essence of man as freedom is required. Next, I shall show how this freedom implies "permission" to be and to do certain things. Finally, I shall show how this freedom also implies restraints on what is permissible, and indeed, clear judgments about the immorality of certain actions.

Rahner's argument for the essence of man has both philosophical and theological aspects. The philosophical argument develops on the basis of transcendental deductions, i.e., it seeks to find the necessary conditions for man to be what man most distinctively is. It also develops on the basis of the historical experience and activity of man. It is no easy task to achieve this knowledge of the human essence, Rahner admits, since more is involved than drawing inferences from factual evidences given in the sciences.[120] But from these processes one comes to a knowledge of the essence of man, which includes knowledge of "the possibilities of nature."[121]

The theological argument is derived from revelation, and the central point of the revelation is the salvation of human beings. Freedom is the necessary condition for human dignity. Human dignity is the goal of human freedom, its salvation or its judgment,[122] which is dependent on the grace and the judgment of God.

The natural being of man is man's "personal nature." The importance of this statement can hardly be overemphasized for its implications for Rahner's moral theology, and for all the criticisms of the "physicalist" bias in the encyclical *Humanae Vitae* and in other aspects of conservative moral theology that have been made by many others. Thus it is important to state at least the major dimensions of "personal nature." In the essay, "The Dignity and Freedom of Man," Rahner lines out the following.

120. Rahner, "The Dignity and Freedom of Man," in *Theological Investigations*, 2:236.
121. Ibid., pp. 236–37.
122. Ibid., pp. 238–39.

While man is always dependent on "the total unity of reality, i.e. on God," man is spirit.[123] This means that persons are "subjects" set off from what is objective to themselves and capable of perceiving and knowing objects.

"Man is freedom";[124] this implies not only the "finite" freedom of choice and action but also those deeper conditions necessary to choose and to act. Even this deeper freedom is not unlimited; it is not "absolutely creative."[125] It is "the *manner* of the appropriation and realization of the person and of his absolute dignity before God and in the community of other persons, using finite, decided materials."[126] But this does not mean that freedom is only instrumental in importance.

> The person and, consequently, freedom are themselves existing realities of the highest order and are, therefore, even in themselves absolute values. Thus freedom is *also* meant to be for its own sake, so that, even if all its results *were* attainable without it (which is not so in reality), it would still have to exist, and the frustration of its exercise would still mean an attempt on the absolute dignity of the person.[127]

The absolute value of freedom is always exercised in specific conditions of both external and internal kinds, and therefore a "concession" to these possibilities and limits is demanded.

Man is an individual, and not merely an instance of the universal. I remarked on the importance of this view in my discussion of the process of coming to a moral choice. The individuality of the person is not merely a negative restriction but shows that he or she "has a valid existence which, as real existence, does not coincide with his [or her] spatiotemporal existence."[128] Each person is immortal, and thus has an eternal destiny. Herein lies what others have called the sacredness of human life; it has normative implications, namely that an individual person "may never be forcibly sacrificed, in a manner which destroys him, for the future of 'humanity,' of the others who come after him."[129]

Human beings are "community-building" persons. Person and community are correlative; as persons we are intended for community with God and other persons, and real community exists only where our nature as

123. Ibid., p. 239.
124. Ibid.
125. Ibid., p. 247.
126. Ibid.
127. Ibid., p. 248. See also Rahner, "Guilt—Responsibility—Punishment within the View of Catholic Theology," *Theological Investigations*, 6:197–209, and "Theology of Freedom," in ibid., pp. 178–96.
128. Rahner, "Dignity and Freedom," *Theological Investigations*, 2:239.
129. Ibid.

persons is protected. Indeed, one is a "perfect person" to the extent that one is open in love and service for other persons.[130]

It has already been noted that persons are embodied; the realization of human nature as a person takes place in the categorical realities of bodily existence and community life—marriage, parent-child relations, the state, the church, and so on. While these realities are in one sense external to our natures as persons, they are the necessary conditions for the self-realization of human freedom and dignity.[131]

In sum, man's essence is freedom. From the description of the essence one determines the end or purpose. Thus the purpose of bodily existence and institutions is to sustain and enhance this freedom. From this purpose one can infer guides to actions and to ends that pertain to human actions in the world. For my purposes two further steps can now be taken.

The first step is to show how freedom grants a degree of permission to do certain things. This was already noted in the discussion of Rahner's view of the moral choice, but here I shall develop it in relation to the possibilities for "self-manipulation" in man. The possibilities of freedom extend beyond simply the perception of what is right in a particular case.

Rahner's essay "The Experiment with Man" seems to open the doors to alarming proportions of intervention into nature and even human nature. Indeed, it provoked Paul Ramsey to write that it "sounds remarkably like a priestly blessing over everything, doing duty for ethics."[132] Careful analysis of the essay, however, indicates that along with the granting of a fresh permission for man to be self-manipulating, there are also indications of the constraints that ought to be placed on such activity.

That human beings are self-manipulating is to Rahner simply a matter of fact, and what is new is the extension of the range and depth of those capacities as a result of modern sciences. This can be seen in developments in physics, biology, biochemistry, genetics, medicine, pharmacology and above all psycho-pharmacology, psychology, sociology, and political science. The matter of fact, however, is no surprise to Rahner, for these activities could not be accounted for apart from understanding the nature of man as transcendentally free. "According to Christian anthropology man is the being who manipulates himself."

> [M]an, as the being who is free in relation to God, is in a most radical way empowered to do what he wills with himself, freely able to align himself towards his own ultimate goal. He is able so to determine and dispose of himself that two absolutely different

130. Ibid.
131. Ibid.
132. Paul Ramsey, *Fabricated Man: The Ethics of Genetic Control* (New Haven: Yale University Press, 1970), pp. 139–40.

> final destinations become possible: man in absolute salvation and man in the absolute loss of salvation. . . . [T]his freedom is creative and what it creates is man himself in his final state, so that the beginning of this history of man's divinely appointed freedom—man's "essence" as we say—is not an intangible something, essentially permanent and complete, but the commission and power which enable him to be free to determine himself to his ultimate state.[133]

In comparison with other created things, "man begins his existence as the being who is radically open and incomplete. When his essence *is* complete it is as he himself has freely created it."[134] It must be noted that the primary reference here is to a person's ultimate final state, that is to being oriented toward or against God.

The same capacity for freedom that man exercises in his option for or against God is also exercised in our earthly existence. The self-manipulation is always in one's categorical existence, but since categorical self-manipulation is "a manifestation of that transcendental self-manipulation" there are many possibilities for its disposal for good as well as for ill.[135] Thus one is to be open to new possibilities, and not, a priori, to react with moral defensiveness to them. This openness is not only backed by the value placed on human freedom, but also by the Christian's belief that the future is ultimately destined by the gracious God.

> [T]he future of man's self-manipulation has begun. And the Christian has no reason to enter this future as a hell on Earth nor as an earthly Kingdom of God. Jubilation or lamentation would both run counter to the Christian's cool-headedness.[136]

There is a "Thou mayest" implied in human freedom and in the grace of God; however, contrary to Ramsey's reading of this essay, it is not "a priestly blessing over everything." For Rahner, the "Thou mayest" is, in my opinion, the first word; the first word is not "Thou mayest not." There are no extensive discussions of particular possibilities of radical human self-manipulation in this essay, and thus it is not possible to judge which possibilities Rahner would most strongly support. But the norm is there: man's action is to be consonant with man's nature. Although one is not able to specify prescriptions based on this norm, another principle seems to follow. Since man's nature is freedom, those actions, social arrangements, interventions into nature, and cultural developments which defend, sustain, and enhance that freedom are permissible. Those which attack, deny, erode, or destroy that freedom are morally wrong.

133. Rahner, "The Experiment with Man," *Theological Investigations*, 9:212.
134. Ibid., p. 213.
135. Ibid., p. 215.
136. Ibid., pp. 211–12.

The second step from the basis of freedom as man's essence is to examine two instances in which Rahner makes clear what is not permitted, indeed, what is condemned. The first instance concerns the public order. To show how certain limitations of freedom are not permitted, I quote another statement of his starting point.

> The moral law as such (in contrast to the forced compliance with it) is not a limitation of freedom, since it does after all presuppose freedom of its very nature and turns to it (since it is fulfilled only when it is obeyed freely), and since it orientates freedom to its own essential goal, viz. the true achievement of the person.[137]

The implications of this point have some similarities to the libertarian tradition. It makes "it impossible to have a total or partial, but unlawful, restriction of some people's scope for freedom by others."[138] An example is the proper use of compulsion in a democratic order: "the freedom of political groupings is conceded only to those who also recognize this freedom in others"; one can proceed with compulsion against the enemies of democratic freedom.

In the educational aspects of personal development, the purpose of restrictions on "the scope of freedom" are finally for the sake of "the liberation of freedom."[139] Indeed, all through life there is the need for some "enforced education" by others, but this does not license the attempt to keep every possible evil "always and everywhere" from happening to a person. In the language of contemporary moral philosophy there is, therefore, a limit to "paternalism."

Freedom of conscience which leads to forms of conscientious objection is guarded. Rahner is quite specific about proper conduct in such cases.

> The one who makes the demand [for performance of a task conscientiously objected to by another] must re-examine the justification for his demand very closely, out of respect for the freedom and conscience of the person who refuses.[140]

The demander is to determine whether he or she has merely the right to enforce the demand or is morally bound to do so. "If the former, then he can desist from enforcing his demand," and often this will be advisable from "general considerations." "If the latter, then he has the right and duty to enforce his demand" insofar as possible, and to use coercive measures in proportion to the importance of the issue.[141] In such a case Rahner admits

137. Rahner, "The Dignity and Freedom of Man," *Theological Investigations*, 2:249.
138. Ibid., p. 250. See also, Karl Rahner, "Institution and Freedom" in *Theological Investigations*, vol. 13, trans. David Bourke (New York: Seabury Press, 1975), pp. 105–21.
139. Rahner, "The Dignity and Freedom," *Theological Invesigations*, 2:250.
140. Ibid., p. 251.
141. Ibid.

that the choice is tragic, for the conflict arises from freedom of conscience on both sides.

> The tragic conflict between the objectively justified and obligatory demand, on the one hand, and the subjective conscience in good faith, on the other, is insoluble in practice. Its tragedy must be accepted with patience and mutual respect as a sign of the imperfection of the order here below.[142]

Implications for the state follow from this. "The state exists for man and not vice versa."[143] Rights of individuals and of smaller natural communities are not granted by the state but arise "from the core of the person."[144] Thus the function of the state is to protect these rights and, "where necessary, regulate and harmonize them with each other."[145] Even duly enacted laws "are only then justified when they do not annul the freedom of the individual in some sector of his sphere of existence or curtail it beyond right measure."[146]

It is clear that "undue" restrictions on individual freedom and on the freedom of natural communities are not permissible. While he does discuss the general conditions in which some restraints are permitted, it is not clear what inferences he would draw for many specific circumstances. It would be interesting to know how his view would be applied to the free-market economy, and to particular instances of vast accumulation of economic power gained as a result of the pursuit of freedom.[147] Or, if the necessary conditions for the fulfillment of individual dignity and freedom were threatened by overpopulation in a given nation-state, would Rahner object to incentives, and in critical situations to coercion, as a means of restricting

142. Ibid., p. 252.
143. Ibid., p. 255.
144. Ibid., p. 256.
145. Ibid.
146. Ibid.
147. In an essay on "The Theology of Power" Rahner rightly argues that power is not intrinsically sinful, and that it is necessary for the realization of freedom. "The real question in a moral theology of freedom is this: in what way, and in what proportions in each concrete case, and with what perpetually revised safeguards, can the right of legitimate power to alter and restrict the freedom of the individual (and of his free fellowship) be reconciled with the higher right of freedom, and the right of the individual to a real, concrete and permanent sphere of freedom? Since the sphere of individual freedom is a variable quantity, and since the tasks of the legitimate authorities, for the sake of which they hold power, are themselves subject to historical change, this reconciliation is not something that can be fixed and firm once and for all: it must be constantly searched anew." In this view the struggle for power is inevitable. There is a "genuine and *materially* irreducible pluralism of representatives and rights—rights, that is of both the upholders of freedom and the holders of power." There are bound to be "cases of conflict which are at least subjectively present and cannot be solved on a theoretical basis." Rahner, *Theological Investigations*, vol. 4, trans. Kevin Smyth (Baltimore: Helicon Press, 1966), p. 400. The essay is subtle, thoughtful, and on the whole commendable, but unfortunately it does not provide difficult concrete examples.

population growth? Certainly purely voluntary restraints would be preferable; this would also be the case from the perspective of my theocentric ethics. Would Rahner be willing to extend the instances of the tragic choice from the case of conflict of individual consciences to matters of population restraint? If his language of "the imperfection of the order here below" is equivalent to "the conditions of finitude," more restraints on the pursuit of freedom than he supports might be morally, but sadly, legitimate.

The second instance in which Rahner quite clearly determines that certain actions and ends are impermissible because they violate the nature of persons is "genetic manipulation." The particular case that is most interesting is that of artificial insemination by a nonhusband donor of sperm. On the face of it, what we have seen about Rahner's views of permissibility would seem to make such a way of conceiving a child to be morally licit, though not preferable. His argument against it must be, and is, on the grounds that it violates the personal nature of human life. He calls to attention the problems that have long been associated with this procedure:

> the obtaining of male sperm, its storage and checking, the age factor, etc., and ultimately the establishment of and whole organization of a "sperm bank" as a public institution in society, documentation of the qualitative characteristics of the sperm, legal questions of the identity or anonymity of the donor, the extramarital use of this material, the necessity of the consent of the male marriage-partner, the question of determining "fatherhood" in such a case, and of course the resultant question of providing instruction and propaganda for heterologous insemination.[148]

He goes on to invoke the specter of planned genetic improvement of the human race.

In my judgment the main lines of Rahner's intricate argument against this procedure are somewhat strained. First, he appeals not to those aspects of man's nature that are free but to those that are determined. "[T]he 'definition' of man cannot deal exclusively with the element of man's self-determination." "[H]e is no less a being whose essence has been predetermined."[149] Here we have a moral appeal to the "conditions of finitude." One is to consent to some of these conditions.

The second line of argument makes a distinction between dealing with things and dealing with persons; in parenthood one is dealing with persons. "[M]an is in a certain respect most free when he is not dealing with a 'thing' but calling into being another, freely responsible person."[150]

148. "The Problem of Genetic Manipulation," *Theological Investigations*, 9:237.
149. Ibid., p. 243.
150. Ibid., p. 244.

> [T]hat means that the freedom to determine another person must remain a clear-cut and radical destiny, which one has *not chosen* but *accepted.* Procreation in particular must not become an act of neurotic anxiety in the face of fate. The other person must remain the one who is both *made* and *accepted*; both an elevating influence, because he has been chosen, and a burden to be accepted and carried. If man, when confronted with his child, saw only what he had himself planned, he would not be looking at his own nature, nor would he experience his true self which is both free *and* the object of external determination. Genetic manipulation is the embodiment of the fear of oneself, the fear of accepting one's self as the unknown quantity it is.[151]

The crucial part of this quotation is that one would not be looking at human nature, nor experience one's self, as both free and determined if one had a child by this procedure. It is not clear to me precisely why this is more the case in this procedure for fertilization than in an intentional impregnation by natural means. To be sure, as Rahner goes on to aver, the child is of the mother and the donor, and the latter does not acknowledge fatherhood as an act of "personal love." But why does this necessarily rob "the child of the right and ability to fulfill the obligation of his existence, namely to accept himself as the child of these particular parents?"[152] This argument seems to rest on a very "physicalist" bias against which much of Rahner's moral theology is directed. Indeed, he takes recourse to unconsidered language when he writes, "Genetic manipulation of this sort is no more 'human,' merely because it produces a human being, than a case of rape."[153] Raising fears of a society in which human life is totally planned, something Rahner sees as "implicit" in any genetic manipulation, is specious. It can just as plausibly be argued that, in individual cases of infertility, artificial insemination by a nonhusband donor extends and secures the individual's area of freedom more than it threatens and encroaches on it.[154] Interestingly, while in other areas Rahner gives assurance of a "feedback" effect which might later restrain what has been innovated, in this area he warns that "there is no guarantee that such feedback effects can be relied upon in social morality in every case." The irreparable harm might occur before the feedback has time to take effect.[155]

I have stated that the critical difference between Rahner's theology and mine is his celebration of the essence of man as transcendental freedom. In volume 1, I argued for a more intricate interpretation of the relationship between human capacities for self-determination and their embodiment in

151. Ibid., pp. 244–45.
152. Ibid., p. 246.
153. Ibid.
154. See ibid., p. 248.
155. Ibid., p. 249.

our physical natures. While Rahner is no more a dualist in his view of human beings than is Barth, his distinction between the transcendental and the categorical aspects of man poses the same problems that Barth's distinction between the phenomena of man and "real" man does. To be sure, Barth does not posit freedom as the end of human activity in the way that Rahner does; the "real" man does not function as the moral end and norm in the same way, though there are interesting similarities even in this respect. Rather by setting transcendental freedom as the essence of man, and thus as the norm of moral activity, Rahner reinforces the strong anthropocentric tendencies of Christian theology and Western ethics. It is not too much to say that man is the only creature who has this freedom, and because of this all things are in the end to protect and to serve this freedom. Categorical existence requires that "concessions" be made to the pursuit of freedom, and aspects of categorical existence are used to enhance and protect freedom. But nonetheless the concern for an ordering of relationships that follows from the theology lined out in my first volume is much subordinated to the pursuit of freedom.

It is the always overriding claim of freedom that leads to ethical differences. This makes a difference in how institutions and their proper functions are to be understood. Rahner concedes, for example, "that there is a *prima facie* opposition between institution and freedom."

> But this must not be allowed to obscure a deeper unity between the two entities and a relationship in which each influences the other. Man, when he has the power, does in fact himself create these institutions of his freedom. They are objectifications of freedom. . . . The situation is, in fact, that freedom creates its own compulsion within itself. It objectifies itself, and creates for itself the external conditions for its own fulfilment, shapes them and so opens out a sphere within which it can operate.[156]

I believe it is only from the conviction that freedom is the essence of man that one can come to this as a sufficient explanation of the origins and functions of institutions. An alternative view would be more complex, and while it needs to account for the human capacity to shape institutions and their ends, it must also show how institutions arise out of our "categorical" existence as ways of fulfilling many needs and ordering relations between persons, among groups, and between the human realm and the wider natural realm. They are as much, or more, grounded in "nature" as in freedom.

It would be repetitious here to expound once again the theological reasons that back a plurality of ends that are legitimate in human pursuits, and that back the inexorability of conflicting choices between justifiable

156. Rahner, "Institution and Freedom," *Theological Investigations*, 13:115.

ends in the conditions of finitude. But some of the implications of such a view run counter to Rahner's theology and ethics, and to some of the particular judgments he comes to. The preservation of human freedom can be very high on a scale of values without finally subordinating all other values to its protection and enhancement. Our interrelationships and interdependencies are part of our "nature," and ends and norms follow from them as well as from freedom.

Paul Ramsey

There are a number of strands in contemporary Protestant Christian ethics, and particularly in recent decades various movements have followed one another like crests of waves hitting the shore. The steadying influence of a theory of natural law has not been present in modern Protestant ethics. If there is one single grounding for the various forms, it is turning to the Bible as the source. In North America Paul Ramsey has been a towering and forceful figure for almost four decades; his writing has forced persons with alternative views to come to grips with his thought, and had a deep impact on a younger generation of authors. He has been a persistent critic of moral fads, a steadfast proponent of the Christian ethics of love, and a vigorous participant in debates about public policy and medical ethics.

Ramsey's first book is his most comprehensive statement of theological ethics.[157] It displays a remarkable range of erudition, and while not everything he has published since is absolutely consistent with every aspect of it, certain fundamental convictions stated there have grounded his subsequent publications. It is, indeed, instructive to read Ramsey's major works in reverse order, from the most recent to the earliest.

Ramsey can be properly called a rigorist in at least two senses. First, he has exemplified and promoted intellectual rigor in the Christian ethical enterprise in reaction to his perception of sloppiness in much of the writing of some of his predecessors and most of his contemporaries. His *War and the Christian Conscience* marks a turn toward his own warlike polemic against the shoddiness of alternatives to his own thought. It is in that book that he attacks Protestant social ethics as "wanderings over the wasteland of utility," and avers that "[p]rudence and contextualism become excuses for lack of disciplined analysis."[158] During the chaotic 1960s he wrote very polemical pieces in response to popular and technical writings in Christian ethics, and passionately attacked the World Council of Churches and other ecclesiastical agencies. His study of contemporary moral philosophers becomes evi-

157. Paul Ramsey, *Basic Christian Ethics* (New York: Scribner's, 1950).

158. Paul Ramsey, *War and the Christian Conscience: How Shall Modern War Be Conducted Justly?* (Durham, N.C.: Duke University Press, 1961), p. 6 and p. 177.

dent, and he enlists various concepts and distinctions from their writings in the service of his own.

The second sense in which Ramsey is a rigorist refers to the content more than to the form of his ethics. Not everyone would agree with this assertion, for his careful defenses of aspects of the Vietnam War and some other judgments can be interpreted as laxist in effect. The justification, however, is his own insistence that the Christian ethical norm of love, *agape*, is the starting point and the ultimately authorizing and controlling reference for the action of Christians. And, in his view, this means that Christian ethics is deontological rather than teleological and consequentialist in character. "Morality," he writes, "has to do with the definition of right *conduct*, and this not simply by way of the ends of action. *How* we do *what* we do is as important as our goals."[159] The same rigorism that is expressed in his critical writings on abortion, fetal research, and genetic engineering also backs his firm judgments about the immorality of the use of weapons that cannot discriminate between combatants and noncombatants.

Another important feature of Ramsey's work is the attention he gives to the relevant "factual" matters in the various moral and public issues he addresses. He is far from satisfied with leaving Christian ethics on a level of general principles, or "middle axioms," though he states such things with care. Rather, he seeks to master enough about weaponry to make particular judgments about particular weapons, about life-support systems and other therapeutic procedures to make particular judgments about their use in particular medical circumstances, or about genetic research to assess with some particularity its possible uses and misuses. His research is not confined to theology and moral philosophy. Indeed, he has done more to introduce casuistry into contemporary Protestant ethics than any other person; he states principles and rules, and applies them to cases, and takes into account as fully as he can the data pertinent to each case.

To use Ramsey's writings as a benchmark which indicates particular features of the profile of ethics from a theocentric perspective, does not require a full analysis and critique of his work.[160] As I have done with the other authors who function as benchmarks, with Ramsey I shall indicate the major points of comparison in content and in form.

First, Ramsey is much more confessionally Christian in his ethics than I am. In studying his work one must take very seriously the commitment he

159. Ibid., p. 6. Also, "Certainly Christian ethics is a deontological ethic, not an ethic of the Good." Ramsey, *Basic Christian Ethics*, p. 116.

160. For critical essays on Ramsey's thought, see James T. Johnson and David H. Smith, eds., *Love and Society: Essays in the Ethics of Paul Ramsey* (Missoula, Mont.: Scholars Press, 1974). The essays by David H. Smith, Donald Evans, Charles E. Curran, Paul F. Camenish, and David Little each are critical analyses. See also Charles E. Curran, *Politics and Christian Ethics: A Dialogue with Paul Ramsey* (Philadelphia: Fortress, 1973).

makes to Christian ethics being biblical ethics, and to obedient love as the central theme of biblical ethics. All of his more philosophical writing is finally in the service of the biblical authorization of love. In the Introduction to his first book he wrote that,

> As a treatise on basic Christian ethics, this book endeavors to stand within the way the Bible views morality. The central ethical notion or "category" in Christian ethics is "obedient love"—the sort of love the gospels describe as "love fulfilling the law" and St. Paul designates as "faith that works through love."[161]

The Christian ethician is warranted to use philosophical materials, as Augustine used Platonism and Aquinas used Aristotelianism. But whatever philosophy is used, the Christian "must first learn not to be used by it or to allow the fundamental Christian ethical perspective to suffer alteration."[162] In his first book Ramsey "employs" philosophical idealism; in subsequent works he uses aspects of natural-law theory and of contemporary moral philosophy. But he is usually quite careful to state that these materials are in the service of the ethics of love.

This starting point and governing perspective is confessional in a special sense. Ramsey nowhere to my knowledge makes an extended defense of it against alternative theological positions, nor does he spell out a view of biblical revelation to support it. From this one ought not to infer that he is unable to justify it! Perhaps it was not necessary to do so at the time of writing, since confessional Christian theology was then a very strong movement in Protestant thought. Nonetheless, one of the differences from my work is highlighted in relation to Ramsey's, namely, that mine does not use the Bible and the deposit of Christian belief in the same authoritative way. My theocentric ethics has a strong biblical base in the creation narratives, in some of the Psalms, in the Wisdom literature, and in some aspects of the New Testament, but for reasons that have been given it is not an exposition of the implications of the grounding it has in the Bible.

It is fair to raise the question of whether Ramsey's work is an accurate depiction of biblical ethics. He makes a good case for obedient love as central to his interpretation of biblical materials from both the Old and the New Testaments, but the case is not argued in detail against alternative interpretations. As I have previously indicated, in the Bible there are many different perceptions of God and God's relations to the world, and many different kinds of moral language. Ramsey is correct to say that the biblical writers "view ethics theologically as rooted in the nature and activity of God."[163] But two questions can be asked about this to which I have given

161. Ramsey, *Basic Christian Ethics*, p. xi.
162. Ibid., p. xiii.
163. Ibid., p. 1.

different answers than he does. The first is internal to the Bible: Within the biblical accounts, is the nature and activity of God as exclusively in focus on God's love as Ramsey's argument claims? I believe that it is not. The second question is: Does such knowledge as human beings can have of God's nature and activity depend so exclusively on the biblical material as Ramsey's does? The line of argument in volume 1 is clearly that it does not.

Ramsey is close to the center of the theological tradition in his Christological reading of the Bible. Critical to his perspective are the following statements.

> Christian ethics stands . . . in decisive relation to Jesus Christ. . . . As a consequence, Christocentric ethics contrasts both with humanism's cutting the pattern to fit man and also with any religious or mystical ethics which may indeed be theocentric and pious enough but in a general or cosmic sense not historically related to this particular man, Jesus Christ. Christian ethics necessarily means a religious ethics "about" Jesus irreducible to the so-called "simple" religious ethics "of" Jesus. The Christian, indeed, is consistently more Christocentric, considerably less merely theocentric, in his religious and ethical outlook than was Jesus himself.[164]

This quotation clearly places the central thrust of my ethics in a critical perspective. It is probably "theocentric and pious enough but in a general or cosmic sense," and not decisively related to Jesus Christ. It might be considered "merely theocentric," and thus not sufficiently an ethics "about" Jesus. It could not, however, be accused of fitting Ramsey's depiction of the ethics of humanism.

The Christocentric character of Ramsey's ethics is not always explicit in his many writings on matters of public policy and medical ethics. But it is never denied, and sometimes it is stated with laudable directness and integrity. For example, in a polemical article about interpretations of death, he writes, "I always write as the ethicist I am, namely, a Christian ethicist, and not as some hypothetical common denominator."[165] In the preface to his first major work on medical ethics he writes,

> At crucial points in the analysis of medical ethics, I shall not be embarrassed to use as an interpretative principle the Biblical norm of *fidelity to covenant*, with the meaning it gives to *righteousness* between man and man.[166]

164. Ibid., p. 23; see also pp. 16–17.

165. Paul Ramsey, "The Indignity of 'Death with Dignity,'" *The Hastings Center Studies*, 2, no. 2 (May 1974): 56.

166. Paul Ramsey, *The Patient as Person* (New Haven: Yale University Press, 1970), p. xii. He reiterates this also in his most recent book, *Ethics at the Edges of Life: Medical and Legal Intersections* (New Haven: Yale University Press, 1978), p. xiii. Rabbi Seymour Siegel, in a paper read on the occasion of Ramsey's retirement from Princeton University, perceptively

The particular principles of medical ethics that he develops are for him grounded in and derived from the themes of *hesed* (covenant fidelity) and *agape* (Christian love), the features central to biblical ethics as he earlier interpreted it. The biblical norm is not unintelligible to those who do not have Christocentric ethics, for a good deal of common human experience also supports it. But Ramsey always writes as a Christian theologian, and the integrity of this stance makes for a sharper alternative to other ethics at many levels of moral discourse than does the present work. Ramsey's work, like John Howard Yoder's, which develops Christian and biblical ethics very differently from Ramsey's, poses a radical North American alternative to the present project.[167]

To establish that steadfast love is the central category of biblical ethics is an exegetical task. I have indicated that a question can be raised about whether Ramsey's view of biblical ethics is fully defensible. Work on the ethics in the Bible by biblical scholars could be adduced to show that the matter is more complex than Ramsey's position states.[168] The effect of his choice, in any case, is what I have elsewhere called a love monism.[169] All further specifications of moral principles and rules must be inferences from the meaning of Christian love. Love is "in-principled" in these further specifications.[170] Ramsey is persistently consistent in making his case that his "special ethics" are authorized by, grounded in, and ultimately controlled by the principle of obedient love. With reference, for example, to the early church, he writes that

> [t]he change-over to just-war doctrine and practice was not a "fall" from the original purity of Christian ethics; but, however striking a turning-full-cycle, this was a change of tactics only. The basic strategy remained the same: responsible love and service of one's neighbors in the texture of common life.[171]

With reference to justice more generally, he says that "love is always the primary notion, justice derivative, since justice may be defined as what

---

pointed out that the covenant between God and man in the Bible is between God and a community and not the individual, as seems to be supposed in Ramsey's use of the idea. Siegel's point would open the way for consideration of the common good in a manner that Ramsey eschews.

167. See Gustafson, *Ethics*, 1:74–76.

168. For a useful analytical review of the literature on biblical ethics and the use of the Bible in ethics, see Allen Verhey, "The Use of Scripture in Ethics," *Religious Studies Review* 4 (1978):28–39.

169. James M. Gustafson, "How Does Love Reign?" *The Christian Century* 86 (1966):654–55. This article is a review of Joseph Fletcher, *Situation Ethics*, and *The Scottish Journal of Theology* edition of Paul Ramsey, *Deeds and Rules in Christian Ethics*.

170. Paul Ramsey, "Faith Effective through In-Principled Love," *Christianity and Crisis* 20 (1960):76–78.

171. Ramsey, *War and the Christian Conscience*, p. xvii.

Christian love does when confronted by two or more neighbors."[172] Further evidence could be cited to back the description of Ramsey's ethics as ultimately a love monism.

Like any other ethical theory with a supreme principle that authorizes all other principles and rules, so Ramsey's has a kind of consistency to it. It is not always persuasive to his readers, however, that love can be "in-principled" to warrant taking human life even for a just cause. Be that as it may, as long as Ramsey can establish to his satisfaction that further principles are derivative from love, his love monism works well. Ambiguous situations still remain, but they are not conflicts of principles or values of equal par. Ramsey often perceives choices to be difficult, and does not deny the costliness of some hard choices that are made. Nonetheless, with obedient or responsible love as the supreme principle, he avoids the severity of some of the moral conflicts that follows from the theology of volume 1. The love monism is theologically grounded for him, and thus, again, one sees how a theological judgment authorizes a view of the content of ethics. My difference with him is not only a scholarly one of whether his biblical exegesis is fully adequate; it is also a theological one. The theology of volume 1 does not warrant a love monism in ethics.

This does not mean that ethics from a theocentric perspective always comes out with different judgments on all particular cases. It does mean, however, that certain actions which love does not permit for Ramsey can be argued as permissible from other theological ethical grounds, and that actions which love requires for Ramsey can be questioned from another theological perspective. One example is clinical research in medicine. It is fair to say that for Ramsey obedient love, or covenant fidelity between persons, is in-principled in the maxim: "Do no harm." Of course, the informed consent of the experimental subject ought to be gained. But there are circumstances in pediatric research, for example, in which the subject is not sufficiently mature to give informed consent, and there is no benefit to that individual from the research. Ramsey's judgment in such cases is consistently restrictive, regardless of the potential benefits to others, including subsequent generations of children. "Do no harm" becomes almost "Take no risks." The infant or child cannot give informed consent to being an experimental subject, and there are no benefits to his or her health from the experiment. Therefore it ought not to be done. From my perspective the canons of informed consent ought to be adhered to as well, but there are circumstances in which for very important reasons of potential benefits to others, one would more readily grant an exception. There are also risks in restricting research too severely, for other persons and future generations might be deprived of a beneficial therapy.

172. Ramsey, *Basic Christian Ethics*, p. 243.

A love monism does not in and of itself lead to the kind of ethics that Ramsey expounds. It is the knitting of love to a deontological method that shapes his particular moral judgments and prescriptions. Love tends to become a rule-term in Ramsey's thought. One could have a love monism in which love is applied to motives; everything that is done from the disposition and affection of love would be justified by its motive. Love might become an intentional term; the self-conscious intention to do the loving thing would justify the act. Love could be a term about the consequences of action; wherever effects that could be claimed to be manifestations of love can be achieved, the actions necessary to achieve them are appropriate. Similarly love could refer to a desired state of affairs; whatever qualities of relationships between persons that could be denominated "loving" are desirable, and the means to such states of affairs are morally warranted. These remarks enable one to see that in addition to the decisive choice of love as the supreme principle, Ramsey has also chosen what he argues is the appropriate ethical method, and particularly appropriate to the working out of *hesed* and *agape*.

I have already cited passages in which Ramsey avers that Christian ethics is deontological ethics.[173] Is this the case? Obviously it is not the case historically and empirically, for there are many patterns of methods and procedures that have been and are used by writers of Christian ethics. Love, for example, has been a motive or dispositional term in the writings of Augustine and Luther. H. Richard Niebuhr has proposed that neither classic teleological nor deontological forms of ethics fully capture what is necessary to Christian theological ethics, and develops his well-known alternative of response and responsibility as the fundamental form of the Christian moral life.[174]

Ramsey has stated that his way of working in ethics "endeavors to stand within the way the Bible views morality."[175] Is biblical morality deontological? Certainly there are moral writings in the biblical material that fit better the modern characterization "deontological" than they fit some alternative appellations. The legal prescriptions of the Torah are a case in point. But even in these the wider context is one of the assurance of rewards if the community is faithful in its obedience to the laws, and thus a "pruden-

173. Whether Ramsey's work is consistently, or even basically, deontological has been questioned. "[I]t is clear that Cahill misrepresents Paul Ramsey's position in saying that it is deontological rather than teleological, although she has at least one predecessor in so misunderstanding Ramsey, namely, Ramsey. For Ramsey's notion of a fidelity to a covenant is at least a partial specification of what he takes to be the *telos* of human life. Such fidelity is a virtue" Alasdair MacIntyre, "Theology, Ethics, and the Ethics of Medicine and Health Care: Comments on Papers by Novak, Mouw, Roach, Cahill, and Hartt," *Journal of Medicine and Philosophy* 4 (1979):437.

174. H. Richard Niebuhr, *The Responsible Self: An Essay in Christian Moral Philosophy* (New York: Harper and Row, 1963).

175. Ramsey, *Basic Christian Ethics*, p. xi.

tial" (in the modern perjorative sense of expediential and not the classic sense of wise) motive is given. The biblical writers were not ethical theorists. In both the moral writings in the Bible and in the theological backings that are given them there is a great variety. There are at least as many biblical grounds for saying that Christian ethics is teleological or an ethics of response as there are for saying that the biblical way of viewing morality is deontological. There are passages that fit nicely into Barth's notion of "points to be considered."[176]

The idea that Christian ethics is deontological ethics, then, must be backed by some other kind of argument. The most coherent theological backing for it would be a theology of God as lawgiver or commander. But even such a theology can lead to different types of ethics. To use distinctions which some contemporary students find helpful, Barth's Christian ethics can be called "act-deontology"; obedience to the command of God is the moral requirement, but the command is for particular acts in particular circumstances. Ramsey's, by contrast, would be a "rule-deontology." I believe Ramsey's theological case is implicit in his first book; ethics viewed theologically must be "rooted in the nature and activity of God."[177] What is known about God is God's steadfast love. Steadfast love in turn entails, or at least implies, a deontological ethics; it converts into covenant fidelity between persons. Fidelity in turn is properly "in-principled" in rules of conduct. Faithfulness to other persons requires principles and rules and not just attitudes and goals. Fidelity that expresses steadfast love is impartial; it is concern for the other for his or her own sake and not because of some preferential relationship or interest of the self or of third parties. It is in this manner, I believe, that Ramsey's ethics takes on a deontologial character, or a kind of Kantian color.[178]

Ramsey's intention to be as rigorously deontological as possible does not mean that he is insensitive to many aspects of human experience that ascend to greater importance from other perspectives. He is concerned with

176. See, for example, 1 Corinthians 10:23–11:1. While the issue is a cultic one, namely the permissibility of eating meat that comes from sacrificial animals, it is not wrong to read it as a way of doing practical moral theology.

177. Ramsey, *Basic Christian Ethics*, p. 1.

178. My impression is that Ramsey has become more rigorously deontological in the course of his writings. Some statements that I believe he would revise from earlier books are these. "Persons who desire rigid allegiance to certain programs for social reform, or the imposition of rules that will remove all doubt about how the individual should conduct himself, will have to go elsewhere than to Christian ethical theory." Ramsey, *Basic Christian Ethics*, p. 80. "Christian love, which often acts within the law and lays down rules or principles for the guidance of action, still continues to exert a free and sovereign pressure—since Jesus Christ is Lord—toward fresh determination of what should be done in situations not rightly covered by the law, by natural justice, or even by its own former articulation in principle." Ramsey, *War and the Christian Conscience*, p. 190. For a very careful critique of Ramsey on the use of rules, see Donald Evans, "Paul Ramsey on Exceptionless Moral Rules," in Johnson and Smith, eds., *Love and Society*, pp. 19–46.

the moral ethos of our culture, in terms both of how it tends to back uncritically certain activities of dubious moral value and of how it is in turn reinforced by such activities. He is also concerned with institutional structures of society. And, as critics have pointed out, his reasons for certain choices are sometimes mixed, with reference to the types of ethical theory. It would be patronizing to say that it is "useful" to have Ramsey's Christian ethical rigorism alive and well to prevent or restrain laxism that could follow from other ways of working. Ramsey seeks to be ethically correct, and not simply to offer an alternative view. Thus, he presents arguments that are forceful; by taking them seriously any theologian or professional person is led to deeper self-criticism even if he or she does not finally agree.

One of the features of Ramsey's work, in comparison to the ethics that follow from my theocentric perspective, is that the description of the morally relevant circumstances in most cases is much more limited. Those limits follow reasonably from the ways in which he has developed a Christian ethics of love in a deontological mode. How a theologian or a philosopher defines the moral or, more sharply, the essence of the moral, is a critical factor in deciding what circumstances are relevant to a moral choice. In at least the ideal-type of deontology, what makes an act morally right is its conformity to a principle or rule of conduct, and necessarily the consequences of an act are of no, or far less, significance. By contrast a "consequentialist" defines the moral in terms of the effects of action that can be judged according to some criteria to be good or evil. In extreme form this is stated in the maxim that the consequences, or the end, justifies the means. A more inclusive description of the circumstances is required; the moralist has to take into account the consequences not only for the principal recipient of the act but also for others, and has to take into account probable effects over a longer range of time for all who are involved.

Ramsey's deontological work, in medical ethics, for example, quite properly attends to the primary relationship of fidelity between a physician and a patient; the covenant requires that the physician be committed to doing what is in the best interests of the patient. But in such an exclusive focus on this relationship, both the physician and the patient are, conceptually at least, severed from their relations to other persons, and other persons are severed from relations to them. The foreseeable bad probable outcomes, for example, of a poverty-stricken unwed adolescent carrying a fetus to full term would not be sufficient to warrant an abortion. The fetus is the primary patient, not the mother and certainly not "society." This follows reasonably from Ramsey's application of love in a deontological mode. He is not heedless about the importance of other matters that follow from moral actions dictated by his content and method. Adolescent pregnancies ought to be avoided, and care ought to be provided for both the mother and the child. But the description of the relevant circumstances of the moral act is stringent, and this follows from his method.

Ramsey's approach has the advantage of clarity and precision that results from the method. More moral ambiguity can be overcome by this method than can be from some alternative perspectives. The "slippery slope" on which a morality finds itself when the circumstances are described in such a way that the relevant relationships are more inclusive, and the time span of probable consequences to be taken into account is longer, can be avoided. From the perspective of theocentric ethics as I have developed it, while one comes to a reasoned choice about the better course of action, one cannot have the moral certainty that Ramsey's Christian ethics provides. This does not mean that one is wandering in the wastelands of utility or that the exercise of prudence requires less disciplined analysis than Ramsey's approach does. The proposal for a procedure of discernment made in volume 1, chapter 7, provides an alternative procedure to Ramsey's deontological one; it demands as much disciplined analysis and clarity as his does. It does not, however, provide the degree of certainty that his does.

Differences in theology, and in the ethics that follow from the theology lead to different procedures in practical moral reasoning. Several features of the profile of ethics from a theocentric perspective confirm this: the interpretation of the human in a more relational pattern than Ramsey's; the derivation of ethics more from the objective ordering given in these relations than from his Christian focus on obedient love; the relationship between part and whole, and the consequent concern for a common good that might in some circumstances override the judgment in favor of the individual; and the less rationalistic interpretation of what is involved in moral choices. I suspect that a further difference emerges, namely, in the criteria for deciding which moral and social issues ought to receive more of the attention of the ethician. Although there are ethical issues in fetal research, one may wonder whether the attention given to it by Ramsey and others is out of proportion to its social and long-term significance relative to other matters.[179]

Conclusion

Karl Barth, Thomas Aquinas, Karl Rahner, and Paul Ramsey have provided benchmarks for a further elucidation of the more distinctive features of ethics from a theocentric perspective. By attending to significant aspects of their ethical thought, it has been possible to show by comparison

179. See Paul Ramsey, *The Ethics of Fetal Research* (New Haven: Yale University Press, 1975).

how both the form and the content of ethics are shaped by theological convictions. To none of these commanding authors has full justice been done; the selection of the aspects of their ethics has been determined by my purposes for this chapter. No doubt there is more agreement with aspects of their ethics than has been accounted for, and on particular moral issues I would often come to a choice similar to theirs, though for different reasons.

It has also been my intention in this chapter to assist readers whose own ethical orientation is informed by, or similar to, those of these authors to see from their perspectives the differences in ethics. In chapter 3 a similar procedure is used with two philosophical benchmarks, utilitarianism and the ethics of Immanuel Kant.

3

Benchmarks from Moral Philosophy

The present work is one of theological ethics. Theological ethics, if done with any effort to be comprehensive and coherent, cannot avoid being philosophical. Moral philosophy, however, does not necessarily have to be theological and, indeed, it seldom is in the modern world. To be sure, moral philosophers make and defend judgments about how some things really are, and what are the fundamental bases upon which their ethical theories are built. It is self-serving on the part of theologians to call these judgments "theological"; they might properly be called the functional equivalents of theology in a system of ethics. It is also the case that philosophical theories of ethics can be fitted into theological frameworks if their authors or readers are interested in doing so.

Kant's famous argument for the existence of God "as a postulate of pure practical reason" is a case in point. It is "morally necessary to assume the existence of God" just as it is morally necessary to assume immortality, in his view, in order to assure the ultimate coincidence of duty and happiness.[1] An ethical theory is developed, and theology is justified as a morally necessary assumption of it. As Kant himself points out, "this moral necessity is subjective, i.e., a need, and not objective, i.e., duty itself."[2] One does not have to assume the existence of God as a ground of moral obligations in general, nor assume that the ordering activity of God is a source for moral principles and norms.

Henry Sidgwick does not accept such an argument as Kant's, but in effect he writes that if one feels the need to have a theology with divine sanctions, utilitarianism can plausibly be fitted into certain theological beliefs.

> If, then, we may assume the existence of such a Being, as God, by the *consensus* of theologians, is conceived to be, it seems that Utilitarians may legitimately infer the existence of Divine sanctions to the code of social duty as constructed on a Utilitarian basis; and such sanctions would, of course, suffice to make it always everyone's interest to promote universal happiness to the best of his knowledge.[3]

It is clear, however, that, like Kant's, the utilitarian basis for morality is established on explicit nontheological grounds, and in itself requires no theological assumptions.[4]

1. Immanuel Kant, *Critique Of Practical Reason*, in Lewis White Beck, trans. and ed., *Critique Of Practical Reason And Other Writings In Moral Philosophy* (Chicago: University of Chicago Press, 1949), p. 228. The extended discussion of this issue is found on pp. 227–34; the discussion of immortality is found on pp. 225–27.
2. Ibid., pp. 228–29.
3. Sidgwick, *Methods*, p. 506.
4. For a careful discussion of Sidgwick and theology, see J. B. Schneewind, *Sidgwick's Ethics and Victorian Moral Philosophy* (Oxford: The Clarendon Press, 1977), pp. 374–79.

Philosophers can also provide grounds for much of the morality sustained in Western culture by the traditions of the biblical religions without having recourse to the theological basis these religions have espoused. Alan Donagan's work is the best example of this.

> [O]ne provisionally accepts as sound and complete the work of the moral theorists (some of them theologians) who shaped the habitual morality that survives in our society, and one tries to isolate the philosophical core of what they had to say about the morality. Fortunately, . . . the part of Hebrew-Christian morality that depends on beliefs about the nature of God . . . is separable from the part that has to do with duties of human beings to themselves and to one another.[5]

Donagan's project separates the "philosophical core" from the religious beliefs that have sustained this common morality, and defends that core on purely rational grounds. These grounds are in the Kantian tradition, but in Donagan's defense of them it is not necessary morally to assume the existence of God.

For theological ethics, as I have argued, the first task in order of importance is to establish convictions about God and God's relations to the world. To make a case for how some things really and ultimately are is the first task of theological ethics. What the theologian writes about ethics must reasonably follow from these convictions. To be sure, it is possible to have a philosophical theology, or a metaphysics, or a cosmology, based on "reason alone" from which follow ethics based on reason alone. In some respects (with qualifications made in volume 1) my work is more in accord with that intention than it is with a view that takes biblical "revelation" as the exclusive basis for theological ethics. In any case the place of theology in the ethics I espouse is different from that of any of the philosophers I have quoted.

The working out of theological ethics, however, requires judgments that are the same as, or similar to, judgments made by moral philosophers. Even in the case of Karl Barth it can be argued that there are certain Kantian, Hegelian, and existentialist influences at work. These render it possible (though that task is not one I have undertaken) to compare Barth's ethics at secondary levels of explication with various philosophers. And, I have shown how particular theological views predispose theologians to adopt certain basic patterns of moral philosophy, for example, how Paul Ramsey's view of love backs his intention to develop deontic ethics. It is also the case that the profile of ethics from a theocentric perspective outlined in chapter 1 can be compared with the views of many moral philosophers. The purpose of this chapter is to do precisely that with reference to two identi-

5. Donagan, *The Theory of Morality*, p. 27 and p. 28.

fiable traditions in modern moral philosophy, the utilitarian and the Kantian.[6]

I have chosen to focus on the utilitarian tradition and on Kant, and to eliminate other possible choices, for several reasons. Natural-law theory, which can be defended on specifically nontheological grounds (though not without the development of a metaphysics or cosmology), has been eliminated because there would be no significant increment to the treatment of it in the previous chapter. I have eliminated existentialist ethics because most of the contrasts with it that would clarify the profile of ethics from a theocentric perspective can be made with reference to other philosophical and theological positions.[7]

The choice of utilitarianism is made not only because the tradition continues to be refined and defended in the literature, but also because its necessary "consequentialism" is an element in practically every proposal for human action and for public policies. Moral agents act purposively; human purposes normally (if not always) are toward the achievement of certain ends judged to be worthy. The achievement of ends requires the assessment of the consequences of alternative courses of action. This does not rule out a "morality of means," nor does it eliminate the prima-facie duties which are not given explicit teleological or consequentialist justfications in each moment of adherence. To put it boldly, human beings seem "naturally" to justify their actions in large measure by their consequences. This, in itself, requires that consequentialism be taken into account, and utilitarianism is a well-developed species of that genus.

6. I have consistently disclaimed the appellation "moral philosopher" when it has been applied to me. There are several reasons for this. I have studied moral philosophy throughout my professional life, but I have never published in the field nor taught it per se. My institutional and personal identity has always been in the area of theology. While I have aspired to make Christian ethics more philosophically sophisticated, as have Paul Ramsey and others, I have always resisted making theological ethics dependent upon the prior acceptance of a philosophical theory of ethics as being correct. I have also adamantly objected to something called "religious ethics" except insofar as that field studies the ethics of particular religious traditions and, particularly, insofar as it engages in a philosophical analysis of the ethics in historically identifiable religious traditions. Indeed, I have often caustically observed that many self-styled "religious ethicists" are persons who have given up on theology but do not have the full credentials of moral philosophers. The theologian must develop ethics with such philosophical care as he or she is able. This does not mean that moral philosophy is "in the service of" theology, as Paul Ramsey has stated. Rather, there are ethical implications of theological beliefs which must be developed philosophically by the theologian. Because these implications are of a theology, whether they fit the standard typology of moral theories, e.g., deontic and teleological, in a consistent way depends on the theology. Although H. Richard Niebuhr did not argue for his view of "man the answerer" in contrast with deontic and teleological models precisely in this way, I believe he assumed and believed this to be the case. His philosophical ethics of "responsibility" follows from his theology of God acting in history, and his correlative view of human agency. That is why his book, *The Responsible Self*, can be legitimately subtitled "An Essay in Christian Moral Philosophy."

7. For a systematic account, see Hazel E. Barnes, *Existentialist Ethics* (Chicago: University of Chicago Press, 1978).

Kant has been chosen because of his historical significance both for moral philosophy and for some Christian ethics. His basic orientation continues to be vigorously defended, developed, and applied by many moral theorists. The moral rigorism that it generally backs can ill afford to be forgotten in the enthusiasms for many courses of action and social and moral reforms that seem to be readily justified on implicit, if not explicit, utilitarian grounds.

In the case of utilitarianism I shall deal with the early tradition. A tradition is named at a particular point in history; Jeremy Bentham is the classical locus for identifying the beginning of a utilitarian tradition, though there are antecedents to its distinguishing features. Kant, obviously, marks the beginning of a tradition; the reader of the history of theological and philosophical ethics also notes affinities between some of his formulations and antecedents. But I have chosen for practical reasons not to use subsequent Kantians in this chapter. It is not within the purview of this chapter to determine, even within my limitations, whether important contemporary moral philosophers adhere to some strict type of each tradition, or how they modify it in specific ways. Nor shall I engage extensive secondary literature about these traditions. The purpose of this chapter is to use the traditions as benchmarks to enable the reader to see, in relation to each, some of the distinctive features of the present work.

Utilitarianism

For my purposes, utilitarianism is to be viewed as a tradition, not as a single theory that commands adherence of all who claim, or are judged, to be utilitarians. Like all traditions, it has evolved as persons have refined, altered, or even abandoned what they have received from their predecessors.[8] To be identified as a tradition, however, there must be some common beliefs or principles. The best way to state briefly the distinguishing feature of a type of ethics is to seek its general answer to the practical moral question, What ought we to do? The utilitarian answer is that we ought to act in the manner that produces the best possible consequences. As stated, the answer leaves many questions open as to what consequences are good, and what criteria are to be used to judge them. It leaves open the question of

8. For the purposes of this project I rely on the writings of the early part of the tradition and use the work of Jeremy Bentham, John Stuart Mill, and Henry Sidgwick. I have not cited important subsequent works, for example, G. E. Moore, *Principia Ethica* (Cambridge: Cambridge University Press, 1903); Stephen E. Toulmin, *An Examination of The Place of Reason in Ethics* (Cambridge: Cambridge University Press, 1950); P. H. Nowell-Smith, *Ethics* (London: Penguin Books, 1954); and J. J. C. Smart, "An Outline of a System of Utilitarian Ethics," in J. J. C. Smart and Bernard Williams, *Utilitarianism: For and Against* (Cambridge: Cambridge University Press, 1973). Nor have I cited any of the voluminous critical literature by moral philosophers.

consequences for whom or for what. It leaves open the question of what rational procedures are to be used to determine the best course of action.

Different answers are given to these questions by persons whose thought is generally classed as utilitarian. For Jeremy Bentham and J. S. Mill, for example, the answer to the first question is that those actions which result in the greatest balance of pleasure over pain are good. For Henry Sidgwick, universal happiness is to be sought. G. E. Moore, who is often classed as an "ideal utilitarian," defends the intrinsic value of such things as beauty and personal affection.[9] On the question of consequences for whom, answers range from egoistic views, to the greatest possible number of persons, or to all sentient beings. With regard to the procedures, a common distinction is made between "rule-utilitarians," who affirm that general moral rules should be followed, and "act-utilitarians," who, in principle, assert that the process of calculating consequences should take place with each prospective action.

While utilitarianism can be viewed as a tradition, it is the case that individual authors have attempted to develop theories, in the sense that they seek to establish an inclusive and systematic view of both the necessary and the sufficient principles for morality, and to propose a supreme principle to determine what is right in prima-facie conflict situations. Like all moral theories, those of the utilitarians rest on some descriptive premises. The critical questions are these: Is the description accurate or true? Is it relatively exclusive or extensive in what is taken to be morally relevant? And, what reasons seem to justify the content and the scope of the description? A comparison of the description that undergirds utilitarianism with that of the present work will highlight the similarities and dissimilarities.

I take it as given that the descriptive basis of any ethical system relies upon some observations and formulates generalizations about them. And since ethics is concerned with the proper action of human beings, a critical feature of any description is its interpretation of human life and of the context in which human life is to be adequately understood. My brief account in chapter 1 of the importance of an interpretation of the place of man in the universe should be recalled. It is certainly the case that classic utilitarian writers, over and over, make appeals to experience in their justifications for ethics. Thus it is relevant to examine briefly what aspects of experience and what context of experience they highlight. One of the differences between utilitarianism and the present work is the description of

9. I never read Moore on these things without shuddering at the social privilege and elitism that they reflect. No doubt he and his friends were enjoying these intrinsic goods and reflecting on them at Cambridge in 1898 when my father, at the age of nine, was employed as a tool carrier during the construction of the Klabböle hydroelectric power dam near Umeå, Sweden.

the place of man in the universe, and the consequent effects of that description on what is morally relevant.

My understanding of classic utilitarianism is that a large, and not necessarily vicious, circle is critical to the position. Without a theological or explicitly metaphysical basis, it bears some formal similarities to the ethics of natural law. The focus of attention in the description is on human beings; observations are made of what it is that they seek as ends; generalizations from these ends in turn are formulated into a moral principle so that one moves from the *is* to the *ought*; and that principle in turn reinforces the circumscription of what is described to be morally relevant. Utilitarians, however, do not take explicit recourse to two arguments made by natural-law ethicians to back the focus on man. One is the metaphysical argument that the lower serves the higher and the more imperfect serves the more perfect; the other is the "revealed" truth that theologians in that tradition claim, namely, that God has created all things for our sake.

One is impressed with the frequency to which appeals to experience are made both to explain and to justify human activity. While Jeremy Bentham is given to more rhetorical flourishes than subsequent writers, the opening paragraph of his most important work, while its content becomes refined (but is never abandoned), boldly supports the impression.

> Nature has placed mankind under the governance of two sovereign masters, *pain* and *pleasure*. It is for them alone to point out what we ought to do, as well as to determine what we shall do. On the one hand the standard of right and wrong, on the other the chain of causes and effects, are fastened to their throne. They govern us in all we do, in all we say, in all we think: every effort we can make to throw off our subjection, will serve but to demonstrate and confirm it.[10]

It is absolutely clear that Bentham believed to be empirically true the assertion that pain and pleasure govern human beings in all they do, say, and think.

Recourse to observations of human conduct as a source for deriving an understanding of the good is not, of course, novel in ethics. Aristotle's argument to show that the end persons seek for itself and not as a means to any other end (*eudaemonia*, happiness, well-being), also is based on observations of human behavior.[11] Thomas Aquinas's conviction that we naturally incline toward the good and away from the evil certainly is based on some observations. Augustine's explanation of action is based on

10. Jeremy Bentham, *An Introduction to the Principles of Morals and Legislation*, in *The English Philosophers from Bacon to Mill*, ed. Edwin A. Burtt (New York: Random House, The Modern Library, 1939), p. 791.

11. See, Aristotle, *Nicomachean Ethics*, 1097a15–30, in *The Basic Works of Aristotle*, ed. Richard McKeon (New York: Random House, 1941), p. 941.

observations that persons act from their desires for certain objects and ends. What is crucial is the judgment of the object or the end of natural desires. And insofar as an ethical theory seeks to develop an overriding end, how that end is stated is critical. If the end is pleasure (or the avoidance of pain) a further decision names the sort of consequences that are pleasurable. Since simply the physical sensations are not sufficient, further qualitative refinement is required. If it is happiness, the various "parts" or forms of happiness have to be described.[12] Some hierarchy of pleasures or of forms of happiness has to be developed to resolve prima-facie conflicts between species of the genus.

In utilitarian ethics pain and pleasure, or happiness, circumscribe the area of the moral; ethics is in focus on man; or, with the extension to all sentient beings, on man and animals.[13] The moral restraints on action are fixed by whether they cause unjustifiable pain, and the positive imperatives are justified by their contribution to the greatest possible pleasure or happiness. Moral relevance, at least of the first order, is confined only to those beings who have developed sufficiently to be able to suffer pain or pleasure. Their existence circumscribes the arena of ethics.

Implicit in this is an assumption that the lower exists for the sake of the higher. To be sure, it would reasonably follow from classic utilitarianism that human beings ought to attend to the fundamental conditions necessary for happiness, but they would be simply that—conditions necessary for happiness. Such proposals did follow; utilitarianism strongly fostered and supported social reforms, for example. That the writers did not take into account problems raised in our time, such as ecological issues, may simply reflect the historical conditions of the nineteenth and early twentieth centuries. Utilitarians could justify restraints on uses of present resources or justify the development of technology on the grounds of whether these things do foster happiness, not only for the present generation but also for future ones.

Certainly utilitarian ethics has a basis for looking to the happiness of future generations. My judgment is that although this basis is there, it was

12. For a discussion of the issue of quality of pleasures, see J. S. Mill, *Utilitarianism*, chap. 2, in Burtt, ed., *The English Philosophers*, p. 901. For the parts of happiness, see ibid., chap. 4, in Burtt, p. 925.

13. "According to the 'greatest happiness principle' . . . the ultimate end, with reference to and for the sake of which all other ends are desirable . . . is an existence exempt as far as possible from pain, and as rich as possible in enjoyments, both in point of quantity and quality. . . . [T]he end of human action, is necessarily also the standard of morality; which may accordingly be defined, the rules and precepts for human conduct, by observance of which an existence such as has been described might be, to the greatest extent possible, secured to all mankind; and not to them only, but, so far as the nature of things admits, to the whole sentient creation." J. S. Mill, *Utilitarianism*, chap. 2, in Burtt, *The English Philosophers*, p. 904. The inclusion of "the whole sentient creation" becomes a basis for defending the rights of animals. See Peter Singer, *Animal Liberation* (New York: Avon Books, 1977).

not exploited with the forethought that it warrants. The orientation toward the future good was generally discussed in the contexts of individuals' pleasures deferred for the sake of future pleasures and of individuals insofar as the achievement of their good requires the good of other present persons and groups. With reference to the future, Sidgwick wrote that "my feelings a year hence should be just as important to me as my feelings, next minute, if only I could make an equally sure forecast of them".[14] The rationality of ethics requires that one seek to take into account impartially all aspects of one's conscious life, future as well as present.

Even if the individual's happiness is the end to be sought, persons have to take into account their relations to others. Persons are all similar parts of "a Mathematical or Quantitative Whole":

> Such a Whole is presented in the common notion of the Good—or, as is sometimes said, "good on the whole"—of any individual human being. . . . The principle [that the present happiness is reasonably foregone with the view of obtaining greater future happiness] need not be restricted to a hedonistic application; it is equally applicable to any other interpretation of "one's own good," in which good is conceived as a mathematical whole, of which the integrant parts are realised in different parts or moments of a lifetime.[15]

Since one's own good cannot be realized apart from the good of others, the implication is that individuals should seek the "Universal Good." Just as the "good on the whole" of an individual is conceived by comparing and integrating successive different goods, so one forms "the notion of Universal Good by comparison and integration of the goods of all individual—or sentient—existences."[16] From "the point of view (if I may say so) of the Universe," the good of any single individual is no more to be preferred than that of any other, unless it is the case that the possibilities of realizing it are greater. From this the "maxim of Benevolence" it is inferred

> that each one is morally bound to regard the good of any other individual as much as his own, except in so far as he judges it to be less, when impartially viewed, or less certainly knowable or attainable by him. [Practically, however,] each man, even with a view to universal Good, ought chiefly to concern himself with promoting the good of a limited number of human beings, and that generally in proportion to the closeness of their connexion with him.[17]

These and other passages from utilitarian writers can be cited to show that in certain respects the social character of human existence is taken into

14. Sidgwick, *Methods*, p. 124, n. 1.
15. Ibid., p. 381. For Sigwick's discussion of posterity see pp. 414–16.
16. Ibid., p. 382.
17. Ibid.

account. The quality of the happiness of others with whom we have relationships is important both to them and to us. Finally, however, the happiness of individuals is the primary end. J.S. Mill, for example, writes that Jesus' Golden Rule and the command to love the neighbor constitute "the ideal perfection of utilitarian morality." To achieve the ideal,

> utility would enjoin, first, that laws and social arrangements should place the happiness, or . . . the interest, of every individual, as nearly as possible in harmony with the interest of the whole; and secondly, that education and opinion, which have so vast a power over human character, should use that power so as to establish in the mind of every individual an indissoluble association between his own happiness and the good of the whole. . . . [18]

Not all utilitarians were as individualistically oriented as J.S. Mill, but in his case the cultivation of individuality was strongly commended. His great work, *On Liberty*, is not only a statement of the philosophical grounds of civil liberties but also a tract in praise of individuality. The liberty of the individual must be limited, "he must not make himself a nuisance to other people."[19] But he goes on to affirm that "there should be different experiments in living." "It is desirable, in short, that in things which do not primarily concern others, individuality should assert itself," and "that the free development of individuality is one of the leading essentials of well-being."[20] This involves a criticism of living merely according to custom, of failing to choose a life plan for oneself, and of failure to use all of one's faculties. Sidgwick, however, expresses some concern about Mill's stress on individuality; it might lead to less than sufficient consideration for the possible risks of evil to others.

> [E]ven supposing that we could mark off the "sphere of individual option and self-guidance" by some simple and sweeping formula, still within this sphere the individual, if he wishes to guide himself reasonably on utilitarian principles, must take some account of all important effects of his actions on the happiness of others. . . . [21]

I have been concerned to point out the important features of a utilitarian description of what constitutes moral life. It is a description of "human nature" that is most important, and this description is affirmed to be empirically true. J.S. Mill makes the point in a forthright manner. As a proof of utilitarianism he states the following.

> If the opinion which I have now stated is psychologically true—if human nature is so constituted as to desire nothing which is not

18. Mill, *Utilitarianism*, chap. 2, in Burtt, *The English Philosophers*, p. 908.
19. J. S. Mill, *On Liberty*, chap. 3, in Burtt, *The English Philosophers*, p. 992.
20. Ibid., p. 992, and pp. 992–93.
21. Sidgwick, *Methods*, p. 478.

> either a part of happiness or a means to happiness, we can have no other proof, and we require no other, that these are the only things desirable. If so, happiness is the sole end of human action, and the promotion of it the test by which to judge all human conduct; from whence it necessarily follows that it must be the criterion of morality. . . .[22]

Human desires are presumably accurately, indeed truly, described. On the basis of observation and generalization, Mill and others judge that what persons desire is happiness, and thus there is a single ultimate end that is not only desired but desirable. The description of the motives for action dictates the end of action, and the descriptive end becomes the normative end. Individual persons are, in my judgment, the final reference point for utilitarianism.

These utilitarians were concerned about implications of their ethics that could be criticized from other points of view. They were concerned about the relations between, for example, justice and utility, duties and rewards. They had read Immanuel Kant, and in part defined their ethics in relation to his thought. They attempted to defend their views against the charge that they did not provide clear and certain standards for morality. I have not taken full account of the refinements of utilitarian ethics.[23] There is what Brian Barry calls a "noble humanism" in their work.[24] They were not utopians who sought to construct an ethics *de novo*; indeed, in Sidgwick's view they had to start with the existing social order and morality and engage in their gradual reform.[25] But there is an ethical "maximalism" entailed in their thought that has some similarities with some forms of Protestant ethics, i.e., beyond specific justifiable duties is always the stringent claim that one

22. Mill, *Utilitarianism*, chap. 4, in Burtt, *The English Philosophers*, p. 926. See also Sidgwick's chapter, "The Proof of Utilitarianism," in *Methods*, pp. 418–22.

23. For example, on the ideal of justice, in relation to utility, see J. S. Mill, *Utilitarianism*, chap. 5, in Burtt, *The English Philosophers*, pp. 928–48. Justice was, for Mill, grounded on utility, and was "incomparably the most sacred and binding part of morality. Justice is the name for certain classes of moral rules which concern the essentials of human well-being more nearly, and are therefore of more absolute obligation, than any other rules for the guidance of life; and the notion which we have found to be the essence of the idea of justice, that of a right residing in an individual, implies and testifies to this more binding obligation" (p. 943). See also Sidgwick's critique of the "intuitional" justification of justice, in *Methods*, pp. 264–94, and his utilitarian justification of it, pp. 439–48.

24. Brian Barry, *Political Argument* (London: Routledge and Kegan Paul, 1965), p. 77, n.2. The comment occurs in the context of Barry's scathing account of T. S. Eliot's essay on "The Idea of a Christian Society."

25. "[I]f [the utilitarian] keeps within the limits that separate scientific prevision from fanciful Utopian conjecture, the form of society to which his practical conclusions relate will be one varying but little from the actual, with its actually established code of moral rules and customary judgments concerning virtue and vice." Sidgwick, *Methods*, p. 474. "The Utilitarian must repudiate altogether that temper of rebellion against the established morality. . . . He must . . . also repudiate as superstitious that awe of it as an absolute or Divine Code which Intuitional moralists inculcate." Ibid., p. 475.

ought to seek the greatest good of the greatest number, indeed, universal happiness.

The richness and complexity of utilitarian ethics are noteworthy, and are executed at the cost of what appears to be confusion in the eyes of modern critics. But the simplicity of the underlying descriptive premises is also noteworthy, and it is this that determines the circumscription of the morally relevant features of life. The good of individual persons is the ultimate good; all other ends are finally justified in terms of their instrumental value to the maximal fulfillment of that good, which is happiness.

What Mill believed to be empirically true (and thus to be a proof of utilitarianism) formed the conception of the good, circumscribed what was morally relevant, and made necessary the method of utilitarianism, that is, the calculation of possible consequences of particular courses of action. The form, or method, of the ethics follows from the content, or substance, of its view of the human good. Thus utilitarianism can be rendered as a moral philosophy with systematic consistency.

The descriptive account of human life in the context of interdependencies in society and nature that is one of the distinctive features of the present work is quite different from the utilitarian one. Insofar as it follows from theological convictions, it is, of course, beyond the pale of the deliberately nontheological, and in some respects antitheological, stance of classic utilitarian authors.[26]

Although utilitarian ethics is, in one sense, ethics in conformity to "nature," i.e., to human nature as described, Sidgwick develops a critique of the idea of nature and the natural as a basis for ethics. He views the idea as assuming a design which can be empirically known with certainty—a design which he does not find. It requires the derivation of what ought to be from what is, something which also occurs (in my judgment) in utilitarianism. He questions how one moves from natural impulses to an order of reason in ethics, but does not consider, for example, Thomas's account of this. He assumes that an argument from some design must run counter to the experience that has developed our desirable social institutions; again he does not take into account sophisticated natural-law theories which readily account for the development of desirable social institutions. Reliance upon a physical view of human nature leads, in his judgment, to trivial conclusions. Natural social relations present to him a problem rather than a solution (though this seems to run counter to one of his previous criticisms); he does not deal with the ways in which natural-law ethics have provided criteria for assessing actual social relations. And finally, he raises the ques-

26. There are several discussions of theological ethics in Sidgwick. One of the most interesting describes three possible types of theological ethics: utilitarian in which God desires the happiness of human beings, teleological in which God desires their perfection, and intuitional in which God's laws are known and are to be obeyed. See Ibid., pp. 79–80.

tion of the significance of the concept of evolution for ethics based on nature—a matter on which I agree. His conclusion is that "no definition that has ever been offered of the Natural exhibits this notion as really capable of furnishing an independent ethical first principle." Thus he sees no way of extracting from the ordering of nature "a definite practical criterion of the rightness of actions."[27]

It admittedly is the case that I cannot provide a single independent first principle of ethics that will in every case resolve moral conflicts. In my judgment the impetus to define such a principle stems in part from the aspiration to have, in the most rigorous and restricted sense, a system of thought. It reflects attempts in other scholarly fields to find the ultimate principle that explains all pertinent data and events; in the case of ethics the single principle must ultimately justify all human actions. To be sure, traditional natural-law ethics could achieve greater success in this regard than the ethics developed in this volume, since it affirmed an ultimate telos not only for the whole of the creation but also for each individual person. The patterns of interdependence in nature and in human community, I have argued, provide indications of the functional requisites that must be taken into account for the achievement of a variety of goods or values. And the interdependence of things valued do not mesh together for the fulfillment of human happiness. With Jonathan Edwards, I have affirmed that there is a proper range of striving for human happiness and well-being, but the limitations of the possibility of happiness must be taken into account. All things are instrumental to the divine ordering, not to human happiness, and the divine ordering does not have human happiness as its final end. There are choices that have to be made which run counter to the fulfillment of human happiness. Sidgwick, it must be noted, was quite occupied with the relations of duties (which, of course are ultimately justified on utilitarian grounds) and happiness, a problem Kant resolved by arguing that immortality is a necessary postulate of pure practical reason. Indeed, there is a kind of darkness of spirit at the end of Sidgwick's *Methods*. It seems, he wrote, "that the inseparable connexion between Utilitarian duty and the greatest happiness of the individual who conforms to it cannot be satisfactorily demonstrated on empirical grounds."[28] He explicitly rejects a theological resolution of this "fundamental contradiction" and admits that it drives one to deeper questions which he finally says belong to "a treatise on General Philosophy."[29]

27. Ibid., p. 83. The discussion of nature is on pp. 80–83.

28. Ibid., p. 503.

29. Ibid., p. 508. See Schneewind's discussion of "The Final Uncertainty," in *Sidgwick's Ethics*, pp. 374–79. Schneewind depicts Sidgwick as heroically adhering to "the service of reason." "His allegiance to it never wavered, even when it meant a final uncertainty about the possibility of a fully rational life" (p. 379).

My understanding of utilitarianism is that any "whole" that has to be taken into account exists for the ends of its individual members. Relationships between parts are to function not for the benefit of the relevant whole but to provide the necessary conditions for the fulfillment of the happiness of the individual parts. Mill's work, *On Liberty*, not only sustains this generalization, but with its emphasis on individual liberty as the principal necessary condition for happiness limits the authority of any collective to intervene into individual life even for the sake of the well-being of that individual.

> [T]he sole end for which mankind are warranted, individually or collectively, in interfering with the liberty of action of any of their number, is self-protection. That the only purpose for which power can be rightfully exercised over any member of a civilized community, against his will, is to prevent harm to others. His own good, either physical or moral, is not a sufficient warrant.[30]

If there can be no justification for the restraint of the actions of individuals against their will for their own physical or moral good, clearly there can be none for the sake of some conception of what is the common good of a human community, not to mention larger "wholes."

Sidgwick's comments on the family also sustain the generalization. He sees in the "common-sense" morality of family life a "latent Utilitarianism."

> [F]or when the question is once raised as to the precise mutual duties (*e.g.*) of husbands and wives, or of parents and children, each disputant commonly supports his view by a forecast of the effects on human happiness to be expected from the general establishment of any proposed rule. . . .[31]

There is a social perspective in this passage and in many others, in the sense that the patterns of interrelationships affect the happiness of those who are related, but I see no way in which one could argue that a "common good" of a family might require restraints against the wills of individual members of the family. While the happiness of each is dependent on the happiness of the others, and certain relations are required to meet the conditions for this, the moral significance of those relationships is not referred to any collective good of the whole.

It is perfectly clear that such a view protects persons from undue interference and from coercive measures instituted by others for the sake either of their individual happiness or benefits of a collectivity. As I indicated in volume 1, one does not move from the protection to individuals that

30. J. S. Mill, *On Liberty*, chap. 1, in Burtt, *The English Philosophers*, p. 956.
31. Sidgwick, *Methods*, p. 436.

such an ethics sustains without good reasons.[32] Nothing in my argument denies the importance of seeking consent of individuals for the restraints on their pursuits for the sake of a whole; nothing has been said that argues for the exercise of coercion as the first means to achieve such restraints. But the interpretation of the relations of parts to wholes given in the present work warrants in certain situations both a "paternalism" with reference to individuals and recourse to restraint with reference to their participation in some defined whole more readily than does the classic utilitarian view. The implications of my view are that some "good" is to be sought; in this respect there are similarities with utilitarianism. The difference is that there are times when the questions of good for whom, or good for what, will be given a different answer. The moral significance of "wholes" is not only that they provide the conditions needed for the well-being of their parts.

Another way to make this point is to indicate that any "good on the whole" that utilitarian ethics, in its classic forms, defends is primarily an aggregation of the goods of individuals. Not only are individual persons actors, as they are in any ethics, but their desired and desirable ends state what is the good. From the viewpoint of the relations of parts to wholes on which the present work is based, it is necessary to argue that the good of a whole, such as the family, is not merely the sum of the happiness of its individual members. The happiness of the individual members is an ingredient, but not the only one. The good of individuals and the common good are reciprocal, but not harmonious. There are various ends that collective life serves, and while one might develop some priorities of ends, the various ends are not seen to be instrumental to the single end of human happiness. When one extends the "whole" to be taken into account, and articulates some of the relationships between human groups and the natural world with which they are interdependent, the aggregative notion of "good on the whole" becomes even more dubious. And the delineation of some right relations between parts of a whole takes on greater moral force than mere usefulness for the happiness ultimately of individual persons.

Utilitarianism has been much criticized because of its "consequentialism." Some of the reasons for the criticism are well grounded. If, for example, the prediction of "good" consequences entailed the notion that any means to achieve them were thereby justified, unmitigated terror and other means would be approved. Classic utilitarians, of course, never argued in favor of such a view. In the case of J.S. Mill, as I have noted, the principle of respect for the liberty of the individual is one restraint on the morally justifiable means to achieve a benefit. A more serious criticism is that there is grave difficulty in determining in many situations just what

32. Gustafson, *Ethics*, 1:99–108. This issue is also addressed in later chapters of the present volume.

consequences are to be deemed good. Highly systematic utilitarians answered in terms of those consequences that made for the greatest happiness of the greatest number of persons, and even (with their concern for the future) over an extended period of time. In principle this single desirable end resolved the problems of judging benefits; in practice it has difficulties. As I noted above, the "good" was largely that of individual persons; a more relational view would press the question of good consequences for whom and for what, and recognize a plurality of benefits and costs for interrelated and interdependent entities as well as for the designated wholes.

The "is-ought" problem was severely raised by utilitarianism. This can be seen as either a logical or a moral problem. As a logical problem the issue was whether one could derive an imperative from a descriptive premise, or how it could be done. As a moral problem the issue was whether and/or how consequences "count"; for example, whether one "ought to do justice though the heavens fall," or whether because deception (i.e., lying) is involved in nuclear deterrence this policy is immoral even if it might avoid a nuclear war. I believe that analysts of moral philosophy are correct when they argue that every deontic ethics takes note of the consequences of action at some point.

A further problem is the lack of consensus about what consequences are desirable. Different parties, with different interests or values, deem different consequences to be justified. This is a very real problem in pluralistic societies, in international affairs, in various realms of public policy, and even within very small communities. Certainly procedures are necessary to attempt to bring greater agreement among persons about desirable consequences, but even with the best procedures I foresee no way rationally to overcome the differences of judgment that will continue to occur. Only if there was universal agreement on a single rationalistic ethical theory, and universal compliance with the logical deductions from it, could such differences be fully resolved.

Consequentialists are always reminded of the difficulty in predicting consequences, especially those over a long range of time and those in very complex circumstances in which many persons are interacting. The reminder is always appropriate, for it is one of the oldest truisms of moral experience that the effects one intends from a course of action often do not follow, and that the further one looks ahead the less secure one's predictions and forecasts are likely to be. Certainly sophisticated consequentialists deal only in probabilities and not in certainties. And they take into account probable undesirable outcomes as well as those deemed beneficial. Skepticism about excessive confidence in current methods of cost-benefit analysis and technology assessment is partially warranted, especially if the conversion of various human values into monetary terms is assumed to be easy. It is also the case, however, that one is less likely to make an error of judgment if one has the best possible projection of probable outcomes than if one simply guesses on the basis of hunches. Foresight is never perfect where human actions are involved, but the absence of perfection does not imply that efforts to improve the capacities for foresight are not warranted.

Ethics from a theocentric perspective, as I develop it, shares with utilitarianism a stress on the importance of consequences. Indeed, it requires an enlargement of the range of probable outcomes, both across space and across time, that need to be taken into account. It is concerned not only for consequences that affect the happiness of individual persons or even the human community. It is also concerned for the consequences for designated wholes such as the common good of the family or of the economy. It seeks to discern patterns of relationships which require compliance in order to preserve possibilities for the future development not only of human beings but of the natural world. It cannot, however, provide a single term for the desirable effects; instead it has to deal with a variety of possible good effects and with the cost to other justifiable ends of achieving those selected. Given the unknowability of God's final end for all things (unless, as Edwards says, they all exist to glorify him), and given good reasons that can be proposed for various benefits that are achievable but not harmonious with each other, the problems of moral ambiguity, and in some circumstances genuine moral dilemmas, cannot be avoided. The major difference with classic utilitarian ethics is precisely that Mill and Sidgwick were certain of a single highest good, and thus could forge a more tightly systematic account of an ethical theory. It is an error based on ignorance, however, to assume that the classic utilitarians were not acutely aware of the difficulties of their position; they attempted with considerable fairness to deal with the problems, and in practical terms their ethical theories were hardly simpleminded consequentialism.

The current distinction between "act" and "rule" utilitarianism was not made by Bentham, J.S. Mill, and Sidgwick, but there are passages in their works in which it is implicit. Indeed, to a considerable extent, Sidgwick's work provided a utilitarian justification for what he called "intuitional" and "common-sense" ethics. I have noted above how modest Sidgwick's proposals are with reference to much of customary morality; as does J.S. Mill, he raises questions about aspects of the received moral tradition and has a reformist tendency, but he is hardly revolutionary. Nor did Sidgwick expect everyone to be able on the spot, so to speak, to give a full utilitarian justification for how he or she behaved. Like all authors of ethics, utilitarians were interested in making moral agents more self-conscious and critical of their reasons for action, and they believed that the world would be better if their own theories were practiced. Finally, I believe, they provided for both "rule" and "act" utilitarianism; that is, they proffered utilitarian justifications for rules such as promise-keeping that normally ought to be adhered to, but also raised the question of how justifications to exceptions could be made in the light of particular circumstances and potentially better outcomes, that is, "act" considerations. The use of reason in ethics pertained not only to the calculation of probable consequences but also to the "principle of generalizability." Sidgwick wrote,

> that even when a moral judgment relates primarily to some particular action we commonly regard it as applicable to any other action belonging to a certain definable class: so that the moral truth apprehended is implicitly conceived to be intrinsically universal, though particular in our first apprehension of it.[33]

Rule-utilitarianism has certain similarities to the process of discernment that I developed in volume 1, chapter 7. First, I agree with Sidgwick that a great deal of customary morality derives from human practices that have been useful to preserve order in the human community and have provided proper benefits for individuals. The moral experience of persons sustains certain moral practices which can be given more sophisticated rational justifications. Neither for the utilitarians nor for me does this entail that customary morality is above criticism.[34] Utilitarians understood that one does not need to be a moral philosopher to live a morally praiseworthy life. They also understood the importance of the processes of socialization in forming moral outlooks. Insofar as they were "rule-utilitarians" they affirmed a strong presumption in favor of adhering to some established moral rules. For a theocentric perspective, although one might provide a different justification for rules, the same presumption holds. Certainly the calculation of probable consequences of various courses of action is part of the process of discernment, though (as I have indicated) there is no single normative end or value to assess them. In these respects the process of discernment has affinities with the procedures described and defended by classic utilitarians.

The difference relates to whether the calculation of consequences is the sole procedure one would use to make an exception to a general rule, and insofar as one did use this procedure whether happiness would be the "substantive" good by which to make judgments. The process of discernment, including elements of utilitarian procedures, brings the range of choices into focus but allows discretion in coming to a final perception of what actions are right and good. It is more similar to what I described Karl Rahner's view to be than it is to the calculative procedures of utilitarianism. Such things as right relations that serve the ordering of life, not only among

33. Sidgwick, *Methods*, p. 34.

34. Indeed, one can hardly read J. S. Mill without being conscious of the extent to which he wrote against the backdrop of repressive aspects of the Victorian era and the casual assumption that what traditional religion supported was right.

human beings but also with nature, have to be taken into account. Sidgwick's puzzle about the relationship between human happiness and the performance of obligations is accepted as part of the ambiguities of living in the conditions of finitude. In sum, the considerations to be taken into account are multiple, and while an ordering of priorities is possible, there is no a priori guarantee that precisely the same abstract ordering is worthy of adherence in all circumstances. The question of generalizability of an action is raised, but it is one of several questions that properly are asked. In any case, it functions as a formal principle rather than as a substantive moral one.

In a general way there are affinities between the present work and the utilitarians on the importance of motives and desires in morality, and consequently for ethical theory. While their ethics is concerned about right action, and the consequences of action, they also recognized more fully than more rationalistic theorists do the importance of desires and even of feelings.[35] Feelings were not infallible guides to value and the good; they were aware of the problems that would occur if feelings and desires were not guided by rational activity. They made the distinction between the apparent good that human desires often have in view and the "real" good, a distinction made by Jonathan Edwards and Thomas Aquinas and many others. Their concern for education and socialization processes was based on the recognition that "character" was an important aspect of morality. Dispositions are an aspect of moral agents, and while they are to be judged by the benefits or harms that issue from them, nonetheless they cannot be ignored. It is an error to view utilitarian ethics as exclusively "act-oriented." Their discussions of motives, desires, and dispositions are murkier than are some subsequent philosophical efforts to deal with these matters, but their recognition of the importance these aspects of moral agency is basically correct.

Finally, there is a maximalist, or strenuous, aspect to utilitarian ethics that has affinities with the present work. For Sidgwick, for example, "Universal Happiness is the ultimate *standard*."[36] It is difficult to find a clear line between an ethics of obligation and an ethics of aspiration in utilitarian ethics. To be sure, something like that is implied in the way in which Sidgwick deals with "special relations," such as those between husband and wife or parents and children. The fact that universal happiness is the ultimate standard does not imply that universal benevolence is the only approvable motive. Nonetheless one finds no clear basis for distinguishing between duties and acts of supererogation. What others might distinguish as moral ideals beyond duty, and thus beyond clear obligation, for utilitarian ethics

35. On feelings, see J. S. Mill, *Utilitarianism*, chap. 3, in Burtt, *The English Philosophers*, p. 922.
36. Sidgwick, *Methods*, p. 413.

have greater obligatory weight. In this respect there are similarities between it and certain forms of Christian ethics, such as those that argue for nonpreferential love as a moral obligation stemming from both the teachings and the life of Jesus, or those that argue that since God is the giver and orderer of all things one has virtually unlimited obligations to God, or those that propose the realization of the Kingdom of God on earth in the form of a kingdom of love.

To be sure, there is an aspect of utilitarian ethics that is markedly different from some forms of Christian ethics, namely, that one's happiness is the end to be achieved. This end, of course, is also deeply imbedded in various forms of Christiam life and thought, as I have noted and criticized in volume 1. The question of whether one realizes happiness by seeking to achieve it, just as the question of whether one receives blessedness or eternal happiness if that is one's conscious intention, was a matter the utilitarians discussed. But the reason for restraint on the fulfillment of a present pleasure is normally the anticipation of a greater happiness (in quality or quantity) in the future; the realization of happiness is consistently the final justification. Self-denial is right only for the sake of future happiness, or for the greater happiness of the greater number of persons.

The strenuousness of ethics from a theocentric perspective is different from that of utilitarianism. To be sure, it is necessary to make distinctions about "degrees" of responsibility and the forms that responsibility takes. These are based upon the ordering of life in "nature" and on the commitments and roles that persons have. Being a parent brings with it natural duties to children, being a clergyman brings with it primary obligations to the members of one's congregation, being a physician carries primary responsibilities for health care of persons. But ethics from a theocentric perspective lays a weight of obligation on persons and communities to deny their interests, and happiness among them, for the sake of the well-being of others—those "wholes" whose common good makes a claim upon us as individuals and as communities. The delineation of right relations as normative lays requirements on persons, and action in compliance with them often entails denial of otherwise justifiable interests. Inconvenience to one's self, or restraint of interests of one's community, or denial of present benefits to humanity for the sake of future generations often follows from theocentric ethics as I have developed it. In this sense, the ethics of the present work resonates deeply with one theme in the Christian tradition, namely, there is a strong obligation to seek to meet the interests and needs of others at cost to one's own. Such acts are not supererogatory, and failure to engage in them properly evokes at least remorse, if not guilt.

It is clear from this discussion of utilitarianism as a benchmark for understanding and developing the features of my ethics from a theocentric perspective that I do not accept the appellation of a utilitarian. Yet it is also clear that I do not view utilitarian ethics as requiring automatic and total responses of derision. To accuse it of being on a slippery slope is to fail to grasp the complexities of the arguments in its classic presentations. While it has a supreme moral principle than shapes the end of human activity, that principle is worked out with more care and complexity than is acknowledged by superficial criticism. And for J.S. Mill, at least, the system did not resolve all problems. I agree with the following statement.

> There is no ethical creed which does not temper the rigidity of its laws by giving a certain latitude, under the moral responsibility of the agent, for accommodating to peculiarities of circumstances; and under every creed, at the opening thus made, self-deception and dishonest casuistry get in. There exists no moral system under which there do not arise unequivocal cases of conflicting obligation. There are real difficulties, the knotty points both in the theory of ethics, and in the conscientious guidance of personal conduct. They are overcome practically, with greater or less success, according to the intellect and virtue of the individual. . . .[37]

I have indicated both the similarities and the disagreements of the present work with the utilitarian "creed." But the disagreements do not entail a blanket dismissal of its insights and arguments.

Kant

In my use of utilitarianism as a benchmark I treated it as a tradition, and referred to various participants in it to make my general points. In the case of Kantianism, the originator is of such complexity and force that one must attend to Kant's ethical thinking in itself. This is, of course, no easy task; nonetheless, one would be derelict in duty not to relate any proposal for an interpretation of ethics from a theocentric (or any other) perspective to the far-reaching work of this quintessential Enlightenment philosopher.

In the contemporary schematization of ethics, Kant is the writer of deontological, or deontic, ethics who fits best the pure ideal-type. That there were antecedents in the Western tradition for this type of ethics is clear; one can suggest, for example, the ethical writings of the late medieval nominalists and aspects of the ethics of Martin Luther. Although Kant had a view of the highest good, and was not unconcerned for the consequences of actions, the principal attention of his deontic ethics is on right conduct.[38] We saw that the utilitarian answer to the practical moral question is that we ought to act in the manner that produces the best possible consequences.

37. J. S. Mill, *Utilitarianism*, chap. 2, in Burtt, *The English Philosophers*, p. 915.

38. See W. D. Ross, *The Right and the Good* (Oxford: The Clarendon Press, 1930), for a very good source to get at the polarity between the right and the good.

Kant's answer to the ought question can be clearly indicated by quoting the principal statements of the categorical imperative. The imperative is categorical; that is, it is not a hypothetical one in which an action is judged to be good only as a means to something else, e.g., happiness.[39] The first statement of the categorical imperative is, "Act only according to the maxim [the subjective principle of volition] by which you can at the same time will that it should become a universal law."[40] This is the formal "principle of universalizability." The "practical imperative," he writes a few pages later, is, "Act so that you treat humanity, whether in your own person or in that of another, always as an end and never as a means only."[41] The third way "of presenting the principle of morality" is "the principle of *autonomy* of the will," i.e., "in the idea of the will of every rational being as a will giving universal law."[42] "Because of the idea of universal lawgiving, it is based on no interest, and thus of all possible imperatives, it alone can be unconditioned."[43]

As every student of introductory moral philosophy knows, this leads to an ethics of duty in which the moral rectitude of action is judged by its conformity to principles, maxims, and rules. It is an agent-centered ethics, in the sense that the primary focus of moral judgment is on the individual agent and his or her intentions, or reasons for action. Backing Kant's views as they are distilled in the forms of the imperative is a description of human agency, and a description of what distinguishes the moral from the nonmoral.

Before analyzing some of the important descriptive premises of Kant's moral theory, one should attend to some of his applied ethical comments to get their flavor. An interesting description from the precritical ethics rhetorically sets the dominant tone of the applications. "Man must be disciplined, because he is by nature raw and wild."[44] Kant's moral intensity and rigor can be seen in his remarks on several issues and circumstances.

A "prescription" for "pastoral care" of the dying that Kant proposes shows how strongly his views run counter to most, if not all, of current Christian ministry.

> The purpose of those who at the end of life have a clergyman summoned is usually that they want him as a *comforter*—not for the *physical* suffering brought on by the last illness or even for the fear

39. Immanuel Kant, *Foundations of the Metaphysics of Morals*, in L. W. Beck, trans. and ed., *Critique of Practical Reason and Other Writings in Moral Philosophy*, p. 74.
40. Ibid., p. 80.
41. Ibid., p. 87.
42. Ibid., quotations from p. 93, p. 90, and p. 89.
43. Ibid., p. 89.
44. Immanuel Kant, *Lectures on Ethics*, trans. Louis Infield (New York: Harper Torchbooks, 1963), p. 249.

> which naturally precedes death . . . , but for their *moral* anguish, the reproaches of conscience. At such a time, however, conscience should rather be *stirred up* and *sharpened*, in order that the dying man may not neglect to do what good he still may, or (through reparation) to wipe out, so far as he can, the remaining consequences of his evil actions.[45]

This remark is backed not only by Kant's view of what is required by respect for the person as a rational being but also by his stress on striving for moral perfection and adhering to moral duties against inclinations. Even in the process of dying the moral agent is to maintain self-control over impulses, and to engage in moral acts.[46]

For Kant suicide is immoral. Indeed, suicide seems to be a test case, since he recurs to it frequently in his ethical treatises. In the precritical *Lectures on Ethics* which, partly because of the textbook on which the lectures are based, have scholastic overtones, Kant adduces evidences similar to those used in the article by Thomas Aquinas on suicide.[47] But he also states the issue in Kantian terms that become refined in subsequent writings.

> Suicide is immoral; for the intention is to rid oneself of all pains and discomforts attendant upon one's state by sacrificing that state, and this subordinates human nature to animal nature and brings the understanding under the control of animal impulses.[48]

In *Foundations of the Metaphysics of Morals*, Kant uses the principle

45. Immanuel Kant, *Religion within the Limits of Reason Alone*, trans. and intro. Theodore M. Greene and Hoyt H. Hudson (New York: Harper Torchbooks, 1960), p. 72.

46. My own most memorable experience with a dying person, while it falls short of Kant's advice, nonetheless indicates something of what respect for agency can be. I learned this not from Kant, but from a wise physician. I spent the last day of a friend's life at his bedside. His physician came in early in the afternoon. He cursed loudly, and shouted rudely at my friend to focus, momentarily to be sure, his attention and get him to respond to the question, "How are you doing?" For the next two hours I tried to infer from the rambling speech patterns what seemed to be most occupying my friend's mind. I guessed it was a book manuscript that had not yet been published but that he had completed under conditions of almost unbelievable adversity. With force equal to the physician's, I called his name, and said, "It's a damned good book." That focused his attention. "Jim, is that you?" "Yes. It's a damned good book. Some students are using the manuscript, and they are excited about it." "Jim, that's the way it ought to be." Then he relapsed into the incoherent and rambling speech of the dying, but the clues I had used for my inference were gone and other words and names dominated. One may not want to go all the way with Kant's advice, but we do not respect the dying as persons if we only sit passively. What was prima facie offensive on the physician's part and mine had a slight Kantian ring, and was the right thing to do.

47. Thomas has three arguments: suicide deprives the community of a member, and thus is against the common good; it violates nature in that all things are naturally oriented toward their preservation; and it is up to God, not human beings, to determine when they should die. Thomas Aquinas, *Summa Theologiae* 2a, 2ae, q. 64, art. 5. Kant adduces the last two. "We shrink in horror from suicide because all nature seeks its own preservation." *Lectures on Ethics*, p. 150. We have a duty to preserve our lives "until the time comes when God expressly commands us to leave this life." Ibid, p. 154.

of universalizability to test the maxim under which one might justify suicide. The person considering suicide has as a maxim,

> For love of myself, I make it my principle to shorten my life when by a longer duration it threatens more evil than satisfaction. But it is questionable whether this principle of self-love could become a universal law of nature.[49]

In *The Metaphysical Principles of Virtue*, the discussion of suicide comes in the section on duties to oneself insofar as man is an animal being. The obligation to preserve one's life is based on the nature of a person, and is a strict duty.

> Man cannot deprive himself of his personality so long as one speaks of duties, thus so long as one lives. . . . To destroy the subject of morality in his own person is tantamount to obliterating from the world, as far as he can, the very existence of morality itself; but morality is, nevertheless, an end in itself. Accordingly, to dispose of oneself as a mere means to some end of one's own liking is to degrade the humanity in one's person (*home noumenon*), which, after all, was entrusted to man (*homo phaenomen*) to preserve.[50]

In the casuistical questions that follow this, he raises classic circumstances in which suicide has been justified, but does not give clear answers to them, e.g., martyrdom for a good cause, avoidance of harm to others, avoidance of the onset of madness due to disease, and the like. The reader is left, it seems, to ask whether he or she could act according to a maxim which would lead to suicide in these circumstances in the light of Kant's moral theory. Since only God, the searcher of hearts, finally knows whether one has done one's duty, perhaps Kant desires to leave the question somewhat open in these instances.

What I wish to stress, however, is that for Kant suicide is immoral. It is immoral because it violates the moral law. The maxim on which a person would act in committing suicide cannot be made universal legislation; the incentive for it is not a moral one, i.e., respect for moral law; one's inclinations wrongly supersede one's rational will, and so forth. No physical or psychological explanation of why a person commits suicide can provide a moral justification for it. This is finally backed by a view of the moral, and a view of human persons to which I shall subsequently turn. An act on which very few of our contemporaries dare to make a moral judgment is for Kant clearly morally wrong.

48. *Lectures on Ethics*, p. 43.
49. In Beck, ed., *Critique of Practical Reason*, p. 81.
50. Immanuel Kant, *The Metaphysical Principles of Virtue*, trans. James Ellington, intro. Warner Wick (Indianapolis: Bobbs-Merrill, 1964), pp. 83–84.

An equal rigor is applied to human sexuality, eating and drinking, luxury, and other realms of experience. One's first duties are to oneself, and these are strict duties. Self-mastery is a fundamental obligation. "Seek to maintain self-mastery; thou wilt then be fit to perform thy self-regarding duties."[51] Self-mastery is "one's highest duty to oneself. It consists in the ability to subject all our principles and faculties to our free will."[52] This is not to be done by the rule of prudence, which puts understanding in the service of sensibilities, but on the basis of a moral rule. The moral issues laws to the sensible. "To exercise a sovereign authority over ourselves we must invest morality with the highest authority over us; it must rule our sensibility."[53]

> By repeated endeavor we must stamp out the tendency which arises from sensuous motive. He who wishes to discipline himself morally, must watch himself carefully; he must at frequent intervals give to the judge within him an account of his deeds; by constant practice he will strengthen the moral grounds of impulse, through self-cultivation he will acquire a habit of desire and aversion in regard to what is morally good and bad. . . . Therefore in self-mastery there resides an immediate worth, for to be lord of oneself is to be independent of all things.[54]

While there are significant qualifications and refinements of this exhortatory rhetoric in subsequent ethical writings, the dominant tone of it persists throughout. It is irresistible to quote the well-known glowing paragraph that one finds in the midst of the abstract discourse of the *Critique of Practical Reason*.

> Duty! Thou sublime and mighty name that does embrace nothing charming or insinuating but requirest submission and yet seekest not to move the will by threatening aught that would arouse natural aversion or terror but only holdest forth a law which of itself finds entrance into the mind and yet gains reluctant reverence (though not always obedience)—a law before which all inclinations are dumb even though they secretly work against it: what origin is there worthy of thee, and where is to be found the root of thy noble descent which proudly rejects all kinship with the inclinations and from which to be descended is the indispensable condition of the only worth which men can give themselves?[55]

This language of awe seems to come from Kant's heart; it sounds like a prayer of adoration or an ascription of glory in Christian liturgy. Backing it, however, is a theory of man and morality that I shall analyze.

51. Kant, *Lectures on Ethics*, p. 138.
52. Ibid., pp. 138–39.
53. Ibid., p. 139.
54. Ibid., pp. 139–40.
55. Kant, *Critique of Practical Reason*, in Beck, ed., p. 193.

The theocentric perspective that I have developed yields a very un-Kantian ethics. The evidence for this can be adduced by showing the contrasting judgments made at various critical points, and their implications. First, it is clear that by comparison, Kant's ethics are very anthropocentric, and indeed, while they are shaped to curb egoism (self-love), they are in an interesting way egocentric and individualistic. The anthropocentrism is clearly stated in the *Critique of Judgment*. Kant distinguishes between a regulative concept and reflective judgment on the one hand, and a constitutive concept and determinative judgment on the other. A teleological concept is regulative; a teleological judgment is reflective. A regulative idea is a heuristic device only. It does not claim to explain the actual workings of nature in themselves as a constitutive idea would, but is warranted as a way by which human beings relate to nature.[56] On the basis of reflective judgment Kant can argue for a teleology of nature, and on the basis of this human construct he is certain that man is the final and ultimate end of creation. This does not mean that our species is especially favored by nature.

> Nature has not taken him for her special darling and favored him with benefit above all animals. Rather, in her destructive operations—plague, hunger, perils of water, frost, assaults of other animals, great and small, etc.—in these things has she spared him as little as any other animal.[57]

Thus in one respect man is "always only a link in the chain of natural purposes."[58] But,

> [a]s the only being on earth which has an understanding and, consequently, a faculty of setting arbitrary purposes before itself, he is certainly entitled to be the lord of nature, and *if* it be regarded as a teleological system, he is, by his destination, the ultimate purpose of nature.[59]

Kant's regulative teleology and his theory of morality are compatible with each other. It is human freedom, another regulative concept, that distinguishes man from the rest of nature, and this grounds morality—the highest human achievement. Lewis White Beck translates a critical passage as follows.

> If things in the world, which are dependent in their existence, need a supreme cause acting towards ends, then man is the final end of

56. For the discussion of a reflective judgment, see Immanuel Kant, *Critique of Judgment*, trans. and intro., J. H. Bernard (New York: Hafner Publishing Co., 1951), par. 69, p. 232. (Introduction dated 1892.)
57. Ibid., para. 82, p. 280.
58. Ibid.
59. Ibid., pp. 280–81, emphasis added.

> creation; for without him the chain of graduated ends would not be perfectly grounded, and only in man (but in him only as subject to morality) is there unconditional legislation with respect to ends. This alone makes him capable of being a final end, to which all nature is teleologically subordinated.[60]

In my estimation, passages such as this are fundamental to Kant's ethics. They develop his argument for man as the final end of creation, a status that often is assumed but not argued by many other moral philosophers.

Kant has an "eschatology" that coheres with these views. It is clearly stated in the precritical lectures, and I believe is not basically altered in his subsequent writings.

> The ultimate destiny of the human race is the greatest moral perfection, provided that it is achieved through human freedom, whereby alone man is capable of the greatest happiness. . . . The end, therefore, for which man is destined is to achieve his fullest perfection through his own freedom. . . . The universal end of mankind is the highest moral perfection.[61]

In *Religion within the Limits of Reason Alone*, this destiny becomes a duty.

> Now it is our universal duty as men to *elevate* ourselves to this ideal of moral perfection, that is, to this archetype of the moral disposition in all its purity—and for this the ideal itself, which reason presents to us for our zealous emulation, can give us power.[62]

The ideal "of such moral perfection as is possible to an earthly being who is subject to wants and inclinations" he describes in the following terms:

> the idea of a person who would be willing not merely to discharge all human duties himself and to spread about him goodness as widely as possible by precept and example, but even,

60. Kant, *Critique of Judgment*, par. 84, in Beck, Introduction to the *Critique of Practical Reason*, p. 39. In the *Critique of Judgment*, Hafner ed., the statement is on p. 268. Also, "[I]t is a fundamental proposition, to which even the commonest human reason is compelled to give immediate assent, that if there is to be in general a *final purpose* furnished *a priori* by reason, this can be no other than *man* (every rational being of the world) *under moral* laws." *Critique of Judgment*, par. 87, Hafner ed., p. 299.

61. Kant, *Lectures on Ethics*, p. 252.

62. Kant, *Religion* p. 54. "First of all, such perfection consists subjectively in the purity (*puritas moralis*) of one's disposition toward duty: when, without any admixture of aims taken from sensibility, the law is its own incentive, and one's actions occur not only in accordance with duty but also from duty. 'Be holy' is here the command. Secondly, such perfection consists objectively in doing one's full duty and in attaining the completeness of one's moral end regarding himself. 'Be perfect!' For man, striving for this goal is always only a progression from one state of perfection to another. 'If there is any virtue, if there is any praise, aspire to it.'" *The Metaphysical Principles of Virtue*, p. 110. Biblical citations are, respectively, 1 Peter 1:16, Matthew 5:48, and Philippians 4:8.

> though tempted by the greatest allurements, to take upon himself every affliction, up to the most ignominious death, for the good of the world and even for his enemies. For man can frame to himself no concept of the degree and strength of a force like that of a moral disposition except by picturing it as encompassed by obstacles, and yet, in the face of the fiercest onslaughts, victorious.[63]

Passages like this lend weight to my judgment that there is an interesting egocentric element in Kant, which is that each individual has a duty to elevate himself or herself as much as possible to the ideal of moral perfection. While this does not imply a positive value to self-love, and thus is not egoistic, it does indicate that the perfection of the individual as a moral being is the highest end. And that perfection requires very stringent conditions. The distinction between the moral and the nonmoral that Kant elaborates and defends reinforces, in my judgment, egocentric and individualistic aspects of his work.

Kant does, however, qualify the individualism by his discussion of an ethical commonwealth in *Religion within the Limits of Reason Alone*. Just as the ideal of moral perfection quoted above is set in the context of Christian beliefs that Kant is altering in the light of his moral theory, so also is the ethical commonwealth.[64] What he proposes is a view of the Kingdom of God on earth, developed within the bounds of, and as an extension of, his moral philosophy. Every individual is in a state of combat against the sovereignty of evil and procures through exertion a measure of freedom from it. But the assaults of evil are not only from the individual passions. A person "can easily convince himself that he is subject to these not because of his own gross nature . . . but because of mankind to whom he is related and bound."[65]

> Envy, the lust for power, greed, and the malignant inclinations bound up with these, besiege his nature, contented within itself, *as soon as he is among men*. And it is not even necessary to assume that these are men sunk in evil and examples to lead him astray; it

63. Kant, *Religion*, p. 55. This is, of course, Kant's interpretation of Jesus. Compare my, "Jesus incarnates theocentric piety and fidelity," in 1:276.

64. It is interesting to speculate whether Kant would have taken his line of argument in the direction he did if he had lived in the more secularized twentieth century than in his time with its Christian culture and particularly its concerns for orthodoxy in doctrine that characterized both church and state. Few moral philosophers in our time feel the need to take traditional Christianity or any other religion into account in their arguments. In the Conclusion to *The Metaphysical Principles of Virtue*, Kant says, "Religion, therefore, as a doctrine of duties to God, lies completely outside the limits of purely philosohical ethics. . . . To be sure, there can be a *Religion within the Limits of Reason Alone*. But this is not derived from reason alone but is also based on truths of history and revelation, and contains only the agreement of pure practical reason with history and revelation (that they do not conflict with reason). Consequently, it is not pure religion but one applied to pre-existing history; and there is no place for such applied religion in ethics, insofar as ethics is pure practical philosophy." P. 158.

65. Kant, *Religion*, p. 85.

> suffices that they are at hand, that they surround him, and that they are men, for them mutually to corrupt each other's predispositions and make one another evil.[66]

To counteract the always tempting forces stemming from our mutual relations there must be communal support for the good. Thus the sovereignty of the good principles requires, within the limits of human possibilities,

> the establishment and spread of a society in accordance with, and for the sake of, the laws of virtue, a society whose task and duty it is rationally to impress these laws in all their scope upon the entire human race.[67]

Thus there is a social moral ideal, namely, "a union of men under merely moral laws." Such a society "may be called an *ethical*, and in so far as these laws are public, an *ethico-civil* (in contrast to a *juridico-civil*) society or an *ethical commonwealth*." Its "special and unique principle of union" is virtue, rather than a set of juridical laws. It would be a "*kingdom* of virtue."[68] It is a duty of the human race toward itself to promote such a kingdom as the highest social good. Just as the highest and supreme good of the individual is virtue, "being the condition having no condition superior to it," so the highest social good is the kingdom of virtue.[69]

To some extent the ideal of the ethical commonwealth, the kingdom of virtue, appears to me to be a concession to the "weaker brethren." Kant says, in the passage quoted above, that a person "can easily convince himself" that the assaults of evil are social in location. His phrasing also indicates a belief that individuals are not deeply interrelated and interdependent with other persons. A person is besieged by the assaults of evil "*as soon as he is among men*." From another perspective, persons are never not among other persons, and while they are agents and actors, who they are and what they do is affected (but not determined) by their social locations. Their natural and social relations are more constitutive of their persons.

I have indicated that I believe that Kant offers an egocentric as well as anthropocentric view of moral life. The ideal is the moral improvement, indeed, the moral perfection of the individual person. Before I turn to analyzing the grounds for this ideal, it is worthwhile to set it in contrast to some other possibilities. If one takes as an example a person widely regarded to be a "moral hero" in recent history, and asks the reasons why such a person is so regarded, some of the lines of contrast are disclosed.

For example, why is Martin Luther King, Jr., so deeply honored by many persons throughout the world? Some of the reasons might be

66. Ibid.
67. Ibid., p. 86.
68. Ibid.
69. Quotation from the *Critique of Practical Reason*, Beck, ed., p. 215.

approved by a strictly Kantian view of morality, and others not. To some extent the ideal of moral perfection quoted above is one that King approximated. He took upon himself affliction even unto death for the good of the world and even of his enemies. He was "encompassed by obstacles" and faced fierce onslaughts, in some senses victoriously. He certainly believed that persons were not to be treated merely as means to ends, and his perception of violations of this principle motivated his actions and his movement. But, I believe it is safe to say, his moral ideal was not his own moral perfection, nor was his social vision one of a kingdom of virtue in a precisely Kantian sense. Indeed, his activity can be interpreted as being justified very strongly by the consequences he anticipated it would have. While there are places where Kant commends certain feelings or sentiments as bestirring persons to morality, in King's case his moral "passion" and the use of powerfully persuasive rhetoric to convince persons of the rightness of his cause exceed anything that Kant's ethical theory would justify.[70] Certainly the use of massive nonviolent resistance was justified on prudential grounds, as an effective means to the ends sought, as well as on grounds of a moral maxim that could be justified by Kant. It is safe to say that King's inclinations, while rationally directed and justified, directed his activity more strongly than Kant's interpretation of the relation of reason to inclination would warrant. A moral rule, or a rational argument, was not, in King's view, sufficient to determine how persons exercised their other powers. King's virtues were more complex than Kant's understanding of virtue would include, though what Kant would consider virtue was among them. My general point is that, from a Kantian perspective, it is doubtful that a person widely considered to be an almost paradigmatic moral actor was truly moral by Kant's standards. Even if much of King's activity could be justified from the perspective of Kant's ethics, I believe that King's own justifications were not Kantian in character.

I have been gradually moving toward what I believe to be the most crucial judgments in Kants's ethics from which my ethics from a theocentric perspective differ. The analysis can be furthered by examining Kant's distinctions between the moral and the nonmoral, and other distinctions he makes which impinge on defining the moral. Previously I argued that how an ethical writer makes this distinction is crucial to what are considered to be the ethically relevant features not only of the circumstances of action but also of the moral agent. The terms that sharpen the contrast are found in the *Lectures on Ethics*, and with refinement and elaboration are used continuously throughout Kant's ethical writings. I shall attend to only a few of the most crucial contrasts here.

70. For Kant on feelings in this regard, see *Critique of Judgment*, par. 59, Hafner ed., pp. 196–200.

The most important distinction that grounds the definition of the moral is that between transcendental freedom and nature.

> [T]ranscendental freedom . . . must be thought of as independence from everthing empirical and hence from nature generally, whether regarded as an object of the inner sense merely in time or also as an object of the outer sense in both space and time. Without transcendental freedom, which is its proper meaning, and which is alone a priori practical, no moral law and no accountability to it are possible. For this reason, all necessity of events in time according to natural law can be called the "mechanism of nature," even though it is not supposed that things which are subject to it must really be material machines.[71]

Freedom, like God and immortality, is a postulate of pure practical reason.[72]

> [T]he possibility of freedom of an efficient cause cannot be comprehended, especially in the world of sense; we are indeed fortunate if we can be sufficiently assured that no proof of its impossibility can be given and that we are compelled (and thus authorized) to assume it by the moral law, which postulates it.[73]

The distinction between the realm of freedom and that of necessity is required for morality. Put in terms I have used, the capacity for self-determination is necessary for holding any person to moral accountability. The differences between Kant and what I have been developing lie in part in the ways in which freedom functions to determine the scope of the moral in contrast to the nonmoral. For Kant, an act is moral only if its "cause" is respect for the law that stems from freedom and reason.

The distinction between freedom and necessity, I believe, in one way or another grounds other distinctions that Kant makes between the moral and the nonmoral. For example, prudential imperatives are "pragmatic"; moral imperatives are ethical. "Prudence is the ability to use the means towards the universal end of man, that is, happiness," Kant writes in the *Lectures of Ethics*.[74] The incentive for a prudential act is always an object, desired consequences, and so forth; the prudent person is always thinking in terms of means to ends, and under Kant's definition such actions are not truly moral. It is prudent to be moral if one's incentive is to avoid punishment under civil law or from God, but such incentives are not truly moral.

Self-respect and self-esteem are morally worthy; self-love is not. "We esteem that which has intrinsic worth, and we love that which has worth

71. *Critique of Practical Reason*, Beck, ed., pp. 202–3.
72. Ibid., p. 235.
73. Ibid., p. 200.
74. Kant, *Lectures*, p. 4. With various refinements the distinction between the prudential and the moral is found throughout his ethical writings.

through its bearing on something else."[75] "Esteem regards the inner worth, love only the relative worth of our fellows."[76] "We love that by which we gain advantage; we esteem that which has worth in itself."[77] The distinction between "the heart" and the understanding is invoked in these early discussions of love. "Doing good from love springs from the heart; doing good from obligation springs rather from principles of understanding."[78] We are to be mindful of the well-being of others from obligation rather than from inclination if our benevolence is truly moral.

Heteronomy leads to spurious principles of morality; true morality is based upon the radical autonomy of the agent.

> If the will seeks the law which is to determine it anywhere else than in the fitness of its maxims to its own universal legislation, and if it thus goes outside itself and seeks this law in the property of any of its objects, heteronomy always results. For then the will does not give itself the law, but the object through its relation to the will gives the law to it. This relation, whether it rests on inclination or on conceptions of reason, only admits hypothetical imperatives: I should do something for the reason that I will something else. The moral, and therewith categorical, imperative, on the other hand, says that I should act this or that way even though I will nothing else.[79]

This legislation that determines human action, if it is truly moral, must be based upon the transcendental freedom of the person; action based on other justifications is prudential, heteronomous, etc. In the ethical writings Kant makes this general point over and over with reference to happiness. To act for the sake of happiness, either one's own or that of another, is to act prudentially, and thus not morally. Happiness is not the ground of morality; it is its corollary. Happiness is the satisfaction that is likely to come from acting for truly moral reasons; it is not a proper moral incentive to action.[80]

"[M]orality requires absolutely no material determining ground of

75. Ibid., p. 135.
76. Ibid., p. 185.
77. Ibid., p. 186.
78. Ibid., p. 192.
79. Kant, *Foundations of The Metaphysics of Morals*, in Beck, ed., *Critique of Practical Reason*, pp. 97–98.
80. It would be redundant for my limited purposes to develop other relevant distinctions. Some of them are empirical and contingent/intellectual and a priori; outer/inner; stimulation/freedom; love of self/love of humanity; juridical/ethical; inclination/reason; counsels/commands; empirical/moral; feelings/duty; world of sense/world of intelligence; pleasure/reason; subjective and empirical/objective and rational; desire/reason; empirical/supersenuous; learned religion/reasonable religion; conditioned purposes/unconditional purposes; phenomenal/noumenal; animality/personality; and others. My general point is that the first term in each relates to the nonmoral, and the second to the moral. I omit about seventy citations of these and other similar distinctions from the ethical writings.

free choice [*Willkür*], that is, no end, in order either to know what duty is or to impel the performance of duty."[81] By drawing on sources that say what morality is not, and by looking at the contrasting terms, we have been pointed toward what morality is. There are descriptive premises involved in Kant's interpretation of what constitutes the moral which in turn determine the extent and the limits of what considerations are relevant to action that is truly moral. It now behooves us to summarize that description.

Moral acts are acts of individual persons. I see no way in Kant's theory that one can speak meaningfully of any kind of collective moral agency, and thus his ethical theory is not directly applicable to institutional choices of political and social policy. Persons have two aspects, the phenomenal and the noumenal. They are bodies with desires and inclinations, and they are transcendentally free; they have capacities for reasons that are considered in terms of their independence from determination by inclinations and desires. What is moral is to be determined by the noumenal aspect of the self using reason to determine moral imperatives, including the maxims that ought to govern particular moral actions. The person has a self-legislating will, and can test the proposed maxims of conduct in the light of the categorical imperative. It is the moral law determined by freedom and reason that determines what conduct is right. "[W]hen we assume any object, under the name of good, as the determining ground of the will prior to the moral law, and then derive the supreme practical principle from it, this always produces heteronomy and rules out the moral principle."[82] Not only do reason, the will, and the moral law direct natural inclinations; they have the capacity to dominate them and, indeed, to act counter to inclination. Either the principle of reason is the determining ground of the will with reference to objects, or desire precedes the maxim of the will. The former marks the moral.

> [T]he law directly determines the will; action in accordance with this law is absolutely and in every respect good and the supreme condition of all good. . . . The paradox is that the concept of the good and evil is not defined prior to the moral law, to which, it would seem, the former would have to serve as foundation; rather the concept of the good and evil must be defined after and by means of the law.[83]

The incentive to act morally needs a bit more exploration.

The moral law itself, and respect for the moral law, are the incentives to action. The moral law, as a formal and objective determination of the objects of human action, "is also the subjective ground of determination."

81. Kant, *Religion*, p. 3.
82. Kant, *Critique of Practical Reason*, in Beck, ed., *Critique of Practical Reason*, p. 214.
83. Ibid., p. 171.

> [I]t is the incentive to this action, since it has influence on the sensibility of the subject and effects a feeling which promotes the influence of the law on the will. In the subject there is no antecedent feeling tending to morality; that is impossible, because all feeling is sensuous, and the incentives of the moral disposition must be free from every sensuous inclination. . . . Since the idea of the moral law deprives self-love of its influence and self-conceit of its delusion, it lessens the obstacle to pure practical reason and produces the idea of the superiority of its objective law to the impulses of sensibility.[84]

Kant goes on to say that,

> [t]hus respect for the law is not the incentive to morality; it is morality itself, regarded subjectively as an incentive, inasmuch as pure practical reason, by rejecting all rival claims of self-love, gives authority and absolute sovereignty to the law.[85]

Respect for the moral law is the sole moral incentive; morality (objectively speaking) is (subjectively speaking) its own incentive or motivation. "The consciousness of a free submission of the will to the law, combined with an inevitable constraint imposed only by our own reason on all our inclinations, is respect for the law."[86] Action that is forthcoming is duty; we are to act "*according to duty* and *from duty*."[87] "The majesty of duty has nothing to do with the enjoyment of life; it has its own law."[88]

Kant's understanding of virtue is in accord with this. Virtue is not, for Kant, the perfection of a power or an inclination which gives it habitual orientation toward its proper end. It is a degree of strength, but of the moral strength of the will. "[V]irtue is the moral strength of the will of a human being in obeying his duty; the constraint involved is moral through his own legislative reason, inasmuch as virtue constitutes itself an authority executing the law."[89] The principle of inner freedom grounds this view of virtue; one must be one's own master in a given situation, and lord over oneself so that one's emotions are subdued and one's passions governed.[90]

His view of evil is also in accord with this understanding. Genuine evil is moral evil. Such evil is possible

> only as a determination of the free will [*Willkür*], and since the will [*Willkür*] can be appraised as good or evil only by means of its maxims, this propensity to evil must consist in the subjective

84. Ibid., p. 183.
85. Ibid., pp. 183–84.
86. Ibid., p. 187.
87. Ibid., p. 188.
88. Ibid., p. 195.
89. Kant, *The Metaphysical Principles of Virtue*, p. 64.
90. Ibid., p. 67.

> ground of the possibility of the deviation of the maxims from the moral law.[91]

In his rendition of some Christian dogmas, Kant can say that man is *evil*, in the sense that the person is conscious of the moral law but has nevertheless adopted into his rules of conduct "occasional" deviation from it.[92] But human beings are always and totally responsible for even their propensity to evil.[93]

The consideration of consequences of truly moral acts is not a matter of complete indifference to Kant. While for its own sake morality requires no representation of an end prior to the determination of the will, "it is quite possible that it is necessarily related to such an end, taken not as the ground, but as the [sum of] inevitable consequences of maxims adopted as conformable to that end."[94] Where and how one takes consequences into account in the determination of moral action is the critical question. They are not to be the basis for the determination of the will, i.e., not to be the end antecedently aimed at, but are to be considered as the result of an action determined by the moral law.

> [M]orality requires no end for right conduct; the law, which contains the formal condition of the use of freedom in general, suffices. Yet an end does arise out of morality; for how the question, *What is to result from this right conduct of ours*? is to be answered, and towards what, as an end—even granted it may not be wholly subject to our control—we might direct our actions and abstentions so as at least to be in harmony with that end: these cannot possibly be matters of indifference to reason.[95]

We are to do our duty and think about "whatever is conditioned, and in harmony with duty, in all the ends we do have."[96] And, the postulate of a higher, moral, holy, and omnipotent Being is made to unite duty and ends in the highest good. But what determines the morality of an act is not its consequences or end, but its being in harmony with duty.

It remains to show more specifically the differences between the distinctive features of my ethics from a theocentric perspective and Kant's. Kant's account of the place of man in the universe, and his understanding of human persons is clearly very different from what I have presented in chapter 1. Kant's delineation of what constitutes the moral is dependent upon both his understanding of how individuals are related to the world in which they live and the sharp distinction between the noumenal and phe-

91. Kant, *Religion*, p. 24.
92. Ibid., p. 27.
93. Ibid., p. 28.
94. Ibid., p. 4.
95. Ibid.
96. Ibid.

nomenal aspects of the self. Indeed, I would argue that his drive to develop and defend an exceedingly rigoristic view of morality affects, if it does not determine, his descriptive premises. For every writer of ethics, including the present one, no doubt one element in the way in which a position gets developed is a predisposition toward a particular cast of morality. Even if this is the case, it does not follow that an ethics is totally relativized, or that a theory is merely a rationalization for a moral inclination. Evidences are adduced and arguments made to delineate the scope of the morally relevant features of human activity. Kant's powerful arguments are thoroughly defended.

Kant clearly recognizes that human beings are in relations of dependence and interdependence with the natural world. Man is, in one respect, "always only a link in the chain of natural purposes."[97] But this linkage is not morally relevant for Kant in the way it is for me. The moral irrelevance of the linkage occurs because the moral has to do with only the transcendental freedom of the individual person. That which determines what is moral is the individual's autonomous will, the exercise of reason, and the capacity of reason, using respect for the moral law, to master and determine the phenomenal aspects of the self and (I take it) the natural world. Since morality is confined to the realm of individual freedom, which by definition transcends nature (which Kant understood in quite mechanistic terms), it follows that natural desires and inclinations, the patterns of natural interdependence of persons with each other in communities and of human beings with the natural order, cannot become a source of moral norms. Kant's ethics thus become individualistic and rationalistic; he develops an ethics of intention (*Gessinungsethik*) of thoroughgoing consistency.

I have indicated above the basic reasons that support his view. Not only does his philosophical anthropology warrant it, but it yields a view of morality that intensifies the moral accountability of the individual agent. It seems to require an acute moral self-consciousness almost constantly. Kant says different things in different places about the relations of reason to inclinations. For example,

> Natural inclinations, *considered in themselves*, are *good*, that is not a matter of reproach, and it is not only futile to want to extirpate them but to do so would also be harmful and blameworthy. Rather let them be tamed and instead of clashing with one another they can be brought into harmony in a wholeness which is called happiness.[98]

But it is not the moral reason that does this; it is prudence. The stringent moral ideal "is completely real in its own right, for it resides in our morally-

97. Kant, *Critique of Judgment*, par. 82, p. 280.
98. Kant, *Religion*, p. 51.

legislative reason. We *ought* to conform to it; consequently we must *be able* to do so."[99] From this we see how for Kant a great deal of the traditional ethics of natural law and of utilitarianism are only prudential; they assume that inclinatons are toward the fulfillment of an end that can be called moral. Kant's moral anthropology in effect says always to distrust your inclinations; they are of the order of mechanistic nature and thus by definition are outside the realm of the moral. It must be remembered that Kant's view of "natural man" is quite in accord with Hobbes's view, a point he made even in the early writings.[100] Moral accountability is intense; not only do persons have the capacity to be morally accountable, they ought to strive for moral perfection. Kant tolerates few, if any, of the excusing conditions normally adduced for immoral acts.

The position I am developing is not, by contrast to Kant's rigorism, a laxism. The differences in judgments pertain to the relation of reason to inclination, the significance of the social character of human life, and the status of our interdependencies in the natural world as a ground of moral norms.[101] I have argued for the capacity of self-determination, but I interpret it within a context of greater continuity and interdependence of what Kant calls the phenomenal and the noumenal aspects of the self. I believe that Kant understood the natural in very mechanistic terms, even though he says that this does not mean that things subject to nature are "material machines." Radical freedom is more readily distinguished from nature if nature is interpreted even regulatively in mechanistic rather than more "organic" terms. At issue is not only a descriptive account of the relations of inclinations to self-determination; the matter of reliability of inclinations as guides to conduct is also at stake. On this point, while I do not agree with Kant that man "is by nature raw and wild," I have argued that our natural desires and inclinations need to be directed by rational activity and the exercise of our powers of self-determination. There are evidences that "natural affections," for example, lead to morally praiseworthy activities. Yet my interpretation of the human fault, while in some respects not as radical as Kant's is in some places, made clear that inclinations do need taming as well as directing. Feelings and inclinations are not infallible guides to what is to be valued or to what conduct is morally right, but as part of human persons they do give direction toward ends and are the necessary conditions for moral activity.[102]

99. Ibid., p. 55.

100. For Kant on Hobbes, see *Religion*, p. 89n; the earlier statement is that "man must be disciplined because he is by nature raw and wild." *Lectures*, p. 249. There is probably some Lutheran theology behind this as well.

101. See Gustafson, *Ethics*, 1:281–93.

102. Max Scheler's criticism of Kant's radical distinction between intellect and feelings is well-taken. Yet Scheler had too much confidence in feelings as a guide to value. See Max

Kant, as I have indicated above, seems to me to give only reluctant concession to the socially interactive character of human life and experience. Certainly it is the case that the social character of human life does not have the descriptive or the normative status in his ethical thought that it does in the present work. The issue at stake is parallel to that of the relations of inclinations to self-determination in the individual. The reason that Kant does not deem the socially interactive character of human life significant for morality is his view of the radical autonomy of individual will, and his radical conception of human freedom. Such communities of interaction as the family or the nation, by definition cannot have truly moral significance as entities. To be sure, the moral law should direct human actions, not only in fulfilling their perfect duties to themselves, but also in their relations to other persons. But the patterns of interdependence, and the patterns of necessary requisites for common life cannot become a ground for moral maxims. Kant's "social" principle is that we should treat other persons as ends in themselves and not merely as means to ends.

That principle can be adhered to within a more socially interactive view of human life, though it would be grounded differently. In an interactive view, and a social view of the self, human relations are never devoid of some use as means to some ends—one's own, those of another, or some ends shared in common. The relation of a parent to a child necessarily involves each being means to some ends of the other. That such is the case is not, in my judgment, morally irrelevant, not to mention morally bad. Parents and children meet each other's needs for affection, for example. That is part of the nature of human persons and of the character of life together in marriage and family. Obligations which I would call moral arise out of capacities and necessities to meet each other's needs. What the Kantian point insures is exceedingly important, namely, that we do not treat others only, or merely, as a means, and particularly as a means of fulfilling our individual interests. Respect for persons is also a part of ethics from a theocentric perspective. But there are "natural" grounds for duties and obligations to one another that are based on interdependence; and our understanding of the requirements for the mutual good and the common goods of communities are a basis for developing moral principles and rules, as well as a basis for determining ends which are, from my perspective, moral.

I have argued that the relations of interdependence between human life and the rest of the natural world are also a basis for ethics. Kant, as I have indicated, would not deny the relationships from a descriptive point of view. It is just that from his understanding of the moral this interdependence

Scheler, *Formalism in Ethics and Non-Formal Ethics of Values: A New Attempt Toward the Foundation of an Ethical Personalism*, trans. Manfred S. Frings and Roger L. Funk (Evanston: Northwestern University Press, 1973).

as such is not morally relevant. One support for this view is his anthropocentrism. In expounding Baumgarten in the *Lectures on Ethics*, Kant says that,

> so far as animals are concerned, we have no direct duties. Animals are not self-conscious and are there merely as a means to an end. That end is man. . . . Our duties towards animals are merely indirect duties towards humanity.[103]

This does not make the treatment of animals a matter of indifference; indeed, Kant says that one can judge the heart of a person by the way he or she treats animals. Our duties toward inanimate objects are also indirect duties to man.[104] Again, this does not justify license. "No man ought to mar the beauty of nature; for what he has no use for may still be of use to some one else."[105]

In the *Critique of Practical Reason* he writes, "Respect always applies to persons only, never to things."[106] Things can awaken inclinations such as love or fear, but they do not arouse respect. Respect, properly speaking, can only be for persons as autonomous will; it cannot be for persons, even, as a result of their achievements and other qualities that evoke admiration. The description of the moral, again, sets the limits to what features are morally relevant: persons, and finally persons as autonomous wills.

From the description I have defended of the interrelations of the human with the wider order of nature, the patterns of those relationships become a basis for developing an ordering of values and for principles and rules of conduct, not only in relation to other individuals but also to "things." Not only are other human beings not to be treated merely as means to our ends. It is, of course, legitimate to use aspects of the natural world for the service of proper human ends. But from our understanding of the relations of things to each other in the natural world, we can infer that most, if not all, things are "means" to other "ends" than their own. I use quotation marks because this statement tends to be anthropomorphic, attributing more to "things" than is proper. Put less anthropomorphically, "things" are interrelated with each other in such a way that they are mutually or functionally interdependent. To affirm this is not to say that these interdependencies exist for the "good" of individual entities and certainly not as ends in themselves; the claim is weaker than that. It is that the survival, development, decline, and death of things (animals and plants) depend upon their functional interdependence with each other. The "end"

103. Kant, *Lectures*, p. 239.
104. Ibid., p. 241.
105. Ibid.
106. Kant, *Critique of Practical Reason*, in Beck, ed., *Critique of Practical Reason*, p. 105.

or purpose we attribute to things need not be "good" with reference to immediate human interests, though it may to a longer and wider range of human interests. Things serve functions (purposes, ends) for each other in the world of nature. Thus whatever we use as means to human ends is also understood to have other functions (ends, purposes) in the ordering of nature. Nothing in nature is, descriptively speaking, merely a means to human ends or purposes. Each is *also* a means to (functional with reference to) other aspects of the creation, not all of which are beneficial to man. Accordingly, I propose the following imperative: *Act so that you consider all things never only as a means to your own ends, or even to collective human ends*. In itself this imperative does not dictate how one treats particular things, but it does expand the considerations that ought to be taken into account in human action. It is possible to state this as an imperative only by having a different account of the status of the natural in relation to ethics than Kant's moral philosophy provides.

In the previous delineations of the differences between judgments Kant has made and those I make, I have not invoked theology, per se. In part this restraint has been exercised to show that an alternative understanding of morality to Kant's can be argued for, without invoking God, on the basis of perceptions of how some things really are. It would be a philosophical task beyond what is needed here to deal with whether the interpretation of nature that grounds these differences is only a "regulative" or hueristic one, and on what grounds such a regulative interpretation is to be judged for its adequacy in the light of a more "constitutive" or determinative one.[107] But clearly the theology that I have developed in volume 1 is from Kant's perspective more a "physico-theology" than an "ethico-theology."[108] Kant has a *very moral* theology; but in the end his God is of utility value to man. God guarantees the ultimate good for man. Again, it is Kant's unrelenting focus on the moral that determines his idea of God, just as it determines what he says about the moral relevance of nature and other aspects of experience. It must be remembered that God, for Kant, is a postulate of the pure practical reason; like transcendental freedom and immortality, the idea of postulates of pure practical reason can never be proven true or false. God is a regulative principle. The idea of God functions more heuristically than constitutively, for God is unknowable in any strong, scientific sense. We do not have knowledge of God in the way we have scientific knowledge of many things; God cannot be invoked as a scientific principle of causation or ordering.

The untheocentric character of Kant's view of religion and theology is clear in the *Lectures*. Morality is to determine religion and theology. "Reli-

107. Neither in volume 1 nor in this volume have I undertaken an adequate development of these philosophical issues.

108. See Kant, *Critique of Judgment*, pars. 85–87, in Hafner ed., pp. 286–304.

gion is morality applied to God. It is ethics applied to theology."[109] Morality and ethics are to determine what can and ought to be said about God.

> [T]o enable us to do our duty it does not matter what notions we have of God provided only they are a sufficient ground for pure morality. The theology which is to form the basis of natural religion must contain one thing, the condition of moral perfection. We must conceive a Supreme Being whose laws are holy, whose government is benevolent, and whose rewards and punishments are just.[110] Religion is the application of moral laws to the knowledge of God, and not the origin of morals. . . . The basis of religion must, therefore, be morality.[111]

Man is the measure as well as the measurer of God. The idea of morality determines the idea of God. These statements do not make belief in God a matter of indifference. "We cannot be moral without believing in God." But one does not need to know for certain that God exists in order to believe in God. It is just that "all moral precepts would be meaningless if there were no being to maintain them."[112] Morality needs the idea of God as a matter of practical necessity. In the *Lectures* he makes points that are refined in later writings, but essentially they are maintained. God is not the ground of morality, but the postulation of God is a practical necessity for morality.

Certainly part of what Kant reacted against is the mentality of "God will get you for that"; such views of God provide only a prudential reason for being moral, namely, the avoidance of punishment. Yet he believed, and argued, that a moral life of doing one's duty had to be rewarded, and while happiness is a corollary of morality it does not always occur in the present life. While Kant rejected religion and theology in the forms he observed around him, because they were prudential relative to morality, his own justification of the idea of God comes close to being subject to the same charge. To be sure, one's reason for acting morally ought never be, in his view, to please God, but the postulates of immortality and God assure the ultimate harmony of duty and happiness, and could easily become incentives for action. The point that keeps them from such is that the assurance comes after, rather than before, moral action, and thus is not a cause of it. Kant, on this point, it seems to me, is very close to a New Testament theme.[113] You ought not to seek the Kingdom of God first in order for "all these things" to be yours; rather you are to seek the Kingdom first, with the assurance that if you do, "all these things shall be yours." In both the New

109. Kant, *Lectures*, p. 79.
110. Ibid., pp. 79–80.
111. Ibid., p. 81.
112. Ibid.
113. "But seek first his kingdom and his righteousness, and all these things shall be yours." Matthew 6:33 (R.S.V.).

Testament and in Kant we see the importance of the intention of the agent; the intention is to be pure; the outcome that favors us will follow.

It is clear that for Kant the first intellectual task is to develop a theory of morality; what can be said about God is a corollary of that moral theory. The fundamental thrust of the present work has been quite different. For the theologian, at least, the first task is to delineate what one can say about God. God is the ultimate orderer and destiner of all things. Morality, then, requires that we relate all things in a manner appropriate to their relations to God. In the previous chapter I have shown how Christian theologians' ideas of God and of how God is known affect both the method and the content of their ethics. For Kant the procedure is the reverse; one first develops the method and content of ethics and in turn this determines the idea of God. God, for the theological ethical tradition, is not simply a postulate of pure practical reason.[114] I noted above that the theology of volume 1 would be, for Kant, a physico-theology. Kant has epistemological grounds for not engaging in such a theology, but another ground is that his definition of the truly moral, and of the role this plays in developing his idea of God, prohibits such a move.

No more than Kant do I endorse the desire to avoid divine punishment as the incentive to morality. Yet to relate ourselves and all things in a manner appropriate to their relations to God is beneficial to individuals, to communities, and to the human species. If, as I have argued, the ordering of nature provides indications of the requirements of the divine ordering of life (and thus guides human action), then the ways in which human activity is related to the ordering of nature will affect human well-being as well as that of other aspects of nature. For example, the moral incentive not to start a nuclear war is not fear of the punishment of God on the agent who would act, nor is it simply a matter of testing the maxims of conduct by the principle of universalizability. The grounding for a prohibition of nuclear war is that such human activity involves a profound disordering of proper mutual relations between persons and communities, and between humanity and "nature." The consequences of such a disordering are reasons for the prohibition: the consequences not only for human beings but also for the rest of nature.

Even to think about this matter requires that the the relations of parts to larger wholes be given more importance than Kant's ethical theory can allot to it. The ordering of life in right relations, the violation of which has destructive consequences, is a proper moral incentive, though in Kant's view such an incentive would not be in itself truly moral. Kant discusses the relations of parts to wholes in nature in the *Critique of Judgment*.

114. There are exceptions to this. Gordon D. Kaufman's argument, discussed in Gustafson, 1:264–67, is basically Kantian.

> For a body then which is to be judged in itself and its internal possibility as a natural purpose, it is requisite that its parts mutually depend upon one another both as to their form and their combination, and so produce a whole by their own causality, while conversely the concept of the whole may be regarded as its cause according to a principle (in a being possessing a causality according to concepts adequate to such a product). . . . In such a product of nature, every part not only exists *by means* of the other parts, but is thought as existing *for the sake of* the others and the whole—that is as an (organic) instrument.[115]

This is, of course, a regulative concept for the reflective judgment which guides investigation; it is not a constitutive concept of reason for a determinative judgment. One could imagine that even as a regulative concept it might provide sufficient understanding of how some things really are and that from such an understanding some moral principles could be inferred. Again, I believe this is not the case for Kant because of his delineation of the purely moral. For ethics from a theocentric perspective, because it does not confine the moral in Kantian terms, the relations of parts to wholes and the idea of a common good are morally relevant.

One cannot develop social ethics or ecological ethics very far, in my judgment, from Kant's theory of morality. In these areas the consequences of alternative courses of action have to take on greater importance than they can, in principle, in Kant's views. Ethics for him, in the end, pertains to the individual's reasons for action. This does not mean that other concepts and categories cannot be employed to deal with corporate matters, but it does mean that the line between ethics and politics, between moral philosophy and political philosophy, is sharply drawn. The sharpness is a function of the descriptive account of what constitutes the truly moral. A construal of the world from a theocentric perspective renders a different descriptive account which makes it impossible to adhere to the precision of Kant's distinction. The effect of this may be, in the eyes of some, a lack of conceptual clarity and precision. But from a theocentric perspective, the arguments which are the basis for Kant's precision and clarity can be brought into question. One may have to sacrifice his kind of clarity and precision because the subject matter that is judged to be relevant to morality cannot yield it.

There is a strong ascetic tendency in both Kant's ethics and those of the present work; there are also differences, and what is common is backed by different reasons. The call to self-mastery which is backed by Kant's understanding of the proper incentive to moral action would, no doubt, in a post-Freudian age, be viewed by many to be repressive and unhealthy because of its possible consequences. The stringent command to do one's

115. Kant, *Critique of Judgment*, par. 65; Hafner ed., p. 220.

duty and the occasions on which this requires going against inclinations are magnified in importance in Kant's ethics. To be sure, one has strict duties to one's self, but these are not for the sake of one's happiness. They are to preserve and enhance one's capacities to be moral. In my judgment, the grounds for Kant's asceticism finally must be self-referential; they enable the individual to be a more perfect moral agent. The end is individualistic and egocentric. If one's self-denying actions are for the sake of (that is justified by) the consequences for others, they are not yet truly moral. The moral law might well require such actions; indeed, it often does. But what makes them moral is the law and not the consequences.

The ascetic aspect of ethics from a theocentric perspective is justified on very different grounds. Self-denial is justified by the ends that it serves, and by the consequences that follow from it. What from Kant's perspective are merely prudential reasons for action are not denigrated as nonmoral, not to say immoral. If to serve God is the end of man, then the reason for self-denying actions is that they serve the ends and purposes in particular circumstances that one (or a community) judges to be consonant with God's purposes. Actions are judged by their service in the ends that are discerned to be effective in larger wholes of which persons and communities are a part. This does not rule out duties to oneself, for Kant is correct that we must sustain the necessary conditions in ourselves (and I would add in our institutions and communities) which enable us to serve wider ends and purposes. But duties to oneself are also ultimately means to ends, namely, to serve what we discern to be the well-being of others, including the wider order of creation.

Ethics from a theocentric perspective cannot be as rationalistically systematic as Kant's ethics, or the ethics of theorists who follow a strict Kantian line. The most rationally systematic ethics always has a single principle from which conclusions can be drawn by deductive logic relative to the circumstances in which one acts. In the *Lectures* Kant already indicates that such a system is his aim.

> [I]t is difficult to establish the general principle of law or of mechanics. But as we all need a basis for our moral judgments, a principle by which to judge what is morally good and what bad, we apprehend that there must exist a single principle having its source in the will. We must therefore set ourselves to discover this principle, upon which we establish morality, and through which we are able to discriminate between what is moral and what immoral.[116]

One way to summarize much of what I have written about Kant is this: the desire to develop a rational system with an ultimate and single principle

116. Kant, *Lectures*, p. 11.

determines not only the method but also the content of morality. The rational system determines what is relevant and irrelevant to true morality, and what can count as a morally justifiable reason for action. Every action that is truly moral must be justifiable by the theory. The premises of the theory, then, become crucial. What determines the premises? Ultimately, as in every coherent body of thought, there is a circle, though it need not be judged to be small and vicious. Kant's premises, largely what I have called his descriptive premises, are coherent, yea, consistent, with the moral theory. A different description, informed by a different way of construing man and man's relations to the world (this description also informed by moral intuitions), leads to a different view of ethics. Ethics from a theocentric perspective can be coherent, but it cannot achieve the kind of rationalistic consistency that Kant's theory does. Because of its reliance on a different description, there will be tensions between warranted values and ends, between justifiable rules of conduct that are not always rationalistically resolvable, that is, resolvable by an appeal to *the* principle of morality. If this is a fault that leads to untidiness and complexity, it is a fault with which theocentric ethics must live.

In my judgment, Kant's moral philosophy has the effect of making every occasion in which a person acts "morally" one which requires Kant's stringent method and content. What is good about this is that one's habits, customs, and inclinations are always called into question. Of course, critical moral self-consciousness is not limited to Kantian ethics; every serious effort to develop ethics requires it, including the present one. What makes Kant's view so stringent is that we are to act not only according to duty, but only from duty, i.e., from respect for the moral law. The ethics of the present work develops duties and obligations based on our relations of mutual dependence, but it cannot as stringently as Kant affirm that duty is the only morally approvable incentive to do one's duty. Duties are grounded in relationships, and relationships serve purposes. This, however, does not rule out in particularly critical events that doing one's duty is to go against one's presently dominant inclination, a point made so strongly, apparently, even in more normal circumstances by Kant. The justification, however, is the claim of the value or end that overrides inclination, and not merely duty itself. And it may be the case that the reasons for doing one's duty differ in different circumstances in which one acts. The justification for one's action does not have to be a single moral principle, as it does in rationalistically systematic ethical theories. There might well be an occasion on which one is called upon to give up one's life—e.g. for the sake of another—but the justification for that is the well-being of the other under a particular set of circumstances, not respect for the moral law as Kant interprets it.

It is also the case that the ethics developed here is more in accord with those of Aristotle and Thomas Aquinas in its view that inclinations toward good ends can be habituated in the course of one's life, and thus actions can flow from them which are judged morally worthy even though the agent cannot or does not rationally justify them at the time. Indeed, "natural" actions that follow from inclinations, such as those that flow from love for another person, can be judged to be morally praiseworthy (at least in their effects and in the quality of relations they sustain) even though they are not in a Kantian sense acts of will. The justification of actions as moral does not necessarily involve the kind of rational justification that Kant prescribes. There are more grounds for some assurance that actions and relationships are morally right than Kant provides. Conversely there are more grounds for judging them to be morally wrong, or disordered, than Kant provides. The procedures for making a moral choice are more complex than they are in Kant's system and, I believe, provide more and sharper direction. It is also the case that an action that follows from Kant's ethics can be deemed to be immoral from another perspective.[117] Of course many actions that could be justified from other ethical viewpoints would not be strictly moral for Kant; "prudential" actions might lead to good consequences, but that, for him, does not make them strictly moral.

In sum, a profile of ethics from a theocentric perspective is quite different from a profile of Kant's ethics. I have attempted to show not only the differences in "profile," but also the grounds on which those differences rest.

Chapters 2 and 3, if they have fulfilled my intention, provide theological and philosophical benchmarks in relation to which the ethics that follow from the theocentric perspective delineated in volume 1 can now be further developed. I have attempted not only to describe differences between the profile of theocentric ethics presented in chapter 1 and profiles of alternatives. I have also attempted to show the points at which there are differences and similarities in judgments, and the reason why those exist. By seeing where the route I am traveling lays in relation to alternative routes that have been well traveled in both theology and philosophy, the reader has, I hope, a clearer understanding of that route and why I have chosen it.

117. An example of this would be Kant's subtle but finally rigoristic negative answer to the old question of whether it is right to tell a lie from "altruistic" motives, i.e., in order to avoid predictable harmful consequences. Kant, "On a Supposed Right to Lie from Altruistic Motives," in Beck, ed., *Critique of Practical Reason*, pp. 346–50.

4

A Brief Transition

In the final chapter of volume 1 I developed the concept of discernment to show the kind of practical reasoning that follows from a theocentric construal of life in the world. The interpretation of moral life that I developed there is grounded in theocentric piety and involves discerning what God is enabling and requiring us to be and to do.

In chapter 1 of this volume I sketched the distinctive features of the ethics that follow from the theology developed in volume 1. The intention was to highlight the differences that the theocentric perspective makes in our interpretation of moral life and of the principles and values that are applicable to the determination of individual and collective courses of action. In chapters 2 and 3 I attempted to make these distinctive features clearer by using significant writings theological and philosophical ethics as benchmarks.

In volume 1 and in the previous chapters of this volume I have largely, though implicitly, fulfilled what I argued, in *Protestant and Roman Catholic Ethics*, are the fundamental requirements for a comprehensive and coherent account of theological ethics. There I stated that comprehensive theological ethics must be developed in relation to four distinguishable base points, or points of reference, and to be coherent there must be an organizing concept, idea, principle, analogy, metaphor, or symbol around which the base points are organized. The base points are: (a) the interpretation of God and God's relations to the world and particularly to human beings, and the interpretation of God's purposes; (b) the interpretation of the meaning or significance of human experience—of historical life of the human community, of events and circumstances in which persons and collectivities act, and of nature and man's participation in it; (c) the interpretation of persons and collectivities as moral agents, and of their acts; and (d) the interpretation of how persons and collectivities ought to make moral choices and ought to judge their own acts, those of others, and states of affairs in the world.[1]

I also stated that Christian theological ethics can be tested for their adequacy with reference to four sources: (a) the Bible and the Christian tradition; (b) their philosophical methods and principles; (c) their use of scientific information and other sources of knowledge of the world; and (d) human experience broadly conceived. Theologians make judgments about these sources, and about the weight or authority each has in the development of theological ethics. Four kinds of judgments are involved: about (a) which sources are relevant, and why; (b) which sources are decisive when they conflict, and why; (c) what specific "content" is to be used from these

1. I believe coherent and comprehensive nontheological ethics also have these base points; for the first one simply substitute assumptions that are made or beliefs that are defended about how certain things really and ultimately are, such as those about the place of man in the universe and the nature of human action.

sources, and what is to be ignored or rejected, and why; and (d) how this content is to be interpreted, and why.

I also showed how judgments about the base points and the sources are interrelated, and how the character of the interrelations differs in different theological ethics. An example of this has been elaborated in chapter 2. Karl Barth chooses the Bible as the authoritative source for his principal base point, namely, the doctrine of God. God and God's relations to the world are interpreted in "personalistic" terms. Everything else about his theological ethics is quite coherently related to the consequences of these choices. Thomas Aquinas made different choices, and his ethics are quite consistent with them.[2]

This pattern has been in my mind throughout the writing of this book. I have not used it more explicitly to organize my analysis of the works of others and my own constructive proposals because it would have excessively schematized the discussions. I state it explicitly here so that the reader can test my work in its light.

The argument of this book is that for theological ethics the base point that ought to be most decisive is the interpretation of God and God's relations to the world, including human beings. In the interpretation of this base point I have relied more heavily on scientific and other sources of our knowledge of the world, and on human experience (e.g., piety) than traditional Christian ethics has. The Bible has not been given the authority that it normally has in Christian theological ethics, though elements of the creation narratives, the Psalms, and the Wisdom literature can be adduced as biblical backing. And, of course, the New Testament accounts of Jesus inform theocentric piety and fidelity. From the Christian tradition I chose one identifiable strand, the Reformed, both because it has informed my theological construal of the world and because aspects of it are supportable from other sources I use. I have, however, selected aspects from that tradition; I have indicated what I reject, what I carry forward, and how I interpret those aspects. My interpretation of man was also informed more by certain philosophical and scientific sources than is the case for some other theologians. Again, I have indicated what sources I have used, and my reasons for using them. The fourth base point was the topic of the final chapter of volume 1, where I delineated a process of discernment by which one comes to moral choices and judgments in a manner coherent with the interpretations of God and God's relations to the world, and the interpretation of man in relation to God and the world. There and elsewhere I emphasized the importance of the second base point, namely, the interpretation of the circumstances in which we are moved to act or to make moral judgments.

The purpose of this chapter is transitional and introductory to the rest

2. James M. Gustafson, *Protestant and Roman Catholic Ethics: Prospects for Rapprochement* (Chicago: University of Chicago Press, 1978), pp. 139–44.

of this volume which is more constructive and illustrative than the two preceding chapters. I shall develop an account of moral life and ethical thought around a central concept of human life. *Man (individual persons, communities, and species) is a participant in the patterns and processes of interdependence of life in the world.* Man is not simply a spectator, though we do and must distance ourselves from the immediacy of particular events and circumstances in order to interpret their significance and reflect upon what action is proper. Man is not the proprietor of the creation, with rights of ownership that authorize us to do with all things what we choose in the light only of our interests. Man is not the all-powerful emperor of the world, with the capacities to determine in detail the course of events and state of affairs. Man is a part of a whole, indeed part of various "wholes" that can be designated. The past brings us to where we are in time and space, providing both limitations and opportunities for new achievements. In the present we are interdependent with many factors, and in our actions are responding to and interacting with other persons and communities, with aspects of culture, and with the natural order. Man has capacities to affect subsequent courses of events and states of affairs, whether in the lives of friends and family members, the conduct of political affairs, or the ways in which nature itself will be developed. But the powers to control the effects of human participation are limited; the consequences of our participation take on their own momentum and direction as they interact with aspects of the world beyond our intentions and control. As participants we are, to use a term often expressed in religious discourse, stewards; we are temporary, responsible custodians of, and contributors to, the realms in which we participate.

Such a view is not novel nor is it esoteric. George F. Kennan echoes it quite clearly in an essay, "A Christian's view of the Arms Race." While the passsage I quote is in focus on civilization, in other places he shows equal concern for the whole of life on this planet.

> This civilization we are talking about is not the property of our generation alone. We are not the proprietors of it; we are only the custodians. It is something infinitely greater and more important than we are. It is the whole; we are only a part. It is not our achievement, it is the achievement of others. We did not create it. We inherited it. It was bestowed upon us; and it was bestowed upon us with the implicit obligation to cherish it, to preserve it, to develop it, to pass it on—let us hope improved, but in any case intact—to the others who were supposed to come after us.[3]

In the statement of the concept of man I did not develop its theological aspects, and I shall simply assume them in most of the rest of the book. Note, however, must be taken of them. In the religious consciousness the patterns

3. George F. Kennan, *The Nuclear Delusion: Soviet-American Relations in the Atomic Age* (New York: Pantheon Books, 1982), p. 205.

and processes of interdependence of life in the world (and not merely in nature) are *signs or indications of the divine power and ordering*. Through them we and all things are sustained; through them we know the powers that bear down upon us, threatening, limiting, and even destroying; through them the conditions of possibility for human activity occur with reference both to man as agent or actor and to the alterability of other persons, events, and states of affairs.

The practical moral question from a theocentric perspective can now be slightly amended. What is God enabling and requiring us, as participants in the patterns and processes of interdependence of life in the world, to be and to do? The general answer can also be slightly amended. We, as participants, are to relate ourselves and all things in a manner appropriate to our and their relations to God.[4]

The concept of man as participant in the patterns and processes of interdependence, and the reasons given to back it, have consequences for how one thinks about ethics itself. This is evident from the previous chapters, and I shall not summarize those consequences here. One does not, from my theocentric perspective, develop an ideal moral theory, or formulate an ethical theory disregarding the implications of our embodiment as moral agents, our bearing of a particular culture, our location and involvement in society, and our interdependence in the ordering of the natural world. Such efforts to develop ideal moral theories assume a posture of spectator that I believe is not finally possible or justifiable, though one appreciates their intellectual brilliance and learns from them. Indeed, as sociologists of knowledge and some philosphers, theologians, and intellectual historians have pointed out, such efforts are themselves part of a cultural tradition; they have their own intellectual history.[5] A theologian who sought to develop such an ideal moral theory would have to have the audacity to assume that he or she could see and evaluate things from God's point of view. It would require a kind of knowledge of God that I believe is not possible to achieve.

The alternative to an ideal moral theory, however, is not existentialism; it is not total immersion in the immediacy of events and of one's

4. The central concept is quite communicable and intelligible without invoking its theological grounding. See my essay, "Ethical Issues in the Human Future," prepared for and discussed at the International Smithsonian Symposium on "How Humans Adapt: A Biocultural Odyssey," in Donald J. Ortner, ed., *How Humans Adapt: A Biocultural Odyssey* (Washington, D.C.: Smithsonian Press, 1983), pp. 491–504. In it I briefly discuss the major consequences for an approach to ethics that follow from the theology of volume 1; this approach to ethics can be defended without the theology, but only by using many of the evidences I adduced to support the theology.

5. Alasdair MacIntyre and Jeffrey Stout have stressed this in recent publications. See Alasdair MacIntyre, *After Virtue: A Study in Moral Theory* (Notre Dame, Ind.: University of Notre Dame Press, 1981), and Jeffrey Stout, *The Flight from Authority: Religion, Morality, and the Quest for Autonomy* (Notre Dame, Ind.: University of Notre Dame Press, 1981), especially pp. 179–255.

self-involvement so that one feels one's way through judgments and choices. The proposal of a theocentric construal of the world as a way to interpret life requires some distance from immediate events and desires. It does not, however, rule out the significance of affectivity, of feelings. But the concept of man as a participant does require the use of symbols and concepts, and rational activity to determine what man ought to be and do. Participants move between disinterestedness and involvement, and the learning and experience of each reciprocally inform the other. Participants are not mere rational spectators but have feelings and sensibilities; both their impulses to act and their perceptions of what needs to be altered or preserved are affected by their involvement. Nor are they merely emotive reactors to their circumstances, relying on immediate emotions and intuitions to guide their conduct.[6]

The following four chapters are illustrations of how human beings as participants in the patterns and processes of life reflect on four areas of human experience: marriage and family, suicide, population and nutrition, and the allocation of biomedical research funding. These four have been chosen for several reasons. First, each of them focuses on a quite different "whole" with quite different relationships among its parts.

Marriage and family are primary relationships and are basically interpersonal in character. They are both natural and covenanted relationships; they involve human affections and sensibilities as well as the meeting of obligations and duties. They are interdependent with other institutions and processes, but experientially are "wholes" within which we are nourished and make critical choices.

6. Some persons in the field of Christian ethics are attempting to work out a theory on the basis of which Christians can participate with secular persons and persons from other religious traditions in matters of moral and social concern. It is as if one had to have such a theory before one could participate. It is ironically the case that in recent American history two of the most influential and vigorous Protestant theological participants in debates about social and moral issues, Reinhold Niebuhr and Paul Ramsey, have had no well-developed theories of this sort. Nor am I persuaded that their participation would have been either more cogent or more influential if they had had such theories. Religious perspectives are historically conditioned, but so are all others, including rationalistic ones. Their historical particularity makes positive contributions to moral discourse as well as limits these contributions, but this is true of Kantian, utilitarian, Hindu, or any other perspectives. While deeper perspectives make differences (as this book attempts to show), participants can agree on many human values, many rules of conduct, and many practical choices without agreeing on (a) a theory of morality, or (b) a theory about how persons from different historical traditions, or with different moral theories, can carry on common moral discourse. Stephen Toulmin has recently published two articles which are based in part on his participation in a commission that dealt with matters of morality and public policy that are much to this point. See Toulmin, "How Medicine Saved the Life of Ethics," *Perspectives in Biology and Medicine* 25 (1981):736–50, and "The Tyranny of Principles," *The Hastings Center Report* 11, no. 6 (Dec., 1982): 31–9. The latter could have been entitled the "Tyranny of Theories." Other scholars are occupied with the relations of practice to theory, or, as we are told is better, *praxis* to *theoria*. There are philosophical problems of importance and interest in that relationship, but I have chosen not to take up the effort to develop a theory of theory and practice.

Suicide certainly must be the loneliest of all human choices and actions. It is an issue to which theologians and moral philosophers have attended, and I take up the ideas of authors discussed in chapters 2 and 3. Since the affective, volitional, and intellective are so deeply intertwined in the motives for suicide, one cannot attend to this issue without engaging in a process of empathetic understanding for the agent. But the lonely agent is still in some relations to others, though they may be warped by many factors. I have chosen to focus on despair as the condition out of which the possibility of justifying the taking of one's own life comes, and on some of the causes and conditions that lead to despair. The major focus of attention in a commending or prescriptive mode is on our interdependence as persons and the opportunities and obligations we have toward each other to attempt to avert conditions that lead to despair and to suicide. Yet our accountability for another's suicide is limited since the other uses his or her capacities for self-determination in choosing the act. And while I argue that we ought always to seek to prevent suicide, if that is possible, there are sufficient reasons for some persons to take their lives. I return toward the end of the chapter to look at the moral arguments against suicide and to evaluate the major ones. Suicide is, in my judgment, the quintessential tragic act; those who take their lives believe they have good reasons to do so, and see no other course of action that will provide for the fulfillment of their interests.

The relation between nutritional resources and human population is chosen because of its vastness, the number and complexity of the variables, and the relationships between human activity, culture, and nature that are involved. In that chapter I do little more than outline a simplified schema, indicate some of the critical matters that are slighted in that outline, and develop the considerations that have to be taken into account both in the increase of supply of nutrients and in the control of population growth. There is no natural balance between human population and nutrition; culture and technology as well as other factors constantly change the contours of the issue. Yet fundamental conditions have to be sustained, and considerations of future generations both of human beings and of the rest of the natural world are required.

Allocation of biomedical research funding is almost as unmanageable a problem as population and nutrition. I have chosen it, however, because it opens up issues of ethics, politics, and economic scarcity within some definable boundaries as well as some matters of clinical medical ethics. Like the previous area, the contours are constantly in flux, and it is not possible to formulate an ideal blueprint of priorities in research, the development of therapies and their distribution. Rather, questions of fairness in distribution of resources and the procedures of consequentialism are commended within the context of historical and scientific developments.

Each illustration requires attention to a very different whole, and each lifts out different features of human experience, requiring attention to traditional ethical concepts in somewhat different ways. Perhaps one reason that moral philosophers have written so little about the family is that the customary abstraction and rationality of much moral theory is prima facie dissonant within the intense and affective relationships that exist there. The conduct of life in marriage and family is more a moral art than a moral science; yet implicit in the relationships are issues of fairness and respect for persons. The motives for marriage and family life necessarily include powerful inclinations—biological, emotive, and others. Duty and inclination are reciprocal in these relationships in ways they are not in political and economic ones.

Most of the ethical literature on suicide has difficulty in coming to grips with the unity of affective, volitional, and rational aspects that must be involved in that choice. Despair, whether caused by loneliness or guilt, by a sense of fatedness or by aimlessness, is not a matter easily addressed in philosophical ethics with its customary separation of rational, objective ethical reasons from the subjective conditions of human agents.

Nutrition and population growth require more specific attention to developments in various relevant sciences and to obligations to future as well as present generations. That topic also enables me to examine briefly, but more particularly, the role that metaphors and analogies have in providing evaluative descriptions of the circumstances.

In the discussion of biomedical research funding more than in the other topics, I am forced to look at the importance of cost/benefit analysis, at scarcity of economic resources, and at political aspects of choices. Traditional concepts of ethics, such as distributive justice, the assessment of probable consequences of alternative courses of action, and the common good are also used.[7]

Each of these chapters is an exercise in discernment of what we are being enabled and required to do as participants in the patterns and processes of interdependence of life. Each is an effort to show how we might

7. These topics are matters on which I have done a considerable amount of research, and about which I have thought for a long time. The depth of research is varied among the four, and the reliance upon personal experience is different in each. None of the chapters indicates in the text or in the citations the extent of the literature that I have explored. None of them is sufficient to meet the standards of a monograph; particularly in the latter two one needs to be involved in a community of moral discourse with persons who have special scholarly competence and who have actual responsibility for making and executing decisions. The chapter on allocation of research funding comes closest to being developed from such a community; it is written on the basis of a research seminar taught with a medical investigator under the auspices of the Committee on Public Policies Studies, and on one occasion with a quite broad representation of students from various fields of graduate study.

relate ourselves and other things appropriately to their relations to God. The signals of the divine ordering are clearer and more precise in some areas than others; this I grant. The features of the profile of theocentric ethics developed in chapter 1, however, do make some differences in one's moral choices and in the order of importance of aspects of social and moral issues. I have not developed theocentric ethics to provide answers to moral questions as they might be given from egocentric or anthropocentric perspectives. The theology of the first volume backs what I have written in each of these chapters; it is a basis both for how and for what I have written.

Following the four illustrative chapters is a conclusion in which I draw together strands from both volumes to depict our being and our doing as moral agents (individuals, communities, and institutions) who seek to discern what God is enabling and requiring us to be and to do as participants in the patterns and processes of interdependence.

5

Marriage and Family

Our question is, What is God enabling and requiring us to be and to do as participants in the patterns and processes of interdependence in marriage and family life? Our response to this will be guided by the general answer, We are to relate ourselves and all things in a manner appropriate to our and their relations to God.

One does not need to read historical and sociological literature to perceive that marriage and family are institutions and communities undergoing significant change in Western societies and in other societies that are becoming industrialized and urbanized. Nor does that perception have to be supported with a great deal of hard evidence, such as the increase in divorce rates over recent time, increase in the participation of women in the work force, the development of new institutions for child care, and so forth. The changes in marriage and family affect other institutions and communities. Changes in family law are only one example: legislatures and the courts in the United States have had to face new questions or resolve old ones in different ways, for example, in the areas of custody arrangements for children of divorced parents, grounds for divorce, from moral culpability to other "faults" to no-fault, and grandparents' visitation rights. The new consciousness of the respect due to women as not merely means to the ends of the husband and family life has effected changes in patterns of life within families, and relations of families to other institutions. The rights of adolescents to secure birth-control means without informed consent of parents have been extended; at the same time parental responsibility for the behavior of adolescents has not significantly diminished.

The ideals of what constitutes a "good" marriage and "good" family life change and are affected by cultural forces. For many North Americans the ideal has been a "suburban" pattern of life: a freestanding single-family dwelling with lawns and gardens, separation from business and industrial areas, the automobile as the chief means of transportation, and schools which prepare children for a college education. This ideal is obviously different from that held when the farm family was a relatively self-sufficient and economically independent unit. Experimentation has gone on in the light of proposed ideals of marriage: attempts have been made to have "open marriages" in which traditional restraints, even in sexual life, are loosened. Panaceas have been proposed, such as "The couple that prays together stays together." Experiments and panaceas often fail, to the dismay of those who attempt to live by them.

Social and economic forces have changed and continue to change marriage and family patterns in many parts of the world. Geographical and social mobility alter relations between the conjugal family and the extended family, and between the generations. My paternal family, for example, for several hundred years, lived in a small area of a single province in Sweden as peasants and soldiers until my grandfather became a construction worker on the Swedish railway system; as a result of that, each child was born in a different place as the rail line went farther north. Immigration patterns to the United States further changed family life both in my grandparents' and my parents' generation. Marriages cross traditional ethnic and cultural boundaries; our own was probably the last generation in America in which persons of Swedish descent usually married each other. Further illustrations are not necessary to suggest to the reader that marriage and family are undergoing change.

It is also the case, however, that marriage and family do not disappear. Couples continue to bind themselves to each other in religious vows and covenants and take the legal step of a civil marriage. Separations between couples who have lived together without eccesiastical or legal sanction often lead to traumas similar to those felt when divorce is undergone. Children are desired, and when born they bring natural duties to parents simply because of the dependence of the young on the older. The basis of relations between persons in marriage and family alters to some extent as a result of distance from extended families, working wives and husbands, and other factors, but some different bases develop in due course. The fundamental patterns and processes of various forms of interdependence do not disappear, though the precise social arrangements that support them change both in particular social classes and in individual marriages and families.

Some changes in marriage and family occur as a result of deliberate choices made by individuals. A married couple can decide what the domestic division of labor will be; they can decide whether and how income and property will be distributed between them; they can decide which of their interests will be pursued together and which separately. Families are also affected by choices. Some families can choose their place of residence in the light of values and ideals that they hold; parents can decide to be more or less permissive in the way in which they raise their children; they can decide how to use their discretionary income and leisure time.

As I noted, many of the changes in marriage and family are the consequences of deeper and wider forces in a given society, in the organization of an economy, and in the culture. It is difficult, if not impossible, to formulate some ideal of the perfect marriage or of the good family, and impose it on the dynamics of the society of which the family is a part. Marriage and family life are "acted upon" in ways they cannot control; they are not merely the result of choices and actions taken by self-legislating persons. What is deemed necessary, or at least desirable, for a good family life is affected by the power of consumer-oriented advertising to which all persons in our society are readily susceptible. Whether the family is perceived as a positive and supportive social unit or one that is repressive and destructive is affected by the portrayals of it in films, television programs, dramas, and novels. How the generations perceive and interpret their relations to each other is affected by popularized behavioral sciences: a term like "Oedipus complex" alerts persons to the slightest indication of the existence of anything that resembles it. Books on child-rearing offer both ideals and practical guidance, and in the middle classes they affect practices and present norms (many of which create parental guilt). Conditions of poverty and job insecurity create psychological pressures which affect relations in the family; there is no guarantee, however, that wealth and security ensure stability. Not only are individual moral agents acted upon as much as they act; marriage and family are also not self-sufficient autonomous social units that can fully control their own ends and destiny.

Perhaps this is one reason why marriage and family have not received attention in moral philosophy, social ethics, and theology in recent years comparable to the attention given other issues of morality and human values. Even the casual reader of literature produced by Christian ethicians, for example, knows that far more attention has been given to homosexuality, abortion, and pre- and extra-marital sexual relationships than to marriage and family as communities and institutions. Perhaps because the order of magnitude of consequences is judged to be so much greater, writers have attended much more to issues of economic justice and world peace than they have to marriage and family. Among Christian writers perhaps there has been a reaction to the highly idealized portrayals of the "Christian family" that churches propagated in their family literature for several decades.[1]

Marriage and family make up a relevant whole, a proper focus of attention, for theology and ethics. They are important for several reasons. First, they are powerful influences on how persons are formed and act. Even before behavioral and social scientists developed their analyses it was clear that the sort of family in which one grew up was decisive in shaping many aspects of the lives of children. Erik Erikson and many others continue to show the significance of the relationships that are developed in infancy as

1. In the late 1950s Robert W. Lynn and I prepared a working paper for a consultation on ethics and family life. It began with a description of a family that came from Lynn's pastoral experience, and focused primarily on two points of tension: between the past and the present, which highlighted geographic and social mobility, and between job and home. The aim of the paper was to interpret American middle-class families in wider social context. This in turn set criteria by which we evaluated the literature on the Christian family that was currently being distributed and used by a major Protestant denomination. On both points of tension that literature was found to be inadequate in the scope of its understanding and, as a result, to idealize the nuclear family in ways that were almost destined to lead to frustration in actuality. Interestingly, it was to the Roman Catholic sociologist, John Thomas, S.J., that we turned to find a more adequate perspective. Thomas, in his *American Catholic Family* (reprinted, Westport, Conn.: Greenwood, 1980) was clear and consistent about viewing the family as affected by other institutions and as dependent upon them to fulfill its purposes. Consequently the effect of his work was more realistic. What I judge to be the best book on family by a Protestant theologian has received little attention: Roger Mehl, *Society and Love: Ethical Problems of Family Life*, trans. James H. Farley (Philadelphia: Westminster, 1964).

well as in childhood and adolescence. And even adults frequently define themselves in relation to the families of their origins. Second, as I have indicated, family is both acted upon and an "agent." One cannot deal with the family from an ethical perspective as if were a fully autonomous unit; one must take into account the impact of social and cultural forces that condition its life and aspirations. At the same time, the family and its members can and do make choices about the quality of relationships within it, what ends will be pursued and how, the rules of conduct that are required, the duties persons have to one another, and how all members will share in the well-being of the institution itself. Third, marriage and family are important institutions for the ordering of human life in the world. The well-being of the wider society is affected by the relationships and qualities of life within them. Fourth, they are grounded in the biological and social natures of man, and thus exemplify ways in which natural needs and desires give some direction to ends as well as ways in which choices of ends give shape to the exercise of natural needs and desires. And finally, marriage and family are universal institutions; although the forms that they take are relative to social and cultural factors, their omnipresence suggests that the ways in which we think about them might give clues to understanding other pervasive social institutions.

An Interpretation

Normative judgments about the morality and human qualities of marriage and family have several bases but most, if not all, of them are finally backed by interpretations of what functions or purposes they have and ought to have. The question is whether a general pattern of family life, or that of a particular family, reasonably fulfills the functions that the family ought to have. Those functions are many; some of them are grounded in our biological natures, and others are grounded in ideal aspirations for both the institution and its members. Thus how one interprets the nature and purposes of marriage and family is critical to the development of any normative ends, patterns of relationships, and qualities of life they ought to have. There is no avoiding the need to relate what is and what ought to be, for what ought to be is grounded in the possibilities and limitations of human biological and social needs, though not without remainder. And since there are several ends of marriage and family, how these ends are interpreted in relation to each other will affect prescriptions of what ought to occur in them.

For example, in Christian literature there have been traditionally three ends of marriage: procreation, mutuality in interpersonal communion, and a remedy for sin. The first and the second are based on biological and "spiritual" human needs. The first is grounded in a species function of survival which human beings share with other species; the institution of marriage is formed to assure that this function occurs within conditions of moral responsibility. The second, while having distinctively human dimensions, is not foreign to some other species; members of these species also show affection for their mates as well as care for their young. But marriage both expresses the desire for mutual sustenance of many sorts and commits persons to reponsibilities for each other to meet those needs. The third end has a distinctive religious moral basis; it is based on the perception that sexual drives are a source of moral temptations, and that they can be responsibly fulfilled only in the binding commitment of marriage. As we have seen in the discussion of official Roman Catholic teaching, if the first end is the primary and overriding one of marriage, the use of artificial means of birth control is illicit, regardless of the consequences. If the second becomes the primary end, a basis is established not only for the use of means of conception control to limit the number of children but also for intentionally childless marriages. If the third end were to become primary, it would be open to making marriage simply a religiously and legally sanctioned device for the exercise of sexual desires. All three ends recognize aspects of "natural" human beings, and on the basis of these aspects a moral ordering is developed. But how the ends are ordered in relation to each other is affected by a choice made in wider and more distinctively moral frames of reference. All three, however, are backed by theology, and particularly by the doctrines of creation and of sin.

I shall not expound all the important ways in which marriage and family are interpreted, or all the possible moral perspectives that shape such interpretations. It serves my purpose, however, to formulate two ideal-types that provide radical alternatives to the constructive position I shall develop. Like all ideal-types, these are not empirical generalizations drawn from evidences which fully support them; they deliberately exaggerate tendencies that I believe are present in some literature about marriage and family, in popular presentations of these institutions in the mass media, and in the ideals or complaints that many persons in our time have.

The first ideal-type I shall call an egocentric, hedonistic interpretation of the ends of marriage and family. The essential feature of the type is this: marriage and family ought to be judged in the light of the extent to which they bring happiness to their individual members. Happiness obviously refers to many kinds of satisfaction; much more than physical pleasure or avoidance of pain is included. The benefits are mutual; the happiness of one member depends in part on the happiness of other members. But the test to which relationships are put is their benefits for the individuals related. The meaning and purpose of relationships is to sustain and foster the self-realization of husband and wife, and of children. When that realization is impeded, whatever specific goals it has, marriage and family are perceived to be repressive institutions. The vows or contractual bonds, the promises mutually made, become open to revocation if the ends that husband and wife have as individuals are deeply frustrated by honoring them.

To state this ideal-type as a foil for the development of an alternative is problematic. It invites the supposition that the only alternative to it is its extreme opposite ideal-type: marriage and family with a clear hierarchy of authority, in our culture male-dominated; a community in which the interests and ends of individual members are totally subordinated to the pattern of authority and sacrificed for the sake of the unity and perceived common good of the particular marriage and family.

By now most persons in our society recognize and acknowledge that an actualization of this second ideal-type can be exceedingly destructive to the persons involved. For the sake of the relationship between husband and wife it is important to acknowledge that distinctive needs and interests of each must be honored in some way. Demands for subordination and obedience can suppress the individuality of each person and destroy the self-respect and autonomy that is proper to each. It is recognized that children become more and more self-determining during the course of their development to adulthood and that total supression of their efforts to do so in the name of a superior wisdom or of the deemed common good of the family leads to hostility or to psychological repression that disrupts the lives of families and of the individual members. To state that the persons married exist for the sake of the institution of marriage, or that they and children are parts whose function is only to serve the well-being of the whole is not the alternative that I shall develop. The assumption that one person's understanding of the good of the marriage and family is to be imposed upon others by the exercise of authority and power is not made in my alternative. But I cannot develop an "ideal" alternative that can be imposed upon the dynamics of family life; indeed such ideals frequently provoke severe frustration and improper guilt. What can be developed is an interpretation of the ethics of marriage and family that follows from what has preceded in this book.

Marriage and family are signs of and evidences for a divine ordering of life in the world. They develop their particular forms in different times and places and under different conditions, but they are grounded in necessary conditions not only for the sustenance and flourishing of life within them but also for relating the life of this social unit to the wider orderings of human communities and even the ordering of life in relation to nature. There is no immutable order of marriage and family that can be traced from an order of nature or from an order of creation that is itself imprinted in the mind of God. Monogamy is the best candidate for a requirement of the order of creation; we can be sure, however, that if the ratio of male and female in our species was not naturally almost 1:1 but 1:4 or 4:1 monogamy would not have the moral status it has. But there are basic individual and communal needs that have to be met by members of the human community and there are relationships of mutual responsibility that must be attended to if human life is to survive and flourish.

Moral reflection about marriage and family seeks to provide direction to natural drives and social needs; it is rational activity based upon what is given both in "nature" and in particular social circumstances in given times and places. Values and principles are backed by these needs, and when they are objicified in rational ways they can provide direction to the ordering of relationships so that these needs are more properly met. Failure to establish and to maintain certain relationships and failure to meet fundamental needs leads to disorder and to consequences which are detrimental both to the institution of marriage and family and to the well-being of individual members. Since relations within the institution are not those of biological cause and effect, or of action and reaction, the importance of human agency, of capacities for self-determination and for directing interactions, obviously has to be taken into account. Interactions and relationships are those of particular and finite human beings, and subject to the possibilities of missing the proper mark, of violating proper relations, and of creating animosity and guilt. While normative patterns of relationships can be developed, principles of conduct can be defined, and more precise rules can be stated, conduct is directed by discernment in the particularities and intimacies of marriage and family relationships. *Function determines form...*

The divine empowering and ordering of life takes place in and through "nature": through human biological relationships first of all. As I noted above, marriage and family are grounded in the biological function of species survival: this is the function of sexuality at the most basic biological level. This function we share with most living species, both animals and plants. Certain conditions must be met for species survival, and these come "naturally" to us as well as to other living things. This function, however, takes a different form among human beings, which is a basis for family life and thus for ethical reflection; I have in mind the long period of parental care that is required. Humans mature more slowly, and thus different needs and relationships are necessary for the care of the human young. And while other animals both care for their young and show affection for them, human animals seem to thrive on caring and being cared for, on showing and receiving affection, in a distinctive way. While other animals instinctively protect their young, and thus fulfill natural duties to them, in human life and particularly in modern cultures this instinct takes more complex forms.

Natural patterns of interdependence become very complex, and thus the patterns of proper relationships, of duties and obligations, become more complex. Human beings, as a result of the biological development of our species, have very distinctive possibilities of development, and thus their needs and desires extend far beyond simple biological survival. The forms of

[margin note: ? form is open to many possibilities?]

care, the patterns of interdependence, serve to provide conditions beyond the almost absolute value of the preservation of physical life; they create conditions which either sustain and enhance or destroy and impede a wide range of possibilities for human life. Recognition of this comes "naturally" to some extent; it also is a basis for articulating various values and conditions that ought to be met in marriage and family.

No religious or moral indignity is cast upon human life by attending to some of the most basic biological needs and drives out of which marriage and family emerge. Indeed, these have great theological dignity since they are indications of the divine ordering of life. To Karl Barth they are part of the phenomenon of man; the real man is quite radically distinguished from the biological needs and drives. To Kant they are inclinations; the real moral life comes only out of human autonomy and freedom. From a theocentric perspective they are signs of the ultimately divine empowering and ordering of life, signs of the radical dependence of human life on powers that are prior, ultimately of dependence on God. The natural condition of biological drives leading to sexual union of male and female is in the service of the creative and ordering powers of God. The fact that love and affection between a man and a woman leads to sexual union, and that sexual life sustains and expresses love and affection, in no way reduces the moral significance of sexuality. The fact that persons enjoy the affection that stems from their natural relationships and have affection for their offspring, some things we share with some other animals, is of theological importance and thus a basis for morality. One can say that human beings are "naturally" ordered to some form of marriage and family life; they participate in the divine ordering of the world.

The more specifically moral questions come to mind when we self-consciously reflect upon what the requirements are for shaping morally responsible relationships in marriage and family. The institution is grounded in nature, but it is not determined by nature; we are participants in the patterns and processes of marriage and family life, and thus can give guidance to actions and relationships in light of "the ought-to-be's" that are backed by the "isness" of nature. The natural bases for marriage and family are not sufficient in themselves to provide an ethics of marriage and family. But ethics provide ways of ordering and directing our natures, even our most deeply rooted biological drives as individuals and a species: biologically grounded drives not only for sexual activity, but also for affection, caring, and well-being for ourselves and those with whom we are so intimately related.

Marriage and family are social *institutions* grounded in our nature as individuals and as social beings. As social institutions, and not only as particular covenants between individuals (as Barth says about marriage), they are part of the ordering activity of God in the world, through nature.

Ethics of marriage and family cannot be developed by defining and imposing extraneous or heteronomous principles and values on to the unordered vitalities of nature. Ethics provides a way of institutionally ordering our natures that is enabled and required by our natures. Those natural vitalities need direction, and apart from it various sorts of morally reprehensible relations and actions can occur. The ethical task is to find those values and principles that direct our natures in a manner appropriate to our relations to each other, and ultimately to God; to provide the institutional patterns that express those values and are guided by those principles. The responses of human beings to their natures are different from those of a field of wheat, subject to the vicissitudes of soil and moisture, sunshine and tornadoes.

Marriage and family also come out of our aspirations for ourselves and others. Beyond the species needs are the additional necessary conditions for the ordering of relations to other marriages and families in a given society and across the generational lines, for bringing a measure of satisfaction to the aspirations of individual members, for a satisfaction of human longings for steadfast love. Within the limits of natural, social, economic, and other constraints human beings make choices. We believe and hope that the choice to marry a particular person and the choice to raise a family (now possible in more cases because of modern medical research) will be satisfying and rewarding to us. To make choices in marriage and family is to express our aspirations as well as to undertake obligations; God is enabling as well as requiring through marriage and family. The fulfillment of aspirations and the meeting of duties and obligations go hand in hand; certain kinds of relationships are required for the aspirations to be fulfilled and certain restraints on aspirations are required for the relationships to be sustained.

Human love entails duties and obligations of persons to each other. The institution of marriage and family expresses and directs those duties and obligations. They exist as necessary conditions for the well-being of individuals who are bound to each other by covenant and natural ties, for the well-being of the institution of marriage and family itself, and for the well-being of the social order of which it is a part. Ordered human relationships and commitments, i.e., institutional patterns, express love and affection; they are necessary but not sufficient conditions for sustaining love and affection; they are a recognition that marriage and family are part of a wider social and legal order. Institutional forms, with their freely undertaken commitments, are forms of contracted or covenantal relations and natural duties through which the well-being of individuals are sustained. They also are recognitions that the enabling incentives that draw persons together are not always sufficient to motivate and direct relationships, that there are temptations to violate commitments and obligations. The natural bases of human love lead to common life, to living together as persons and communities. These require pledges and restraints on individuals for the sake of life together. Institutional forms, commitments, and obligations are enabled and required by human love. They are grounded in the patterns and processes of interdependence of human life; they are ways of meeting some of the necessary conditions for its sustenance and well-being.

The family is not an organism; the forms of functional interdependence do not automatically develop so that the well-being of the whole and of the parts are in harmony. But one can use the organic analogy (recognizing that as an analogy it always breaks down) to highlight the relationships of parts to wholes within it. Nor is the reality of marriage exhausted by defining it as a contractual or convenanted relationship; it is a legal and religiously covenanted relationship, but in at least most Western marriages the contract is the fulfillment and expression of interpersonal relationships that are prior in time and in reality. Marriage and family are based on both natural inclinations and tendencies on the one hand, and on consent and commitment, i.e., on contracts or covenants, on the other. The relationships of parts to the whole entail both the more organic and the more contractual aspects of the institution. The junction of the "natural" community and the covenanted community is the focus of most of the ethical issues of marriage and family.

As natural communities, marriages and family are more than the sum of their individual parts, more than the aggregate of the persons who belong to them. Yet it is the case that the parts do not exist solely for the sake of the whole any more than the whole exists solely for the sake of the parts. The relationships are reciprocal, but not naturally harmonious. Because of the intricate interrelationships of the parts and the whole, attention must be given to the well-being of individual members, to the "goods" that are shared in common in the reciprocal relationships, and to the common good of the marriage and family as identifiable social entities. The "good" of marriage and family is more than the sum total of the happiness or other "goods" of its individual members, and the pain and suffering that sometimes occur is more than the aggregate of that of individuals.[2] But the well-being of the whole cannot be sustained apart from some realization of the well-being of the individual members. And the good, or well-being, that is involved is not merely physical sustenance, the conditions for biological survival; in the intensity and intimacy of life together it is much more: the

2. Novelists and dramatists write poignantly of the spreading infections or the cancerous growths that debilitate and often destroy both persons and the institution of marriage and family. One thinks, for example, of the opening chapters of D. H. Lawrence's *Sons and Lovers* (Baltimore: Penguin Books, 1948) which describe the rapid atrophy of romantic love and its replacement by deepening bitterness and hatred between husband and wife. The effects of this change on the husband, who is a coal miner; on the wife, whose education and social standing are higher than his; on the children, who live in anxiety and fear; and on the institution of marriage are vividly and painfully disclosed.

sense of worth, freedom from excessive anxiety, the joy of mutual love freely given and freely received, and being cared for and caring.

Nor is it the case that the patterns and processes of interdependence that sustain or threaten well-being are precisely the same over time. They change through the course of the life cycle: with the birth of children, with the development of children, with changing economic and social conditions, with upward or downward social mobility, with the coming of the "empty nest," with the aging process. Individual well-being, the "goods" shared in common, and the common good of the particular marriage and family are all affected by these and other changes which are part of the natural history of every marriage and family. The participation of persons with each other in interaction is altered through the course of time. Just as the health of the human body is judged in relation to the age of the person, so the "health" of marriage and family are proportionate to different periods in the life cycle. Certain conditions are necessary throughout, for example, respect for one another and readiness to forgive one another, but the occasions which meet them undergo change.

Persons inchoately sense that they are parts of a whole in marriage and family. They sense that the quality of the life of the whole suffers when persons do not properly participate with each other in it. One reads from time to time about persons who resign from the demands of professional responsibilities because their family life is suffering. Excessive preoccupation with work affects the relations of persons in family life. The signs of "suffering" are many: guilt for duties and obligations not properly fulfilled; putting excessive burdens on others by failure to do one's share; unhappiness as a result of missing opportunities in family life; tensions and signs of estrangement as the result of benefits not shared; unresolved conflicts of loyalties and many more. Other social relations perhaps suffer from the same things, but the intimacy of family life intensifies the sensitivities.

The contract or covenant of marriage, if not nourished by the more "organic" relationships, becomes a heteronomous requirement which is either a burden upon the family or a moral and legal obligation fulfilled for duty's sake alone. In most Western marriages the contract is an expression and certification of natural relations that precede it in time. It is a specification of obligations and responsibilities that are freely undertaken, involving restraints upon the pursuit of individual interests and ends and the formation of relationships by and through which individual, mutual, and institutional common goods are served. The contract signifies not only that persons accept responsibilities for each other; it also signifies that they have undertaken to be the custodians of an important social institution both in its own right and in relation to the wider society of which each marriage is a part. Vows are time-binding commitments; they represent obligations undertaken to be trustworthy to others. They are assurances of faithfulness, pledged out of inclination but binding when inclination is not strong. They are, in a sense, a specification of the order of human love, of the character of relationships which appropriately express and direct love. They illustrate the forms of mutual reliance which must be met for the sake of individual well-being, the mutual well-being of the partners, and the common good of the marriage and family as a whole. They represent the human participation in the social ordering of life, and ultimately in the divine ordering of life in the world.

Our Being in Marriage and Family

Marriage and family are both gifts and tasks; they enable forms of joy and fulfillment but require effort; they are signs both of the "grace" of God and the "law" of God given through nature. The image of life as a gift has a long and deep history in the Western religious traditions, and is backed by the theology I have developed, e.g., the significance of the senses of dependence and gratitude. Those whom we love are in a proper sense gifts; their coming to be and their special relations to us flow not from the application of a moral principle or the fulfillment of a duty. We are drawn to others in special ways as part of the processes which meet our needs and bring a measure of fulfillment and joy in human life.[3] They are gifts which bring satisfactions to us. We receive them as gifts, and thus are grateful for them; they bring responsibilities to us for their care, and thus our relationships are a basis for duties and obligations to them.

God is enabling and requiring us, as participants in the interdependence of marriage and family, to be stewards, deputies, or custodians of one another and of life itself. We are agents of the divine ordering and empowering of human life in the world. We are "called" to be stewards of many

3. "Special relations" such as the love of marriage, the intensity of love between parents and children, and friendship do not require the kind of distinctive justification from my perspective that they do for those Christian theologians and ethicians for whom *agape*, or Christian love, becomes virtually synonomous with Kant's principle of respect for persons. It is the case that in the Bible and throughout much of the history of Christian thought Christian love is deemed to require that the particular characteristics of individuals be transcended in love, that love be nonpreferential. One is to love another person even though he or she is one's enemy; one is to love another person regardless of their particular features and accomplishments. If this becomes *the* principle of Christian ethics, and if Christian ethics is understood to be exclusively the application of moral principles and the maxims that they support to individual cases, then the justification of special relations is a problem. If, however, the "natural" ordering of life has theological and moral dignity, i.e., if God is ordering the world through special relations between persons, they are not morally problematic in the same way. Part of the problem in Christian ethics that centers on love exclusively is that the term either has to have a univocal meaning which creates the difficulties with special relations, or it becomes an umbrella term under which are put all sorts of relationships that can and ought to be distinguished. If I were to develop this I would propose that love of enemies requires respect for them as persons regardless of their particular characteristics, and I would reserve the term love for other uses.

aspects of life through the commitments we make to one another, the duties that arise naturally from our mutual dependence, and the obligations we ratify in the covenant or contract of marriage.

We are stewards of our species; indeed one can state this more dramatically by saying that we are stewards of the "gene pool" of our species, among other things. While the consequences of a given couple's reproductive activity on the gene pool as a whole is infinitesimal, its consequences for immediately subsequent generations can be significant. The studies of human genetics and the clinical possibilities they create enlarge our accountability in this area.[4] The enlargement of human accountability does not imply that coercive and intrusive methods are warranted to get genetic profiles of all prospective parents, and that the carriers of severe genetic defects ought not to be permitted to bear children. The knowledge does, however, raise the possibility of responsible moral choices about child-bearing that can be accepted and acted on for the sake of the well-being of one's progeny. We are stewards of human biological life, and the well-being of some future persons is in part dependent upon the choices that we make. Science and technology enable us to be better stewards.

We are the stewards of each other's lives in marriage and family, whether we accept such a "call" or not. The intimacy and interdependence of life together is intense in these relationships; the fact that others are so "causally" affected by our actions and attitudes deepens and strengthens our moral accountability to each other. Both common observation and the research and writing done by various scholars point to the patterns and processes, sometimes elusive to precise definition, which back the need for a sense of responsible stewardship. The ordering activity of God through the natural needs of persons as individuals and communities enables and requires a sense of moral responsibility, and certain dispositions and attitudes. It enables them: to some extent they arise naturally out of experiences of the giftedness of the lives of others to us, and out of the actions and attitudes that these gifts evoke which express gratitude and love. It requires them: while no recipe book of family ethics insures that the natural stewardship will be properly exercised, our errors of judgment and our attitudes have consequences for the well-being of others to whom we are intimately related. There are rewards to our stewardship: the responsiveness of others in love and gratitude. There is pain and suffering in our stewardship: the anxiety

4. When our children were small we were privileged to have an exceedingly wise and compassionate pediatrician. In a jocular, but nonetheless poignant, way he told us that if he were to attend the wedding service of any of our children, when the question was asked "If anyone knows any reason why this couple cannot lawfully be joined together, let him speak now or forever hold his peace" he would like to stand up and say, "His (or her) father has severe allergies." If he thought that this comment was relevant, one can be sure that if he knew a mother was a carrier of hemophilia his intervention would have greater urgency.

and sufferings of others become our own; our intentions for the well-being of others are sometimes misunderstood, and sometimes are misguided.[5]

Our being together in marriage and family is under severe restraints of finitude; yet it is the particularity of given persons and relations that provides the possibilities of a measure of human fulfillment in family life. Restraints of particular economic conditions limit the possibilities for almost all families relative to their own aspirations and those evoked by the society and culture of which they are a part. Our stewardship of marriage and family involves our stewardship of whatever material resources we have and earn, our choices about their allocations, if we are fortunate enough to have discretionary income, and the ways in which they can sustain and enhance common life and individual well-being.

But the constraints are not only material; they are physical and personal. The intimacy of relations of individuals each of whom is distinctive, with distinctive possibilities and shortcomings, backs certain attitudes required for common life: trust and trustworthiness, patience and tolerance, mutual understanding, readiness to be forgiven and to forgive, willingness to sacrifice one's own interests for the sake of the interests of others and of the common good. These can be subsumed under the term "mutual love"; it is a love which we are enabled to share by virtue of our natures and by the sustaining care of others; it is a love we are required to share by being participants in the intimacy of interdependence in family life.

The limitations of the distinctiveness of individual members provide the distinctive possibilities of each. We are the stewards of each other's development during the childhood of our progeny and with different degrees of responsibility for each other throughout the various stages of the life cycle. An alertness is required to the potentialities and opportunities that come about by the distinctive individuality of each member of a family. In marriage and family, persons are not only members of classes about which we can generalize: wives, husbands, parents, children. Each has unique features which require particular sensitivities in our relationships. The moral stewardship of family is not conducted by the logic of syllogisms but by the discernment of the needs and possibilities given in many different relationships and intersections of interactions. A sense of stewardship is a condition that serves delicate discernment.

We are the bearers and thus the stewards of culture in family life. Social, moral, and aesthetic values and other aspects of culture are carried to some extent from generation to generation through the medium of family life. To be sure, in this regard family is acted upon as well as acting; in our

5. A penetrating account of the family can be found in Gabriel Marcel's essay, "The Mystery of the Family," in *Homo Viator*, trans. Emma Craufurd (Chicago: Henry Regnery, 1951), pp. 68–97.

culture it is not a closed community within which the influences of other communities can be shut out. But through the interactions of parents and children, the qualities of relationships that are established, the ends and activities that are pursued, and the sensitivities and values that are implied, something of the ethos of culture is transmitted from generation to generation. Traditions are kept or forgotten, memories are sustained or fade, various symbols of values are vitalized or wither in significance, moral and religious beliefs are exemplified or hypocritically displayed. Through the patterns and processes of family life some of the ethos of culture is carried; family life is a steward of culture.

We are stewards of an important social and legal institution in marriage and family. Contra Karl Barth, family is an important concept in theological ethics. Marriage is not only a covenant between two persons but a formed social relationship into which two persons enter. Family is not only a community but also an institution necessary for the orderly function of human relationships within it and for the organization of the society of which it is a part. To be a member of a family is to be a custodian of an institution whose significance is more than its benefits for its members.

To perceive and conceive of our life in marriage and family as a stewardship is a way of being; stewardship is a basic disposition that affects the qualities of our relationships, our sense of moral responsibility, and the sorts of specific duties to others that we adhere to. Stewards can never treat other persons and things merely as means to their own ends; a sense of accountability to others, and in the religious consciousness ultimately to God, qualifies self-understanding and the ways in which one relates to others. Stewardship is the personal basis for an attitude of caring for what is given and for the forms of caring that are appropriate to it. It is to be a "mask of God"; it is to have a calling in marriage and family that is ultimately in the service of the divine ordering and caring for the world.

The exercise of our stewardship is always in the conditions of finitude, the inexorable limitations but also possibilities of being the particular individuals we are. This is true in all our social roles but has a special poignancy in family, where the intensity and intimacy of relationships are so strong. I have long been persuaded that many tensions and a great deal of misplaced sense of guilt occur in family life because persons cannot accept the conditions of finitude, i.e., the limitations that follow from our physical natures, from the limits of interests and capacities, from the complexity of loyalties and duties, and from limits of economic and other resources. Idealizations of what we and others ought to be as husbands, wives, parents, children, and siblings lead to aspirations and expectations that exceed the particular limitations of each person as an individual and of a particular family as a community. But the particularities are also opportunities; the possibilities of specific forms of enrichment of human life are given because of the distinctive aspects of the persons related in family life. The conditions of finitude are "natural," and have to be accepted for their limits and possibilities.

It is also the case, however, that the "human fault" can infect, debilitate, and sometimes destroy marriage and family. Egocentrism, the failure to fulfill duties and obligations, the breakdown of trust and trustworthiness, all of which are more tolerable in less intimate relationships and interactions, within the family cause instability and deep pain. They corrode the bonds of love, heighten animosities and anxieties, and create suspicions which affect the well-being of individuals and the common good of the whole. There are good reasons for guilt that occurs in family life: casual insensitivity and heedlessness to the particular needs and interests of others, inconsideration of natural duties and obligations to others that occur from the pursuit of egocentric interests and ends, delicate betrayals of trust, outbursts of anger, failure to communicate, the silent nursing of bitter memories and grudges, aggressive and abusive physical treatment. The intimacy of relations intensifies our guilt and the pain to others that is inflicted by our expressions of the human fault.

Being together in family requires a readiness to forgive and to be forgiven; it requires those healing powers that cannot be commanded as a duty or obligation, a humility that can acknowledge fault, a strength that can accuse another and that can take being accused. Being together in family requires that persons see and seek the possibilities for overcoming the pains and weaknesses, develop conditions which sustain, renew and enrich the bonds in which we participate for the sake of individuals and of the common good. Here too, we can participate in the sustaining and renewing powers of God that come to us through our natures and capacities as human persons.

What Gabriel Marcel aptly called "creative fidelity" is a necessary condition for good stewardship in marriage and family.[6] Fidelity that comes only from a decisive act of will to adhere to vows and to apply principles of respect for persons will not sustain the qualities of caring and love on which marriage and family thrive. To do one's duty to others in these intimate relations solely for the sake of duty can erode the inclinations that draw persons to each other in mutual fulfillment. To treat others solely from the "law" impedes the nourishing graces which are beneficial to individuals, to mutual relations, and to the good of the whole.

But fidelity is a necessary condition for these nourishing graces. The vows of marriage and the acceptance of natural duties of parenthood confirm a ground of deep trustworthiness of persons to each other. Even when the mutual trust and trustworthiness fail or do not take the expected forms there remains a deeper commitment to faithfulness. The "creative"

6. Gabriel Marcel, *Creative Fidelity* (New York: Crossroad, 1982).

powers of life have to flourish for the fidelity to remain more than a heteronomous duty. They have to flourish because the precise actions and expressions of faithfulness change in the course of a marriage and family life; they are different before the coming of children and after it, in health and in sickness, after children come to adulthood, and in the process of aging. The enabling and the requiring go hand in hand; we are enabled to be faithful stewards of each other and of the institution of marriage and family; we are required to be faithful. Meeting the requirements sustains and nourishes the enabling; the powers of life and caring that enable breathe vitality into the requirements.

Our Doing in Marriage and Family

I have stated that the ethical issues are located at the junction of the "natural" communal aspects and the contracted or covenanted aspects of marriage and family. In this section I shall explore a few ethical dimensions to illustrate what issues come to consciousness from my theocentric perspective, and how some resolutions can be made.

I have already alluded in other terms to the puzzling duty to love. In traditional marriage vows the couple pledges to love and to cherish each other. In the biblical traditions, there is a command to love. In much modern literature, however, love is cast as antithetical to duty and as not subject to command. Love is to be given freely and even spontaneously; if it does not well up from inclinations, it is not love. Its requirement cannot enable it. We confront again the ambiguities of the term "love," a matter which I shall not analyze deeply here.[7]

7. I quote fully what I consider to be one of the finest statements of the meaning of love in theological literature. "By love we mean at least these attitudes and actions: rejoicing in the presence of the beloved, gratitude, reverence and loyalty toward him. Love is rejoicing over the existence of the beloved one; it is the desire that he be rather than not be; it is longing for his presence when he is absent; it is happiness in the thought of him; it is profound satisfaction over everything that makes him great and glorious. Love is gratitude: it is thankfulness for the existence of the beloved; it is the happy acceptance of everything that he gives without the jealous feeling that the self ought to be able to do as much; it is gratitude that does not seek equality; it is wonder over the other's gift of himself in companionship. Love is reverence: it keeps its distance even as it draws near; it does not seek to absorb the other in the self or want to be absorbed by it; it rejoices in the otherness of the other; it desires the beloved to be what he is and does not seek to refashion him into a replica of the self or make him a means to the self's advancement. As reverence love is and seeks knowledge of the other, not by way of curiosity nor for the sake of gaining power but in rejoicing and in wonder. In all such love there is an element of that 'holy fear' which is not a form of flight but rather a deep respect for the otherness of the beloved and the profound unwillingness to violate his integrity. Love is loyalty; it is the willingness to let the self be destroyed rather than that the other cease to be; it is the commitment of the self by self-binding will to make the other great. It is loyalty, too, to the other's cause—to his loyalty." H. Richard Niebuhr, in collaboration with Daniel Day Williams and James M. Gustafson, *The Purpose of the Church and Its Ministry: Reflection on the Aims of Theological Education* (New York: Harper, 1956), p. 35.

Love, if it is not simply a fleeting moment of deep emotion, takes forms of relationships which entail mutual obligations and duties to one another. The emotions cannot be commanded, but the relationship of love is more than feeling love for one another. What can become a duty, indeed, what can be commanded, is attentiveness to those relationships and obligations that are the forms of love; this attention sustains the conditions for more profound interpersonal experiences and makes possible their further flourishing. Faithfulness is an obligation as well as an inclination; fidelity is a duty of love. The forms of mutual fidelity in marriage and family are many: reliability in keeping promises and in attending to mutual needs, readiness to serve others at inconvenience to one's own interests, and many more. Breaches of faithfulness occur in those small and large betrayals that corrode and often destroy mutual love. Mutual love motivates fidelity; persons are inclined to do their duties to each other. As I shall demonstrate in the last section of this chapter, the traditional marriage service wisely portrays the interrelations between love and duty.

To participate in marriage and family is to be a part of a whole. In my judgment the intimacy of interdependence in such a relationship comes closer to being "organic" than any other in human experience. It is not the case, however, that the well-being of individual parts naturally follows from the common good of the whole any more than the common good is the aggregate to the well-being of individual members. The tension, so perceptible in all forms of social life and organization, between the pursuit of individual interests and the good of the group can be even more dramatic in marriage and family. The interrelations are dynamic; there is no static equilibrium that can be ideally and abstractly formed and applied to the interactions.

There are moral norms that pertain to the relationships of persons in marriage and family: respect and reverence are due one another, the individualities of each are to be honored by the others, patience and forgiveness are to be exercised, willingness to develop new conditions of human relationships is required as changes occur through the life cycles of individual members, and fairness in the distribution of duties and rewards must be adhered to. These norms point to both what is beneficial to individuals and to "goods" shared in common. Sharing these goods in common, fulfilling these moral norms are necessary conditions for family life. Duties and obligations are also undertaken for the well-being of the institution per se.

As parts of a whole, however, the individual members are often, if not always, means to the ends of others and means to the end of the common good, the good of the institution itself. Persons are functionally interdependent in family life. They meet each other's needs for love and affection, for common necessities of physical sustenance, for edification and mutual correction, and many other things. If they are treated only as means to the ends of others and the common good, a natural resistance is often manifest; thus persons are due a respect that transcends their utility to each other. But that respect cannot be merely respect for each other's autonomy; life together requires restrictions on the exercise of self-legislation. Restraints are necessary for the sake of the mutual well-being and for the sake of the common good. In family life self-denial is not a supererogatory norm; it is a moral necessity for common life. While there may be some special virtue to voluntary restriction of one's own interests and desires for the sake of others and the family, the exercise of authority is often required to enforce it. The autonomous pursuit of justifiable interests by individuals seldom automatically coheres with the interests of others or with the requirements for the well-being of the whole. While reasons can be given for restrictions and for the ways in which duties and responsibilities are distributed, the persons involved are never merely members of a class (spouse or children). Proper choices do not follow from a moral syllogism; a fine discernment is required to make them. Ambiguity is often never fully resolved.

An effort to apply the concept of distributive justice illustrates this. Justice is a principle applicable to the treatment of children; particularly, equals should be treated equally. As children of one family, they have a claim to equal treatment. But what does equal treatment require? At certain levels of fundamental needs the answer is quite clear: each should be provided with physical sustenance, and equal opportunities should be provided to develop their individual potentialities. Favoritism based on irrational preferences is unfair.

Justice requires that each individual receives his or her own due, and not simply as a member of a class; each child is different. To apply the principle, however, is by no means easy, nor will its application necessarily satisfy all members of the family. Suppose, for example, that a particular child has a talent that can be developed only by giving her unequal attention and an unequal share of the family's common resources. Justice seems to require preferential treatment not for the least but for the most advantaged. To do so, however, might deprive another child of the resources to realize his lesser or other potentialities. Should equal regard for each child, or love of each child, warrant preferential or discriminatory treatment? Should parents take into account not only differences in capacities but also the prospective differences in the benefits that each child might contribute to others and to the human community? Surely the principle of distributive justice has to be exercised through the virtue of equity, through the discerning and discriminating judgment required by individual cases. One might rationally determine that preferential treatment is justified, but in my judgment this does not rule out ambiguity or eliminate the possibility of justifiable resentment on the part of others who bear the cost of the discrimination.

Different choices will also be ambiguous. Parents might in the name of an egalitarian concept of distributive justice deny preferential treatment. They could determine to treat each equally by an equal distribution of family resources. Or they might determine that justice requires preferential treatment of the least-advantaged child. Such applications of the principle of fairness can lead to the deprivation both of particular children and of benefits to the wider community. Parents might avoid the resentment of those family members who would bear the cost of the discrimination by adhering to a principle of strict equality, but the consequences would be the failure to achieve distinctive benefits for particular persons and for society. Preferential treatment of the least advantaged would lead to similar losses.

Marriage and family are contexts in which traditional ethical concepts are applicable to define obligations and to guide choices. Marriage vows traditionally have been unconditional; they have been time-binding, "till death do us part." The seriousness with which vows are taken has eroded in many institutions in modern life, and conditions are stipulated in some contemporary marriage vows. The Christian tradition has historically been very negative toward divorce for many reasons, including that vows bind persons over time and changing conditions. It is clear that in marriage as in other intimate relations the keeping of vows purely for the sake of legal and religious fidelity when the natural and spiritual conditions that brought them about have withered away can be destructive to persons as individuals, to the benefits they share in common, and to the common good of the institution. Hyprocrisy occurs, bitterness and hatred often follow, and marriage becomes destructive. The wellsprings that nourished the intentions at the time vows were taken become dry.

Marriage is not unlike other aspects of moral life; there is a very strong presumption in favor of keeping vows; they are not to be taken "unadvisedly, lightly, or wantonly." But subsequent consequences, if they are unbearably destructive and evil, do provide reasons for dissolving them. The ethics of marriage are, one can say, presumptively deontic. The duties, however, have a wider justification in terms of prospective beneficial consequences to persons, the institution, and the wider society. The ethics of marriage are also consequentialist; in the light of effects that are evaluated to be destructive, persons can be absolved from duties in extreme circumstances. But a temporally prior task is part of the duty of marriage, namely, to nourish the conditions of creative fidelity that sustain the fulfillment of vows. And even under the most ideal conditions marriage implies duties that sometimes go against inclination. Luther, a mask of God in his role as father, seems not to have been inclined to change those stinking diapers.

Vows, general rules, presumptions in favor of certain values, the application of moral principles such as distributive justice, the assessments of probable consequences of various courses of action, and other procedures of moral life are applicable in the relations of marriage and family. But the interdependence is so intimate and intense, the awareness of particular features of self and others so detailed, and many of the consequences of action so sensitive that it is often not possible to avoid moral ambiguity. Persons are more than members of classes that can be dealt with in rational moral syllogisms. Feelings as well as reason enter in, and thus the process of discernment is required.

"Schools" for Piety and Morality

Family life is where we first and most formatively develop as persons, and where we come to early recognition of duties and obligations to others, as well as of the obligations others have to us. Family is the earliest school for the senses of dependence, gratitude, obligation, remorse and repentance, possibility, and direction that ground piety and ultimately theology, and morality and ultimately ethical thought. Thus the quality of married and family life is crucial.

Our earliest experiences of dependence occur in infancy and childhood: for the physical sustenance that enables us to survive, for the affection that gives us a sense of well-being, and for the stimulation that develops our minds. We have come into being without any choice of our own; we cannot sustain and nourish our lives, even in adulthood, without reliance upon powers beyond our capacities to control. In marriage as well, there is mutual reliance in mutual dependence. Gratitude flows from the consciousness of the contributions each makes to the well-being of the other and to the well-being of family. There are obligations in our mutual expectations that others will fulfill their roles and sustain our human spirits. Our earliest experiences of remorse are evoked by familial relations. We realize that we are not self-sufficient beings as individuals, and that we come to some completion in binding ourselves in interdependence with others. The most basic senses that are central to theocentric piety and morality are developed, sustained, and nourished in marriage and family life.

The significance of these very natural experiences is expanded in religious and moral life. The wider and deeper meanings of them extend beyond the intimacy of family to become the basis for application in religious life: not only in family do we depend upon powers beyond our control and recognize that our destiny is not fully in our own hands. We gain insight into the interdependence of other aspects of life and things with each other, and are led to experience the reality of God as the ultimate power that brings all things into being, sustains them, bears down upon them, and creates conditions of possibility for them. The moral meanings also extend beyond family: the forms of interdependence in which we learn gratitude and obligations, the possibilities as well as restraints placed on our lives and those of others, are more universal in reality. We gain insight into the much wider significance of what we experience in family, and we abstract from these experiences to articulate ends, principles, and ideals.

From a theocentric perspective, then, family and marriage are communities and institutions of extraordinary significance. In them we have our most intimate experiences of what is ultimately the divine ordering of life in the world. The quality of those experiences is formative for our religious and moral lives. They can be construed theologically and given generalized ethical significance. Marriage and family are "schools" of theocentric piety and fidelity.

Marriage, Family, and Social Ethics

I have noted that marriage and family are institutions interdependent with other institutions of society. They are affected deeply by the social ordering of which they are a part, as well as affecting it in some ways. They are not self-sufficient communities and institutions. This perception is a basis for moral and political concerns about the relationships and qualities of life in the wider society of which any family is a part. Families are "acted upon" as much as they are agents, and thus the relationships through which they are acted upon and the institutions and values that act upon them must be taken into account and attended to. Because families are parts of larger wholes the relations within, and quality of, the larger whole is a matter of deep concern for the sake of the family. It is in the best interests of the designated whole—the wider society—to provide conditions for the well-being of the part—family life. If the well-being of individual persons and families suffers deprivations, there are affects upon the whole, the wider society. Such is the divine ordering through the patterns and process of interdependence of life in the world.

Many inferences can be drawn from this. As part of a larger social whole, the life of the family is affected by the values that are generated and propagated by educational institutions, mass advertising, the media of mass communication, religious institutions, and others. It is not possible in a pluralistic society, especially in one that has developed powerful means of communication, for the family to insulate itself against wider cultural forces even if it desires to do so. Very few culturally isolated communities, such as the Amish, survive in our society. In my judgment it is a mistake to permit such current movements in American life as the Moral Majority to monopolize the concern for the effects of social and cultural institutions on marriage and family life. To say this is not to agree with all the values they wish to defend and certainly not with the means they use to defend them. But it is to recognize that there are difficult and complex issues to be analyzed and responded to if the family is to have the formative influence it has a right to have on the development of children.

I shall cite only one example, moral education. It is no accident that in both the social-scientific literature and in discussions of educational policy the subject of moral education has become more prominent in recent decades.[8] Whether correctly or not, it was long assumed that the family and religious institutions together with what was an admittedly Protestant-dominated public education system transmitted the moral values that were deemed worthy. The Roman Catholic Church and some Protestant bodies, e.g., some Lutheran and Reformed denominations, recognized that an alternative to the public education system was essential for the distinctive features of their religious and moral outlooks to be kept alive. American society, legally and socially, accommodated to this need. The Protestant characteristics of the public schools, with their prayers and religious celebrations had to be altered in the face of large numbers of Jewish, Roman Catholic, and secularized children attending them. Religious communities saw a decline in their proportionate influence in the culture at the same time. The power of the mass media, and particularly television, made it increasingly difficult to isolate families from the very effective portrayals of alternative values and life-styles to those they wished to sustain. Necessarily the issue of moral education took on new importance, including the development of programs and curricula for moral education in the public schools. The recent development of Protestant "Christian schools" is a defensive response to what is, from my perspective, a very real problem in North American society.

I shall not attempt to propose a solution to this problem here. I do, however, stress its great importance. Any proposed solution runs quickly into conflicts of values in North American and all modern Western societies. The freedom of the means of mass communications is properly defended as essential to the political and social well-being of the society; the line to be drawn on the right to censor is difficult to determine, and the difficulty is apparent in the decisions of the courts on controversial matters. The shifting balance of power from church and family to educational systems and particularly to mass communications in regard to the generation, sustenance, and propagation of moral and social values is difficult to alter given legitimate protections for the freedom of institutions that are gaining increasing influence. Certainly one effect has been to place a different strain on the functions of marriage and family in regard to their stewardship of the moral values they seek to sustain. The problem is real, and it is an error to permit only the most reactionary religious forces to raise and provide solutions to it.

8. For a recent symposium on moral development and moral education, see *Ethics* 92, no. 2 (April 1982).

Another inference from the analysis of the relation of the family as a part to the wider whole of the society pertains to social policy, particularly to the fair distribution of rights and benefits. The civil rights movement was a response that had some effect on the application of distributive justice in the areas of education, access to public facilities, and health care. Families were deprived both by social custom and by legal restraints of "equal" access to the same quality of resources available to other families, and this affected the opportunities they were able to provide. Necessary conditions for certain aspects of family life and development, especially visible when comparisons with other groups were made, were unfairly inaccessible to many families by virtue of their ethnic identifications.

Some of the arguments for the enlargement of the range of application of more egalitarian concepts of social justice are made on relatively deontic ethical grounds. Equals should be treated equally, and with reference to the conditions necessary for respect of persons, equal opportunities should be provided. Fundamental human needs have to be met for the sake of the capacities to be moral persons, and when the families and individuals concerned cannot meet these through no fault of their own it is the duty of the wider society to do so. In Roman Catholic social thought this is recognized in the principle of subsidiarity: if the family, a subsidiary social unit in size and social power, cannot meet the needs of its members, the state and also voluntary institutions have an obligation to do so.

But concerns for social justice also have consequentialist backing. Failure to provide certain necessary conditions is detrimental not only to families as parts of a larger society but also the the common good of the society as a whole. Thus the ethics of family life has to extend to the public-policy sector; the concern for social justice is essential. It necessarily confronts the conditions of limited resources and the limit of the right of external institutions to intervene in individual family life; moral conflicts are unavoidable. Both for the sake of the common good of disadvantaged families and the good of the society of which they are a part, a heightened concern for distributive justice is required. This concern is backed not only be deontic principles but also by consequentialist concerns and by the "natural" interdependence of the processes and patterns of life which are a manifestation ultimately of the ordering power of God. Ambiguity and conflicts of values are bound to be met in every particular context in which justice is applied to policies that affect family life. But such are the conditions of finitude. Social institutions have a collective moral responsibility to attempt to reduce the ambiguity, resolve the conflicts, and see that the costs of the pursuit of justice are fairly distributed. Political and social institutions of wider scope and power are essential to carry out the ordering of life in the world, even for the sake of the family, and the well-being of family life affects wider political and social institutions and processes.

The Religious and Moral Wisdom of the Marriage Service

The traditional Christian marriage service continues to bear important wisdom—religious and theological, moral and ethical. The social circumstances of most modern marriages are different from assumptions of relatively stable and self-contained parishes, and certain biblical analogies that are used are of significance only from more traditional points of view. But the recognition of the social character of marriage, and thus of the relationships of the married couple to wider communities, continues to be of great importance. The service expresses what persons are enabled and required to be and to do in the patterns and processes of interdependence in married and family life. While from the perspective of contemporary individualistic libertarianism some aspects of the service that I shall praise are judged to be undue interference on the freedom of the two principals, I shall argue otherwise.

I have chosen "The Form of Solemnization of Matrimony" from *The Book of Common Prayer* as a basis for expounding the significance of the tradition.[9] I shall not quote the entire service, only portions of it that pertain to my interpretation of marriage.

Prior to the actual marriage service is the publication of the banns. On three Sundays before the marriage the priest says, "If any of you know cause, or just impediment, why these two persons should not be joined together in holy Matrimony, ye are to declare it." This is the first point to which individualistic libertarians might object; from that perspective it appears to be an invitation to undue meddling in the lives of two individuals. The publication of the banns, however, takes account of the relationships that the couple already have to the members of their parish community, and the recognition that they will continue to be related in interdependence with others beyond themselves. The request that persons declare any knowledge of impediments to the marriage is, I believe, intended to serve the well-being of the couple as well as that of the community. Marriage, while surely a covenant between two persons, is a concern of the community. The interests of the couple and of the community are interrelated.

On the day of the marriage the couple "shall come into the body of the Church with their friends and neighbours." Again the sociality of marriage is taken into account; the vows are taken in a community of those with whom the couple have especially close relationships. Not only do the friends and neighbors celebrate the event with the couple; they are also the social witnesses to the vows. The vows are not secret and private, but public. The community can expect compliance with them.

The service begins with the familiar words of the priest. "Dearly beloved, we are gathered together here in the sight of God, and in the face of

9. *The Book of Common Prayer* (Oxford: Oxford University Press, n.d.), pp. 341–45.

this congregation, to join together this Man and this Woman in holy Matrimony, which is an honourable estate, instituted of God in the time of man's innocency." Following this, the union of Christ and the church, the miracle at Cana, and the commendation of St. Paul are adduced, "and therefore [it] is not by any to be enterprised, nor taken in hand, unadvisedly, lightly, or wantonly, to satisfy men's carnal lusts and appetites, like brute beasts that have no understanding; but reverently, discreetly, advisedly, soberly, and in the fear of God; duly considering the causes for which Matrimony was ordained."

The religious and theological significance of marriage is invoked in these words. To be gathered "in the sight of God" is to call attention to the place that the human life of marriage has in the wider and deeper ordering of all things. It invokes a consciousness of the fact that what is about to take place is not merely of significance to the two principals, or even to the society of which they are a part, but also to the divine ordering. To the religious consciousness there is already both a note of thanksgiving for life that is brought together in a new way and a note of awe in the public recognition of the event. Marriage is "instituted of God in the time of man's innocency." It is, as many theologians have expounded, an "order of creation" even before the "fall"; or in keeping with the thought of the present work, it is part of the ordering work of God through the patterns and processes of interdependence in life. Its functions are far deeper than merely the joys and pleasures of the principals and even of the society. To be married is to participate in a distinctive way in the creative, sustaining, and ordering work of God.

The moral and ethical significance is also invoked in these words. The gathering is not only in the sight of God but also "in the face of this company," the friends and neighbors of the couple. The seriousness of their commitment to each other is vividly stated: it is to be taken in hand "advisedly, soberly, and in the fear of God." Time-binding commitments, like oaths, are matters of utmost moral seriousness. (There is an interesting archaism in what I have quoted. Marriage is not to be "enterprised" "to satisfy men's carnal lusts and appetites, like brute beasts that have no understanding." Actually, the sexual activity of the "brute beasts" is naturally more restricted to the processes of procreation than that of man, and thus the simile is badly chosen.)

What are the "causes" or purposes for which marriage is "ordained" by God? "First . . . for the procreation of children, to be brought up in the fear and nurture of the Lord, and to praise his holy Name." One notes that the purpose of species survival is not the sole end named here; the children are "to be brought up. . . ." A specific religious intention of their nurturing is the only one indicated in the service, but it warrants extension to other aspects. The responsibilities of parenthood are basic to what is stated; parents are not merely the transmitters of species continuity but are the stewards of their offspring. There is a "charge" here to be the caretakers of the spiritual and moral welfare of children. In modern conditions one might draw from this the possible conclusion that if the couple for significant reasons cannot become responsible parents they ought not to have children. Intergenerational responsibilities come naturally from the interdependence of life, and to procreate is to undertake those responsibilities.

"Secondly, It was ordained for a remedy against sin, to avoid fornication; that such persons as have not the gift of continency might marry, and keep themselves undefiled members of Christ's body." "Nature" is recognized in two of its aspects here; "continency" is not expected of all persons, but is rather a "gift"; only those who have the special gift are expected to remain continent. But those who do not have the gift are subject to sexual temptation, and thus "fallen" nature is taken into account. Sexual intercourse is a moral matter; conditions of moral responsibility must be met. Contemporary sexual mores are obviously very different from the expectation to avoid fornication, and, interestingly, even in some Christian ethical writings not only mores but the ethics of sexuality condone (if not encourage) sex outside of marriage for sake of self-fulfillment. Certainly, however, even to modern sexual mores this "cause" of marriage charges that moral accountability is important, that sexuality is not amoral because it is "natural." It also indicates a concern for "purity," that is for a proper dimension of individual moral and spiritual integrity, in sexual life.

I note that even in the liberation of sexual activity that Western societies have undergone, justified in part by the presumed bad consequences of sexual repression, there are new forms of "sins" that disturb persons. While fornication is not as generally judged to be immoral, the exploitation of persons for the sake of sexual gratification alone is judged to be morally wrong. It is demeaning to the meaning of personal life, and surely not a solid basis for sustaining human relationships, for persons to treat one another merely as objects for physical gratification. The "sexual sins" are now properly seen to be more than the breaking of traditional rules of moral conduct; a purely "act" morality relative to moral rules does not get at the deeper human faults that sexual activity can manifest. The sins, whose subtlety was always present, are now brought to consciousness so that harrassment and exploitation are seen to be morally irresponsible not only in casual relationships but even in marriage itself. I note this to indicate that liberation from traditional sexual morality has not eliminated the need for remedies against sin; nor is marriage a remedy against such sin. Those protests against exploitation are evoked not so much from a morally high-minded principle such as treating others never merely as means to an end but as ends in themselves, though this is applicable. They are evoked by a deep natural revulsion on the part of some persons, especially women, who have been subject to sexual exploitation; there is a violation of their "natures" as human persons. Indeed, from the perspective of the present work, these are violations of the ordering of life that is required for proper relations between persons, and the proper self-fulfillment of persons in their relations to each other. Sexuality remains a locus in which the human fault finds ready manifestation; remedies for sin are not antiquated. Conditions of moral responsibility are properly indicated, and attitudes, principles, rules of conduct, and moral ideals follow from them as much now as they did in earlier times.

"Thirdly, It was ordained for the mutual society, help, and comfort, that the one ought to have of the other, both in prosperity and adversity." If the end of procreation is based on Genesis 2:28, "Be fruitful and multiply," this is based on Genesis 2:18, "It is not good that the man should be alone; I will make him a helper fit for him." It recognizes the social character of human existence; the mutuality of relationships in the intimacy of marriage meets human needs. The fact that persons have deep needs for each other is not a mark of human weakness; it is not as if the partners of a marriage could be self-sufficient so their relationships to each other would overflow from the superabundance of their individual strengths. Indeed, the statement says that "mutual society, help, and comfort" are part of the ordering of life by God. The purpose is not simply procreation but a mutual fulfillment that comes from all aspects of the common life that they share.

It is on the basis of this end of marriage that most Protestants and in practice many Roman Catholics take a very positive attitude toward sexual relations within marriage without the intention of "being open to the transmission of new life." Sexual intercourse is both an expression of this mutual society and means of fostering its vitality. Indeed, in the Puritan tradition "mutual society" was seen to be the first end of marriage. John Milton in fact laments the fact that the church made the vows of marriage so unbreakable that persons must remain married who "through their different tempers, thought, and constitutions . . . can neither be to one another a remedy against loneliness, nor live in any union or contentment all their days." For Milton, "God in the first ordaining of marriage, taught us to what end he did it, with words expressly implying the apt and cheerful conversation of man with woman, to comfort and refresh him against the evil of solitary life" and only afterwards mentioned "the purpose of generation . . . as being but a secondary end in dignity."[10] Whether the biblical interpretation is right is not a concern here; the position that Milton represents in making mutuality the prime purpose of marriage acknowledges a profound aspect of the divine ordering of life through the interdependencies of nature.

If life with and for each other is central to marriage, then the forms and

10. John Milton, "The Doctrine and Discipline of Divorce," in *Complete Poetry and Selected Prose of John Milton* (New York: Random House, The Modern Library, n.d.), p. 625.

patterns of common life which nourish mutuality have to be sustained. In a sense, what follows in the questions that the priest asks the couple is a statement of the conditions not only for the sake of children but also for the good shared in common. The failure to nourish and meet these conditions is destructive both of individuals and the common good of the marriage.

Before these questions are asked, however, there is another query that recognizes the communal or public character of marriage that the banns express. The couple have come to be joined in a "holy estate." "Therefore if any man can shew any just cause, why they may not lawfully be joined together, let him now speak or else hereafter for ever hold his peace." This is in effect a moral command; the friends and neighbors have been given their final chance to inform all gathered of any impediments to the marriage. A temporal transition is recognized; if they have nothing to say or dare not say what they might desire to say, they are thereafter not to interfere, gossip, or in other ways denigrate the couple and their marriage. (When I conduct marriage services I always scan the congregation and remain silent long enough for persons to respond. The embarrassing silence, I believe, makes the point.)

Next follows a similar charge to the couple. "I require and charge you both . . . that if either of you know any impediment, why ye may not be lawfully joined together in Matrimony, ye do now confess it." The priest then declares that if there are impediments, the marriage is not valid in the eyes of God or in the civil law. There is a history in Christian thought about the impediments to a valid marriage, and so the charge has a basically legal connotation both with reference to canon and civil law. But the implications can be broadened; the couple have a final opportunity to confess reasons why they believe the marriage is not proper for them. Here too one can infer that the forthcoming vows are so serious that reasons for not taking them should be considered one more time, and that once they are taken, in a sense, the past is past and should not be brought in to disturb the present and the future.

The instructions in the order I am using are very specific, if any impediments are stated. "[I]f any man do alledge and declare any impediment . . . ; and will be bound, and sufficient sureties with him, to the parties; or else put in a Caution (to the full value of such charges as the persons to be married do thereby sustain) to prove his allegation": then the marriage is deferred until the truth is "tried." This requirement has the value of indicating the seriousness of raising charges at this point; the presumption is that the couple have cleared all possible impediments and thus anyone stating any must have solid proof.

Only after "the air has been cleared" does the priest ask for a declaration of intention and will. To the man, and then to the woman (with changes in wording), he asks,

> Wilt thou have this Woman to thy wedded wife, to live together after God's ordinance in the holy estate of Matrimony? Wilt thou love her, comfort her, honour, and keep her in sickness and in health; and, forsaking all others, keep thee only unto her, so long as ye both shall live?

The form of love gets specification in this question. The couple will enter into an "estate" which is "prior" to their commitment to each other; they undertake to meet the requirements of a social status and institution, namely, marriage. To do so is to accept the claims of that status and that institution, to live together according to its requirements. The second question specifies further the obligations that are undertaken in that status: love and comfort of one another, honoring one another, keeping each other in both adverse and easy circumstances, and confining one's most intimate relationships (more than sexual intercourse) exclusively to the other for the rest of one's life. Each consents to accepting these conditions and obligations; each answers "I will." A voluntary binding occurs to meet the requirements that tradition and experience sustain for a faithful and loving relationship. Mutual trustworthiness is consented to, which becomes a basis for mutual trust; the enabling love is explicated in its requirements to be sustained for the sake of each other and for the sake of the institution of marriage.

Next comes the question that ought more properly be asked of the parents of both the bride and the groom. "Who giveth this Woman to be married to this Man?" That the service as it is implies a traditional lower status of the woman cannot be denied, but even as it is, there is wisdom and power in this moment. It acknowledges a profound shift in primary loyalties and in social identification. In the past each "belonged" to their parental families, and duties and obligations as well as loyalties that were part of that relationship are now significantly altered. The parents and the couple both symbolically acknowledge that shift, a temporal and social one, in this moment in the drama of the service. This is further symbolized by actions that are never visible to the congregation. "The Minister, receiving the Woman at her father's . . . hands, shall cause the Man with his right hand to take the Woman by her right hand" before the vows are taken. What has normally already taken place between the couple, namely, a love which alters the ordering of their other loves, here is sealed. Restraints of intervention on the part of parental families are implied. The declaration of intention wisely comes before it. The vows wisely follow only after this. It is a decisive step between the declaration of intention and the actual taking of vows.

I quote only the man's vows; the woman's are identical except for the substitution of "husband" for "wife."

> I (Name) take thee (Name) to my wedded wife, to have and to hold from this day forward, for better for worse, for richer for

> poorer, in sickness and health, to love and to cherish, till death us do part, according to God's holy ordinance; and thereto I plight thee my troth.

The vows succinctly express what I described earlier in this chapter as the conditions that have to be met not only to fulfill obligations to one another but also to sustain the enabling powers of love in marriage. The variety of conditions stated indicate that faithfulness is assured in adverse as well as pleasant circumstances. The vows provide the order of faithful love; they include a vow to love and to cherish, that is to maintain the conditions in which love can be sustained and can flourish. The stipulation of these conditions, including "till death do us part," has the effect of making the vows virtually unconditional; that is, none of the adversities are to be excuses for breaking them as long as both live.

The vows are followed by the ring ceremony. The service I am using provides only that the man gives a ring to the woman, another indication of the subordinate status of women that was assumed at the time it was composed. But the contemporary double-ring service bears the same significance. The instructions at this point are intricate and have symbolic significance. After the woman takes her vows, the couple again separate their hands. The ring is placed "upon the book" and the priest takes it to "deliver it unto the Man, to put it upon the fourth finger of the Woman's left hand." The fact that the ring is "delivered" by the priest suggests the social and religious sanctioning of the relationship. The ring itself is a public, visible sign of the commitment: to all who see it the commitment is known. "With this Ring I thee wed, with my body I thee worship, and with all my worldly goods I thee endow," is said by the giver of the ring. Again we have stipulations of what are judged to be requirements of faithful love.

This is followed by an intercessory prayer which reads in part, "So these persons may surely perform and keep the vow and covenant betwixt them made, . . . and may ever remain in perfect love and peace together, and live according to thy laws. . . . " This is the only point in the service where perfection is invoked, but even here it is to be a gift of the blessing of God; it is not stated as an ideal to which the couple is to aspire on their own.

Then the priest again becomes the actor, and joins their hands and says, "Those whom God hath joined let no man put asunder." The congregation of friends and neighbors are not to sunder the relationship that has been conscientiously and voluntarily undertaken before God, nor are the couple to permit this to occur.

The pronouncement follows.

> Forasmuch as (Name) and (Name) have consented together in holy wedlock, and have witnessed the same before God and this company, and thereto have given and pledged their troth either to the other, and have declared the same by giving and receiving of a

> Ring, and by joining of hands, I pronounce that they be Man and Wife together. . . .

This pronouncement recalls what has gone before, and stipulates the conditions that make the marriage binding. The couple have consented, they were not coerced; they have made public witness of their consent before God and the people; they have both given and pledged their faithfulness to each other; they have exchanged a visible sign of their vows in the rings. All that is left to do is to offer the blessing.

I have expounded on this traditional "Solemnization of Matrimony" to show that it bears lasting significance not because it is part of a religious and social tradition but because in its words and movements it articulates what God is enabling and requiring persons to be and to do as participants in the patterns and processes of interdependence of married and family life. Its religious and moral wisdom is deep and well-grounded, and that is no doubt why it has become traditional. It is not archaic but timely, and is backed by the theocentric perspective and the ethics following from it which have been developed in this book.

6

Suicide

The ethical arguments against suicide are cogent, and like ethical arguments about other matters they differ according to the moral and religious perspectives of the writers. On various bases one can argue that suicide is an immoral act. In the religious contexts of the West it has been interpreted as a sin against God as well. Indeed, in some traditions it is a mortal sin, one that so disorients the person from his or her fulfillment in union with God that eternal punishment is merited. Yet there are probably very few persons in our society who are prepared to make a strong moral condemnation of a person who takes his or her own life. Explanations that are given for the act in particular cases border on or become, if not justifications for it, at least excusing conditions. It is quite properly seen to be a tragic act; the person does what is irreversible and irrevocable, i.e. dies, because he or she thinks it is the right thing to do, and has no other choice. Or it is seen to be an act of a person who has by virtue of "mental illness" lost the capacities to think rationally; it is an act done under the domination of passion rather than reason, and like other such acts the agent has limited accountability for it. Limitation of accountability means limitation of culpability, and thus our judgments are not harsh. It is precisely the ambivalence that many, if not most, persons have about judging suicide on strictly moral grounds that makes the issue worth pondering. Indeed, ambivalence toward it may reflect a certain kind of moral ambiguity about the act itself.

I shall in this chapter review briefly the arguments about suicide made by some of the authors who have served as benchmarks.[1] Following that I shall discuss several important issues that complicate the matter, and engage in an empathetic description of some of the circumstances in which persons who take their own lives find themselves. Finally, I shall interpret the circumstances in a way that follows from the present work, and indicate some of the conclusions.

Arguments from the Literature

Karl Barth

Karl Barth's assessment of suicide would be maddeningly equivocal to most philosophers. Yet the ambiguities which he does not resolve reasonably follow from his theology, and perhaps other theological positions must be satisfied with less than definitive conclusions as well. The basic theological grounds for Barth's ethics were discussed in chapter 2, but some rehearsal of them is proper here since one cannot understand his discussion of suicide without having them in mind.

1. For a philosophical analysis, see David Novak, *Suicide and Morality: The Theories of Plato, Aquinas, and Kant and Their Relevance for Suicidology* (New York: Scholars Studies Press, 1975).

"[L]ife is a loan from God entrusted to man for His service."[2] We do not own it, free and clear; we are stewards of life.

> Temporal life is certainly not the highest of all goods. Just because it belongs to God, man may be forbidden to will its continuation at all costs. He may be ordered to risk and expose it to varying degrees of danger. . . . Wanting to live on at all costs can then be only an elemental, sinful and rebellious desire. . . . It may be that he must offer himself.[3]

The stage for ambiguity is already set by this. The question is why or why not suicide is justifiable when temporal life is not the highest good, when it is given to be in service of God's purposes. The moral question is necessarily set within a theological construal of life; it is a religious as well as moral, a theological as well as ethical, issue. To convey the sense of Barth's discussion I follow the order he has given it. Barth comes to ethical conclusions not by moral syllogisms but by a dialectical process of "on the one hand" and "on the other hand."

The first descriptive statement is of the freedom that distinguishes man from animals. Man "can freely dispose of his life. He is so strictly the subject of his life that he is under no compulsion to continue to live." "He can will and achieve his own non-being." Suicide is the "most radical means of procuring for oneself justice and freedom." The capacity is a mark of human freedom; the paradox involved is that the act by which one asserts one's freedom throws it away.[4]

In the light of this paradox, theologians have adduced that a religious issue is involved. The self-sovereignty that the suicide exercises is a refusal of the divine sovereignty, and particularly of the help of God. This is a ground for the unqualified No that most of the theological tradition has given to suicide.

According to Barth, some mistaken inferences have been drawn from this No. "From this unqualified No, of course, there ought not to follow, as there has, an absolute condemnation, with subsequent ecclesiastical and civil discrimination against suicide."[5] We cannot know what is involved in the choice to take one's life. "But what right have we to isolate the last moment of human existence from that which precedes, and to judge a man by this moment alone?"[6] Human beings cannot know or even assume as probable that the act was taken in rebellion against God, "and therefore whether every case of self-destruction is really suicide in the sense of

2. Karl Barth, *Church Dogmatics*, III/4, p. 402.
3. Ibid., p. 401.
4. Ibid., p. 403.
5. Ibid.
6. Ibid., pp. 403–4.

self-murder."[7] Indeed, Barth casts aspersion on theologians and moralists who really do not know what human affliction goes on because they are occupied with exegetical, dogmatic, and pastoral theory.

After these warnings, however, Barth seems to become unequivocal again.

> We must start with the unequivocal fact that when self-destruction is the exercise of a supposed and usurped sovereignty of man over himself it is a frivolous, arbitrary and criminal violation of the commandment, and therefore self-murder. To deprive a man of his life is a matter for the One who gave it and not for the man himself.[8]

Human beings are not to decide for themselves whether their lives are successes or failures, tolerable or intolerable, worthwhile or worthless. Because we are not authorized to be our own judges, we are not free to take our own lives.[9]

A counterpoint, however, follows. "[E]ven suicide in this sense is not as such unforgivable sin." "If there is forgiveness of sins at all . . . there is surely forgiveness for suicide."[10] God weighs the whole human heart, and the judgment of his righteousness is mercy. "He judges the content of the last hour in the context of the whole."[10] Even a morally righteous person or a very sincere believer might be thrust into confusion and uncertainty, and thus commit suicide.

Counterpoint follows. "Here as elsewhere, however, God's forgiveness is no excuse, much less justification, for sin." By taking one's own life, one takes what does not belong to oneself, and thus violates the commandment against murder. Forgiveness does not make this legitimate. "Suicide cannot be extenuated, excused or justified." Freedom before God is not freedom to take one's own life.[11]

Barth then turns to an empathetic account of the person who contemplates suicide. Just to think about it evidences that a person is "in some way in the darkness of affliction."[12] The affliction is theological and religious; God is hidden from the person as his or her God; the person sees himself as alone and sovereign, as surrounded by a dreadful void. In these circumstances what is going to prevent the person from acting? "Certainly not an ideal, nor a mere imperative however serious, nor an empty prohibition even though it be taken from the Bible, where incidentally we look in vain

7. Ibid., p. 404.
8. Ibid.
9. Ibid.
10. Ibid. p. 405.
11. Ibid.
12. Ibid., p. 406.

for any express prohibition of suicide, nor a moral argument, however conclusive."[13] Nor can one accuse the person of being a coward, since to take one's life might require more courage than not to. Indeed, persons might have good reasons for suicide; they might see it as serving the good of society or of their neighbors, relatives, and friends.

Suicide comes out of darkness, but into the darkness "shines only one light." "It is not a 'Thou shalt live' but a 'Thou mayest live' which none can say to another nor to himself, but which God Himself has spoken and continues to speak."[14] The will to live is derived from God's gracious Yes to man. The truth of life is not that we must live, but that we may live; the will to live is the will to be what we are permitted to be. Barth continues to describe, in terms familiar to his readers, the glorious grace of God to whom man belongs; indeed, "all the angels of God are on our side, and there is for us inexhaustible, illimitable and unfailing forgiveness, help and hope."[15] Suicide is seen in the light of this grace not only to be reprehensible; "it is already rejected."[16]

Again, however, what seems to be an unequivocal No is qualified. There are exceptional cases. "Self-destruction does not have to be the taking of one's own life. Its meaning and intention might well be a definite if extreme form of the self-offering required of man."[17] The first possibility of this is that in a particular case the act might not be the assertion of self-sovereignty over God's sovereignty or an act of futility, but might be an act of obedience. "Who can really know whether God might not occasionally ask back from man in this form the life that belongs to Him?"[18] One cannot arbitrarily deny that this might occur; it seems to have occurred in the case of Samson. But an even more arbitrary assumption would be that exceptions are common; "[t]hough not impossible, the exception is rare and extraordinary."[19] And even where the exception might be valid, it does not mean that human beings can decide it. Occasions for martyrdom are the second possible type of exception. Barth raises an example used by Kant; whether one is justified to take one's life if under torture one might betray others and a cause. Barth says, "He can indeed have the freedom to do this if

13. Ibid.
14. Ibid., pp. 406–7.
15. Ibid., p. 408.
16. At this point Barth has a lengthy excursus in which he adduces evidence for his conviction that nowhere in the Bible is suicide explicitly forbidden, a point which he sees to be painful for all who want to interpret the Bible moralistically. He discusses the suicides of King Saul, David's counselor Ahithophel, and Judas. Only subsequently does he briefly note the death of Samson which for him, as for Augustine and Thomas Aquinas, is a suicide secretly commanded by God. I shall not elaborate on Barth's exegesis of these passages.
17. Ibid., p. 410.
18. Ibid.
19. Ibid., p. 411.

God gives it. And he should then use it joyfully, resolutely and with a good rather than doubtful conscience."[20]

The final point, however, echoes the more stringent aspects of the discussion.

> If a man kills himself without being ordered to do so, then his action is murder. God may forgive him, but it is still murder, so that none can will to perpetrate it with uplifted head if he has faith in the gracious God who forgives sins. This warning may aptly be our last word on the subject.[21]

Barth's position can be summarized in a non-Barthian manner as follows (although logical difficulties cannot be eliminated). There is a No given to suicide. The backing of that No is not made on some of the Aristotelian grounds adduced by Thomas Aquinas,the utilitarian grounds that Sidgwick offers to support common sense morality, or grounds Kant adduces in the critical ethics. Barth backs the negative in the following ways: (a) life is a loan from God; it is on loan to man and thus man is not self-sovereign; (b) life is to be used for the service of God, man is a steward; (c) God is gracious and thus commands "Thou mayest live"; (d) man is not the judge of the worthwhileness of any human life. There are three grounds which create the possibility of suicide: (a) man is free and thus has a sovereignty over his or her life out of which a decision for suicide might come; (b) continuation of physical temporal life is not the highest good, and therefore suicide could be done for a higher good; (c) since the purpose of life is to serve God, conceivably God might be served by the self-destruction of a human person. Yet none of these possibilities implies a divine Yes to suicide; it is always a sin.

There might, however, be two exceptions: (a) suicide might be an act of obedience to the command of God because God might choose this way to end a particular person's life; (b) acts of martyrdom might be justified, but only if commanded by God. There are possible excusing conditions: the affliction and confusion of the person at the time he or she acts. Because of these possible exceptions and excusing conditions, because of the necessary ignorance of human beings about why a person chooses to take his or her life, and because God forgives and certainly does not judge a whole life by its

20. Ibid., p. 412.

21. Ibid., p. 413. It is not Barth's last word in this volume. In his discussion of euthanasia he affirms that self-inflicted death, even when the means are indirect, is suicide. Ibid., p. 426. In the discussion of war Barth writes, "War reveals the basically chaotic character of the so-called peaceful will, efforts and achievements of man. It exposes his radical inability to be master without becoming not merely a slave but his own destroyer, and therefore fundamentally a suicide." Ibid., p. 452. Developments since Barth wrote this underscore this point.

last moment, Barth takes a very nonjudgmental attitude toward those who commit suicide.[22]

Like all of Barth's moral arguments, this is a theological one. While one might attempt to extract the moral argument from its religious context, a radical alteration would be required. One might say that there is a strong presumption against suicide and that the conditions for overriding the presumption are stated, or that there is a rule against it with applications to show how it does not apply in certain circumstances. Barth's own language of "points to be considered" is of course most appropriate. But all of these, if wrenched from the theological and religious context, radically alter the significance of the act of self-destruction. God's relation to man, not ethics, is the proper context for Barth. With Barth's discussion as a benchmark, one can look at other writings to see how they resemble or differ from it.

Thomas Aquinas

Thomas's principal account of suicide comes in the "Treatise on Justice and Prudence" under the vice of murder. I shall not analyze the argument in full detail, but expound its main points.[23]

Thomas's third principal argument against suicide is a purely theological one based on revelation and is the same as one of Barth's. "[L]ife is God's gift to man, and is subject to His power, Who kills and makes to live. Hence whoever takes his own life, sins against God." God alone has the right to decide the time of death. The argument at this point is explicitly backed not by a theology of creation, though one is implied, but by a biblical citation: Deut. 32:39, "I will kill and I will make to live." The first two principal arguments are drawn from Aristotle, though in the first Thomas uses both natural law and charity. "[E]verything naturally loves itself" and thus naturally keeps itself in being. Thus suicide is "contrary to the inclination of nature, and to charity whereby every man should love himself." It is always a mortal sin, "being contrary to the natural law and to charity." The second is a part/whole argument. "Now every man is part of the community,

22. Barth adduces Dietrich Bonhoeffer's discussion of suicide in partial support of his own position. Bonhoeffer, like Barth, notes the importance of freedom. "Without freedom to sacrifice one's life in death, there can be no freedom towards God, there can be no human life." The wrongfulness of suicide "is to be arraigned not before the forum of morality or of men but solely before the forum of God." The sin involved is lack of faith, and "[l]ack of faith is not a moral fault." In the lack of faith "man seeks his own justification, and has recourse to suicide as the last possible means of his own justification, because he does not believe in a divine justification." Thus Bonhoeffer strikes a more Lutheran theological note than does Barth. Like Barth, however, in the end he is very nonjudgmental about particular occasions in which the act is committed. Dietrich Bonhoeffer, *Ethics*, ed. Eberhard Bethge (London: SCM Press, 1955), pp. 122–28. Quotations are from p. 122, p. 123, and p. 124.

23. Thomas Aquinas, *Summa Theologiae*, 2a, 2ae, q. 64, art. 5; Benziger ed., 2:1468–70. For a fuller analysis of Thomas on suicide, see David Novak, *Suicide and Morality*, pp. 43–82. It has been suggested that by using materials from other articles in q. 64 and from q.40 (on war) one might make a case for ambiguity about suicide.

and so, as such, he belongs to the community." Hence the person who commits suicide injures the community.

In the replies to the objections, other arguments are made: suicide is contrary to charity and to justice; only a public authority can lawfully put a person to death, and thus no individual is to judge himself or herself; to bring death on oneself in order to escape affliction is to adopt a greater evil in order to avoid a lesser one; one deprives oneself of the time needed for repentance; it is not true courage to take one's life to avoid penal evils. To take one's life is a greater sin than being "violated," and thus a woman is not justified to commit suicide to avoid sexual sin. "Evil must not be done that good may come." In the case of Samson, Thomas follows Augustine and states that the Holy Spirit issued a secret command.

The form of the argument is palpably very different from Barth's. Thomas's conclusion is unequivocal; suicide is always wrong, and there are no excusing conditions and no self-justifying exceptions. Barth and Thomas share two principles based on the biblical material: life is a gift or loan from God, and God can command that the life of a particular person be taken by suicide (Samson). The theological difference that most marks their discussions is the meaning of God's grace and forgiveness. For Barth the judgment of God is not on the last moment of life but on the whole life, and the grace of God is sufficient to forgive the sin of suicide. For Thomas suicide is always a mortal sin, and since there is no time to repent there seems to be no possibility of forgiveness.

Barth is clearly more sensitive to the "affliction" and the confusion in which a person contemplates suicide. Indeed, Thomas's account is one of those on which Barth casts aspersion; the theologian is so interested in theory that he does not have the capacity to empathize with the situation of the person. Suicide becomes a class of actions the morality of which can be judged syllogistically, without any discernment of why the subject might consider it. There can be no excusing conditions because the choice is assumed to be a rational choice, i.e., one which can be made without the person making it being affected deeply by the anguish of human spirit out of which the choice generally comes.

While Thomas's arguments are mostly based on natural reason, one needs to note the theological grounding of nature that I discussed in chapter 2. God has ordered life so that every being seeks to perpetuate itself in life; God has ordered life so that persons are parts of wholes. As a moral argument, however, Thomas's makes several different appeals. Suicide is not only counter to nature, but to *caritas*, it is counter both to our natural love of being and to Christian love. An argument about the nature of social authority is adduced: only duly constituted authorities have the right to pass judgment on life. There is a religious appeal: one needs time to repent of one's sins, and this is precluded by suicide. Consequences are appealed to:

on the basis of the gradation of sins, suicide is a greater evil than sexual sins, and thus the consequences of committing it are graver. He makes a distinction between the appearance of courage and true courage; true courage faces the consequences of action regardless of the infliction of penal evils. Suicide is a misuse of human freedom; this basic point Thomas shares with Barth, and also with Bonhoeffer. To show why suicide is wrong, Thomas makes this variety of appeals, all in a mode of argumentation quite different from more biblically centered Protestant theology. The rule against suicide is unexceptionable; the language of "presumption against it" and "points to be considered," or "general rules," is not licit.

Mill and Sidgwick

In *Utilitarianism* John Stuart Mill discusses self-sacrifice without mentioning suicide as a possible form of it. He writes that it is noble to resign entirely one's own happiness if it is done for the sake of one's fellow creatures.

> All honor to those who can abnegate for themselves the personal enjoyment of life, when by such renunciation they contribute worthily to increase the amount of happiness in the world; but he who does it . . . for any other purpose, is no more deserving of admiration from the ascetic mounted on his pillar.[24]

The sacrifice is in itself not a good; one that does not tend to increase the sum total of happiness is wasted. I take it that one can infer from this that a suicide that can also be described as an act of martydrom would have a utilitarian justification on the basis of its consequences for the increase of good in the world.

Mill has very stringent proscriptions of any kind of paternalism in *On Liberty*. He writes that general rules for the most part ought to be observed so that persons know what to expect from each other, "but in each person's own concerns his individual spontaneity is entitled to free exercise." One can exhort others, but each agent is to be the final judge. "All errors which he is likely to commit against advice and warning are far outweighed by the evil of allowing others to constrain him to what they deem his good."[25] If this is taken to be a governing principle of social relations, it implies that the honoring of the liberty of another to commit suicide is a greater good than restraining him or her. In a sense the principle of liberty overrides the calculation of consequences.

Henry Sidgwick discusses suicide under the heading of "self-regarding virtues" and states that common sense, at least in modern Europe, recognizes a strict duty to preserve one's life even when its prospects are for

24. John Stuart Mill, *Utilitarianism*, chap. 2, in Burtt, *The English Philosophers*, p. 907.
25. Mill, *On Liberty*, chap. 4, in ibid., p. 1009.

more pain than pleasure. It would be praiseworthy to encounter death in the performance of a strict duty, or to preserve the life of another, or for an important gain for society, "but not merely in order to avoid pain to the agent."[26] Can this "commonsense" morality be justified?

Sidgwick is unwilling to give up the "apparent absoluteness" of commonsense morality, at least where the conditions stated above do not pertain. Yet it is not fully apparent whether other conditions might not justify self-destruction, such as those in which a life is foreseeable that is both miserable to oneself and a burden to others. Under such circumstances "the universal wrongness of suicide is at any rate not self-evident." But reasons apart from revelational theology can be adduced, and they are, of course, consequentialist in character. Sidgwick adduces two: one is a generalizability argument, namely, "that if any exceptions to the rule prohibiting suicide were allowed, dangerous encouragement would be give to the suicidal impulse in other cases in which [it] would really be a weak and cowardly dereliction of social duties." The second is that the toleration of it would probably encourage secret murders.[27]

It is clear that on the basis of utilitarian ethics the increase of good consequences in the world does justify forms of self-sacrifice. It is not precisely clear whether the agent's initiation of his or her own death for the sake of others is to be absolutely forbidden. If suicide as an act comes under the larger heading of self-sacrifice it would seem to be permitted in certain circumstances. The act would be described as martyrdom. But Sidgwick suggests other consequences that might be forthcoming from permitting suicide, especially if it is done to relieve oneself from pain and suffering. The permission might encourage suicide in less restrictive circumstances and increase "secret murders." One can at least infer from this that Sidgwick would find probable cause on consequentialist grounds for restraining the liberty of another to take his own life. He seems to be readier than Mill to justify the "common sense" morality of the West. Mill, it would seem, would permit a person to take his or her life in recognition of the person's liberty. He does not, however, extol suicide as the greatest possible act of human freedom.

Kant

In chapter 3 I noted Kant's discussions of suicide as evidence for the stringency of his ethics. Like Thomas Aquinas, Kant has strong moral arguments against it, but unlike Thomas his "casuistic questions" at the end of a late discussion seem to leave the issue unresolved in some particular cases.

26. Sidgwick, *Methods*, p. 327.
27. Ibid., p. 356.

One of the most extensive discussions is in the precritical *Lectures on Ethics*. Here Kant states and refutes two arguments that others have made to permit or tolerate suicide. One is the argument from freedom. As long as one does not violate the rights of others, one is a free agent and thus is free to take one's own life. Kant's rebuttal is that we have rights of disposal over our own bodies so long as our motives are for self-preservation, i.e., to preserve our persons. But taking one's life does not preserve one's person; it destroys it.[28] Man has the freedom to dispose over things, but when one disposes over oneself one has made a thing of oneself. This is a degradation of human life below the level of animal life. To be sure, it is better to sacrifice one's life than to violate one's morality and honor, but "[w]e can at all times go on living and doing our duty towards ourselves without having to do violence to ourselves."[29] We may be miserable in preserving our morality, but misery is no ground for suicide.

The second argument others have made for suicide is that one might find oneself in circumstances in which to continue to live is to deprive life of all value and virtue. Kant cites the case of Cato as the only plausible example. Cato took his life rather than fall into the hands of Caesar; if he had submitted, others would also submit, and the Romans would give up their defense of freedom. Kant writes, "had Cato faced any torments which Caesar might have inflicted upon him with a resolute mind and remained steadfast, it would have been noble of him; to violate himself was not so."[30] Freedom is the condition to be preserved, and it cannot subsist "except on a condition which is immutable. This condition is that man may not use his freedom against himself to his own destruction, but that . . . he should allow nothing external to limit it. Freedom thus conditioned is noble."[31]

In the discussion in the *Lectures* Kant argues against suicide on various grounds, some of which are similar to Thomas's. "We shrink in horror from suicide because all nature seeks it own preservation."[32] In the context of religion suicide opposes God's purposes; it is God's intention to preserve life, and we are to conform to that "until the time comes when God expressly commands us to leave this life."[33] But suicide is not abominable because God forbids it; God forbids it because it is abominable. The common-good argument that Thomas uses is, however, notably absent here.

In the critical writings the arguments are more economical and rigorous. In the *Foundations* he shows that a maxim by which one justifies suicide cannot be universalized; if it were to be done from a principle of self-love,

28. Kant, *Lectures on Ethics*, pp. 148–49.
29. Ibid., p. 152.
30. Ibid., p. 153.
31. Ibid.
32. Ibid., p. 150.
33. Ibid., p. 154.

that could hardly become a law of nature.[34] Suicide also violates the statement of the categorical imperative that one should treat humanity (including one's self) always as an end and never as a means only[35] In *The Metaphysical Principles of Virtue* a similar argument is made under the heading of duties to oneself. To dispose of oneself as a mere means to an end is to degrade one's humanity; care of one's phenomenal nature is a necessary condition for morality.

The casuistical questions that follow the above are of great interest, for they open the possibility of exceptions or justifications.[36] At least in this section Kant recognizes that there are possible ambiguous cases. The five types of cases can be stated in question form. Is self-murder in order to save one's country to be condemned, or is it a heroic act of martyrdom? Is it permissible to commit suicide in anticipation of an unjust sentence, even if one's superior permits it (as Nero permitted Seneca)? Is a person in authority culpable of intending suicide if he carries with him the means to take his life, in case of capture in war, in order to avoid harm to others? Can one take one's life to avoid inevitable madness and avoid bringing misfortune to others as the result of an illness (in Kant's example, the result of being bitten by a mad dog)? Is it suicide to risk one's death by consenting to an experimental medical procedure, in Kant's example, by submitting to the then uncertain results of smallpox vaccination? (If it is, Jonathan Edwards committed suicide, since his death was the result of inoculation.)

In each of these cases the intention of the agent is toward an end that can be reasonably defended, and the taking of one's life or putting it at high risk is a necessary means to achieve the end. A teleological ethics is suggested by each case, an ethics that might qualify the stringent deontic ethics central to Kant's thought.

Kant does not do what a Roman Catholic moral theologian would when facing these questions, namely, analyze them in the light of the principle of double effect. Although one is never to do an evil act for the sake of the good that might ensue, the following analysis could be explored. Is suicide "intrinsically" evil? If it is, it can never be done for the sake of a good effect. Kant's casuistic questions suggest that he might be agnostic about the intrinsic evil of suicide or putting life at risk in the circumstances he describes. Does the person sincerely not intend the evil effect, that is, his or her death? Are the good and evil effects caused simultaneously, so that the evil is never a sequential means to the good? And is there a proportionately grave reason for permitting the evil effect? Kant's "casuistic ques-

34. Kant, *Foundations*, in Beck, ed., *Critique of Practical Reason and Other Writings*, p. 81. This argument is also found in *Critique of Practical Reason*, in ibid., p. 154.

35. Kant, *Foundations*, in ibid., p. 87.

36. Kant, *The Metaphysical Principles of Virtue*, trans. James Ellington, pp. 84–85. See also Novak's discussion of this section in *Suicide and Morality*, pp. 104–7.

tions" could be further examined in the light of this more refined casuistic method. Whether the outcome would decisively avoid the moral ambiguity of the act, however, depends upon one's confidence in the principle of double effect to resolve all doubt. Perhaps Kant's failure to come to decisions indicates that each of his types has a possible moral justification in the light of an end, but that he cannot provide certainty about it. Mill and Sidgwick would say that the possible justifications would be utilitarian.

For Barth and Bonhoeffer the question of suicide is a religious question; for Kant, in his critical ethics, it is a strictly moral one. The relationships to be considered do not include man's relationship to God or the state of a person's faith or unfaith. It is to be resolved on purely rational grounds. Nor does he take into account the despair and affliction that Barth cites as possible excusing conditions; what follows from afflictions would be in Kant's ethics a matter of inclination, and in his most stringent passages duty goes against inclination. Nor do Kant's arguments elaborate the part/whole language that Thomas takes from Aristotle; to be sure, one's duties to others require that one adhere to duties to oneself, and thus they require a No to suicide, but the more organic mode of thought is not invoked. Kant is clear that virtue does not necessarily bring happiness in this life, and thus one ought to tolerate pain and suffering for the sake of virtue. One ought not to be motivated to adhere to virtue by the anticipations of rewards for it in a future life, but as a postulate of pure practical reason he states that such will be the case. Kant's theological argument invokes the justice of God, not the gracious mercy and forgiveness of God, as does Barth's.[37]

An Interpretation of Suicide

All actions of persons are susceptible to explanation and judgment both from the agent's own perspective and from that of observers. Psychia-

37. Other moral and religious perspectives on suicide could be elaborated. Two which I shall not develop are of special interest and importance. The first is not simply that one ought to recognize the liberty of another to take his or her life, and thus not intervene. Rather, to take one's own life is the greatest act of human freedom. Fyodor Dostoyevsky portrays the character of one Kirolov, who proclaims this view and ultimately acts on it. "Everyone who desires supreme freedom must dare to kill himself. . . . He who dares to kill himself is a god." Fyodor Dostoyevsky, *The Devils (The Possessed)* trans. David Magarshack (Baltimore: Penguin Books, 1953), p. 126. For Kirolov this affirmation, which he later avers in the proclamation that his self-will is his attribute of divinity, is part of an intense religious and theological struggle. For some modern existentialists it is the expressive act of the highest human freedom.

The second perspective is that of Judaism. In this tradition the issue of martyrdom as well as suicide is very important. For a brief survey of the history of the suicide literature, see Fred Rosner, "Suicide in Biblical, Talmudic and Rabbinic Writings," *Tradition* 11, no. 2 (1970): 25–40. An interesting account of the history and the teachings about martyrdom is W. H. C. Frend, "Judaism and Martyrdom," in his *Martyrdom and Persecution in the Early Church* (Garden City, N.Y.: Doubleday Anchor Books, 1967), pp. 22–57. One of several incidents in Jewish history that is much discussed is that of the Masada martyrs; for an account of its various interpretations, see Louis I. Rabinowitz, "The Masada Martyrs according to the Halakhah," *Tradition* 11, no. 3 (1970): 31–37.

trists and sociologists can provide explanations of a suicide which the person would not accept as adequate. Moralists can use the theories of Thomas Aquinas or Kant to judge the immorality of the act, but it probably occurs most often because the person believes at the time that it is the only possible course of action, if not the morally right one. For the agent the explanation is the justification, and the justification is the explanation. For the observer, whether social scientist or moralist, an explanation of why a person commits suicide does not necessarily justify the act. From an ethical observer's perspective every qualification of a judgment that suicide is morally wrong seems to be made on the basis of either the agent's intention and justification, or on the basis of excusing conditions from which the agent cannot extricate himself or herself, e.g., Barth's "affliction." All of Kant's casuistic questions justify the act, if they do, on the basis of the intention of an end that the agent seems to have in mind. From Thomas's arguments one can find no possible moral justification, and he reduces possible ones to moral errors on the part of the agent, e.g., believing that it is better to commit suicide than to be sexually violated. In the light of the "objective" moral argument against suicide, Thomas can find neither justifications nor excuses, it seems. Yet, as I indicated at the beginning of this chapter, few if any contemporary persons make harsh moral judgments about self-destruction. That suggests a deep compassion, or at least a deep ambivalence on the part of observers. Both of these might well be evoked by a deep ambiguity in the act itself under most circumstances, an ambiguity that is perceived through empathy for the conditions and/or the intentions of the agent.

Of course traditional moral distinctions are useful to assess the extent of culpability and the possible justifications from the standpoint of the observer. In one sense, suicide is self-murder. Teutonic languages make this clear: *Selbstmord* in German, for example. Physically the agent is the cause of the act, and intentionally the agent wills the death. This is the clearest and most precise description. If an agent is the cause of his death but does not intend it, we do not call it suicide; it is an accident. The distinctions become more ambiguous if the agent intends death but does not cause it. What counts as causal accountability normally affects what counts as moral accountability. This kind of issue has been discussed in medical ethics; if a patient intends death, and death follows from refusal to accept therapy, has the patient caused his death, i.e., committed suicide? Is this suicide by omission rather than by commission? Few persons, to my knowledge, are ready to make a moral accusation of suicide if an aged and very ill person refuses treatment in order not to prolong life.

The question of mental competence is often raised both in the precise cases and in the ambiguous ones. The judgment of competence is important both morally and legally; if the person, for example a patient, is judged incompetent, the physician can intervene to save life without the informed consent of the patient. The difficulty is in drawing the precise line between a competent person and the next nearest case which is judged incompetent; competency is a concept with graded relevance, but for many legal and moral purposes precise lines are drawn. With reference to suicide, incompetence is a sufficient excuse to avoid all moral and legal culpability, and in one form or another recourse is taken to it to excuse the agent and to assuage the grief of others. Indeed, from some standpoints no suicide is done by a fully competent person; it is a intrinsically irrational act.

Kant's casuistic questions and similar ones raise the question of the intention of the act. To what end is the agent's intention? If the end is praiseworthy, as in the case of a soldier who deliberately falls on a grenade to save the lives of others, is the act one of martyrdom or of suicide? Or is pure martyrdom achieved only when one is not the immediate "cause" of one's own death, but permits others to take one's life? If the taking of one's own life for the sake of an admirable end can be justified, can the observer assess the reasonableness of the agent's calculations of the efficacy of death as a means to the intended end? Hunger strikes as means to the end of some political or social change are cases in point. In Gandhi's case, his intention to permit himself to die was an efficacious means of securing changes in the British policies in India. More recently, in Northern Ireland, men died from their hunger strikes without their intended outcome occurring. Some Roman Catholic priests were reported to judge their deaths to be suicides. During the Vietnam War there were instances of self-immolation both in the United States and in Vietnam. Does one evaluate such actions differently if they are described as expressive acts of indignation or protest, or as acts which were intended to affect a causal linkage to actually end the war? What sort of end is sufficient to merit the designation of an act of genuine martyrdom? We have seen that Kant and others would not consider suicide for the sake of avoiding misery to be justifiable, but perhaps for the sake of avoiding death to others it is. St. Lucia of Christian legend committed suicide to avoid being "violated"; Thomas Aquinas would have morally preferred a sexual act by force to suicide.

Kant's final question is about putting oneself at a probable risk, in his case by a smallpox innoculation. Since daily life almost inevitably requires that we put our lives at some risk by exposing ourselves to the possibility of accident, is the moral observer to distinguish between the probabilities of risk to which persons deliberately put themselves in judging whether the intention is suicidal? Is a "stunt man" who crashes cars for movies more "suicidal" than I am when I cross a busy street while the "Don't Walk" sign is blinking to warn me of danger? Or since neither of us intends our death by taking the risk, is the adjective "suicidal" inapplicable? I, and I believe most observers, would say that it is. Yet the judgment is a bit ambiguous, because while the stunt man does not intend his death he intentionally engages in actions which could easily cause it.

Some persons destroy themselves because they have been, or believe they have been, causally accountable and therefore morally culpable for the death or misfortunes of others. While no moral observer would, I believe, say that suicide for such a reason is justifiable, would one wish to say that in instances where the evidence indicated strict accountability the guilt which led to suicide was more "understandable" if not justified?

These observations and questions from an observer's perspective are important, and while I have not given precise answers to the questions, it is possible to use casuistic procedures to do so in some cases and to narrow the range of judgment in others. I reiterate the point, however, that even when it has been determined that an act is suicide in the most precise definition, moral judgments are seldom made about persons who take their lives.

From the agent's perspective suicide must be a very lonely choice and act. Its awesomeness could hardly be ignored, for death is irreversible and irrevocable. It is the choice not to be rather than to be. To chose not to be must be very compelling in the thinking and feeling of the moment. In my judgment it is irreverent for an observer flippantly to dismiss the agent as always being irrational or mentally ill. It must be the case, as Barth suggests, that in that time no appeal to a moral imperative, however well argued, or to an ideal is likely to be efficacious. If others have an opportunity, however, they ought to attempt persuasion and engage in coercive action to prevent a suicide. The continuation of life is the condition sine qua non for the realization of any values not only for the individual but for that individual's participation in the larger realms of life. And there are good reasons for being less disturbed by the suicide of an aged and very ill person than by that of an adolescent or a person who could be an active participant in life and who has responsibilities for, and to, others on which their well-being is dependent.

Interpreted from the perspective of the present work, many suicides follow from, though they are not directly caused by, conditions which cannot be overcome by acts of will based on objective moral arguments. There are conditions of the human spirit, not all of which can be laid to the accountability of the person, which can make suicide appear to be a good, if not a right, choice. In a sense, then, spiritual or religious factors are involved; there is disorder in the life of the person or in the person's relations to others which leads to despair. The religious dimensions are not so much those of belief, such as Bonhoeffer suggests when he states that suicide comes from the failure to accept God's justification and the attempt to justify one's self. They are more of what Barth calls affliction, or what I think can more aptly be termed despair.

Despair seems to me to be the condition of hopelessness, of not seeing possibilities for life for oneself. It is not often, I believe, the result of the absence or failure of convictions about the big questions—the ultimate meaning of life, or whether God and the forces of life sustain the human good in toto. These might enter in when experiences in detail seem to run counter to such cosmic aspirations; from my perspective the problem then is that the cosmic aspirations are in error. One does not have to find "the meaning of life" in order to find meanings and significance in the more immediate realms of life and experience. Many suicides, I believe, develop from conditions of despair about more limited and more immediate contexts of both the life around one and one's own life. Cognitive aspects enter into this, though they are not of the sort that would resolve a moral syllogism. They are, rather, how life is interpreted, what explanations one accepts for the conditions of one's tribulations, how the immediate realities of life are understood, and how the possibilities or impossibilities of one's personal and social future are conceived.

One can only imaginatively reconstruct what might be the perceptions of the self and the world that despair both confirms and evokes in persons who choose to take their lives. What I develop in the following paragraphs is only in part the result of reading literature about suicide; it is an attempt to empathize with persons overwhelmed by despair. It is the result of a process of *Verstehen*, that is, attempting to place oneself empathetically into the life, feelings, thoughts, and conditions of another so that one might interpret the act from an agent's perspective. No empirical claim is made that all suicides are caused by despair. But I believe that many persons have troubling experiences which are similar to those of persons who take their lives; only the intensity of them is different. Thus, in a sense, to understand the subjectivity of others involves the use of analogy from one's own experience. I shall use several terms as a basis for describing the sense of tribulation, affliction, or despair.

The first is a sense of impossibility, or of fatedeness. To be sure there are persons who believe in divine determinism, in cosmic determinism (a secular version), or in the power of the positions of the stars to determine events and personal destiny. Such beliefs might well be a source of comforting resignation in conditions of affliction. My interest, however, is in more immediately "caused" senses of impossibility or fatedness. The relations in which one lives are perceived to be determined and immutable; there is no possibility of altering them. The events in which one is called to respond are subject to powers beyond one's control. The state of one's own spirit is perceived to be unalterable. The course of life appears to make the person totally a patient rather than an agent, totally a victim of an unalterable sequence of events that are beyond his or her, or anyone else's, capacities to control, or even to alter significantly. Despair occurs when the powers that bear down on one seem to be totally against one's own interests or others' interests about which one is concerned and in which one is involved. If the course of life is in accord with one's own best interests, one might still believe one is "fated," that is, that the immediacies of a religious or secular providence are carrying one to fulfillment or satisfaction. It is when the powers beyond human control appear to destine one's immediate circumstances in ways that are counter to one's ends and aspirations that despair is evoked. What bears down upon one both from within and without is a "too-muchness," a complexity, inexorability, or unmanageability that offers no opportunities for action that can lead to change, that provides no "handles" to grasp to meet one's own needs and interests. What bears down upon one seems not to be amenable to personal initiatives that might change the course of events or alter the state of affairs. All foreseeable outcomes are maleficient with reference to one's own future, and any gradations of greater or lesser between them are indistinguishable.[38]

Despair can be evoked by a deep conflict of loyalties. A conflict of loyalties is not simply a conflict of ends, or a conflict of duties and obligations. Loyalties signify our personal identities; they affect our perceptions of who we are. They are not simply contractual commitments rationally made, but affective bonds to persons, groups, or traditions which condition our sense of identity and well-being. Not all loyalties are of equal significance, and generally we can maintain a number of them without unbearable tension between them, without being driven to an either/or choice. But severe conflicts of loyalties are excruciatingly painful; they are disturbing in ways that conflicts of social roles and duties are not. Despair can follow when a person perceives and feels an irresolvable conflict between loyalties to different persons, different communities or groups, different "ways of life," and different traditions. Such conflicts are not readily dissolved by objective analysis or by rational argumentation. The choice of fidelity to one seems absolutely to exclude all others. Conflicts of interests, rationally undertaken obligations, natural duties and even many values can be negotiated in our own minds or with others. Deep conflicts of loyalties are perceived to be nonnegotiable. One's deepest integrity is at stake; one's own sense of wholeness is in jeopardy. The despair and affliction that results can make self-destruction appear to be the only possible course of action.

Despair can be evoked by aimlessness or purposelessness. There are persons for whom their own lives, or the lives around them, are literally non-sense; life makes no sense. Whether as a result of their own sloth or of circumstances in which they live, there seems to be no significant pattern of

38. In one of the most profound recent books on despair and hope, William F. Lynch, S.J., discusses the significance of the loss of imagination as a source of hopelessness. One cannot imagine a variety of possibilities for oneself, or various courses of action that events could take. To be able to imagine, to dream, is from one perspective a dawn of hope. Imagination, however, is ambiguous, for the person in despair, like any anxious person, can imagine that only the worst is possible, can construct powerful scenarios of fatedness as well as of possibilities. Imagination can lead to terror as well as to hope. See William F. Lynch, S.J., *Images of Hope* (Baltimore: Helicon, 1965).

continuity in life, no direction that circumstances take or that one can take for oneself, no meaningful goals for achievement. One cannot see oneself as a significant part in any scheme of things or any whole either as a recipient or as a contributor. Satisfactions might be sufficient to make drifting temporarily worthwhile, but for some persons aimlessness and drifting can lead to a profound sense of the absence of any significant meaning and thus to despair. The perceived aimlessness of external events and affairs can be turned inward on oneself; the strength to bear the perceived chaos outside one's self ebbs away. Or the chaos within, the directionlessness of one's own life, erodes the strength to participate in the life of the world of which one is a part. Not to be, rather than to be, seems a reasonable and responsible choice. Indeed, in a spiritual sense one is not being when there are no aims and purposes to one's life; the step to not being physically might be perceived to be a very small one. For some persons the crisis or the small step is a response to big events—the perceived aimlessness of a world at war or preparing for war, for example; for others it is a response to little events and immediate circumstances—the seeming meaninglessness of the boring round of daily duties and obligations or of relationships in which one lives day-to-day life. Aimlessness is avoided by removing its most necessary condition, life.

I have already noted what I now wish to develop more fully; despair can come from the sense that one has no capacities *within oneself* to determine the course of one's own life or the course of immediate events in which one participates. This loss of a sense of self-determination is not merely the result of restraints upon one's freedom of action by external circumstances and forces. It is a sense of inner weakness; one cannot see that one might become in the future what one now is not; one's capacities do not enable change in oneself or in relationships even when changes are externally possible. There are no significant "interstices" in one's own selfhood when a choice and action could alter what is a deeply unsatisfactory life. This sense of weakness might well be engendered by external circumstances: ill health or extended unemployment might be examples. One's own dignity, which is dependent in part on the inner capacities to determine to some extent one's immediate destiny, is offended. The futility of one's efforts to exercise one's capacities of self-determination can lead to their atrophying or to a desperate conviction that one no longer has any. So, for some persons, the question is, Why live?

Despair can follow from isolation, from the rupture of the relations of mutual interdependence that are necessary to sustain meaningful life. Isolation can come from overt betrayal. Others sometimes break their promises and commitments, and thus betray one; the isolation that follows is accompanied by bitterness. Or the agent can betray others by breaking vows and commitments; the isolation is accompanied by guilt. Or isolation can come from a presumption of self-sufficiency which denies the need for interdependence; the self-sufficiency with its sense of pride collapses of its own limitations if not impossibility. There is a loneliness that comes not so much from conscious betrayal of the opportunities and obligations of interrelationships as it does from heedlessness that leads to neglect. Surely, for example, the despair of many aged persons in nursing homes is fostered at least in part by nonmalevolent inattentiveness of family and friends preoccupied by their own more immediate interests and obligations. Sustaining physical life is not sufficient; the failure to sustain the interdependence of minds and affections which brings worth to the lives of individuals can lead to desperation, to a loneliness that makes life seem not worthwhile.

Despair can be evoked by an excessive sense of moral scrupulosity, by an excessively scrupulous conscience. It can be evoked by a sense of total accountability both for one's own painful condition of life and for the sufferings and untoward circumstances of others. It can be evoked by failure to accept the conditions of human finitude. Despair comes from misplaced guilt. On the face of it there appears to be something morally honorable about an intense moral conscientiousness which accepts responsibility for events and states of affairs for which one has little or no causal accountability. During the Vietnam War it was fashionable on the part of many protestors to charge persons and institutions only remotely related to the events themselves with guilt for them. It was not uncommon for individuals to be persuaded that they were somehow accountable for, and thus guilty of, all that was portrayed to be wrong. Yet many accusations and a lot of guilt were misplaced. Moral responsibility reasonably is related to causal accountability; to be sure it is more strictly attributable to actual acts of intervention, acts of commission, than to failure to act, acts of omission. But the error of the excessive scrupulous conscience is often that it assumes moral responsibility where there is no causal relationship between the person and the course of events. Some persons are even led to feel responsible for the actions of their ancestors; surely this is an intellectual error that leads to a moral error. The failure to accept the conditions of finitude can lead to misplaced guilt; the failure to recognize that one's own actions are only a small part in the ongoing processes of interaction in which many others exercise powers can lead to unbearable senses of responsibility. The excessively scrupulous conscience is often unwilling to consent to realities and powers beyond its control. If misplaced guilt is not the result, there might be an unbearable frustration of not having the capacities to do what one thinks one ought to do, of not having access to those forms of power that are sufficient to alter a course of events. Persons can be burdened with an extravagant sense that certain events would have been different if they had done otherwise than they did in the past, that their actions could have made a decisive difference. They are unable to distinguish between what happens to them or to others to whom they are related, and what occurs or could occur as a result of their interventions. Probably every person who has ministered to the afflicted conscience of another has confronted despair that is based on a failure to accept the conditions of human finitude. Such despair can lead to suicide.

If living is perceived to be only a task or requirement, and never a gift or enablement, dejection and despair can follow. Events that could be perceived as occasions for joy are interpreted as occasions for temptation and strenuous duty. Persons on whose presence one depends become the objects of worry rather than gratitude. One's own life is perceived not to be a gift properly to be nourished and fulfilled but only a task to be carried out in the service of duty. Humor and joy become rare; laughter at one's self becomes impossible. Dejection and tribulation can follow; deadly seriousness can be a condition that leads to seriously contemplating one's own death.

Of course persons often are morally accountable for various sufferings of others, for courses of events and states of affairs that are properly judged to be wrong or immoral. Not all guilt is misplaced. Despair comes when there are no perceptible sources of forgiveness and renewal: when there is no other to console the sense of guilt, and to make clear that if the past cannot be redeemed the future presents conditions to "atone" for one's misdeeds, to do other than what one has wrongly done, to compensate for failures in the past. Guilt and its remission have been near the center of much of the biblical religions as well as others. Cultic rites and theological assurances have been consoling and renewing to persons, and the assurance that God is merciful, as well as just, is part of the traditional faith. No doubt some persons have been deterred from taking their lives by the conceptual and verbal assurance that the ultimate power is a loving person who forgives and renews life. There surely have been others, however, for whom such assurance is only a verbal formula and a theological abstraction apart from the forgiving and renewing efforts of other persons. As Barth points out, even the most religiously faithful person can in the end be in a state of affliction that leads to the taking of his or her own life. The absence of subjectively meaningful forgiveness and renewal, whatever their ultimate source, can lead to despair. Forensic acquittal is often not enough; the assurance that one man died for the sins of all, and thus all (or at least those who believe this to be true) are justified in the eyes of God is no sure preventive for the moral guilt that leads to despair.

I do not claim that it is only conditions of tribulation, affliction, and despair in which suicide appears to be a reasonable choice for an agent. Nor is my description of the aspects of despair and the occasions that lead to it exhaustive. Other writers prefer other vocabularies and concepts. No doubt my account is colored in part by a theological and religious perspective, but I believe it is not esoteric. It remains now to develop the kinds of responses to these conditions and to suicide itself that follow from the theology and ethics of this book.

Response from a Theocentric Perspective

We are participants in the patterns and processes of interdependence of life. What is God enabling and requiring us to be and to do in relation to human despair and acts of self-destruction? Do the patterns and processes of interdependence give us signals of the kinds of relationships and interactions that can alleviate severe tribulations? Are there ways in which persons can be more rightly related to each other, and are there patterns of interaction that can be fostered which appropriately sustain human well-being?

From my theocentric perspective the first requirement and possibility is to attend to the patterns and processes of interdependence, to attempt to discern from them the conditions that are necessary to mitigate despair, and to govern actions and relationships accordingly. Because the act of suicide is that of an agent exercising his or her powers of self-determination; because it is, in a limited sense at least, an act of freedom (or even an act of self-legislating, self-judging, and self-executing—a truly "autonomous" act), there is no guarantee that attention to the broader conditions of life which dispose persons to despair can ultimately avoid it. Indeed, one peril of attending to human responsibilities for the conditions of despair is that this approach might create the illusion of total accountability in others for a person's self-destruction: itself a condition that leads to despair. (I shall return to this issue subsequently.) Nonetheless, within limits, others have capacities to sustain and alter conditions and relationships so that deep affliction is less likely. It is also, within limits, possible for desperate persons to interpret and understand the possibilities for altering life conditions so that they perceive themselves not to be fated.

The person who in lonely desperation takes his or her life is a person who also is related to others by various social ties: husband, wife, parent, child, sibling, friend, professional associate, fellow student, housemate, or what have you. Some of these relationships are natural and some result from commitments; some are intimate and some are casual; some are personal and of long standing and some are role relationships of brief duration and little intensity. Not all of them have the same subjective and affective significance; the possibilities and requirements of mutual caring are relative to the degree of intimacy.

In my analysis despair is in large part, if not in toto, the absence of hope, that is, the absence of any sense of the possibility that the person's inner life, relations to others, or external conditions are subject to improvement. One feels fated by one's own history, by one's relationships, or by events. Conflicts of loyalties seem irresolvable. One cannot find a sense of direction for one's activities; one's inner weakness seems to make one always the victim and never the actor. There seems to be no possible way to overcome loneliness or one's sense of guilt, whether misplaced or proper.

What is God enabling and requiring us to be and to do in these circumstances? We are to be faithful in our relations to others. We are to sustain relations with others which mitigate conditions that might lead to ultimate desperation. We are to relate to them so they sense possibilities for their lives, so that they can negotiate if not resolve conflicting loyalties, so that they can grasp realistic but satisfying aims. We are to keep company with the lonely, and be agents of forgiving and renewing powers. In these and other ways we relate to others in a manner appropriate to their relations to God; we contribute to the conditions which sustain life and create conditions of possibility for it.

While the construal of life in the world from a theocentric perspective highlights the persisting patterns and processes of interdependence, and points to limitations of human action, it is not deterministic. There are "interstices" in events and relationships and in the history of the self in which capacities of human agency can be exercised to alter conditions, relationships, the course of events, and state of affairs. For both the primary agent and for those to whom he or she is related one task is cognitive, namely, to interpret circumstances in the light of their alterability—realistically, to be sure, but nonetheless firmly. What one experiences oneself, and what one experiences with others in moments of grave disappointment and grief indicate how easily possibilities seem to be foreclosed. Most persons have experienced what the desperate person experiences more intensely.

All conscientious teachers and pastors have talked with persons who see no viable course of action in a moment when the relations on which they have most relied are broken or the aspirations which have meant the most to them are demolished. A marriage breaks up, a death occurs, a critical application for a job or for graduate school is rejected, an examination is failed, a natural catastrophe destroys one's possessions. Father William Lynch is profoundly correct to suggest that in such moments of grave disappointment there is often a failure of imagination, a failure to be able to "image forth" ways of coping with and renewing life, alternative prospects of employment or education, steps that can be taken to rebuild life after it has been damaged and apparently destroyed. One of our moral tasks, a possibility and an obligation, is a cognitive one. It is to help the other to see and foresee possibilities beyond the disappointment and despair. It is to assist the other from foreclosing possibilities which, even if they do not meet aspirations and expectations held dear, provide occasions for worthwhile life.

Hope, as Lynch argues, is a sense of possibilities. But to the desperate person those possibilities must be "tangible"; they must be near enough and real enough to provide the first steps out of deep affliction. In my judgment it is relatively useless to preach abstractions about all things being possible for God, or that God is the future of infinite possibilities, to most if not all deeply despairing persons. To be sure, the divine ordering of the world is such that there are conditions of possibility in life, but the moral task is to see and help others to see actual and specific opportunities to better one's condition of life. It is to help someone to see that their present state of mind and spirit is not chiseled in marble, that other relationships than those which they find broken can be established, that others can act to open possibilities for them. It is not enough to give verbal assurances that life is not foreclosed; our responsibility is to act on behalf of the interests and needs of others in order to develop conditions of possibility.

Desperation is often based upon an inaccurate interpretation of how one has come to the state in which one finds oneself. How I explain myself to myself in times of introspection may be incorrect, or only partially correct. Alternative interpretations of the past can lead to different explanations of the present, and in the light of them new possibilities for the future might be seen. This is, I take it, what therapists seek to do for those who are in their care. To be able to see that the present could have been otherwise, and is what it is in part as a result of contingencies, might well enable persons to see that the future also is not foreclosed, but can be affected by one's own initiatives, by those of others, and by contingencies to which one consents or which provide opportunities for action.

Both despair and hope are, however, not the result of the sum total of available facts or of a construal of circumstances. Both are deeply affective. Despair often exceeds the realistic accounting of its causes and reasons; it is a matter of the human spirit which argumentation and the imagination of better possibilities cannot always dispell. Hope, as well, is a condition of the human spirit; it might be backed by reasonable beliefs but often exists in the face of bleak realities.

Alas, for all too many persons there are good and realistic grounds for the deepest despair: persons facing unrelievable pain and suffering of body and spirit, persons facing the bleakness of continuous poverty and unemployment, persons facing the loss of simple human dignity. No ringing ideals, no cogent argument for an imperative of a duty to oneself, no charge of self-justification, and no counsel of possibilities will bring relief or hope. To deaths of such persons by suicide one must consent. The powers that bear down upon them are greater than the powers that sustain them. Neither moralists nor God ought to be their judge. The tragedy of their deaths flows from conditions of life beyond their powers to control.

I have argued that actions are governed both by our affective and our rational capacities. Surely the choice to take one's own life is a cogent example of this. And the moral response thus must be multifaceted; ethics requires not only reasons against taking one's life but actions to sustain human relations and subtle forms of counsel to which the whole self of the afflicted person can respond.

If a seemingly irresolvable conflict of loyalties is the locus of the despair, one's duty (if one has an opportunity to exercise it) is to aid the other to sort out feelings as well as reasons, to help the person to find those overlapping and mutually inclusive grounds which can mitigate the perception of an either/or choice. Aimlessness is seldom, if ever, overcome by exhortations to get one's life together, to formulate goals and purposes that are realizable, to subdue one's sloth by an act of will. Relief of aimlessness requires patient, sustaining support as well as nudging and provoking interventions. One never overcomes another's inner weakness simply by exhorting the person to be strong, to exercise their capacities for agency. The weakness is often conditioned by factors over which the person has had no control and which are not now susceptible to a command of the rational will. To strengthen persons may require professional therapy; it at least requires sympathetic understanding and the sustaining of trustful and trustworthy relationships.

Loneliness and isolation are not simply descriptions of physical relationships. We all know that one can feel loneliest in a crowd of strangers, and most isolated in the midst of intense interactions. The desperation of loneliness has to be met by affectively sustaining relationships, by communication with those whose relationships are more than technical role functions, by signs of affection. Trustworthiness or fidelity to others is an obligation not merely to keep promises and vows but to be present with the other, to be attentive to the other. No simple observation that one is not physically alone can overcome the isolation of the human spirit. One might counsel another to take initiatives to relate in some significant way to those around him or her, and one might take initiatives to open such possibilities. But loneliness is an affliction that runs contrary to deep natural human needs: to care for others and be cared for by them, to love others and be loved by them, to be taken seriously as a human person by others and not merely as the object of technical and functional social duties. The proper ordering of relations and processes of mutual interdependence is being violated when unbearable loneliness occurs.

Misplaced guilt on the part of the desperate person can be cognitively explained away, but the sense of affliction is not necessarily dispelled. Persons can be shown the limits of their causal accountability for what they are and have become, or for the sufferings of others and of the world for which they feel responsible. Surely this is necessary to bring relief to the afflicted scrupulous conscience. False self-understanding leads to a false sense of guilt; more accurate self-understanding can lead to some relief. But the excessively scrupulous conscience does not easily accept the conditions of finitude; it may take extended patience and sustaining love to bring the troubled human spirit into equilibrium with an accurate account of events.

Perhaps those who have been brought up to believe that no actual guilt can separate them from the love of God find some comfort in hearing that assurance. It is certainly preached often enough to many congregations of Christians. In my limited experience, however, many persons who accept such assurance as an article of traditional religious faith are as plagued by their moral failures as are persons for whom the assurance is only a bit of religious superstition. And there are traditions in Christianity in which guilt is intentionally intensified to drive persons to despair so that they are prepared to hear the word of divine grace and forgiveness. Martin Luther's experience seems to be one example of this possibility; only when he knew himself to be a breaker of God's law and had unsuccessfully confided in his own strength to overcome his guilt did he come to the assurance that in relation to God he was justified by the atoning death of Jesus. My suspicion is, however, that most persons are not relieved of guilt simply by proclamation of the gospel, but need the forgiveness of the human victims of their moral failures.

Etched in my mind is the memory of a child in Musselshell, Montana, many years ago who chose as her recitation for a children's program the following words, "Jesus said we must forgive, we must forgive, we must forgive. If we would be forgiven we must be forgiving too." The moral wisdom of the second sentence is backed by deep human experience. The relief of guilt comes from the reciprocal acknowledgment of guilt; to be forgiven requires the capacity to be forgiving. Rationalistic views of morality simply ignore the affective dimensions of guilt and the need to be forgiven. Guilt before the law can command retributive justice and compensation for injuries that one has caused. But the nature of the human persons is such that affective aspects of the self are seldom if ever assuaged without subjectively meaningful experiences of not having moral wrongs endlessly held against one. The possibilities of renewal are dependent in part upon having the past excused—not by an account of "excusing conditions" that mitigate culpability, but by genuinely not holding a deed against its agent. But this seems to require deeper bonds of love and loyalty in the most intimate human relationships, bonds which can sustain persons through the tribulation of guilt to a sense of being forgiven. Such relationships are barriers against the depths of despair.

We are by nature as well as by "calling" the stewards of each other's lives. We are participants in the patterns and processes of interdependence. Those patterns and processes that are most intimate are the most fragile as well as the most fulfilling. Trust and trustworthiness are types and qualities of human relations by which we sustain significance in each other's lives: caring and being cared for, forgiving and being forgiven, creating possibilities for others and permitting them to create possibilities for us. Life together in intimacy provides both opportunities and requirements to develop and sustain conditions which can alleviate the desperation that leads to suicide, and conditions which can bring hope out of affliction.

We are, however, finite participants in life. There is no blueprint of precise relationships and interactions that can avoid desperation in ourselves and others. Often the conditions that create it are beyond human control, and often it is beyond relief. We can err in our judgments, we can intend to sustain life but not be knowledgeable enough to achieve our end. The other always remains an other; as persons others are not simply objects controlled by our best intentions and manipulations. Their responses to our relationships and initiatives are inexorably their own, determined within limits by their own agency. As stewards of the lives of others our capacities and our accountability for what they do are limited. To recognize the opportunities and obligations we have does not entail our total accountability for what occurs.

All persons who are intimately related to those who destroy themselves are prone to a sense of failure and even of guilt. Because of our natural and committed relations to them we interpret ourselves as part of a causal nexus out of which tragedy has come. For more than most other modes of death, we feel a vague sense of total accountability for what occurred. But we must accept our own finitude; we must recognize our own limitations of abilities, roles, and causal accountability. We are sustainers of the lives of one another, but we are not the only powers that sustain and bear down upon persons and create conditions in which they make their own choice about whether not to be is better than to be. There are possibilities for us, sustaining and renewing ones, in and after the affliction of grief for the death of another for whom we feel responsible. There are sources of forgiveness for us; for our errors of judgment, our insensitivity, our failure of courage, and all those proper and improper self-accusations we make. There are possibilities for the living even in the face of the death of those who destroy themselves.

Our first order of moral responsibility from a theocentric perspective is to be participants in the patterns and processes of interdependence that sustain and support the lives of others—in this case especially those who are intimately related to us. If ethical reflection on suicide is confined only to the act, and excludes the conditions in which the act appears to the agent to be a good or even right one, it is morally myopic if not blind. From the theology and ethics developed here, attention to relations out of which acts in part come, to our perception of what God is enabling and requiring us to be and to do with and for one another in times of affliction, is the first locus of moral opportunity and moral obligations.

What is to be said about the morality of the act of suicide itself? I return to this question, answers to which I have discussed from some of my theological and philosophical benchmarks, only after having considered the possibilities and obligations we have to mitigate conditions of tribulation, affliction and despair. Self-destruction is understandable, excusable, and forgivable, but is it ever morally justifiable?

From my theological standpoint the first word is similar to a word from Karl Barth. "Life is no second God, and therefore respect due it cannot rival the reverence owed to God."[39] The preservation of physical human life is not an end in itself. Its almost absolute value stems from the fact that it is the condition sine qua non for the individual to value anything else and to make contributions as a participant in life. The seriousness of suicide is basically the same as the seriousness of any other untimely death; the condition sine qua non for a person to experience what is of worth in life and to participate in life is taken away. There are occasions when the exposure to risk of life is morally justified for other ends; again, war is the classic example. Are there occasions when the taking of one's own life is justifiable in the light of other ends? Are there occasions when one ought not to intervene even when it is possible to keep another from self-destruction? Is the right to dispose of oneself either by an act of commission or by refusing the means to sustain or heal life an absolute right, so that the freedom to take one's own life ought never to be interfered with?

We can begin with one of Kant's casuistic questions as a way to consider these questions. Is it suicide to do what entails certain death in order to save one's country? Few, if any, persons are so important that their country could be saved by their suicides, but the general issue raised by this is whether suicide can be an act of martyrdom, that is, an intentional act of self-sacrifice for the sake of other persons, one's integrity, or other good ends. Any act of martyrdom worthy of the appellation is a voluntary act; the agent at least consents to it, if he or she does not initiate it. Thus the moral status of one life voluntarily being given for many, or for a cause, is different from an occasion in which some external authority determines that if he takes one life others will be saved. If permitting one's life to be taken for some end is justifiable, that same end would justify taking one's own life. The moral query is about what ends and potential consequences are sufficient to justify the suicide. What ends or consequences are commensurable with the loss of a single life?

The first question is whether there are other means short of suicide to achieve the desired benefit for others. The answer to this will be context-

39. Karl Barth, *Church Dogmatics*, III/4, p. 342.

bound; rarely would the giving of one life save one's country, as in Kant's example. It is more likely that a less eminent person than a king could jeopardize the lives of others by betraying information under torture that would cause many deaths. For the sake of the others, I would argue, a suicide in such circumstances is justifiable. The principle of double effect would require that the good and evil consequences occur simultaneously, and thus that the suicide not be a means in an extended sequence of causality for the desired effect. This, like the intention sincerely not to desire the evil effect, only the good, is a distinction made for the sake of preserving the moral rectitude of the agent. I have already indicated that I believe this is a questionable consideration in the circumstances one can imagine here; the morally proper concern is not for the self but for the others. The assurance that the means, a suicide, will have the desired effect is always a matter of probability. Where there are low probabilities there would be no justification for the act. If persons who immolated themselves during the Vietnam War believed that somehow their action would stop the war, or would even hasten the ending of the war, they were in error, and their suicides were not justified. Perhaps Gandhi's first hunger strikes assured to a greater extent his desired outcomes, but that was relative to the power he had achieved as the leader of a movement. Hunger strikes by prisoners in Northern Ireland did not bring the desired outcome. The question, never one which can be answered with certainty, is whether suicide will be a significant "causal" factor, a means to the desired benefits for others. The judgment of any agent is by no means risk-proof.

Is suicide not only understandable and excusable but also justifiable when a person takes his or her life in the face of what is reasonably perceived to be unbearable and unrelievable suffering for oneself? Persons who suffer anguish physically and mentally with courage and patience do evoke the admiration of others. The fact that they are praiseworthy, however, does not imply that there is an obligation to endure unbearable and unrelievable suffering. Kant argues that the taking of one's life to avoid misery to oneself is not justifiable. I argue to the contrary; physical life is not of ultimate value; many persons who suffer acutely are in no way accountable for their sufferings. Suffering is inflicted upon them, and it can be a morally proper choice to seek the relief of death for their own sake and for that of others.

Again the conditions in which one would justify such a suicide are context-bound. The case of an adolescent boy whose aim in life is to be a great athlete and who is permanently disabled by an accident is quite different from that of a person who has undergone years of suffering, whose capacities to value life and contribute to others have been largely spent, and for whom there are no courses of action available which can relieve the suffering. Such a person need not be demeaned with a judgment of incompetence in order to establish the propriety of the decision.

A special set of cases occurs where patients exercise their legal and moral right to refuse life-sustaining or even life-restoring medical procedures. Their passivity is a factor in their dying; they do, however, intend their deaths. Again, physical life is not of ultimate value, and the consent of the person honors the capacity of self-determination. One can assume in most modern medical contexts that the consequences of refusal have been made clear, and that the judgment of the persons is informed by the physician. A moral evaluation is again context-bound; the case of an aged person who is ill and of a patient who can no longer tolerate the effects of a kidney dialysis regimen are different from that of a young adult whose injury precludes that one aspiration can be filled but does not rule out others. In the latter case, from my perspective, the patient's present and future possibilities for participation in life for his own sake and for the roles he can have in human communities would morally warrant an intrusion even against the patient's will. This, I know, raises legal issues and issues of medical morality as it is dominantly viewed in our time and culture. But like Thomas Aquinas, I believe that when a member of a human community who has prospects of functioning in significant ways in life is lost to the community this deprivation violates a common good and is a warrant for intervention.

In every case one can be directed by general rules and presumptions; any exceptions to them require careful consideration; a final judgment is a discernment. In every case there is no avoidance of the possibility of tragic consequences; in every case something of value is taken for the sake of ends for oneself and for others. From the ethics developed in this volume the occasions on which exceptions might be made and presumptions overridden can be backed by good reasons. The first obligation, however, is always to prevent suicide; death is irreversible and all prospects for the person and the community are ended.

I believe that the fact that few if any persons morally condemn any given suicide, and particularly one by a person to whom they have been intimately related, both reflects compassion for the conditions which led to the act and an ambivalence that mirrors a moral ambiguity inherent in the act itself. Suicide is always a tragic moral choice; it is sometimes a misguided choice. But it can be, I believe, a conscientious choice. Our first responsibility from my theocentric perspective is to sustain others and the relationships which make life worth living; another is to restrain persons from the act if we have opportunity to do so; but finally we often must consent to its being done—justifiably, tragically, and mournfully.

If I am correct that there are morally justifiable suicides, that datum has to be taken into account in piety and theology. If the powers of destruction that bear down upon individuals are insurmountable, if there is no other reasonable choice for them to make in the face of unbearable and unrelievable suffering, if persons are not significantly causally accountable for the bleakness of their lives and the circumstances in which they live, and if there is nothing or almost nothing that those in whose care they are can do for them, there is reason to quarrel with God. Life is a gift, and is to be received with gratitude, but if life becomes an unbearable burden there is reason for enmity toward God. Traditional religious assurances can become glib abstractions to those who suffer deep tribulation, and to those who grieve such a tragic death. That God not only does not guarantee the good of the afflicted persons, but also that conditions of possibility to meet their reasonable interests do not exist should raise again traditional theological difficulties that are sometimes easily ignored. The experiences of persons from which reasonably follows their self-destruction, and the experiences of grief through this most tragic form of death, are crucibles in which claims about the benevolence and beneficence of God are severely tested. Finally one has to consent to the reality that the powers that bring life into being do not always sustain it but can lead to its untimely and tragic destruction. No rationalized theodicy or facile assurance of grace removes the pain and the sorrow of the victim and the grieving survivors.

7

Population and Nutrition

Population growth in relation to resources for human nutrition on a global level is an unmanageable problem in actuality and as a thought experiment. The factors involved are so many and so diverse that no person or government has the wisdom, knowledge, and power to resolve the problems that emerge. The variables are virtually countless when one considers the specific conditions of each of the countries on our planet, and the ways in which everything from meteorological conditions and soil conditions on the one hand to simple human greed on the other can affect the course of events. Nonetheless, by simplifying some factors to create a more manageable thought experiment, I shall attempt to show how one would think about these matters from the perspective of the present work. Since malnutrition and famine are matters that appeal deeply to human compassion, and since in the biblical traditions there are such clear mandates to care for the hungry, it is an especially poignant issue. Most persons in the world feel compassion toward those whose lives are disabled or lost as a result of malnutrition, even if they cannot give a complex argument to support their feelings. The Golden Rule is sufficient. It is an intractable problem that will not go away; human beings suffer, and one needs no sophisticated argument to sustain some sense of obligation to persons and communities that are in such straits. If we have obligations to all sentient beings, whether as direct or indirect duties, surely we have obligations to our fellow human beings to try to keep them from starving or being subjected to diseases as a result of inadequate nourishment.

Religious and Theological Reflections

This general area is worthy of attention not only because it requires thought about moral and political responsibilities but also because it bears on the theological aspects of ethics. There are probably few places in the world where failure to feed the hungry is the effect of some evil will, either in individuals or in some collective entity such as the United States or other national governments. There is evidence that food shipped to areas of great need have been diverted by agencies to the profit and advantage of persons in power; this must be acknowledged. But I believe that the presence of evil wills, in the strict sense in which Kant defined them, is a negligible causal factor relative to the vastness of the problem. If we knew persons who took delight in seeing starving children, we would probably judge them to be mentally ill. Indeed, even if there were significant numbers of persons of evil will or of sadistic temperament, their capacities to control events would not be large. The variety of actions required to meet critical needs both of population control and of food distribution are so many, and the interrelations between them so complex, that no concentration of power, whether good or evil in intention, can control the events in all places and at all times.

There are, however, interests which persons, groups, and states protect that have costly consequences for others in these matters. At the time of this writing, for example, a vast number of acres of American farmland are being taken out of production in order to reduce the large surplus of grains and other agricultural produce that is now in storage. The reasons given are economic. In order to keep grain prices above a certain level the federal government will reduce the costs of storage of surplus grains it has purchased in past years; individual producers will by growing less grain, keep the market price at a level that better insures their profits. Such interests have plausible justifications within the designation of a particular whole, a particular set of circumstances. For the sake of the well-being of individual farmers, the agricultural sector of the American economy, and the economic obligations of the federal government, this policy is being pursued. Of course other interests even in this country will bear some of the cost; the depressed farm-machinery industry will find that the market for its products will be further reduced in the short and long runs. If, however, a given farmer in Iowa takes land out of grain production this year, it is not because he thinks it is a good thing for persons in other parts of the world to suffer malnutrition; the farmer does not intend such evil.

The victims of the malnutrition that results from overpopulation and from inadequate agricultural production are seldom causally accountable for their plight. In the most critical circumstances those who suffer are innocent. God has not so ordered the world that even the minimal provisions for survival and health can be made available to many persons. Meteorological changes in the upper atmosphere affect climatic conditions, which in turn affect sources of food for human beings. The failure of monsoons, the encroachment of deserts, and other forces are beyond human control, and thus certainly beyond the control of those individuals and communities who are their primary victims. Poverty-stricken lands are sometimes without sufficient resources to purchase or trade for the basic rudiments needed to sustain human life under critical conditions. None of the victims chose to be born, and probably none of them chose to reside where they do. Poverty and legal restrictions reduce their mobility.

To be sure, landowners, governments, and others have sometimes taken courses of action in their economic interests which are causal factors in the shortage of nutrition. Land has been used for products that are internationally marketable in order to increase financial capital resources as well as profit. The victims of such policies are largely powerless. One can charge that injustice has been done, and that this needs to be rectified by changes in policies and practices; yet the victims at any given time are innocent with regard to their plight due to their relative powerlessness.

There may be occasional signs of very admirable human qualities that emerge as persons deal with their adverse conditions in dignity, or even meet the needs of others at great cost to themselves. Such signs, however, never justify the suffering, and never compensate for it. Christian theologians, including Thomas Aquinas, have argued that the taking of food when one is starving is not theft, and thus not a sin. But when there is nothing more to share, not to mention to steal, even that course of action is removed.

Such circumstances have to be thought about theologically, and not just ethically; one cannot ignore them when one attempts to understand and conceive God's relations to the world, and particularly to human beings. Religious people and theologians have, of course, thought about natural evils from biblical times to the present. The story of Job is only one such account. In non-Western religions, as well, natural evil is accounted for. Conceptual escapes have been devised to reduce the dissonance between this sort of experience and the presumptive love of God who cares for each human being. But for large numbers of persons to be subjected to intense suffering and untimely death as a result of powers that bear down upon them, powers insufficient to sustain even their basic biological needs, powers beyond their control and sometimes beyond any human control, is something too easily glossed over both in Christian theology and piety. To be sure, there is human responsibility to attempt to so order life in the world that human suffering can be mitigated if not relieved. Some courses of action are available to persons, institutions, and groups though they are limited by established economic and other relations. But the exercise of human wisdom and power according to good intentions has not been able to save people from the consequences of imbalance between human population and available nutritional resources in all times and places on our planet.

One can glibly say that "life is unfair," and that no one, including God, can be held accountable for chance. In my judgment, however, life's unfairness in critical matters of massive suffering of innocent persons is not something easily explained away theologically. To presume too facilely in the face of such events that God is for man and cares for each individual, or that while God's will is inscrutable we know that God's chief end is the salvation of man, is religiously seductive and morally numbing. To focus on human disordering is a proper step, but to question whether the divine order cares for, not to mention guarantees, the well-being of man is also legitimate.

It is my reasoned conviction that as in the past history of our species so also in its future there will be times and places in which a satisfactory balance between human population and nutrition will not occur. The human task is to seek to avoid such occasions; there are ethical reasons for so doing. But the victims will always be tragic; untimely illnesses and deaths will occur due to forces they cannot, and sometimes no human powers can, control.

Some Variables

In this chapter I can only show how one can think ethically about this issue from a theocentric perspective. The two foci chosen for attention, population and nutrition, already involve a simplification. The explanations for increase and decrease in birth rates are complex, and discussions occur among specialists as to which are most critical. Population increase over the past decades has resulted not only from an increase in birth rates but also from a decrease in death rates and the extension of the life span. Decrease in death rates and extension of life span are due more to better public health measures than they are to advances in high-technology medical therapy. Sewage control and purer water supplies extend more lives than kidney dialysis and artificial hearts. A fuller interpretation of the circumstances that I can give here would involve much further analysis of the effects of public health measures and medical advances.

Another dimension is the organization of the world's economy. New forms of economic interdependence have been developed; as a result societies that were more or less self-subsistent at a relatively simple state of technology are being brought into contemporary world-trade patterns. Industrialization in many parts of the world has required the accumulation of capital resources; in order for such resources to be acquired traditional patterns of subsistence farming in many nations have been altered. The poverty of rural existence, industrialization, and the attractiveness of the products of a more technologically sophisticated way of life have drawn masses of people into urban areas. The economic power and interests of particular nations affect their relations with other nations and their domestic economic life. Multinational corporations have been developed with ambiguous outcomes in the lesser-developed nations in which they locate their production and marketing operations. Economic interests of particular groups within nations affect the flow of resources between nations. I have indicated already the example of the ways in which the economic interests of the agricultural sector of the American economy are met by the reduction of food production while the need for food increases on a worldwide scale.

For many persons, and for very vocal segments of the Christian churches in the world, the patterns of international economic relations are deemed to be the most crucial of all in causing poverty, malnutrition, and starvation in parts of the world. The choice of economic institutions is understandable; they have great power to pursue their self-interest; they are subject to collective decisions made by responsible persons and thus can be held morally culpable; they are highly visible in the world and thus make good targets for moral blame. But the tendency toward simplified causal analysis and therefore toward simplified moral responsibility distorts interpretation in many cases. The outcomes of international economic relations are a mixture of costs and benefits and thus their status is more ambiguous than some Christians assume. For persons and groups who need a personification of evil in the world overly simple causal analysis serves a purpose. To analyze the causes of poverty, malnutrition, and starvation, however, is a more complex task than fixing blame simply on economic institutions and their international relations.

Political interests are involved. The distribution of surplus food from the United States has been, from time to time, in the service of the political ends of various national administrations. It has been a tool for international politics. Political interests are also involved in recipient nations; those in control of distribution have been known to direct it in ways to serve their own political interests.

No manipulation of technological, economic, political, and other factors, however, will guarantee freedom from malnutrition in many parts of the world. India is extolled again and again as a nation that has achieved a self-sufficiency in grain production as a result of modern agricultural technology. Yet the failure of monsoons for one or two seasons could easily jeopardize that achievement; all the forces of nature are not under human control. And the extent of illness due to less success in achieving public health goals and in distributing food to all who need it remains an enormous problem.

I have stressed the importance of the evaluative description of the circumstances we address in our ethical reflection. The time and space boundaries we construct around the problem are critical choices. To address the issue of the existence of one hungry family near one that has a lavish diet is quite a different moral problem than that of the relations of nations with surplus grain to those deficient in food supplies. To think about what constitutes responsible parenthood in a single middle-income family in the United States relative to its resources for caring for children is quite a different matter than to think of global population growth relative to the present resources of the planet. Time-spans and space-spans are very different in each; causal analysis becomes much more complex in the enlarged problem; "blame" has to be more widely spread, including "blame" on nature and even on the ultimate ordering power of life; courses of action to meet the issue are varied, and there is no single "actionable" center of power to resolve the perceived evil conditions. We are participants in very complex patterns and processes of interdependence: those within the "natural" order; those that relate human activities to what occurs in the natural order; those that are historical and cultural, and create political, moral, and other limits or possibilities for action. Just as victims of malnutrition and starvation in various places are powerless to control their destinies, so also the requirements to meet their needs are so broadly distributed that the actions of individuals are without desired effects. There is moral merit in adopting simpler patterns of food consumption and limiting family size as expressive or representational acts, and there is merit in donating the savings achieved to agencies seeking to relieve world hunger, but the magnitude of the largest whole, the global one, is so great that these have limited effects.

Different evaluative descriptions and different causal analyses will lead to different prescriptions of policy. The decision by an analyst as to what kind of problem, basically, is to be dealt with will make a difference in the recommendations that follow. What one determines is a "relevant whole" and what one judges to be the principal determinants of the well- or ill-being of that whole and its parts are critical judgments. To frame the problem as the relations between population and nutrition is not to have determined precisely what factors are actionable, and what means of action are to be recommended. It is only to state that population growth should be controlled and the amount of nutritional resources increased. To focus on two important variables, however, provides some limitations, some degree of manageability, to our thinking.

I have previously in this work noted the importance of the symbols that are chosen to interpret events. The selection of symbols, analogies, and metaphors is critical to the circumscription of a problem, to how it is represented, and to the solutions that follow. Metaphors and analogies can elucidate and help us to penetrate into difficult issues; they can also limit us, blinding us to possibilities of understanding and action. Thus they must be chosen and used with great care, and their limits as well as their contributions have to be understood.[1]

Garrett Hardin has proposed two images which have widely affected the discussion of moral responsibility and policy proposals, and provoked a great deal of critical response. In "The Tragedy of the Commons," he proposed a way to get a fix on the proportions of resources to population.[2] A historical analogy is used: just as the commons on which residents of a given area had a right to graze their livestock has fixed limits, so also the world has fixed limits. Just as additional livestock using the commons would work to the disadvantage of all, so growth in human population will work to the disadvantage of all. The commons becomes a metaphor that seems to be enlightening; it has the advantage of simplicity and of visualizing an extreme

1. The literature on the use of symbols, metaphors, analogies, and similes to achieve knowledge and understanding is growing. My research and thinking in this area is very limited. See, however, David Tracy, *The Analogical Imagination* (New York: Crossroad, 1981), George Lakoff and Mark Johnson, *Metaphors We Live By* (Chicago: University of Chicago Press, 1981), and the important symposium volume, Sheldon Sacks, ed., *On Metaphor* (Chicago: University of Chicago Press, 1979), with papers by, among others, David Tracy, Donald Davidson, Paul de Man, Wayne Booth, and Paul Ricoeur.

2. Garrett Hardin, "The Tragedy of the Commons," *Science* 162 (13 December 1968):1243–48.

situation. As such it evokes a sense of the seriousness of the problem, and for some people the sense of impending doom. It pictures the problem in a dramatic way. Many critics, however, have pointed out that it is overly simple because it tends to foreclose various possible courses of action. The number of livestock can be limited or even reduced; also the commons can be expanded and the productivity of it can be increased. The adequacy of the metaphor is challenged; it does not convey the full story of the human possibilities in our interrelations with the natural world.

Hardin's second contribution to the symbolism of the population issue was the notion of a lifeboat. The lifeboat example has an interesting history in ethical and legal thought. The sense of crisis evoked is perhaps even greater than in the case of the commons. The critical choice is who shall live and who shall die when not all can live; if all were given the resources to live on an equal basis all might die. Does a nation with resources for its own survival and well-being have a strict obligation to share them with nations and peoples in danger of starvation? Or can it morally protect its self-interest regardless of the fateful consequences to others? Is it the responsibility of each nation to attend to its own interests, to its own "carrying capacity," and thus to have no claim on another nation when life is threatened? The symbol of the lifeboat has great rhetorical power; like all hard cases in moral thought its extremity forces difficult choices. One foresees the most drastic situation, and from that one thinks not only about what ought to be done if that situation becomes a reality but also about what are the possibilities and obligations of all nations to avoid its becoming a reality. It is, at least, thought-provoking; its impact, however, is often to convince persons that the crisis exists now and that extreme measures are now justified.[3]

A related symbol is that of triage. An analogy is drawn from emergency medical situations in which there are insufficient resources to save all who are in need and choices must be made about which persons are most worthy of treatment. One of the most frequently cited examples of this comes from World War II; those soldiers who were most likely to recover rapidly and thus could be returned to battle were given preference in treatment. If medical triage is justifiable in such circumstances, by analogy (so the argument goes) social triage is defensible. Powerful and wealthy nations and societies are to decide which populations will be consigned to

3. Among several collections of essays that deal with the issues involved in food and population and that discuss Hardin's metaphors are Ian G. Barbour, ed., *Finite Resources and the Human Future* (Minneapolis: Augsburg Publishing House, 1976), which reprints Hardin's essay, "Lifeboat Ethics: Food and Population"; George R. Lucas, Jr., and Thomas W. Ogletree, eds., *Lifeboat Ethics: The Moral Dilemmas of World Hunger* (New York: Harper and Row Forum Books, 1976). For a careful ethical analysis of many of the issues, see Robin Lovin's review-article of nine recent books, "Self-sufficiency or Equitable Development: Moral Issues in World Food Policy," *Religious Studies Review* 7(1981):328–32.

suffering and death if meeting their need threatens the standard of living of the powerful nation. Like the commons and the lifeboat, triage provides a symbol for an evaluative description, and if its use is judged to be appropriate certain courses of action are backed by it. The reasoning is consequentialist; the desired end, however, is not the greatest happiness of the greatest number, but a "sociocentric" or even nationalistic understanding of whose good is to be served.

Every interpretation of the problem gives certain information special weight; other information does not get equal attention or is ignored. We have passed the mid-1970s when some alarmists predicted world famine of tremendous proportions. Those predictions failed to take adequate account of certain actual and possible developments. The precise character of the problem is constantly shifting as a result of many factors, and thus alterations in perception, description, and analysis have to be made regularly. Following from them alterations in the courses of action are required.

There is no "natural" balance between world population and the global capacity to produce nutrients. The world has changed since the time of Malthus as a result of developments in various sciences and technologies. Science and technology enable human beings to intervene into nature in ways that serve human needs and interests; culture exists between human bodies and their natural environment. Man is a participant in the patterns and processes of interdependence in nature; man is not merely a reactor to natural forces utterly beyond control. Those patterns and processes of interdependence change as a result of cultural developments; the ways in which human lives can be sustained or threatened vary with scientific and technological (cultural) developments. The state of technology is a source of operational moral norms; both the possibilities and requirements of action shift, and the rate of cultural development is rapid in our time. There are new methods for controlling population growth and for increasing the supply of nutrients; thus there are new possibilities and new obligations to attack the problem.

In the twentieth century there has been amazing success in avoiding famine. In 1975 the international agricultural economist D. Gale Johnson wrote as follows.

> Both the percentage of the population afflicted by famine and the absolute numbers involved during the past quarter century have been small compared to what has prevailed during the period of history for which we have reasonably reliable estimates of the number of famine deaths. There appears to have been a rather steady reduction in the incidence of famine. In the last quarter of the 19th Century perhaps 20 to 25 million died from famine. Adjusting for population increase, a projected figure for the third quarter of the 20th Century would be at least 50 million and for

> the quarter century we are entering, at least 75 million. In reality, for the entire 20th Century, famine deaths have probably been only about 12 to 15 million and most were the result of deliberate governmental policy or due to war.[4]

This is an astounding human achievement; catastrophes that could have been predicted on Malthusian calculations have been avoided. While this evidence ought not to harden human compassion or lead to complacency, it stands as a measure of hope for the future. It confirms that there is in modern culture no "natural balance" between human population and nutrition on a world-wide scale. Both are subject to human intervention.

Yet no one, to my knowledge, has proposed that our planet can sustain all the possible persons that could be born, nor that there are sufficient resources to sustain the standard of living of technologically advanced nations for all persons in the world. It is because of such limits that the papal teaching on birth control, affirmed in the encyclical *Humanae Vitae* by Pope Paul VI, and reaffirmed over and over by some of the church leadership since then, is of very questionable morality. As I have previously indicated, the argument is flawed by interpreting the "whole" in such a way that certain features of the human situation are denied moral relevance.

Any forecast of the future growth of world population has a significant margin of error since so many different events and developments could alter the outcome. With this caveat it is still worthwhile to remind readers of some forecasts, all on the assumption that all other things would remain equal. The following figures are drawn from the *1981 World Population Data Sheet*; the use of the doubling time of population growth in nation by nation has a rather dramatic rhetorical effect.

In the United States, with a population of about 230 million, the process of doubling would take 95 years. In Sweden, with a population of a little over 8 million, it would take 1,155 years. In Mexico, with a population of 69 million, it would take 28 years. In India, population of 687 million, 33 years. In Iran, population of about 40 million, 23 years. In Belgium, popula-

4. D. Gale Johnson, *World Food Problems in Perspective* (Chapel Hill, N.C.: Institute of Nutrition, University of North Carolina), Occasional Paper Series, vol. 1, no. 6 (1975), p. 3. In a personal communication to me, dated November 6, 1981, Johnson wrote about the above: "These figures reflected what I thought we knew about 1973. If I were writing the paper today I would raise the estimate of 12-to-15 million famine deaths to a somewhat higher figure. There are two reasons for this: First, at the time of writing I accepted the general view that China had not suffered a famine in the early 1960s; this assumption now appears to be incorrect. Second, there have been famines of some significance during the 1970s—Bangladesh in 1973, Nigeria in the early 1970s, Sahel, Uganda, Cambodia, Ethiopia-Somalia more recently. Each of these famines was the result or aftermath of civil war or could have been prevented by prompter action by the governments involved.

"On a basis comparable to the figure of 20-to-25 million famine deaths for the last quarter of the 19th Century, I would put the estimate of famine deaths for the first eight decades of the 20th Century at approximately the same absolute number." Quoted by permission.

tion of about 10 million, 578 years. In East Germany, population of about 17 million, 6,930 years. In Gaza, population of .4 million, 19 years. In the world as a whole, with a population of about 4.5 billion, it would take 41 years for the population double.[5] No one believes that other things will remain equal. and thus these forecasts are fallible; they nonetheless provide a rough account of what might be anticipated in the future.

The number of articles published in *Science* is not necessarily an accurate indication of the state of research in various areas, but it may indicate something important. In the seven months before this writing there were no articles on new developments in birth control, but there were at least seven which addressed various problems and possibilities in the area of food production. I dare to infer from this that there is a great deal of research going on with reference to the production and utilization of nutrients; perhaps there is less new research on birth control. The practical issues in either variable, however, are not resolved. If known means of conception control were used, the birth rate could be decreased significantly; it is also not easy to change the eating customs and habits of people even when more efficient use of agricultural products is known.

Some Ethical Approaches

Various ethical approaches can be taken to come to some recommendations about population growth and nutrition. One can be inferred from the morality of birth control as espoused by the teaching authorities of the Roman Catholic Church. The argument can be developed as follows.

It is undue interference into the intimacy of relationships in the primary community of the family to use any procedures which can be interpreted as coercive in order to have couples limit their family size. It is permissible for couples to limit the number of their children, but self-restraint of sexual activity is the only morally licit means. Every act of sexual intercourse in marriage must be open to the possibility of the transmission of life; nothing that the church judges to be an artificial means of birth control is approved. Thus, as I indicated in chapter 2, consideration of the common good of the human species within limits of production of nutrition on our planet is not, in this argument, a moral justification even for the use of artificial means for conception control.

It is also the case that every human being deserves to have his or her life sustained and preserved; each has a right to the resources needed for personal well-being. In Catholic social encyclicals arguments were made in favor of wages being based upon family need rather than on earning capaci-

5. "1981 World Population Data Sheet," (Washington, D.C.: The Population Reference Bureau, n.d.).

ties of working members of the family; it was recommended that family allotments and other devices be developed by the state to supplement the earnings of a family.

In the strongest interpretation of this position there are two inalienable rights: to procreate and to have life and health sustained. An implication for policy seems to be that parents can have as many children as they choose, that the necessary food be produced to care for all, and that public policy is morally bound to see that food is distributed to all who need it. If families cannot sustain their offspring it is morally obligatory for others, including social institutions, to assist them.

From the perspective of the present work the basic flaw in this position is the limitation of the whole whose common good has to be taken into account. A number of important factual matters, as well as future probabilities, are judged to be morally irrelevant. The well-being of the family is a common good that is worthy of support regardless of family size. The well-being of a nation of families or of the species is not of sufficient weight to warrant the use of artificial means of birth control. The common good of the human community is not a morally approved entity, at least when an adverse ratio of population to nutrition suggests birth control as a means to ameliorate the problem. (The common good of humanity is appealed to at least implicitly, however, in the concern of many church leaders for the possible consequences of a nuclear war.) The undue restriction of circumstances deemed to be morally relevant is dictated by what is determined to be *the* critical moral issue, namely, the means used to prevent conception. No artificial means are licit; at this point the biological law of nature and the moral law of nature are the same. While it is appropriate to intervene into nature "artificially" for many other ends, including the increase of food production, it is not appropriate at this point. The consequences of interventions are considered in other cases, and their potential beneficial or harmful consequences assessed. But in this case a "deontic" weight is given to the proscription of a particular action.

If the obligation to sustain the lives of all who are born (every human being having an inherent right to such sustenance), is coupled with this proscription of the use of artificial means of conception control, the only policy options are to increase the amount of nutrients available and distribute them to all who are in need. Thus technological innovations that increase food production are lauded, as they should be. But this, it seems to me, becomes the primary, if not the only, morally approved course of action. Only one of our two variables is subject to a morally approved practical course of action. From the perspective of the present work, the official teachings of the Roman Catholic Church on this matter, while understandable, are wrong; indeed, they are immoral. A relevant whole that ought to be considered is current humanity and future generations. And in thinking about this large whole considerations have to be taken of many variables such as ecological effects of modern agricultural technology required to produce more food.

A second ethical approach would be as follows. Just as individuals have indirect, but nonetheless strong, obligations to act beneficently for others, so do social groups and nations. But duties of beneficence to others require first of all strict duties to oneself. This is a generally Kantian argument, extended from the sphere of individuals to social entities.

The argument for duties to one's own community and nation are not based upon fellow-feeling, natural kinship, or loyalty. Rather the individual or community must maintain the necessary conditions for it to act in its own proper self-interest, whatever that may be. This is a prior condition for acting on behalf of the interests of other groups and nations. Weak analogies from arguments about suicide can be drawn to illustrate this. It will be recalled that one of Kant's arguments is that persons have strict obligations as moral beings to sustain the necessary conditions for human action. By analogy, a nation or community has strict obligations to itself not to weaken the conditions required to meet its own proper interests; and it cannot be beneficent to other nations and communities if its own strength and capacities weaken. One of the arguments against suicide by Thomas Aquinas was based upon the contributions that individuals make to the good of the community; for a person to destroy himself or herself deprives the community of a participant as a part of a whole. By analogy, a group or nation that participates in the common good of the whole human community through its production of food must attend to its own productive resources, for to fail to do so would vitiate its capacities to participate in the common good. Duties of beneficence and participation in a common good require duties to oneself to maintain the capacities and strengths to pursue proper self-interest and to meet obligations of beneficence to others.

Something like this argument might be used to justify current American agricultural economic policies, though it is likely that economic self-interest and political considerations are the operative reasons. On the basis of this kind of moral argument the primary obligation of internal farm policy would be to maintain a healthy, economically profitable agricultural sector in the United States. Whether the capacities to maintain high agricultural productivity back a strict obligation to meet the food needs of other nations would depend upon the applicability of different principles. For example, if one country is obliged to provide the necessary conditions for the well-being of another only so long as there is no comparable cost to itself, one policy might follow. If, however, given limited capacities to produce food, it can only sustain the lives of others at some cost to its own economic profitability or to the customary diet of its citizens, a further principle would have to be invoked. In either case, however, figuratively speaking, the United States,

Canada, or any country that can produce surplus food would be under no obligation to mutiliate itself, or commit agricultural suicide, in order to feed the whole of a growing world population.[6] This would be especially the case if other nations are not doing what they can to restrain population growth or increase their own food supplies. Our capacities to meet the needs of others are dependent upon our own strength; our first duties are to ourselves. Duties to others exist. On Kantian grounds they are "imperfect duties" and on Thomistic grounds one might say they are grounded in our membership in the human family; both arguments require the prior condition of strength in ourselves.

This kind of argument is more defensible from my perspective than are the policy inferences I draw from the official teaching of the Roman Catholic Church. That teaching quite properly supports agricultural growth on the part of highly productive nations; but in itself it does not precisely address the issues of "duties to oneself." That it could, in principle, I think is the case; at least some Roman Catholic moral theologians, for example, have argued that if one has constructed a survival shelter for a nuclear war one has a right to ward off any who have not provided for themselves and who might wish to share it. I know of no use of this kind of argument, however, with reference to population and nutrition.

What is appropriate about the foregoing argument is that (a) it recognizes the importance of any highly productive nation to sustain and develop the capacities of its own food production both for its own sake and that of others, and that (b) other "agents," i.e., nations, have obligations to themselves to increase their own nutritional resources and control their population growth. Agents are accountable for themselves, as well as being recipients of the beneficence of other nations that can meet their needs.

The temptation that follows from this kind of argument is the erosion of compassion for the victims of malnutrition in other nations. It becomes all too easy to hold governments and other social units fully accountable for their plight when their capacities to meet their needs either through increase in food production or restraint of population growth are limited. More painful is the possibility that one becomes insensitive to the innocent suffering of persons who suffer malnutrition and starvation through no causal accountability and therefore no moral responsibility of their own. The question that must be placed to the highly productive nation is, What standard of living is judged to be necessary to sustain its own survival or well-being and its capacities to produce food which will sustain the lives of others? Complacency can easily set in; doing something for others at no comparable cost to oneself can lead to the assumption that there are no reasons to alter present patterns of consumption (that would be of some

6. In extreme form this becomes the lifeboat argument.

cost) for the sake of the well-being of others. If a nation justifies its policies in terms of duties to itself both as prior to and as a ground for meeting obligations to others, the outcome is likely to create innocent victims in pursuit of a justifiable end; tragedy is virtually unavoidable.

A third kind of argument is that persons, groups, and nations should have such good-will, i.e., benevolence, toward those in need that they would voluntarily assist them even at the cost of some of their individual and collective interests. This is the traditional prescription of philanthropy or charity. It might be backed by appeals to the sense of compassion in the face of the suffering of others, by the Golden Rule, or by historic religious appeals. These latter might be (a) God has given us the good things of life beyond our deserts, and thus we should be willing to share them with those who suffer due to no fault of their own, or (b) in imitation of the form in which God's love was shown in the life and death of Jesus, Christians should be ready to sacrifice their interests for the sake of the needs of others.

Although it can be argued that persons ought to be benevolent toward one another, goodwill, and especially willingness to sacrifice one's own interests for the sake of others, can hardly be commanded. The religious tradition has understood that love of neighbor is a matter of the heart as well as of moral duty. It is even more difficult to argue that collectivities, for example, nations, have a duty to be benevolent toward others. Certain groups and even nations have had reputations of being voluntarily generous toward those in need, but insofar as this exists in a collective form it is a matter of culture rather than command. On the basis of reason alone one cannot obligate persons to be of goodwill as a necessary backing for beneficence to those in need, though goodwill can be appealed to in individuals and groups as a way of supporting policies that are publicly justified on other grounds.

I have indicated in several places that there are both motives and duties that are characteristic of particular communities, and that within ethics from a theocentric perspective there are explanations and justifications for Christians being motivated and obligated to meet the needs of others at cost to themselves. Indeed, voluntary giving of resources to meet the hunger of others has a deep appeal and, I would say, an obligatory weight for the Christian community. Compassion is human and thus can be appealed to without religious backing, but the Christian story and the church as a community in the service of others strongly support the opportunity and the requirement to be self-giving.

The limits of the efficacy of the appeal are historically apparent. Christians are not particularly notable for undertaking inconvenience to themselves, not to mention self-sacrifice, for the sake of the needs of others. Giving of our "surplus," and not at cost to our necessities, is relative to our standards of living. And even Christians cannot be utterly heedless in their giving; as early as the *Didache* we have admonitions to "prudence" directed to the Christian almsgiver.[7] Indeed, Christian groups have been concerned not only to meet emergency needs but also to enable others to achieve greater self-sufficiency in food production. Neighbor love is expressed in helping others meet their own needs. Theocentric piety and fidelity enable and require religious persons and groups to try to help others to avoid malnutrition and starvation. But even at best such benevolence and its fruits will not be sufficient to meet present and highly probable future circumstances.

A fourth kind of argument is from a principle of distributive justice. In the Western moral tradition there are two formal principles of distributive justice: equals shall be treated equally (or similar cases treated similarly), and to each his or her due. Each of these requires that other questions be raised. With reference to the first, Who are the equals who are to be treated equally? On what basis or principle does one decide who they are? What is to be distributed equally among them? The questions with reference to the second are, What is due to any given person? On what basis or principle does one decide what is due to whom? Our concern here is about the distribution of nutrients.

No one would argue for an arithmetically equal distribution of available food to all persons in a given community, not to mention all who populate the earth, i.e., that each person should receive an equal amount of wheat or rice or beef or oranges. There are, however, strong arguments to support distribution of food according to need. Who are the equals to be treated equally? All persons, because all need food to survive and be well-nourished. Why ought their needs to be met equally? Various ethical positions would give different answers: they are sensate beings and others ought to help them to avoid pain and suffering; they are human persons who deserve equal respect, and respect for their persons requires that the necessary conditions for their existence be provided; they are all God's children, all are in the "image of God," and all equal in the "eyes" of God; the Golden Rule applies to all persons, and so forth. What is due to each person? At least those provisions which enable them to survive and have a measure of physical health. If there is a basis for the ultimate equality and worth of all

7. "Give to everyone that asks, without looking for any repayment, for it is the Father's pleasure that we should share His gracious bounty with all men. A giver who gives freely, as the commandment directs, is blessed; no fault can be found with him. But woe to the taker; for though he cannot be blamed for taking if he was in need, yet if he was not, an account will be required of him as to why he took it, and for what purpose, and he will be taken into custody and examined about his action, and he will not get out until he has paid the last penny. The old saying is in point here: 'Let your alms grow damp with sweat in your hand, until you know who it is you are giving them to.'" *The Didache*, 1, in *Early Christian Writings*, trans. Maxwell Staniforth (New York: Penguin Books, 1968), p. 227.

persons, there is a basis for arguing that distributive justice mandates that the fundamental needs for living be met for each and for all.

Distributive justice requires nonpreferential treatment of others. Whether they live in an agriculturally productive society or one that is marginal, whether they belong to families that practice birth control or not, whether their government is engaged in responsible policies of food production or birth control or not—each person deserves the nutrients to survive. Whether they live in socialist countries or in those that are politically allied with the United States, whether they are Muslims, animists, Hindus, Christians, or Jews is irrelevant. Those who are undernourished have a claim on those who have more food than they need as a matter of strict distributive justice. Whether the meeting of needs is motivated by compassion or Christian love is irrelevant; their claim is based on a moral principle. Ought implies can; there is a moral obligation on the part of nations to produce the food necessary for all persons, to make the economic and political arrangements necessary to get it to those in need, and to engage in all other practical procedures to fulfill the obligation.

This is a position that ought to be defended; and it is backed by the theocentric perspective I have developed. But the achievement of distributive justice is always related to various conditions of finitude. To say this, however, is not to warrant self-satisfaction, to say that present perceptions of the conditions are fixed and that there is no obligation to extend the possibilities both of production and distribution of nutrients. The use of food as an instrument of political purposes, if it involves suffering and loss of life in other nations, is morally abominable, no matter what justification there is for the political ends. But if the common good of humanity is a proper moral whole, it is also the case that responsibilities are mutual, and that within their capacities all nations have obligations to increase their own self-sufficiency in food production and to encourage methods of birth control. The acceptance of responsibilities as being mutual is an aspect of how communities are related to each other in a manner appropriate to their relations to God. Various courses of action have to be explored and developed between the extremities of the ideal of distribution according to need on the one hand and the doomsday scenarios of triage and lifeboat ethics on the other. Tragedy and suffering, however, cannot be completely avoided.

If basic need is not the material principle of distributive justice, various forms of desert, or deserving, necessarily become the material principle. The idea of desert is preferential, though the principle of equal distribution, or of giving to each his or her due, is still applicable. Those who are to be treated equally are those who deserve to be treated equally because of some merit they have achieved: accountability they have taken for themselves, contributions to the well-being of some larger whole, and so forth. The pertinent argument with reference to food and population growth is that those nations and communities that do not exercise any duties to themselves in this regard can lay no moral claim on those who are more responsible in food production and birth control. Such a view is supportable within the pattern of reciprocity of obligations for the sake of the common good, and of acceptance of accountability for individual and collective actions. The difficulty in application is clear: the variables that make merit possible, and the judgment of what is sufficiently meritorious are by no means fixed or easy to formulate. The morally relevant "facts" are bound to be disputed by various persons.

The oversimplification of assumptions in what I have written about the uses of these ethical arguments has to be acknowledged. The patterns of interdependence in food production and distribution that already exist render some of the arguments very problematic. At least two important qualifications have to be made with reference to achieving greater degrees of national self-sufficiency in food production. One is that insofar as world trade is regulated by the competitive price structures of the free-market system, nations will produce those commodities and goods that are most profitable to them and purchase those things they need, including food, from others who can produce them more cheaply. The whole that needs to be considered as self-sufficient in food production is no longer marked by national boundaries. One of the complaints against some international corporations is that they encourage the use of imported food products through effective advertising and marketing and thus contribute to the erosion of production, especially in developing countries. The second qualification is the development of economic communities such as the Common Market in Western Europe. Such pacts intensify interdependence between nations, and result in dislocations or relocations of agricultural production. One hopes that these forms of interdependence will be a restraint on the outbreak of war, but the specter of war or some other catastrophe looms and the consequences could be more disastrous than in the past because of the reliance of various nations upon others for their fundamental nutritional needs.

I have already indicated respects in which the kinds of arguments briefly presented above are compatible with ethics from a theocentric perspective. It remains in this chapter to develop a more coherent interpretation of population and nutrition from a theocentric perspective.

The Approach from Theocentric Ethics

The issue of population and nutrition highlights multiple forms and levels of interdependence. The threat of malnutrition and famine, like that of earthquakes and tornadoes, gives the lie to assertions of man's domination of nature. Human life remains dependent upon natural forces and powers that are not fully in human control. The number of children could be controlled: sterilization, conception control, abortion, and infanticide are all means to this end. The use of most of these means is very old in human culture. There are, however, both practical and moral restraints upon their efficient use. The supply of nutrients can be increased and their distribution improved, but the deepest reliance upon nature as their source remains, and some parts of the world are more vulnerable than others to nature's vicissitudes. I have stressed that there is no natural balance between nutrition and population; human intervention, culture, has long been a factor in the circumstances of any particular group. Nonetheless, any human policies and activities to improve conditions have to take into account natural limitations and possibilities. Though the signals of an ultimate ordering beyond the powers of man to control are not clear, and though the destiny of the species is not fated in the foreseeable future by inexorable natural forces, patterns and processes of interdependence of human life with the wider order of nature necessarily must be taken into account. The general obligation based upon our participation in the patterns and processes of interdependence is that the production and distribution of food on the one hand and the size of the human population on the other ought to be correlated so as to avoid malnutrition and famine in any given generation and place, but also so as to avoid possible severe outcomes in the future. But, as I noted, no person or government has the power to control all the variables involved; for many reasons it is not desirable that any ought to have such power. Creating, sustaining, or limiting the numbers of human beings are not ends in themselves.

Human values and ethical principles give guidance to the course of events that is taking place. Ideals, such as every human being having sufficient nutrition, or principles, such as distribution of nutrients according to need, can be formed and provide aspirations, but the limits and possibilities of various courses of action require special attention in this area. For purposes of development of this section, I shall first discuss some relevant wholes and then separate the two variables I have chosen in order to indicate what seem to be possible courses of action, and what moral considerations must be taken into account in pursuing them.

To think globally about the problem requires that the earth's ecosphere be taken into account, not only with reference to the needs of the present population but also with reference to the short- and long-range future probabilities both of population growth and development of food supplies. We are not now in a zero-sum game, and will not be in the foreseeable future.[8] Recall the observations of D. Gale Johnson, cited

8. "A zero-sum game is any game where the losses exactly equal the winnings." Lester C. Thurow, *The Zero-Sum Society*, p. 11.

above, as evidences of what human participation has been able to achieve. The future consequences of various technological innovations have to be assessed as accurately as possible. The possibilities for development of food ought not to be underestimated, nor should one underestimate the concern of investigators for future outcomes of the use of their work. Aspects of the ecosphere are malleable and can be developed to meet human needs without destroying it.

The moralist concerned about these matters has to be informed about current and prospective scientific developments. To indicate both possibilities and concerns for limits I quote from the summaries of recent articles published in *Science*; the articles go into much greater detail. As is to be expected, not all of the authors agree about which possibilities are most promising, and which limits are most formidable; nonetheless a range of investigation to meet the food needs of the world while being sensitive to ecological matters can be illustrated.

An article by Norman E. Borlaug, who received the Nobel Prize for his work that led to the present success of the green revolution, is summarized as follows.

> Within a relatively short geological time frame, Neolithic man, or more probably woman, domesticated all the major cereal grains, legumes, and root crops that the world's people depend on for most of their calories and protein. Until very recently, crop improvement was in the hands of farmers. The cornerstones of modern plant breeding were laid by Darwin and Mendel in the late 19th century. As the knowledge of genetics, plant pathology, and entomology have grown during the 20th century, plant breeders have made enormous contributions to increased food production throughout the world. . . . Since it is doubtful that significant production benefits will soon be forthcoming from the use of genetic engineering techniques with higher plants, most research funds for crop improvement should continue to be allocated for conventional plant breeding research.[9]

An article in the same number of *Science* acknowledges that the state of research in plant genetics does not promise immediate results, but the summary adds the following.

> However, the benefits to be gained from all aspects of plant improvement are stimulating research into both the development of plant transformation technology and the isolation and characterization of genes responsible for valuable traits. As scientists develop greater knowledge of plant molecular genetics, we can expect to

9. Norman E. Borlaug, "Contributions of Conventional Plant Breeding to Food Production," *Science* 219 (11 February 1983):689. An interesting comparative analysis could be made between the articles cited here and those in *Science* 188, no. 4188 (9 May 1975), on food.

> see practical applications in such diverse areas as improvement of plant nutritional quality, decreases in fertilization requirements, and increases in resistance to environmental stresses and pathogens.[10]

One area of investigation is the relationship between plant productivity and environmental factors. J.S. Boyer's article on this is summarized as follows.

> An analysis of major U.S. crops shows that there is a large genetic potential for yield that is unrealized because of the need for better adaptation of plants to the environments in which they are grown. Evidence from native [plant] populations suggests . . . opportunities for adaptation to such environments are substantial. Genotypic selection for adaptation to such environments has already played an important role in agriculture, but the fundamental mechanisms are poorly understood. Recent scientific advances make exploration of these mechanisms more feasible and could result in large gains in productivity.[11]

After demonstrating that the great increase in food production in developing countries has been based on chemical technologies, Nyle C. Brady shows beneficial possibilities for the future even in areas not well endowed with natural and economic resources.

> Innovative chemical and biochemical approaches must be called upon to produce crop varieties, animal strains, and associated technologies to overcome constraints such as insects and diseases, acid and alkaline soils, and drought conditions. Genetic engineering will probably be a primary mechanism to achieve this goal.[12]

Other investigations deal with native plants, for example, cassava, and can lead to improvement in their quality and efficient usage in various parts of the world.[13]

Together with the research reports that indicate prospects for increasing nutrition are those that warn of problems in present agricultural

10. Kenneth A. Barton and Winston J. Brill, "Prospects in Plant Genetic Engineering," in *Science* 219 (11 February 1983):671. It is worth noting here that concern has been expressed about excessive specialization in the development of grains which might render them susceptible to destruction in the future in ways not now anticipated. In anticipation of such a possibility "banks" are being organized and developed to preserve a large variety of natural grain seeds. Even the foresighted concern for the future of our species leads to a greater respect for nature. See D. L. Plucknett, N. J. H. Smith, J. T. Williams, and N. Murthi Anishetty, "Crop Germplasm Conservation and Developing Countries," *Science* 220 (8 April 1983):163–69.

11. J. S. Boyer, "Plant Productivity and Environment," *Science* 218 (29 October 1982):443.

12. Nyle C. Brady, "Chemistry and World Food Supplies," *Science* 218 (26 November 1982):847.

13. James H. Cock, "Cassava: A Basic Energy Source in the Tropics," *Science* 218 (19 November 1982):755.

methods. One is soil erosion in the United States; as the following summary indicates, both the national interest and wider ecological concerns demand attention to this problem.

> National increases in row crops at the expense of hay and pasture crops, particularly on steeper slopes, have made the control of erosion a difficult prospect. Management practices that fit the various field conditions are needed to accomplish effective erosion control. These measures should be selected on the basis of soil characteristics, landscape type, and the amount of ongoing erosion. The maintenance of a cropland base adequate to our needs must be a primary national goal.[14]

I have quoted these summaries extensively to adduce evidence for the contributions that scientific research and technology can make to the maintenance and increase of the supply of nutrients for the world population in ways that seem not to lead to ecological doom. Of course they do not address issues of economic organization, political interests, and others that can affect both production and distribution, but they give good evidence that humanity is not in the foreseeable future in a zero-sum game in this regard. Man is a participant in the patterns and processes of interdependence; scientific investigations and technology are means of preserving and enhancing nature's own gifts. The moralist must be alert to these possibilities in order to avoid foreclosing the future by using simple metaphors, i.e., in order to have as accurately informed an evaluative description of the circumstances as possible.

The impact of agricultural and other technologies on the environment is evidence for the interdependence of life within which interventions occur. While there are areas of large geographic effects, such as the impact of acid rain on soil and freshwater streams and lakes in North America and Northern Europe, there are also more limited geographic affects from the use of herbicides and fertilizers. Policies directed toward sustaining a future human population have to be informed by these limiting factors as well as by the investigations that show promise for greater food productivity. There is no way for the moralist to avoid efforts to calculate possible outcomes from various innovations in policy and practice; consequentialism is necessarily a major part of the ethical method. And since there are unforeseeable consequences, measures to monitor outcomes and revise policies and programs are constantly needed. The ecosphere, or more accurately various limited ecospheres, in which the human action to sustain a large population takes place, is one of the wholes that has to be taken into account. Interaction takes place among the parts, and the good of the whole is sustained or

14. W. E. Larson, F. J. Pierce, R. H. Dowdy, "The Threat of Soil Erosion to Long-Term Crop Production," *Science* 219 (4 February 1983):458.

adversely affected by human interventions. Parts are affected by the good of the whole. There is no escaping man's being part of wide and long-ranging patterns and processes of interdependence in nature.

I have already noted that the world economy has become a relevant whole when population and nutrition are the focus of attention. The economic well-being of various nations has been interdependent in many parts of the world for centuries, but modern technology and industrialization have deepened and extended it. It is possible for a bloc of nations to affect in unpredicted ways the future course of events, as the historic oil embargo in 1973 made clear. This event had impact upon food production in part because developing countries were dependent upon oil for various aspects of their agricultural production. Fewer countries are self-sufficient in their food production now than was the case a few decades ago, partially as a result of the operations of the market system on a worldwide basis. I only note the importance of the world economy and call attention to economic interactions within it to indicate that innovations in food production and distribution are both affected by and affect economic institutions and policies. The interdependence of this aspect of human culture with the requirements of natural human needs increases in complexity in the modern world. It is intellectually naive for moralists not to attend to these complex patterns and processes just as it is naive to isolate within them a single set of institutions as responsible for the famine, malnutrition, and poverty that exist on earth. Just as there will always be some imbalance at various times and places between population and nutrition, so there will be outcomes as a result of the world economy that are costly to some peoples and beneficial to others. To mitigate these consequences is the moral dimension of the policy-maker's task. Yet, even though modern communications and transportation make possible more rapid responses to famine when it occurs, it is not likely that a moral ideal will be achieved.

I have noted that nation-states are relevant wholes, but also that with growing economic and political interdependence their capacities to determine policies even within their boundaries are qualified. They do, however, have sufficient power and authority to encourage, if not determine, certain policies and actions that aid in avoiding massive starvation. India is a much-studied case in point. The green revolution has been marvelously successful, and that nation has avoided famines that were predicted with considerable assurance a few decades ago. Distribution remains a problem; malnutrition and diseases that often follow from maldistribution continue to take a toll of untimely deaths. Population control has been less successful than increase in food production, and for many reasons: resistance to coercive measures engaged in by the government during the mid-1970s, the absence of any social security system and thus the necessary reliance of parents on surviving children to care for them, cultural factors including massive illiteracy and beliefs by some that birth control is immoral; the continuing absence of a fair and reliable distribution system of wealth that keeps masses of people at the poverty level, and others. No central government has the knowledge, wisdom, or even the power to control fully all the variables involved, however, and the concentration of authority and power that would be required to be effective leads to infringements on individual aspirations and liberties.

The individual family is a relevant whole, although the effects of its self-restraint in family size and food consumption have only minuscule effects on the global scope of the issue. Families can make choices both about their size and about their patterns of consumption. These choices can be morally conscientious. They can take into account the resources required for their own well-being, and can make judgments about the required limits of consumption to achieve it. Even though the consequences of restraint in one family's size and consumption will not have wide-ranging global effects, an understanding of that restraint's small part in the larger whole can lead to moral choices that serve the wider ends both of present and future generations. Self-denial, if not self-sacrifice, of some interests and desires beyond those for the basic human needs, for the sake of the well-being of other present and future persons as well as of the natural world, is appropriate. Theocentric vision extends the range of considerations taken into account in family choices; it backs a moral consciousness of the consequences for others of choices that are made and can instill the motivation to take them into account in the conduct of family life.

Any whole that is designated to be relevant is interrelated with others, and ultimately could have some relationship to the planetary whole. It is this complexity that makes the problem of nutrition and population so unmanageable. Actions in any given sphere seldom if ever have decisive consequences for the larger spheres in which they interact. The development of culture creates new ways of relating to nature, new economic incentives and disincentives for various forms of action, new and different political and other relationships of power between groups and nations. There is a plurality of values to be considered: sufficient supply of nutrients cannot be achieved at the cost of possible disaster for future generations; the means used to achieve effective control of births is technically limited and there are moral reasons against the use of coercive measures; consequences of particular courses of action done with good intentions are not fully predictable.

If the control of human population growth and the increase of nutrition supplies are both desirable ends within various relevant wholes, how do we think about the morally defensible means to achieve them? The first question asked from the theocentric perspective is not whether certain means of action are immoral in and of themselves, as seems to be the case in the official teaching of the Roman Catholic Church on the matter of birth control. Theocentric ethics does come to the question of the immorality of means, and can judge that certain means are not licit for the ends that are justifiable. But it comes to that after the exploration of various courses of action and of human values and moral principles that are backed by the theocentric perspective; no single value and no single moral principle is sufficient as a basis for resolving complex moral and social issues. To some extent the question of morally defensible means is context-bound, as in the case of medical triage; in the most extremely critical circumstances certain acts of omission and even commission are justifiable that cannot be justified when there are several possible courses of action.

If the ends of increase in the supply of nutrients and control of the rate of growth of human population are justifiable, what means are morally as well as technically permissible to begin to realize them? Are there certain means that are fundamentally immoral and cannot be justified regardless of the desirability of the end?

I have quoted summaries of articles which show that the prospects for the increase in available food supply are by no means closed. Biochemical research on plants and soil points toward long-range promise without foreseeable disastrous ecological outcomes. In the light of this no massive anti-scientific or anti-technological bias is ethically warranted from a theocentric perspective. While the ultimate destiny of the species is not in human hands, man's capacity to be a participant in the natural processes of life creates possibilities for the relief of suffering due to malnutrition and for the continuation and extensions of resources for human physical well-being. When increase in aggregate supply of nutrients reaches the level of human need the moral issues become those of distribution. Indeed, with reference to present capacities for food production in the world, the moral issues are already located there.

Persons responsible for the development of research and technology show concern both for increasing food and for the environment of future generations. While soil erosion has been intensified with the mechanization of agriculture, it is to science and technology that one turns to find ways to reduce that problem. "Seed-banks" have been developed to preserve wild seeds that have no known immediate beneficial value for human life but which might be developed in the future. Erosion of tropical soils as a result of deforestation and imprudent agricultural methods is becoming a concern even in various developing countries. It is to science and technology that we turn for knowledge of the effects of acid rain, of the importance of tropical rain forests for the maintenance of good air, and for other matters which will affect the human future in relation to nature. The concern about nuclear war is not confined to the potential losses of human life and artifacts, but also to the outcomes for other aspects of the natural world; again it is to science that we turn for precise understandings of what these might be.

Ethics from a theocentric perspective does not support a naturalistic romanticism which would return to a more primitive stage of culture. Culture has developed as man has participated in the ordering of nature to develop means of relief from suffering and possibilities for significant enrichment of life in the world. But this is no license for complacency about our relations to nature. There is no return to a mythical Eden, and there is no assurance of a risk-proof and tragedy-free future.

Different wholes evoke different issues for thinking about the growth of nutritional resources. Some of them are quite purely speculative in the foreseeable future. From my theocentric perspective it cannot be argued that all things were created for the sake of man. The need for food for the human species is not the sole end to be realized in human interventions into nature; attention must be given to the conditions of possibility not only for the continuity of human life but also for other forms of life to be sustained and developed. Persons who develop resources for the human population have to be sensitive to the natural needs for the sustenance of the rest of nature both because of human dependence on it and for the sake of nature's own flourishing. This does not imply that every endangered species of plant or sea life has to be preserved, though attention to the extinction of forms of life is a valid concern. Nor does it suggest that a critical point has now been reached in the development of culture which requires drastic measures of human population reduction for the sake of sustaining other aspects of nature. But warnings about long-range effects on nature of some possible innovations in food production, and in other aspects of industralization, modern culture, and human-life patterns, are signals of the necessity to remain within some limits of ordering of life in the world. The more that scientific investigation understands about the interdependence of the natural order, the more signals can be given about points to be considered for the sake of future generations of human beings and the rest of nature.

There are no moral reasons to restrain investigations of plant genetics and other similar matters that show promise to increase the production of nutrition. If their utilization were to become a threat to the rest of nature, if some process had deleterious and irreversible outcomes for the well-being of the natural world, there would be cause for questioning their use. The concern for loss of irreplaceable soil, by contrast, is worthy of grave moral attention. Currently critical moral concerns are less with scientific and technical developments than with the economic and political interests that can be brought to bear against intensive monitoring and correcting processes that are required. There is no political or economic power bloc serving the common good of nature and future generations of the human species. The level of consumption and gratification that requires inordinate amounts of the world's food, and the economic and political interests which militate against its distribution to many persons in dire need are more immediately pressing problems.

To tackle these problems requires more than a simple moralism, or moralistic idealism. Where there are dire human needs for nutrition there are valid claims on those with sufficient resources to meet them. There is a proper oughtness to devising political and economic measures so that avoidable human suffering does not occur. Social organization is in disorder when persons who are in no significant way accountable for their lack of food, who are susceptible to natural, economic, and political forces beyond their control, are starving. Human actions such as war or political power-struggles that are major causes of starvation are susceptible to moral judgment and to moral action. To develop political and economic policy proposals for such remedial actions is beyond the scope of this project and of my competence.

The goal of population control is more achievable because the means to it are fewer and simpler. Scholars do not agree about what factors have been most crucial in the reduction of birth rates in various parts of the world. There is evidence to indicate that when a people begin to achieve a higher standard of living their birthrates decline, though the precise causal relations between these two factors are not fully understood. Parents are probably more willing to have fewer children when their own sustenance in old age is not necessarily dependent upon the support of surviving children. What can most efficiently control population size is, of course, intervention into the processes of human reproduction. Various stages in the human reproductive process are susceptible to interventions which can effectively control the number of children. The constraints on various interventions are moral and practical. Alternative courses of action for the end of population control raise some similar and some different moral questions.

Infanticide has apparently been practiced as a means of population control since the dawn of human culture. Its use in particular families and groups can be interpreted as a matter of survival of the mature in the face of desperate shortages of food. Perhaps those have been triage occasions in which the judgment was made that not all could survive and therefore some must die. There are, no doubt, other explanations for instances of infanticide, for example, sex preferences in children or parental unwillingness to care for an infant; our concern is limited to population control.

The issue of infanticide is raised in modern medical contexts in which a choice is made to permit certain radically defective infants to die. Justifications for such deaths are most often made in terms of what is considered to be the best interests of the infant in the light of the predictable future circumstances of its life. Sometimes a larger whole is also invoked, such as the predicted effects upon relations in the family if the child is kept alive and needs highly specialized care, or the economic burdens that will be created for the family and even for the community. Reasons given in these circumstances do not invoke the end of population control.

From a theocentric perspective human physical life is valued because it is the indispensable condition for the person to realize any proper self-fulfillment and to participate in the human community. Infanticide either by neglect or by overt aggressive action is thus a very grave matter. The infant is powerless to defend its own life and unable to make a case for its future if it would be permitted to live. It is conceivable that circumstances have occurred and might occur in the future in which a genuine triage choice is required with reference to a social unit like a family, and thus the sacrifice of the life of an infant could be tragically and mournfully justified. It is also the case, however, that the self-interest of others can predispose them to rationalize the choice, and thus extreme scrutiny of motives is necessary.

As a policy of population control in a given nation or in the world, however, there is no justification for infanticide. At least in cultures and societies that have modern medical technology available there are alternative means of birth control that do not involve killing a newborn infant. As long as alternative courses of action are available, or can be made available, infanticide for purposes of population control is morally wrong. An action that can be justified in the most extreme conditions is not justified when those conditions can be altered or when courses of action that are morally preferable are possible.

Abortion is another human intervention in the reproductive process. It is widely held that rapid population growth in Japan was restrained in the 1950s as a result of loosening the legal prohibitions against abortion.[15] There are currently reports that in the People's Republic of China abortion of pregnancies after two live births is being used as a means of population control. In many Western countries legislation and court decisions have extended the range of legally permissable abortions so that the desire of the mother is a sufficient reason for the procedure.

I shall not rehearse and analyze the ethical arguments about abortion here. The choice is always a morally serious one because fetal life has the possibility of developing into a unique human being with capacities for self-fulfillment and for contributions to the human community. There are circumstances in which it is morally justifiable, though it is always a tragic choice. Among those circumstances might be a familial situation in which the birth of another child and the resources needed for its care would severely jeopardize the survival and well-being of the family and its other members. Other courses of action for relieving such dire straits, however,

15. To realize the extent of research that has been done on population growth and policy one needs only to glance through the relevant shelves in a university library. The literature on the ethics of population control is also quite extensive. For a study that did not receive the attention it deserved and deals with postwar Japan, see Richard M. Fagley, *The Population Explosion and Christian Responsibility* (New York: Oxford University Press, 1960). The most recent publication I have examined is Daniel Callahan and Phillip G. Clark, eds., *Ethical Issues of Population Aid: Culture, Economics and International Assistance* (New York: Irvington Publishers, 1982).

ought to be taken by the family and by the community of which it is a part. With the availability of means of contraception in many parts of the world a morally preferred preventive technique is also available. Thus if a nation determines that a policy of birth control is essential for the sake of the common good and of the individual members of its community, the use of contraceptive means is morally to be preferred. This, however, does not solve the practical problems of distribution, education, and use, which are formidable.

Contraception is the most morally preferable intervention for the sake of population control. The expectation that couples can and ought to refrain from sexual intercourse not only runs counter to deep biological drives but also can be detrimental to the interpersonal values of companionship and love that sexual relations both express and sustain. Sexual relations conform to the "nature" of marriage, and thus are basically good. It is not necessary here to list various means of contraception that have been devised historically and those more effective and refined ones that have been developed in recent decades. There are no reasons, from the perspective of the present work, why contraceptive means are not morally licit for the sake of the human species. Indeed, with the distinctive emphasis on the common good that is a feature of this book, the use of contraceptives has an authority that is little short of an imperative.

Sterilization is the most efficacious means of population control. There are circumstances in which it is morally justifiable, as when the health of the mother is at special risk with pregnancy or where the couple has conscientiously determined that they have achieved the family size that is desirable for them. The irreversibility of known means of sterilization makes this choice especially serious. It forecloses the possibility of future pregnancies that might be desirable in altered conditions.

The issue of population growth in relation to nutrition raises a fundamental issue of ethics that is especially recognizable from my theocentric perspective: the conflict between individual rights and liberty on the one hand and the common good of larger wholes, including the whole of the human species, on the other. Does a couple have a right to have as many children as they desire, or even as they can afford to raise? Or, in the light of population growth, is limitation of births in a family or nation morally obligatory, or at least morally desireable? Even the most simple perceptions of the problems of population growth sense a conflict between the liberty of individuals to pursue their own interests and the potential outcomes of unrestrained pursuit of individual interests upon the well-being of other persons and the common good of various communities, including the species as a whole. From the perspective of theocentric ethics the common good is more readily appealed to as a basis for a moral restraint on the activities of individuals than it is in the individualistic libertarian tradition. That appeal is clearly applicable to the present concern. A theocentric construal of the world expands the human perceptions of the wholes of which persons are parts; it is spelled out in patterns and processes of interdependence of life which are the basis for human values and moral principles. There is, from my perspective, no automatic harmony of values that will be achieved by "letting nature take its course," or by permitting individuals to pursue their own claimed individual rights and individually defined interests.

Nor is it the case that there is a blueprint of the ratio of population to nutritional and other resources imprinted in nature from which fixed allotments between the common good and individual interests and rights can be issued. This concern is one that has developed dramatically over the past decades.[16] Malthus published his theories in 1798, and as I have noted science and technology have been used to avert or delay the outcomes he foresaw. Nonetheless recent growth and forecasts heighten the concern about possible future threats to the well-being of individuals, communities, and even the species. And since human life is interdependent with the ordering of nature, there is proper concern for the common good of all of life on the planet. Consideration of particular wholes cannot be avoided in considering courses of action appropriate to individual couples and to public policy.

I argued in volume 1 that the human fault can be conceived of primarily in terms of contraction of the human spirit: of empathy, vision, understanding, and will. The narrowing of interests and values beclouds human perceptions of the interrelationships of interdependence, and the pursuit of these narrowed interests and values can be detrimental to the outcomes of life for countless other persons and communities. The theocentric interpretation portrays both the requirement and the possibility of restraint in population growth. Persons can be enabled voluntarily to restrain their family size for the sake of the whole; there are also prospects of natural perils for all of humanity at some future time if they do not. This does not imply that coercive means are legitimated as the course of action at the present time; the support that theocentric ethics gives to the value of capacities for self-determination, while not as absolute as that backed by the libertarian tradition, requires that these capacities be honored as long as is possible.

Theocentric ethics backs a preference for voluntary restraints. To relate to persons in a manner appropriate to their relation to God requires the honoring of their capacities for self-determination. These capacities are part of the nature of human life. The range of control that individuals and families have over their actions is part of the distinctiveness of human life,

16. When I first learned the population of the United States it was 122 million, the 1930 census figure. My grandchildren will first learn the figure when it is over 230 million.

and thus of its distinctive value. Holding fast to the value of capacities for self-determination and of accountability for one's own actions honors the distinctive feature of the human animal. It is also a bulwark against tyranny. Voluntary consent to restraints is preferable not only to coercion (which practically requires compulsory abortions or sterilization) but also to inducements and "disincentives."

In this matter as in all others there is a continuum between pure rational autonomy (which I have viewed as impossible to realize in its ideal form), persuasion, inducements, disincentives, coercion, and outright physical duress. Rational persuasion with voluntary consent not only requires the presence of certain knowledge-conditions but also a readiness to act contrary to some inclinations that couples might have. But other conditions, when present, make that action more feasible; these conditions are in effect inducements. In circumstances of sustained poverty which make significant family savings and communally guaranteed social security impossible it is difficult to persuade couples who will be dependent upon their own offspring for their care in old age to limit the number of births. Assurance of some social security is an inducement to be rationally persuaded that limitation of births can meet a larger common good. This fact explains in part the reduction of birthrates that often accompanies greater prosperity and higher living standards. The offering of overt inducements, such as transistor radios, for sterilization is a form of bribery, and while it might be immediately gratifying it can be in the long run resented as unfair. Disincentives are on the line between inducements and coercion. Examples of such are the requirement of increased taxes or of other expenditures, such as paying the cost of education for more than a certain number of children.[17]

The judgment by a government that coercive means of population control are needed is dependent upon the evaluative description of its circumstances accepted by those in power. From a moral standpoint coercion or duress in this area, as in all others, ought to be the court of last resort. In the just-war tradition, resort to arms is justifiable only when all other courses of action to settle a dispute have been exhausted; so in this area, all other courses of action must have failed to a critical degree to justify coercion. Some cultural traditions and state ideologies support the use of coercion at a point that other traditions and ideologies do not, in the interest

17. Singapore is an example of a nation-state that uses "disincentives." Its population is about 2.4 million; its doubling time in the forecasts I have used is 58 years. It is a very distinctive place: its geographic size is small, it has almost no resources other than its human population; it is economically dependent on world trends in a most vulnerable way; it even gets part of its water supply from another nation, Malaysia. Although its population is not as culturally homogeneous as that of some other small nations, it seems to be quite successful in reducing population growth. Its use of disincentives, I would judge, is a morally appropriate policy that is bound to its own context and conditions. There is an aspect of unfairness that cannot be eliminated; those with more income can better afford to have larger families. The restraint and therefore the "cost" is unevenly distributed.

of what those in power determine to be the common good. But even in such circumstances there is evidence of resentment against it, particularly when the intimacy of marriage and family is disrupted. Only in the most extreme circumstances would coercive means of birth control be warranted from the perspective of the present book. But a moral appeal to the common good is more readily invoked in this perspective as a justification for intensification of persuasion, inducements, and disincentives than is the case in some other views of morality.

What is God enabling and requiring human beings to be and to do in the circumstances in which there is imbalance between nutrition and human population in various parts of the world? How are they to relate themselves and all things in a manner appropriate to their relations to God? To be a participant is to be a steward; it is to see and feel subjectively the responsibility not only for individual persons and families but also for larger human communities and for the nautral world. It is to recognize the critical significance of personal and policy choices for other existing persons, for future generations of human beings, and for the life of the world. To see and feel oneself as a steward, and to grasp the consequences of possible courses of action through the patterns and processes of interdependence, is to accept responsibility for larger wholes than the immediate interests of a couple, their family, their community, or their nation. The acknowledgment and conviction of this responsibility are induced and sustained by a theocentric construal of the world. Apart from this acknowledgment there is limited inclination or incentive to participate in or support those activities that will increase nutritional resources or reduce population growth when there is some cost to defensible self-interests. There may be inducements, such as economic advantages, that motivate participation, but the larger sense of vocation will be weak.

The area of nutrition and population shows how developments over the course of human affairs alter the problems that individuals, communities, and institutions have to face. There are perduring principles such as distributive justice and respect for individual life; there are almost absolute values such as that of physical life. But these are not sufficient as a basis to determine what courses of action are preferable in the light of finite and changing natural and cultural conditions. The signals of the divine ordering are not as loud and clear as might be preferred but to relate human activity to the ultimate ordering power is to see that various conditions must be met or created in order to avert potential suffering to present and future generations of humans, and to avoid irreversible and deleterious outcomes for the natural world of which we are a part. The ratio of nutrition to population is not fixed in an eternal and immutable law of God; human participation and the results of natural events alter the possibilities and requirements. Yet in particular contexts fundamental human needs have to be met; they back ends such as increase of nutrients and control of population growth and principles such as distributive justice; they order the morality of the means to achieve appropriate ends such as the preference for voluntary participation over coercion.

The moral task is to avoid potentially disastrous outcomes globally and in areas of particular need. But even to do this is to negotiate between conflicting claims and values, to make choices whose outcomes are of cost to some defensible interests for the sake of the needs and interests of others. God has not ordered the world so that the pursuit of morally justified ends and means can be fulfilled without cost and sometimes suffering to particular groups of persons now and in the future.

8

Allocation of Biomedical Research Funding

The ultimate justification of all stages of medical research and health care is the benefits they will have for persons and for a human community. In the division of functions in society "medicine" has the end of attending to health, just as other professions, social roles, and institutions have their ends.[1] There are arguments about the proper ends of medicine that I will not explore in this chapter.[2] For example, ought it to be limited to the elimination or restraint of bodily ills or ought it to be concerned about improving natural capacities? What constitutes a disease? If medicine is to minister to disease, is cosmetic surgery a justifiable medical activity? For the purposes of this chapter it is sufficient to state that the purpose of medicine is to sustain human physical and mental well-being. While there are those who argue on the basis of particular distinctions between the moral and the nonmoral that health is not a moral value, it is clear by now to the readers of this book that the more generous interpretation of ethics which follows from my theology includes well-being or qualities of life. Things which from other perspectives are only "necessary conditions" for moral life are from mine part of the ethical. Health is not an end in itself; it is a necessary condition for human functioning to realize other purposes, and for the capacity to exercise human agency. It is a proper concern of ethics. The backing for economic support of biomedical research, for development of screening and diagnostic techniques, for preventive counsel, and for intrusive therapies is necessarily consequentialist. Within the larger end of "health" particular activities are justified on the basis that they have various degrees of probability of success to benefit individuals and human communities.

As in other spheres of activity in which the calculation of potential consequences justifies the basic enterprise, so in medicine other moral concerns are applicable. There are arguments about whether certain means to achieve the end are immoral. Regulations governing research on human subjects, for example, require the informed consent of the person on whom the experiment is conducted or who is part of study to test the comparative efficacy of particular therapies. Some very stringent medical moralists raise the question of whether certain biomedical research is immoral per se even though it might lead to benefits for certain individuals; arguments of this sort have taken place over the procedure of in vitro fertilization and the use of human fetuses in research. Matters of distributive justice have occupied many medical moralists in recent decades. Who are the similar persons who are to be treated similarly? What criteria are to be used in the provision of access to various procedures of health care? What is the ethically proper procedure to be used when there is more demand for a medical resource

1. "Medicine" is used in this chapter as a shorthand term to cover the entire activity of biomedical research and care.

2. See, for example, the controverted article by Dr. Leon R. Kass, "Regarding the End of Medicine and the Pursuit of Health," *Public Interest*, no. 40 (Summer 1975):11–41.

than is available? The concept of human rights has been important to the discussions of health care as it is to other areas of human activity. Is there an equal right to health care? Is everyone entitled to equal health care, i.e., to the same standard of care and the same therapeutic procedures when they are needed?

The resources available for biomedical research and health care are not infinitely expandable in the light of competing claims. The question of allocation necessarily raises the question of equity or fairness.[3] There are tragic policy choices as well as tragic individual choices.[4] The allocation question is faced not only at the point of patient care but also at the point of choices about research funding.

To make the discussion of medical ethics more manageable, but complex enough to be realistic about the problems, I have chosen to write about the allocation of biomedical research funding. Within the limits of this chapter I can do little more than examine the agenda to be used to come to policy choices that are made by governmental agencies. The chapter is based upon much more extensive and intensive research than is manifest both in the text and in the citations.[5]

3. An editorial by Peter L. Frommer, M.D., in *The New England Journal of Medicine* 305 (1981):1646, states the issue. "Expensive technologies are not new to the medical science, but they must be assessed on the basis of their benefit as well as their net cost. Cost-benefit decisions are intrinsically difficult and unpleasant when they deal with human life and with the quality of human life. Decisions on the use of expensive technologies are difficult because they may appear applicable to patients who would derive widely differing degrees of benefit. Hence, the cost and benefit will not be specific for a therapy but will vary in subgroups of patients from the clearly acceptable to what most would consider unacceptable. As we develop further advances in medicine, we will face such problems with increasing frequency. We must develop the means of making such decisions as equitably as possible. Society must come to accept the fact that all the stops cannot be pulled out on every patient all the time, even in the difficult situations in which emotional or familial bonds are involved.

"Resources must always be allocated among competing needs with care and equity, and the research dollar must likewise be allocated among competing opportunities and needs in a balanced fashion. From the perspective of cost-benefit analysis and from the perspective of relieving suffering and averting early death, there is much truth in the old cliché that an ounce of prevention is worth a pound of cure. Thus, research aimed at prevention and the disseminaion of the message about proved approaches to prevention deserves the highest priority, but these approaches are not our only priority. We do not have all the answers to prevention, and we cannot expect to identify them in the near future. The acquisition of a better understanding of the biology of disease is a prerequisite for successful research on prevention and is also fundamental to our other major research priority—i.e., the development of widely applicable, cost-effective therapy. It is a question of balance in the allocation of resources—a problem with which we will be dealing for many years."

4. See Guido Calabresi and Philip Bobbit, *Tragic Choices* (New York: W. W. Norton, 1978).

5. This chapter is based chiefly upon the work done in a seminar I have taught with Dr. Clifford W. Gurney, professor of medicine, under the auspices of the Committee on Public Policy Studies at the University of Chicago. There is no way in which I can clearly mark and acknowledge the extent and points of my indebtedness to Dr. Gurney and to students from various fields who were members of the seminar. Suffice it to say that I could not have written this chapter without reliance upon the collaborative efforts.

The research done for that seminar was more detailed and technical than is evident in

Some Social Analysis

The patterns of interaction are very complex in which various agents exercise powers in accordance with their interests and intentions to affect the allocation of biomedical research. Nonetheless it is worthwhile on the basis of studies of past events to isolate some of the critical points at which choices have been made that have affected outcomes of allocation. The ethical significance of this is that it notes the junctures at which reasons, including moral reasons, are or can be given for particular choices. One has to be able to interpret what is going on in order to know at what points intentional interventions do and can occur, and thus at what points some possible alteration of a course of events can be made if that is desirable.

I have chosen to order the analysis by distinguishing various processes that are occurring which do affect the outcomes, but I shall not detail all the many points at which significant determinations are made within each distinguishable process.

In the United States the political process is very significant in the allocation of biomedical research funding.[6] The United States Congress is one of the places in which critical choices are made. It is Congress that authorized the National Institutes of Health as an institution which does research and which is in charge of the allocation of research to other institutions that serve the interests of the public's health. Congress also allocates the funding for biomedical research that is distributed through the NIH, the National Science Foundation, and other federal agencies. The political processes that affect the actions of Congress occur at various levels. Historically it is clear that the lobbying efforts of various interest groups

this chapter. Here I shall generalize and not back my reflections or even illustrate them with economic facts and figures, technical medical information, and other specific data. A brief description of the purpose and pattern of the collaborative exploration however, is in order.

Our question has been whether and how ethical principles and moral values can give guidance to choices about the allocation of biomedical research funds. We chose to do this by engaging in a retrospective study of the policies and practices developed at various institutional levels on research and therapy for kidney disease. On the basis of this we analyzed what seem to have been the most crucial choices, and the various reasons—moral and nonmoral—that were given for them. We also explored alternative choices that could have been made both with reference to the conditions that lead to end-stage kidney disease and with reference to the allotment of funding for this disease in comparison with others. A parallel study of heart disease was made to provide a more prospective dimension. What would be involved if policies parallel to those used to provide kidney dialysis and transplants were to be used to provide implantable artificial hearts and heart transplants? Only the general patterns of analysis and very general conclusions of this more detailed research are used in this chapter; it is a simplification of a previous but more complex simplification.

I also draw to some extent from my experience as a member of the Advisory Committee to the director of the National Institutes for Health during the middle 1970s.

6. See Stephen P. Strickland, *Politics, Science, and Dread Disease: A Short History of United States Medical Research Policy* (Cambridge, Mass.: Harvard University Press, 1972). A more journalistic account is Natalie Davis Spingarn, *Heartbeat: The Politics of Health Research* (Washington and New York: Robert B. Luce, 1976). Many articles have been published since these books, as well.

have been important. What have come to be called "disease lobbies" are formed, frequently by those who suffer from certain illnesses and their relatives and friends. They are able to make poignant appeals to various members of Congress, and especially to those from areas in which the disease lobby has strength or special ties to the representative. Individual lobbyists have had an inordinate impact on the congressional choices; Mrs. Mary Lasker is the most notable of such individuals. In addition to the disease lobbies there are the efforts of members of the scientific community; investigators take the initiative, or are called upon, to support various interests. Chairpersons of the relevant congressional committees who for political as well as other motives become well versed in the needs of the biomedical community exercise potent political power over critical decisions. Persons in charge of the administration of the NIH and other federal agencies necessarily play political roles in justifying the allocations they believe ought to be made; often they play these roles in seeking to maintain greater autonomy for their agencies in these determinations, against congressional and public pressure for mandated funding for particular diseases.

Even at this point of possible intervention various ethical questions are pertinent. What constitutes an equitable allocation of funding among various disease lobbies, and what criteria should be used to determine what is fair? Who provides a vision and analysis of the whole health-care area, of which particular diseases are parts? To what extent can cost/benefit analyses of the probable outcomes of various allocations be made? What factors can be quantified in monetary terms, and which ones ought to be decisive? I shall return to the problems of criteria.

Another point of intervention is in the administrative process of research funding. Quite elaborate processes of peer review have been established to guarantee, insofar as possible, the wise allocation of limited resources with reference both to the quality of the research and to its possibilities of success. Questions about the fairness of the peer review panels are raised by some scientists and institutions. One of the arguments against the mandating of specific dollar sums for research on particular diseases at the level of congressional appropriations is that wiser choices about allocation can be made by institutions and persons who have more technical knowledge about the criteria that ought to be used. Here, as well, the question of forecasts and predictions of likely success are relevant, as well as questions about fairness in distribution. Attention has to be given to the current state of knowledge about a particular disease, as well as to more basic research from which might come the knowledge that is more significant in meeting the health need.

A third point of intervention is the choices that individual investigators make about the research they desire to do. Here the decisions are relative to many factors: the state of research in a particular area, the interests and training of investigators, the equipment and other aspects of their research facilities, and so forth. Quite understandably, investigators are sensitive to what areas are for various reasons currently receiving funding, and some of them find ways to develop their own lines of investigation so as to contribute to these areas. To make a case for basic research is sometimes difficult when a considerable measure of the allocation is dependent upon special-interest groups in society and their impact on congressional decisions.

A fourth point is of quite a different order and involves scientific judgments which have consequences for allocation of research and for the development and distribution of therapies. The question is, for what point in a sequence of disease processes should the research be targeted, or how should research funding for a particular disease be allocated among various stages in the process? The significance of this point of judgment is readily seen from the examples of kidney and heart disease. With remarkable success therapies have been developed to extend the lifespan of persons with end-stage kidney disease; the development of mechanical artificial hearts as well as improvement in the success of heart transplants indicates that further progress will be made in end-stage therapies for heart disease. Consequent upon the development of these "half-way technologies" (to use Lewis Thomas's term) is a range of economic and ethical questions about their distribution to those who need them. The allocation question is whether a fair proportion of funding for kidney and heart disease is being made to those health problems which are causes of the dramatic end-stage when the critical question is to save a life and extend a lifespan by use of high technological therapies. I have in mind such things as investigations into preventive health care, hypertension that can cause both kidney and heart crises, and so forth. If fairness were to be a criterion in the determination of the points in disease processes at which resources would be targeted, is cost/benefit analysis the way to secure information on which to make such decisions?

The last moment of intervention to which I call attention is that of determining how and to whom various forms of therapy will be provided. Normally this is the last in a sequence of decisions. Investigations are made, applications tested, therapies and technology developed, and then the fruits of the research are distributed to those who need them. The general assumption is that, if there is a health problem, study of its causes can and ought to be conducted, and therapeutic procedures developed. The question of to whom the therapy will be made available is not considered until it is available. The history of the development of end-stage therapies for kidney disease make this abundantly clear.[7] The question of just distribution in that

7. My work at this point and others has been very much informed and in other ways affected by Renée C. Fox and Judith P. Swazey, *The Courage to Fail: A Social View of Organ Transplants and Dialysis*, 2d ed. (Chicago: University of Chicago Press, 1978).

case was resolved by guarantees that virtually every person who needs the therapy will be provided access to it regardless of the cost. I call attention to this point of intervention to raise the question, hypothetically at least, of whether forethought should be given to the sources of payment and the criteria for distribution earlier in the sequence. If distribution in our society were based on the market principle, i.e., the ability to pay for the therapy, one resolution would take place. This does not occur and will not occur not only because of the extension of funding for health care to all persons in the society but also because public funding has supported research and development, and therefore privileged access to its fruits would be unfairly preferential. An illustrative question can be asked. If the similar cases to be treated similarly are persons with end-stage diseases, whether of the kidney or the heart, and if precedent has been set in the case of kidney disease so that the therapy is provided to virtually all who need it, ought artificial hearts, when they are perfected, be made available on the same principle of distribution? If they are, what are the costs and who shall bear them? If they are not, what criteria will be used to determine who will have access and how the costs will be borne? The painful question is whether one should take account of the policies for distribution and payment of therapy earlier in the process of investigation and development of technology, and make judgments about what research ought to be supported in light of that.

This kind of social analysis is important for the ethics developed in this volume. One could, of course, begin with a general principle, such as equals shall be treated equally. From this one might determine in theory who are the equals and make a moral claim for the development of research, therapies, and institutions that would distribute the results to meet the needs of all judged to be equal. My approach does not avoid the claim for justice; it comes later in the sequence of analysis. Cultural and institutional developments have occurred and are occurring which issue in certain possibilities and requirements. The contexts of these must be understood; while they need not be morally accepted as they are, and require attention in the light of certain values and principles which might lead to some alteration, the contexts to a large extent determine the possibilities for action.

Ethics gives direction to events that are occurring and makes claims for the development of events and outcomes that ought to occur. There are points to be considered at various stages of the process of policy formation and application; they are to be considered with forethought for the issues that are likely to follow sequentially. Given scientific, economic, cultural, and other developments in a society, it is at least incomplete to think that the function of ethics is to develop a theory devoid of serious consideration of the conditions of its applicability. And the ethical reflection in the area of biomedical research funding necessarily is pluralistic in the points that have to be taken into account. There is the general end of medicine, namely, to engage in those activities that make for better health of persons and communities. This surely authorizes the whole enterprise. But choices within that require attention to predictions and forecasts of future outcomes of alternative actions both in research and in the development and distribution of therapies; consequentialist thinking is necessary. And questions of justice pertain at every point of choice: What is due to persons? To what persons? What criteria are to be used to determine this? Who are the the equals who shall be treated equally? What criteria determine this? From the special emphasis on the common good that is a feature of the present work, there is a greater force to the issues of distribution since the resources available for medicine are finite. Because of limited resources, what hard choices have to be faced about a distribution that shares costs and benefits fairly, and that contributes to the well-being of the relevant public or community as a whole? An even larger question is how resources are to be distributed between various ends (medicine, education, defense, the arts, etc.) in such a way that the common good of society is served.

Types of Criteria

In sorting out the processes in the course of which important choices are made that determine the outcomes of biomedical research policy I have already suggested some of the sorts of criteria that are and must be applied. Here I shall, in a quite schematic way, explore four types of criteria: medical, ethical, economic, and political. In my judgment research policies in the biomedical field follow from the ways in which these types of criteria are applied, what valence is given to each, and how some of the particular criteria under each type are used. The actual history of the development of research policy leads to incremental choices based upon present and immediate past achievements and policies. There is, however, some merit in distancing oneself from the social realities and lifting out more objectively at least the points to be considered. No one of the types is absolutely decisive, and in them no particular criterion is any more decisive than another.

In order to establish policy in any area certain knowledge-conditions have to be met and, as I have indicated, the relevance of certain kinds of information to the policy is a matter of judgment. When several criteria are applicable, there is some weighing of each, but it is not possible to establish an ideal pattern that can be imposed upon actual funding of research. Here I am particularly concerned with various medical criteria.

One is the frequency of the disease. It can be argued that those illnesses that have the highest degree of frequency in a community deserve priority. More persons suffer, more persons lose more time from their work and other activities, and so forth. There would be less claim for funding research on a very rare disease that afflicts only a small number of people. If frequency were the only criterion we would, of course, have tremendous sums of money allocated to research on the common cold, and persons with very rare but severe or fatal diseases would be left to the course of nature. Frequency is obviously inadequate as the only criterion, but frequency does come in for consideration. Knowledge of increasing frequency of a disease stimulates research, especially when the disease is fatal. At the time of writing no disease is more in the public eye in the United States than the acquired immune deficiency syndrome, a disease about which little is known at present, and which is found most frequently among a specific population in society but which seems to be communicable.

Mortality is a second medical criterion. Diseases that are life-threatening receive high priority. One can be sure that if the common cold were a fatal disease a greater allocation of funding would go to research on it. Surely the principal reason why so much money is allocated to cancer research is that cancer is generally fatal; the same is true for heart disease and for respiratory diseases. The threat to life brings its own demand for intervention. In terms of policy the combination of frequency and mortality establishes the priority that governs a great deal of allocation. Research that leads to therapies that can prolong life under threatening conditions receives wide public attention and support. Chemotherapies and radiation therapy for cancer, dialysis technology and transplants for kidney disease, surgical interventions, transplants and the development of the artificial heart for heart disease are all examples.

Morbidity or severity is a third medical criterion. Those diseases that severely impair normal human functioning and significantly lower the quality of life of persons do and ought to receive greater attention in research. Kidney disease does, but the common cold does not. Two points of human functioning have a normative status here. One is the normal functioning of the human organism; those diseases that more severely lower the functioning deserve greater attention. The second is social functioning, for which physical functioning is a necessary condition. The concern is to respond to diseases so that the patient is able to participate as normally as possible in human activity and relationships. The criterion of severity lowers the claims of the common cold and all but the severest allergies, for example, but raises those of kidney and heart diseases.

A fourth medical criterion is age at onslaught of the disease. Illnesses that commonly strike persons of all ages and particularly persons who are quite young claim more attention than those which normally affect mostly the very old. Pneumonia and tuberculosis indiscriminately attacked persons of various ages, and this probably affected the intense and successful search for therapies. Heart and kidney diseases are not confined to the aged, but impair the functioning and take the lives of persons in their prime, and thus receive strong research support. Childhood diseases that potentially have long-range deleterious outcomes, such as polio and some of the more common communicable diseases, have properly warranted special attention. Although one application of the principle of distributive justice, namely, that each person is equal and deserves equal attention when ill, would make age at onslaught morally irrelevant, within the limitations of resources for research and care it rightly becomes a point to be considered.

I have already introduced a fifth medical criterion, the point in the sequence of the disease process at which therapy is likely to be effective over a long range of time. The question of equity is how research funding is to be divided between end-stage therapies and therapies for earlier medical indications of a disease. Clearly, attention is given to both; the progress made in the treatment of hypertension in the past decades, for example, no doubt has reduced the incidence of stroke, heart attack, and end-stage kidney disease. At the same time dramatic developments in end-stage therapies for kidney and heart disease have been developed. The arguments for more attention to the medical indications of the onslaught of these diseases is basically consequentialist; more normal physical and social functioning over a longer period of time is enabled, and it is less costly economically to develop relevant therapies for earlier stages than to provide expensive high technology care which does not always issue in fully satisfactory outcomes. Surely there is some public pressure for greater support of the dramatic end-stage therapies; the news media thrive on the dramatic cases and arouse a great deal of public interest. People eagerly count the days and months of extended life that result, and these extensions of life are used to justify the costs of such procedures. Lives are snatched from certain impending death, and the patients involved in experimental end-stage therapies become heroic figures. The issue of equity, however, presses for a more disinterested calculation of potential outcomes of allocation of resources; the quantification of indications that are not readily translated into dollars, for all its difficulties, is required. The attention given to normal health care as a preventive means of avoiding some diseases indicates that there is public recognition of the issues involved both for individuals and for society.

The final criterion I shall note is the state of biomedical research. It is clear that those points in the state of research that seem to promise the most immediate developments that will benefit patients deserve the greatest attention. The judgments about this are, of course, subject to a wide margin of error due to the unpredictability of the possible efficacy of various investigations. Even where a choice is made for research funding targeted on a particular disease, in contrast to basic research, it has been the case that the knowledge acquired is of as great or greater benefit for persons suffering other diseases. Also, arguments are very strong for the support of basic biological research in areas such as genetics because of the potential general applicability of the new knowledge to a wide range of human diseases. Both basic and disease-targeted research are, of course, supported. The justifications for the distribution between them are, in the American political system, largely made in terms of potential beneficial consequences of each. Clearly, the evidence adduced to support a choice is rather conjectural, given the nature of biological research. No simple principle of fairness is readily applicable.

I have called these medical criteria. Each involves judgments based upon the conditions of knowledge that exist at the time the choice of allocation of funding is made. The knowledge is the result of various types of scientific investigations: epidemiological, basic biological, medical engineering, pharmaceutical, and so forth. These knowledge conditions are continually changing as investigations develop and as concerns for particular diseases are strengthened. With developments in both basic and applied research come reorientations in the allocation of funding. Outcomes are unpredictable in a precise way; there is no absolutely certain way to predict the efficacy of a great deal of research. But assessment and judgment of the existing states of knowledge is a necessary aspect of the choices that are made in the allocation of biomedical research funding. Other types of criteria have to take into account the present and relevant knowledge-conditions. The possibilities of further action directed by scientific purposes and by human value-ends are set by them.

The second type of criteria, the ethical, I have already introduced. In this area as in all others of public policy there is a necessary interplay between four related patterns of moral reflection: distributive justice and its fine-tuning in equity; calculations of possible outcomes of certain choices in terms of a variety of "benefits" and "costs"; the question of the moral limits of research, i.e., whether there are investigations that ought not be undertaken for moral reasons regardless of their potential benefits for others; and the common good, e.g., how can concerns for the well-being of larger whole be taken into account? There is a vast amount of literature written about these issues by moral philosophers and theologians, by political scientists, sociologists, and economists, and by biomedical investigators and physicians. Since the issues are of public concern and affect public policy there have been presidential commissions which have done research, conducted hearings, and written proposals on these matters. There have also been NIH special panels that have produced reports on specific matters, such as the artificial heart; there are documents produced by interdisciplinary research institutes dedicated to the study of these matters; there are statements by religious leaders and denominations. In addition the advisory committees for the NIH and various of its institutes have been extended to include persons who can presumably represent the "public interest." Indeed, "medical ethics" has been an intellectual growth industry in the United States since the late 1960s.[8]

It is the function of an ethician in the process of policy formation to call attention to the moral issues involved. This, I believe, is done in various ways: by showing what values are implicit in allocations that exist, e.g., by analyzing what principle of distributive justice is actually now operative; by raising questions about whether certain ethical issues have received sufficient attention, e.g., in the way in which the circumstances have been described or whether criteria of fairness have been taken into account; by demonstrating to others what the outcome of allocation would be from various moral points of view, e.g., by showing how various material principles of justice would affect the policy in different ways or by showing how a utility calculus would work; and by aggressively making a case for his or her own moral point of view as applied to the relevant circumstances. None of these implies that the moralist is the final determiner of that issue; all of them point to the need for a community of moral discourse in which ethical concepts are used and moral issues are considered seriously in the mix of criteria that are required for careful formulation of policy.

The question of what constitutes just, fair, or equitable distribution of research funding is forced upon us simply by the fact that the resources to be allocated are limited. Since funding for research covers basic biological investigations, those targeted on particular diseases, and the development of therapies, some forethought is required about the ways and means of distributing successful therapeutic outcomes of the research as well. It is doubtful, for example, that in the foreseeable future the questions of fair distribution will be resolved by increasing the aggregate amount of funding so that all qualified claimants can receive the attention they desire. Simply on economic grounds it is doubtful that the precedent set by providing renal dialysis for almost all who need it can be followed for artificial hearts and all other prospective therapies for end-stage diseases. The problem of fair distribution cannot be avoided since there are limits to the aggregate of public resources that can and should be devoted to biomedical research and health care.

I have previously noted that the context in which choices are made is a matter of first-order importance. The development of a formal and ideal system of just distribution in which equals are treated equally, or in which

8. I was a participant in various groups and an occasional contributor to the literature on medical ethics for approximately a decade, but I have not attended to this area with the same concentration in recent years. The literature has become enormous and medical ethics has become, somewhat unfortunately from my perspective, a field and discipline in its own right. I have chosen not to cite extended bibliography even of the materials with which I am most adequately acquainted, nor to develop my own views in relation to many arguments about medical ethics by others who publish in this field.

each is given his or her due, requires material judgments about what is to be distributed and on the basis of what principle. In my delineation of various medical material criteria it became clear that no single one, such as frequency or severity, is sufficient. From the perspective of the present work, including the interpretation of the circumstances in which choices are made, one does not deduce from a theory of justice how limited funds are to be distributed. Rather, at various points in the development of research policy it is necessary to consider whether the distribution is reasonably fair in the light of the various medical criteria. It is necessary to inquire whether diseases of comparable frequency, severity, etc. are being ignored because of present public interest or scientific interest in a particular disease. But the claims for a fairer distribution will not be absolutely decisive in the light of the multiple medical criteria.

The assessment of possible outcomes of various distributions is clearly part of the task; consequentialist procedures are unavoidable in the development of public policy. In other places in this book I have acknowledged the difficulties that are commonly stated in discussions of consequentialism in ethics. Consequences for whom? Consequences over what period of time? How these questions are answered is critical. In research and even in normal medical care the prediction of outcomes of particular innovations is hardly a matter of absolute certainty. Assessment has to be made of potential costs as well as potential benefits.

How these questions are answered makes a great deal of difference in policy. If the "whole" to be taken into account is the class of patients whose lives are threatened, there is little restraint on the impulse to forge ahead with research for high technology lifesaving therapies. Life-threatening diseases make dramatic claims on quite substantial grounds since the preservation of life is the condition sine qua non for any other values for that person. The original heart transplants were justified as desperate measures in desperate circumstances, as was the use of an artificial heart in 1969. If, however, there is an enlargment of the range of potential outcomes to be taken into account, matters become more complex. Even the prospective quality of life of the individual patient complicates the issue of the avoidance of death as the end in view. Further consequences for the medical establishment and its limited resources, for the family of the patient, for subsequent developments of research and therapy that can build from high-risk interventions, and so forth, cannot be avoided. As I have stressed, forethought is required also for the potential outcomes for the wider society and its use of resources.[9]

9. In the mid-1970s I participated in a consultation held at the Salk Institute on the question of whether increased research funding should be allocated for the investigation of the basic biology of the aging process in human beings. Human beings are genetically "programmed," normally, to die at approximately the biblical "three score and ten" years. Papers

Are certain forms of biomedical investigation immoral regardless of the possible beneficial consequences? The modern concern for the ethics of medical research received a great impetus from the disclosure of human experimentation done during the Nazi regime in Germany. Among the many horrors of that regime were the coerced use of human beings for research purposes, many of which were scientifically poorly grounded, and for trivial ends of knowledge. The dramatic revelations of that experience led to the famous Helsinki Declaration on the ethics of experimentation on human beings, to retrospective examination of experimentation on human beings in many nations prior to that period, and to the development of standards and surveillance procedures for experimentation in most of the world.[10] The possible horrendous outcomes of unreined utility calculus have been properly restrained by the establishment of regulation and surveillance procedures not only for experimentation but for other ends. Persons were treated as only means to ends, and not as ends in themselves; the Kantian principle would have been a bulwark against such activity if it had been adhered to in the nation that had nurtured Kant's mind a century and a half earlier. The requirement of informed consent by the human subject of experimentation is directly grounded in the Kantian principle; only by respecting the autonomy of the person, and thus gaining his or her voluntary consent based upon adequate and relevant information, is it morally justifiable to experiment.

The literature on the ethics of experimentation on human beings is vast. Two different kinds of argument are involved. One is based upon forecasting possible long-range outcomes of either the uses of the research

were presented by leading genetic investigators who were attending to this area, by various social scientists working in gerontology, and by others. The valued end that was proposed was the extension of the life span without drastic losses of normal functioning. As one prominent participant put it, "it would be wonderful to be able to function at the chronological age of eighty like persons normally function now at the age of sixty." It takes little imagination to suggest relevant questions about this kind of research. Is aging a disease? Has the calling of biomedical research been expanded considerably if one alters the primary criterion from the elimination of threats to health and life to the amplification of the life span? What would be the social outcomes if the investigations led to interventions that extended the range of normal human functioning for a period of twenty years? What would the outcomes be for the labor force and the economy? For family structures and functions? For a whole range of institutions that now exist? In the light of the difficulties now encountered in providing care and meaningful life to the aged, is there a warning to be sounded with reference to future difficulties? Where in an order of priorities for biomedical research should such investigations be placed? Would they be justified by the right to extend the range of human knowledge regardless of prospective uses of that knowledge? Given health problems of many of the poor in the United States and of countless others throughout the world is it just to proceed with this research? The extension of the range of possible outcomes to be considered is sufficient to flash at least a bright amber light of caution, and for some commentators a red stoplight. It would, to say the least, be foolhardy to proceed apace with such investigations without considering the breadth and length of probable consequences.

10. The most comprehensive book I know on the topic of experimentation on human beings is Jay Katz, *Experimentation with Human Beings*, (New York: Russell Sage Foundation, 1972).

or of permitting exceptions to stringent controls in a particular case. The qualms that have been expressed about pushing forward with research on the biology of aging are an example of the first. "Slippery slope" considerations are examples of the second: if one permits experimentation on aborted human fetuses for some end, has one opened the way to permitting experimentation on newborn infants? These arguments involve the forecasting of potentially bad outcomes and using those forecasts as grounds for restraining present investigations.

The second kind of argument is deontic in character. There are investigations that are deemed immoral no matter what benefits might be forthcoming from them. The circumstances in which this is most frequently addressed is that of using human subjects who are not competent to give truly informed consent to participation in an experiment. Of this class of cases one of the most frequently discussed is the use of children in pediatric research when there is no potential therapeutic benefit to the subject. The degree of risk to the subject is taken into account in any proposals that might require the use of such children; clearly a proper distinction is drawn between an experiment that might impair the health of the persons and one that has only a minimal risk of harm. Arguments have been made for proxy consent; for example, where there is a minimal risk, *if* the patient were of age or competent, he or she would consent to the participation. Another factor that is taken into account is the significance of the potential findings of the experiment; a distinction is drawn between confirming a hypothesis of no or relatively minor benefits for health and, for example, testing a vaccine which might largely eliminate a communicable and life-threatening disease.

My assessment of the ethics of biomedical research is that not only the principles and regulations but also the review procedures that have developed over the past decades are quite adequate to make investigators morally accountable for their work. We do not know, to the best of my information, whether they have inhibited the development of therapies that would be given a very high priority according to medical criteria. The regulations and procedures are effective because they have worked out ways to take account of values that do not fall into an automatic harmony, e.g., honoring the capacity and right of self-determination of individuals, and gaining knowledge that will benefit the health of individuals and of groups. The tensions between these are never resolved in hard cases to the satisfaction of persons who have a strong moral interest in one or the other. That some risk is inevitable and necessarily must be taken to establish the efficacy of innovative procedures is simply a fact. At some point in the development moral responsibility requires that some persons be put at risk to test the effectiveness for human beings. The spectrum I introduced in the chapter on "Population and Nutrition" between the ideal of fully informed and purely free consent on the one hand, and coercion and physical duress on the other, is equally applicable here. The hard question is whether persuasion and inducements such as compensations are violations of voluntary informed consent. I know of no case at present for which the therapeutic significance of what might become known is sufficient to violate the regulations and procedures that are now in force. And the dramatic instance of the 1983 artificial heart patient at the University of Utah indicates that, with careful screening and informing, volunteers are willing to take risks both for the sake of possible benefits to themselves and to others.

The common good of a society's health is not something that can be delineated with precision. In the area of biomedical research, as in other areas, seeking to determine the common good evokes reflection on the larger wholes of which particular pursuits are a part. There are various aspects of the common good that have to be taken into account. If, for example, one attends only to the limitations of resources for biomedical research and health care in a given society, higher priority is likely to be given to education in health care and other preventive measures as a way of serving the common good. Concern will be shown, as it now is, for technologically induced threats to normal human functioning, for example, in industrial work-places. The relations between human functioning and the environment ascend in the order of priority. There is no definable ideal of the common good of human health, but the expansions of the considerations to be taken into account in the funding of research is strengthened by the extension of the whole that attention to the common good evokes.

The third type of criteria is economic. The concern for the economics of health care is, indeed, pressing. The cost of research and health care has increased greatly as a result of many factors: complex technology required to do research; the development of high-technology screening, diagnostic, and therapeutic procedures; the expansion of access to modern medical care based on an extension of the range of human rights and entitlements; and others. The high percentage of health care costs devoted to the latter stages of illness has been noted in various countries. No way to restrain the costs without doing injustice or harm to persons who need health care has been devised.

The economic criterion that is relevant is efficiency. Efficiency refers to calculation of the use of means to achieve a desired end; it is an aspect of technical reason; clearly it is not an end in itself. Obviously if the aggregate of resources for research and health care were limitless the issue of efficient use would not be critical. Efficiency as a criterion is, to many persons, morally offensive when dealing with biomedical research and the health care of human beings. The saving of human lives and the sustenance of health cannot, or at least ought not, it is argued, be quantified in monetary terms. Ought should determine can; when life is threatened all the possible resources available ought to be used to save it. When many lives are impaired or threatened by a disease, all possible resources ought to be marshaled to relieve the problem. If a defective newborn's life can be saved by the use of modern medical technology, in the view of many it ought to be saved regardless of the economic costs incurred at the critical time and that will be incurred in the future as a result of the need for continued expensive medical care. Whether the same costs could be used more effectively for other medical purposes is not an appropriate question. Thus there is on the part of many persons a moral repugnance at the introduction of economic efficiency as a criterion in determining the allocation of resources for medical research and health care.

In addition there are inherent difficulties in applying efficiency standards in medical research. Duplication of research efforts to attack the same problem, whether in basic biology or in the development of therapy, is not necessarily inefficient since many investigators are needed to explore various possibilities. Communication among research projects through the media of professional journals, seminars, and conferences provides mutual stimulation and information which can function to avoid blind alleys. Although the public learns only about "successful" investigations, it is essential to success to have shown that other hypotheses and modes of investigation fail to achieve the sought ends. What counts as wasted effort and expenditure is not easy to make, since the elimination of hypotheses is a step to success and since important findings can occur in this process that are incidental to the primary intention of a project. The peer-review process used by funding agencies is an institutional means that restrains some possible inefficiencies in the use of resources by not awarding grants to inferior research protocols and by assessing the qualifications of the applicants. Yet the freedom to be somewhat inefficient, to be able to explore insights and possibilities that do not promise immediate results for medical therapy, contributes to the achievement of the general end of the expansion of biological knowledge that might issue in therapeutic procedures.

One grants legitimacy to the moral offensiveness of using criteria of economic efficiency in determining policies for the use of lifesaving interventions, and to the ambiguity of those criteria when applied to research funding. Descriptively it is also the case that policies are developed in small increments, and that one stage is a response to what has resulted from the previous stage. I again use the example of the development of policy about end-stage kidney disease; the issues of fair distribution of both dialysis machines and transplants plagued medical teams from the beginning. A good argument can be made that the policy decision to make dialysis available to virtually all who need it was motivated in part by the desire to avoid the difficult distributional choices. It is not clear, however, that significant consideration has been given to the precedent that this policy set. The policy was formed incrementally for kidney disease without due consideration of both potential fairness in relation to other life-threatening diseases and to economically efficient use of the limited whole of resources available for research and health care. Incremental choices that do not take account of the efficient use of limited total resources generally face the questions of cost at some stage; they do not avoid it but merely delay its consideration.

A thought experiment can suggest how the economic-efficiency criterion requires attention.[11] One can project a sum of money as the total to be allocated by the federal government for biomedical research and health care. Economics deals with the allocation of finite resources, and in this thought experiment they are at a fixed amount. The question becomes what is the most equitable and efficient distribution of the limited resources. Economic efficiency becomes morally relevant; there is no virtue in wasting finite resources, and there is merit in attempting to increase the beneficial outcomes at the lowest possible cost. The term "waste" is used simply as a rhetorical device to force us to the unpleasant task of thinking about criteria of distribution. It is offensive to assert that a disproportionate amount of health care dollars are wasted because they are spent on behalf of patients in the last stages of illness. It is offensive to calculate the costs of surgery and medical care entailed in saving the life of a radically defective infant for whom technology and care are available, and to many it is even more offensive to use predictions of the subsequent costs of medical care for that child, its family, and either the state or insurance companies. It sounds hardhearted to say that this money is wasted.

Yet from the perspective of the thought experiment in which we are engaged attention must be given to the context of the health needs of others: to the defensible claims of other patients or other diseases for a fair share of the resources. The aggregate sum available cannot be expanded indefinitely; funding for research and health care is in competition with other needs and claims for funding within a total budget of which all are parts. Whether the proportion allocated to medicine relative to other claims such as national defense, education, environmental concerns, etc. is itself fair is an argument I shall not address. But fair and efficient allocation will force very hard choices since the needs of all who have claims on research and health care funding cannot be fully met.

To make these hard choices requires consideration of principles of justice, the calculation of potential consequences for alternative policies, and some proposals about what constitutes the common good of the society. One may not desire to say that the high proportion of medical costs that are

11. For a general study of this problem, see Arthur Okun, *Equality and Efficiency: The Great Trade-Off* (Washington, D.C.: The Brookings Institution, 1975). My thinking throughout this chapter has also been informed by Lester C. Thurow, *The Zero-Sum Society*.

expended on the last stages of life is wasted, since various arguments can be made to support the claims of individuals to the available technology. But the thought experiment forces consideration of the criteria that would be used to make discriminating decisions. I am not implying that such an exercise would be decisive in particular instances, or that triage thinking is called for. The triage pattern presumes a forced choice between two alternatives, life or death, whereas the circumstances under consideration here allow for a variety of courses of action.

Economic efficiency is at least a point to be considered in biomedical research policy. With the general end that backs the whole enterprise, the improvement of human health, there are literally thousands of particular ends, from basic biological research (biochemical research, for example, that has no particular therapeutic end in view) to the delivery of services to those who need them. It is also the case that in the course of both investigations and delivery of services procedures are developed which lower costs; improvements in bioengineering are a case in point. But to consider efficiency within the projected finite total resources requires that the whole be taken into account, something which is both intellectually and practically difficult. We do not have an agency responsible for thinking about, not to mention allocating, resources in the light of efficient as well as fair distribution. The arguments against the establishment of such an agency in a democratic society are strong: the wisdom required is not confined to a collectivity of technicians; the concentration of power to allocate could lead to stagnation of individual initiatives; the interest groups that have claims could be stifled. Without some consideration, however, of economically efficient distribution of finite resources, there are other "costs"; interest groups without sufficient power to make their claims heard might be ignored, and preferred interests with power can get an undue share of resources which can be wastefully used. While it is not decisive, economic efficiency in the allocation of biomedical research funding is a point that needs to be considered in policy formation more than it is at the present time.

The final type of criteria is political. I have noted the importance of the political processes involved in determining allocations of publicly funded research. As long as the procedures we now use in the United States continue, a relevant consideration will be what can gain public, and therefore political and economic, support. The interests of various disease and research lobbies are legitimate; they represent the health needs and scientific strength of particular groups in society. The power of particular groups, however, can become disproportionate to the importance of their needs, on the basis of the medical criteria I have enumerated. The process, however, is also political in beneficial ways. Legitimate research and health interests are able to organize sufficient power to have their claims taken seriously in the allocation of resources. And various legitimate interests are overlapping. A disease lobby cannot pursue its ends without sustaining and strengthening the more general and basic interests of the biomedical research community and of those concerned for better health care.

The political process is in accord with the American tradition: various groups can organize voluntarily to make their rightful claims. They can gain access to Congress or other institutions in which their claims are adjudicated relative to the claims of others with competing or overlapping interests. I believe, however, that the "democratization" of dialysis indicates that the political processes lead to quite mixed outcomes. The question of equity in the distribution of research funding and the subsequent delivery of services can be avoided for reasons of expediency, i.e., unwillingness to face difficult choices and to see the importance of precedents that are set. Excuses can be found to avoid the development of agencies with the authority and power to make decisions of allocation based on more equitable principles. But the tactics of expediency cannot be sustained forever in the face of finite resources. The practical question is whether to continue to use the present political processes and muddle through with a quite favorable record from these procedures, or to establish agencies with power and authority to make allocations more in accord with the medical, ethical, and economic criteria I have drawn. The system now is, of course, already mixed; funds are granted to the NIH and the NSF for certain categories of research and these funds in turn are distributed through application and review processes. There are clearly risks in increasing the authority of agencies which determine allocation in the light of a vision of a common good and principles of equity, but further steps in this direction need support.

These four types of criteria are, descriptively, now taken into account in the process of allocation. No one type is sufficient to determine what policies ought to be pursued in the social conditions of common life. The ethical task is to contribute to the direction of events that are taking place. An understanding and interpretation of various "factual" matters is an important aspect of any move toward recommendations or prescriptions. The knowledge-conditions are constantly changing: research continues at a rapid pace, the availablility of economic resources fluctuates with the state of the economy, different interest groups attract public and political attention, and so forth. Even if one addressed the allocation issues from an ideal ethical theory, e.g., that similar health needs should be given similar access to resources, policy would not be affected without taking into account the other types of criteria.

One sees in this chapter the way in which the designated whole complicates the task of ethics. If, for example, medical ethics is confined to the determination of right conduct of experimentation only in the light of the established principle of informed consent, a resolution of the ethical issue becomes relatively clear; where informed consent cannot be given, and particularly if there are no possible health benefits to the experimental subject, the research is morally wrong regardless of potential benefits that might be forthcoming. In contrast with this position, if one begins with the sphere of ends for which medicine has responsibility within the division of functions in human society a larger set of circumstances must be taken into account in ethical reflection. Although the individual patient is a "whole," he or she is also interrelated with others in a larger whole, and there can be justifications for some risks being taken with the individual for the sake of others. The first question is not what research would be intrinsically immoral, but what are the necessary conditions for the end of medical research to be reasonably approximated in a given society. Within this way of working, one would come to a point at which a moral judgment must be made about a particular research protocol: Can the objective be achieved morally through the procedure that is proposed? But cognizance of the consequences of making that judgment would highlight a tragic aspect of a moral choice.

A question to be put to the moralist whose primary focus of attention is on the morality or immorality of the act of experimentation is this: Would one deprive the whole population of children susceptible to a communicable and life-threatening disease of a probably successful vaccine because children as an experimental population cannot give fully informed consent to participation? Of course, if the answer to this is negative there is also a painful aspect of the choice; persons who cannot fully consent are put at risk for the sake of benefits to others. Life in the world is not ordered so that there is a preestablished harmony of all the ends, values, and principles that are worth of support and that are applicable to a complex policy choice. Like personal moral choices, policy choices are made in a process of discernment in which a variety of points have to be considered.

Reflections from a Theocentric Perspective

The aspect of man as participant comes to the fore in especially significant ways in the previous chapter and in this one. Human capacities are extended and developed through culture, and particularly through science and technology; intervention into natural processes for human ends—activity as old as humanity itself—takes on new dimensions. Human reproduction can be controlled; the supply of nutrients can be increased. Interventions into "natural" processes bring benefits to persons and communities. Man's dependence upon nature and interdependence with it are radically altered through culture.

In biomedical research man is investigating patterns and processes of life both in minute proportions and in extensive dimensions. Through research and through scientific concepts and symbols the operations of nature are perceived, conceived, and explained. The knowledge that is yielded makes possible the more normal functioning of human life and the delaying of human death.

What "naturally" occurs, that is, what occurs apart from human intervention, threatens and destroys proper human good and values as well as sustains them. Nature is the enemy as well as the friend of man. Disease impairs that vital and normal functioning of aspects of human life. Untimely deaths take the lives of persons who have responsibilities, whose lives are quite full and rich, and who have great potential to make contributions that would benefit others. Medicine, as a part of culture, is a means of warding off the debilitating and death-dealing consequences of natural processes. To be sure humans are mortal; death comes to all; in the end nature and God will not be defied. Indeed, in the end all persons must consent to their own natural mortality. But natural processes do not provide immutable laws to which human activity is to be conformed. Values of human life, those of some personal fulfillment and those that contribute to the community, cannot be realized apart from a level of necessary health conditions. The moral choices in the allocation of biomedical research funding have to be made by taking cognizance of personal and social ends; the sustaining of health and life is a condition for the meeting of those ends. Nature is still the source of sustenance of life; interventions reorder natural processes that are occurring and thus there is still a basic dependence on the powers of life that are beyond human control. But the preservation of physical life is not an end in itself from the perspective of theocentric ethics.

The weight of the argument of this chapter is on the need for more careful forethought about the social and individual ends to be served by biomedical research and medical care. The effectiveness of medical science and technology in part creates new human and social problems, quite unintentionally. For various reasons human longevity has been extended in a dramatic way in recent decades. The outcomes are mixed, for there are those for whom a longer life has some richness and meaning in activity and many for whom it is meaningless and even burdensome. The social consequences of this extension of longevity have not been adequately dealt with; many of the problems that come with an increasingly aged population are due to the effectiveness of modern medicine. There is no single moral end to be the lodestar guiding medical research and practice. The preservation and extension of human life in certain afflicted groups in the population is not without its costs to others and to the resources that might be allocated to serve equally defensible objectives.

I have, in effect, argued that the natural course of events is not necessarily morally or humanly normative in the light of the ends that life and health serve. An interesting moral and even theological question is, however, the moral relevance of what can be judged to be the *normal* course of events. In medical research and practice there is a sense in which descriptive judgments of the normal do function as norms of value. Interventions are justified to return the bodily functioning as nearly as possible to that which is normal for the patient, relative to age and other factors. Disease is, in a sense, a deviation from the normal, both in a descriptive and evaluative sense.

Judgments about what constitutes a genetic defect is but one example. Certain prenatally detected defects are judged to create sufficient impairment to justify the abortion of a fetus. In judgments of what is normal appeals are made to other values than simply biological survivability. Fetuses with prenatally detected Downs syndrome, for example, have been aborted. The criterion is not biological survivability but judgment about the potential capacities for normal human functioning in a society whose values and family structure place premiums on intelligence and on capacities to be individually self-reliant. A similar issue arises in other circumstances; the question is whether the "normal" is only a biological criterion, and what is it if that is the case? Is it relative to age? To what? Or should the normal take into account various capacities for meaningful human functioning that are personal and social in character? I have already referred to the interest in investigating the biology of aging with the prospect of slowing the now normal aging process. Should what is now "normal" in a biological and statistical sense be altered?

In my judgment, both medical research and medical care ought to consider more than the extension of physical survivability in evaluating possible outcomes. To be sure, even the biologically normal shifts as medicine develops. Those outcomes of hypertension, for example, which were statistically normal (the number of strokes and heart attacks attributable to hypertension) a few decades ago have been drastically changed as a result of medical research and therapy. But this change sustains not only an extension of life but also personal and social human functioning. Other interventions, however, do not issue in outcomes as beneficial to the primary patient and to others.

Given limitations of resources, and a serious effort to allocate research funding among persons and groups who have at least equal claims to therapy, the consequences of rapid technological advances in a given area of medicine have to be given forethought. Theologically, at least, it is necessary to consider that the good is sought under finite conditions. While the conditions are not, as a result of scientific and technological development, in a zero-sum state, it is also the case that in the foreseeable future the needs of all individuals cannot be fairly met. Inequities in the quality of health care might well be intensified, particularly if certain results of research are available only to those who can afford their high costs. If public funding has supported the research, however, equal access to the fruits of that research is a significant moral claim.

These reflections follow from ethics from the theocentric perspective developed in this work. We are to relate all things in a manner appropriate to their relations to God, but there are no divinely initiated or infallibly revealed prescriptions of proper actions. What we as participants are enabled and required to do cannot, so to speak, be read directly off the patterns of interdependence of life. There is no precise moral blueprint in nature to which actions are to be conformed. The theology of volume 1 provides a basis for a theological interpretation of human experience and activity, and theological backing for certain values and ends. It does not provide a harmonized set of values in which all things work together for the good of individuals or even of the human race. It does not provide an immutable hierarchical ordering of values from which priorities can be deduced in all possible circumstances. But the theology backs certain ends and values, and sets the significance of human life within the larger context of the ordering of life in the world. It provides signals or indications of points to be taken into account in making personal and social choices.

As I have noted, in the area of biomedical research the significance of human participation in nature and the consequences of this for society are particularly dramatic. With the gaining of new and more fundamental understanding of the workings of the human organism as well as of the relations of various environments to it, the course of the natural can be directed by human interventions. Medicine is an area in which culture very dramatically "stands between" human possibilities and the natural course of events. Though death is not finally defied, it is warded off; though debilitation and impairment of functioning are not fully in human control, they are remarkably reined. Dependence upon nature continues even in the course of interventions, but the interventions are not governed by some presumed morally valid ordering of the natural course of events. Theology and ethics do not provide an infallible moral guide, but the theology does support an interpretation of life and of various ends and values that have to be taken into account in thinking about the allocation of biomedical research funding. These ends and values provide some clues as to how this arena of human activity can be reflected upon so that policies are more appropriate to the relations of all things to God. All the features of the profile of theocentric ethics in chapter 1 pertain to some extent to this area, and without explicit citation most of them have informed this chapter.

Individual persons are not of absolute value, and thus continuation of physical life is not of ultimate value. Physical life, while the indispensable condition for all human values, is not an end in itself. As Barth so nicely said, we do not owe the same reverence to life that we owe to God. From my perspective individuals are interpreted in their relations to other persons and to the communities of which they are a part. The pursuit of justifiable individual ends occurs in the patterns of interdependence. Interdependence carries mutual responsibilities so that persons and policies have to take into account how the consequences of the pursuit of particular valid objectives of research and therapy affect other persons and other objectives. What I have called the time- and space-spans that are morally and socially relevant have to be extended; the "whole" has to be enlarged. Calculation of probable outcomes not only for individual recipients but also for health care institutions, costs and payments of health care, and social arrangements have to be taken into account. While such an expansion will not yield a precise moral or social imperative applicable to the allocation of research funding, it will at least force forethought and enable choices to be more appropriate.

The common good of the society with reference to health care is not achieved simply by aggregative benefits to particular individuals with particular needs. Equity has to be striven for even though the types of criteria required to formulate research policy are varied and complex. Given all the elements that make up a vision of the common good of a society and the limitations of resources that can be allocated for medical research and health care, research that leads to prevention of severe diseases has priority over that which dramatically and at high cost is targeted to end-stages of disease. There is no avoidance of conflicts; the legitimate needs of all persons cannot be met. The progress of biomedical research itself puts certain classes of persons (those with certain diseases) at a potential advantage over others. Choices to allocate funding for one objective rather than another necessarily entail neglect of those whose diseases are given less attention.

From the perspective of the present work, the ethical writings on biomedical research which focus almost exclusively on the issues of possible violations of informed consent and similar matters are ethically shortsighted. I have indicated that those concerns are valid; the present work does not license the use of any possible means to achieve valid and desired ends in research. The present work requires multiple points of consideration, the formulation of complex criteria, and careful assessment of long-range and broad outcomes to discern what policies are most appropriate. It does not guarantee that perfect fairness is achievable; choices will have to be made which are painful and even in some circumstances tragic. The task of ethics is to assist in directing courses of events; it is to seek to discern what man, as a participant, is enabled and required to do within particular circumstances; to call attention to limitations and possibilities that emerge in the course of events.

From the theology of the present work an even more painful question is worth asking. Does the pursuit of health and the extension of physical life tend to become an idol—an idol whose worship skews other valid ends both for individuals and for societies? Of course the question cannot be answered in general; as an almost absolute value the responsibility to care for one's body as well as the pursuit of research and therapy which aid in keeping persons healthy is unquestionably legitimate and important. Life is given, and it is sustained out of gratitude for the qualities and activities that it provides. If man is a steward of life in the world the bodily conditions for the exercise of that calling must be sustained. Karl Barth, Thomas Aquinas, and even Kant, in the precritical ethics, stated in effect that the moment of termination of life was for God to decide, not man. Technology clearly has made such statements obsolete; it is in human power to sustain life under increasingly desperate circumstances. Yet in the end the powers that create and sustain human life also bear down upon it and destroy it. Nature and God will not be defied; disease and death come to each and to all whether we consent to them or not.

9

Conclusions

So little knows
Any, but God alone, to value right
The good before him. . . .
Milton, *Paradise Lost*, Book 4

It remains to draw strands from the previous chapters of this book to conclusion. To do so I return to some of the fundamental themes stated in both volumes. The practical moral question from a theocentric perspective, once again, is: What is God enabling and requiring us, as participants in the patterns and processes of interdependence of life, to be and to do? The general answer is: We are to relate ourselves and all things in a manner appropriate to their relations to God.

The previous four chapters have shown how ethics from a theocentric perspective addresses some areas of human life and choices. I remind the reader again that the first question of theological ethics is about God and God's relations to the world; it is not to establish theological backing for an ethical theory. Thus the ethics has to be congruent with the theology. The ethics that follow from the theology may not be sufficiently precise or systematic to meet certain standards of a philosophical ethical theory. If I have not lapsed seriously in the processes of reasonable thinking, however, I have delineated ethics in the manner that the theology requires and permits.

I have divided this chapter into two sections, man's being and man's doing. The distinction is only a practical one. Who we are affects what we do; what we do shapes who we are. Thus in the first part I draw conclusions about what God is enabling and requiring us to be, about the manner of life that is appropriate to man's relations to God. In the second part I draw conclusions about how we discern what God is enabling and requiring us to do, i.e., about criteria for ordering our participation in life.

Man's Being

The concept of man as a participant in the patterns and processes of interdependence of life is a way of self-understanding, not only for persons as individuals but also for communities and for the human species. By "understanding" I mean to include both our more rational or intellective and our more affective capacities. The concept has implications both for how we *see* man and how we *sense* or *feel* our place in the scheme of things. These two can be distinguished for purposes of exposition, but they cannot be separated.

What are some of the implications of the concept for how we see ourselves as individuals, communities, and species? One is that we are parts of more inclusive wholes, and in the condition of interdependence with them. This is the case of ourselves as members of families and as professional persons in institutions; it is the case of the institutions and communities in which we participate as they are interrelated with other institutions and communities; it is the case of our species within the ecosphere we inhabit, and it is even the case of our planet with the cosmos.

This understanding qualifies our perception and conception of our place or our "roles" in life. It makes us take seriously the condition of human finitude with reference to our knowledge, our capacities to predict the effects of our activity, and our capacities to control the interventions we make into the lives of other persons, into social processes and orderings, into historical events, and into nature itself. Not all deleterious outcomes (with reference to our intended beneficial achievements) are irreversible, not every wrong action is subsequently uncorrectable; there are possibilities of rectifying the unintended consequences of our actions. But it does sound a warning signal; the limits of our knowledge and our control of events lead almost inevitably to costly consequences for other persons and things; the interventions that have the deepest and farthest-reaching consequences require grave reflection and the strongest possible justification before power is exercised; and those that are irreversible ought not to be done except for very powerful reasons that support compensating laudable ends. "So little *knows*/Any, but God alone, to value right/The good before him. . . . "

The concept of man as participant not only discloses our limits; it also affirms our powers and capacities to intervene in the patterns and processes in accordance with our intention to achieve beneficial ends. As participants, Bach and Beethoven created music and Michaelangelo and Picasso created art; Fleming discovered penicillin and Watson and Crick discovered the double helix structure of DNA; Frank Lloyd Wright and Mies van der Rohe designed architectural treasures; Watt advanced the harnessing of steam and Edison harnessed electricity; Aristotle and Wittgenstein changed philosophy and Thomas Aquinas and Luther changed theology. As participants, human beings are exploring the development of renewable sources of energy and means to increase sources of nutrition for humankind. The capacity to participate is part of our nature; even animals exercise their capacities purposively to use other aspects of nature to build nests and to feed themselves. The human capacities are qualitatively distinctive, of course, and when our natural ones are cultivated and extended by developments in science and technology, our interventions reach deeper and farther—whether into the lives of other persons through psychoanalysis, into biological nature through recombinant DNA, or into the course of history through mass communications or war. As I argued in volume 1, the benefits we achieve rely upon processes and patterns of interdependence even as we intentionally control them. Our capacities testify to our being only a little lower than the angels, as the Psalmist wrote. A commonplace needs a constant emphasis, namely, that with the increased ability to understand

and to control our interventions into the lives of persons, history, society, and nature, comes the inevitability of deeper and wider consequences. The selection of ends to be served becomes a matter of greater moral seriousness. The concept of man as participant does not imply that there are things we ought not to know; there is no way to predict that what is learned might not benefit both human life and the rest of life in the world. Recent scientific developments indicate that pursuit of an intended target in research often yields unintended knowledge which is beneficial for the relief of human suffering.[1]

Whether the weight of accountability for the ordering of life has shifted, in a sense, from God to man, that is, whether we now have each achieved such knowledge and such capacities for intervention that man and technology control the destiny of our planet, is a matter of debate. Certainly the balance has shifted to some degree since primitive times, and is shifting more rapidly in this century than in all the previous centuries of human culture combined. The difference in the possible consequences of a major war is a case in point; nuclear weapons have far more destructive power and longer and wider range effects than any armaments used in World War II. To see ourselves as participants who can use presently available technologies to control human emotions through drugs, control values and ways of thinking through mass communications, affect the course of world history through economic interdependence, and affect the course of civilization and even nature through the use of nuclear weapons qualitatively alters the seriousness of our participation in the patterns and processes of interdependence.[2]

1. It is an error to determine a universal evaluation of "human nature" and then read all experiences in the light of it, as is done in a Hobbesian view, or a theological view that all persons are utterly depraved, or an unambiguously "optimistic" view. Judgments about the reliability and unreliability of participants, whether persons or institutions, need to be made with reference to more particular experiences and information. It is a truism, but worthy of observation, to say that some persons and institutions deserve more of our confidence than others, and there are usually evidences on which we can base our judgments. Yet these predelictions to universalize color our responses to persons and events. Much of the sharp difference of opinion about the uses of genetic research, for example, rests not on scientific information and extrapolations from it to various practices, but on whether the investigators, clinicians, and various institutions that determine policy are to be trusted or not. If one has a fundamentally distrustful attitude toward a class of persons such as scientists, then restraints, regulations, and surveillance of a high and detailed order are called for. If one takes a more benign view, less restrictions are called for. There is some wisdom in thinking from the worst possible case of misuse for the sake of the protection of persons; many of us think in this way, for good reasons, about the possibilities of nuclear war. But it is also the case that in some other areas of human activity worthwhile work by reliable persons is hampered to some extent because critics take a totally and unambiguously Hobbesian view of human nature. There are also, however, "cosmic optimists" whose confidence in certain classes of persons or even in "man" impairs their seeing and feeling potential risks and dangers in activities they judge to represent progress.

2. Over the past twenty years I have, in a lay person's way, attempted to grasp the main lines of genetic and neurological research because I believe that in biology these have the

In one sense all of this is commonplace; it simply recognizes our distinctive features as agents. But I believe that the perception and conception of our activity in the processes and patterns of interdependence qualifies our self-understanding in a way that seeing ourselves as agents in a very circumspect "time and space" boundary does not. Certainly it is appropriate for a physician, for example, to be primarily concerned about the immediate needs of the patient. The lines around the relevant interaction are quite properly confined. But even in such conditions a larger whole—both in "space" (the numbers of persons, for example, affected in secondary ways by the care of the patient) and in "time" (the long-range consequences for the patient and for others)—must be envisioned. The interactions stimulated by our intended actions have to be considered; probable outcomes of our intended consequences have to be taken into account. There is never only one outcome of a human action; there may be one immediate recipient but in the subsequent interactions there are many "recipients" in the larger patterns and processes of interdependence. Our perception and conception of ourselves, our place, and our roles are qualified significantly by the concept I have proposed; we are enabled and required to *see* man as a participant in larger roles.

What are some of the implications of the concept for how we sense (or feel about) ourselves? Our affective capacities are also involved in our self-understanding; our valuation of ourselves as individuals, communities, and a species is qualified by seeing man as a participant. Theologians and others have long been concerned about the self-evaluation of human life. "So little knows/Any, but God alone, to *value* right/The good before him, but perverts best things/To worst abuse, or to their meanest use." The disordering of life described in Genesis 3, the loss of paradise, itself is an account of a false evaluation of the place of the human in the ordering of the world. The prophetic indictments of the people of ancient Israel and Judah are based upon the failure of the people to acknowledge the laws of God which order history. The preoccupation with the pride of man throughout Western religious history and thought is grounded in the perception of excessive certitude, on the part of man, in human capacities rightly to order life. The preoccupation with sloth, with the resignation of man to being merely the flotsam and jetsam floating on biological needs or on the events of history, is equally based on an evaluation of the human—its denigration below the distinctive capacities it has. Different concepts have been used to describe the grounds for these errant valuations: for example, man is both

---

deepest and widest implications for future human participation. Man, in my judgment, will come closer to being the ultimate orderer of life through the uses of these investigations than through the matters that preoccupy so much of the attention in clinical medical ethics. Of course in practice it will not be "man" but those persons and institutions that have the power to control the use of such investigations.

"spirit" and "nature," and in the freedom that is ours by virtue of "spirit" we have a deep dread or anxiety which leads us either to strive for a false security in that which is less than God or to deny our freedom and lapse into sloth and sensuality.[3]

Our valuation of ourselves deeply conditions our valuations of other persons, of things, and of nature. If we believe (and believing here combines intellective and affective aspects) that as individuals we are the center of value in our little world, that as a nation we are the center of value in the world of nations, that as a species we are the center of value in nature, others become simply means for our interests and desires, tools for our achievements, and objects whose own place in the scheme of things is denied by reducing them to their utility value to us. At the other extreme if we do not sufficiently respect our distinctive human capacities we undervalue ourselves as persons, communities, and a species. We deny our "nature" by refusing to accept its distinctive place in the wider ordering, with its possibilities and responsibilities for sustaining, cultivating, and developing the world of which we are part.

From the theocentric perspective I have developed, just as the ordering of life in the world can be indications or signs of the divine ordering, so also proper valuation of man's being involves a proper assessment of ourselves in relation to God. Piety, evoked by the senses of dependence, gratitude, obligation, remorse and repentance, possibilities, and direction, is thus an essential aspect of theocentric morality. Piety involves feelings or affectivity. Theocentric piety and fidelity shape our sense of the value of the human in relation to the patterns and processes of interdependence in which we live. It "moves" (motivates) our participation as well as grounds some of our reasons for it.

We not only *see* ourselves as parts of larger wholes, but we *value* ourselves (individuals, communities and institutions, and species) as parts of the larger wholes. I shall only indicate some reminders of what I have written previously.

No individual and no generation of human beings creates its own limits and its own possibilities. We are the heirs of the past—an ancient biological and physical past, and a historical past that bequeaths us our institutions and culture. We are parts of a larger whole; we are recipients, as well as agents, dependent upon what we have been given. We cannot, in such a perception feel that as individuals or as a generation our life and our time is the center of value. If subsequent generations blame us for the problems that are our legacy to them, so also they must thank us for benefits that are theirs. Our "sense" of being participants qualifies our assessment of ourselves and of

3. Reinhold Niebuhr, *The Nature and Destiny of Man*, 2 vols., (New York: Scribner's, 1941 and 1943), 1:178–240.

the value of things relative to those who will come after us. To be a "steward" is a matter of our feelings as much as it is a matter of conceptually locating ourselves in life.

In the present we are sustained and impaired by other persons, by the social institutions of which we are a part, by the vitality or poverty of our culture, and by the ordering of the natural world. Our individual autonomy, the extent to which we can and ought to be self-legislating, is of limited scope. Both our powers as participants and the issues of how to use those powers are framed in large measure by our contemporary interdependence. A young adult often seeks the counsel and approval of parents on crucial matters. We are conditioned by family life, and family life is deeply affected by the larger institutional relationships of which families are a part. The history that has brought us to a preoccupation with nuclear deterrence gives us problems unique to our time and place. The air we breathe, the water we use, and the land we till are matters that raise our ecological consciousness. Our self-understanding in these relationships is as much a matter of our "senses" as it is a matter of our idea of the place of the human in the world. Dependence and gratitude, remorse and hope, all affect our valuation of ourselves as individuals, communities, and species.

There are possibilites for altering ourselves and our world; our choices and actions are not bound by inexorably determined laws. But we sense our finitude, and recognize that what we do will be caught up in processes and patterns beyond our control. As we grasp our power to affect the future, the anxiety that comes from our self-understanding is fitting. Risks are inevitable, and the requirements of courage to act, to live with risk and with remorse and even guilt, are part of our self-understanding. The imperative that I articulated, "Act so that you treat all things never only as a means to your own ends, or even to collective human ends," is grounded not only in a perception and conception of ourselves as participants but also in the qualification of our valuation of human life.

Humankind is not the exclusive or ultimate center of value in creation. Our capacities enable us to participate in the cultivation and sustenance of many values that are proper to ourselves, and we rightly value things in relation to our proper interests. But our interdependence qualifies our tendencies to anthropocentrism. We can be sure that if many aspects of the natural world could speak and claim rights they would say that the activities of many are frequently detrimental to them and their world. While such a thought may be fanciful, it points to something valid, namely, the interdependence of things in the world in which each sustains or relies on the being and value of the other. This recognition should at least evoke greater modesty about the claims, explicit and tacit, that our superiority in capacity renders us of such superior value that all things exist for our sake. There are no gains for persons and humanity without some costs to others—persons and things.[4]

The central concept of participation evokes an understanding of man as a steward of God, and part of that stewardship requires that we care for ourselves, as individuals, as communities and institutions, and as a species. To participate in the patterns and processes of interdependence, to act in cooperation with and in the service of worthy wider ends and purposes, requires attention to our capacities to be participants, to sustain and develop the necessary conditions to function in our roles. Kant was correct to stress the importance of duties to ourselves for us to be able to fulfill obligations to others. Not only our duties and obligations toward other persons, but also our aspirations for the species, society, culture, and even nature cannot be met without developing the necessary resources and strengths to be participants.

The development of our capacities to be participants always brings its own temptations; it almost necessarily leads to ambiguities. The temptation for individuals is egocentrism and pride; the conditions we cultivate can lead to excessive self-confidence, and to excessive advantages for ourselves. It is a small step in Kant's ethics from a stringent morality of primary duties to oneself to the idea of individual moral perfection, and then to an insufferable self-satisfaction (which Kant, of course, does not commend). It is a slight shift from developing the necessary powers in oneself to serve wider ends and purposes to using that power for one's own undue advantage. In communities and institutions the temptation is corporate pride and aggrandizement of institutional and group advantages. A nation's fitting concern for its self-defense can tempt it to aggressions. The ambiguity lies in the fact that justifiable attention to developing the requisite conditions for participation of any designatable "self" invites the temptation to excess.

Refusal to accept responsibility to be participants is equally tempting for individuals and communities. It is easy to hold others totally accountable for all the ills and deprivations that persons and groups suffer, and to assume there is nothing that agents can do for themselves. It is easy to let nature and historical events take their courses on the assumption that there is nothing that human beings can do to direct them. It is easy to let oneself be sustained by the activities of others, so long as one survives. It is easy to find excuses not to develop our powers and exert our efforts. Sloth and self-debasement are as tempting as pride.

Important to our being before God is the sense of calling that the

4. Another fanciful notion comes to mind. What if there are beings in some other galaxy who would sometime find their way to our planet, and whose capacities have developed in ways "superior" to ours? How would they value human life? If they are as ——centric as we are anthropocentric, would we be judged to exist only for the sake of their interests?

Reformation fathers developed. In Luther's language, persons, and by extension communities and institutions, are "masks of God."[5] They are, so to speak, deputies responsible for carrying out the purposes of the divine ordering of life, insofar as that is within human powers. The sense of calling not only directs human minds to the larger purposes which each individual's modest efforts can serve, but also evokes in a person a sense of dignity, a sense of worthiness, and impulses to fulfill one's capacities. To be sure, the sense of calling can be romanticized; social arrangements and conditions of life and work often militate against the purposiveness that a calling induces. It was no easier for a serf in the Middle Ages, or a woodcutter in Reformation times, to feel a sense of calling than it is in the modern world for the operator of a word processor or a worker on an assembly line. No guarantee of immediate satisfactions can be given; as Luther liked to point out, to be a parent, and thus in this role a mask of God, required that one change the stinking diapers. But to interpret our being from a theocentric perspective is to both see and feel ourselves as being called—being given opportunities and responsibilities to participate through our roles in the ordering of life in the world.[6]

To see and to feel oneself as called is to accept responsibility to sustain and develop one's capacities to participate. This implies the development of the skills required for our various roles in life, and those required to assume different roles. It also involves the development of dispositions, or readiness, to act toward proper ends, that is, it involves the development of virtues. The idea of virtue has a long history in the secular and religious moral traditions of the West, and there is no consensus among the scholars as to whether ultimately virtue is one or many, or what precisely it is. For Kant, as we have seen, virtue is the moral strength of the will to do one's duty, especially against one's inclinations. For Erik Erikson, virtues are "ego strengths." For the natural-law traditions virtue is the perfection of a natural power toward its natural and proper end—in a sense the direction and perfection of an inclination. The preference that follows from the present work is for the latter understanding.[7]

5. For example, "Thus the magistrate, the emperor, the king, the prince, the teacher, the preacher, the pupil, the father, the mother, the children, the master, the servant—all these are social positions or external masks. God wants us to respect and acknowledge them as His creatures, which are the necessity for this life." They are, however, only masks, and not to be confused with God. See Martin Luther, *Lectures on Galations, 1935*, trans. Jaroslav Pelikan, in *Luther's Works*, ed. Jaroslav Pelikan, 56 vols. (St. Louis: Concordia Publishing House, 1963), 26:95.

6. I have developed the importance of the sense of calling as well as its problematics in "Professions as 'Callings'," *Social Service Review* 56 (1982):501–15. This was a lecture given at the invitation of the faculty of the School of Social Service Administration of the University of Chicago.

7. For Erik H. Erikson's discussion, see *Insight and Responsibility: Lectures on the Ethical Implications of Psychoanalytic Insight* (New York: W. W. Norton, 1964), pp. 111–57. See also James M. Gustafson, *Can Ethics Be Christian?* (Chicago: University of Chicago Press,

To be a responsible participant is to attend to the development of those dispositions that issue in actions toward worthy ends. And those dispositions of our being are developed in considerable measure by our doing. Again a temptation is met; one can focus with smug satisfaction on oneself as a "good" person. But from a theocentric perspective the worthiness of persons must refer both to the capacities that they have developed and the ends that their participation serves.

Whether one focuses on "skills" or on dispositions to act in certain ways, we are cultivating "natural" capacities that are given us. Human beings can take only limited credit for such virtues as they have. Some of the conditions for their development are beyond the control of individuals. If, as Erikson argues, the capacity to become a faithful or a loving person is dependent in large part on experiences in infancy and childhood, i.e., on having had one's needs faithfully met, and having been loved, a person with these characteristics cannot take full credit for them. It is equally the case, and one of the tragic aspects of human life, that some persons are deprived of the necessary conditions by genetic defects, by the family conditions in which they were reared, and by social and cultural factors. Their deficiencies are thus to some extent excusable. With whatever gifts and deprivations persons have, however, they are enabled to have a sense of calling; to be called is to accept responsibility for sustaining and developing our capacities to be participants, purposive agents, in the patterns and processes of interdependence of life.

What is true for individual persons is also true for communities and institutions. They also must assemble, sustain, and develop the resources and capacities to achieve worthy ends in their roles in the patterns and processes of interdependence. They are also, in Luther's term, "masks of God" in the sense that their functions are necessary for the ordering of life in the world. To do what they should properly do they must be; they must have the means to exercise their functions. As with individual persons, so also for groups and institutions—there are unavoidable temptations and ambiguities. And the characteristics of institutions and communities alter in the course of history and in the light of different conditions in different places.

The nuclear family is one example: in certain social conditions it has been more intimately related to multigenerational and extended families, and this has affected its resources for fulfilling its functions. In industrialized and urbanized societies, deeper changes in the economic and social ordering significantly alter these conditions, and thus the various resources required for the nuclear family to exist and function are changed. In societies with high technology the needs of health care are met in very different ways than those in which they were met a few decades ago, or in which they are met in

1975), pp. 25–81, and Stanley Hauerwas, *Character and the Christian Life* (San Antonio: Trinity University Press, 1975).

less industrialized societies in the world. What is required to be a "mask of God" in order to fulfill the purposes of family life and health care is affected by many historical and social changes. But the fundamental requirement to assemble, sustain, and develop resources remains.[8]

For many morally sensitive persons, and particularly Christians, moral ambiguities are imbedded in the requirement of institutions to assemble, sustain, and develop resources needed to function. An example in this regard is the need for capital accumulation in industrialized economies, and the role of the market in determining the allocation of resources. Whether an economy is managed more by the market or more by state planning, the accumulation of capital is essential to the means of production, and thus to the provision of industrial employment. In more capitalist and mixed economies significant income discrepancies are required for some persons and institutions to have sufficient resources to invest. Gross income-discrepancies are unfair; while to some extent they may reflect a distribution based on merit or on the significance of the contributions of persons to society, often they exceed tolerable ranges in the light of more egalitarian conceptions of distributive justice. Yet it is not clear that a more egalitarian distribution of wealth would guarantee the capital accumulation that is required in an industrial economy. In more centrally managed economies capital accumulation comes from the reservation of wealth by the state, wealth which thus also cannot be distributed in a very egalitarian way. Changes occur in technology and in the desires of persons and groups; competition occurs for scarce resources; dislocations in the economy and society occur which cause hardships to persons and families; sufficient remedial means are not available to meet the needs of all those who are burdened through no fault of their own. Issues of distributive justice are imbedded in the need for institutions to accumulate the resources needed to achieve both worthy and unworthy ends, but so are issues of efficiency. There is no ideal arrangement that can be implanted upon the dynamics of the economy which will meet the worthy ends of all persons and communities. Yet institutions are required to develop the resources to function in the ordering of society.

The improvement of health requires resources to develop science and medicine and the institutions to distribute preventive and therapeutic health care. The feeding of a growing world-population necessitates the development of many resources and institutional arrangements to produce and

8. From the room in which I write this I can observe a landfill project in Lake Michigan. Whether the project is worthy, I shall not judge. But the technology assembled to complete it is certainly radically different from that available for more extensive landfills in Chicago in the nineteenth century and the early part of the twentieth. What tractors, front-loaders and mammoth dump trucks are doing would probably be done in India by hundreds of women, some with infants on their hips, carrying baskets of dirt on their heads.

distribute food. The natural and cultivated curiosity to know the moon and other planets in our solar system, to know how life has evolved, and to know about ancient cultures requires that institutions find resources to pursue these ends. Ambiguities are involved in supporting each of these proper incentives. Medical research leads to both the elimination of smallpox, a disease that affected large numbers of people, and to expensive end-stage therapies for a few patients or nations that can afford them. Expansion of food production can deplete irreplacable topsoil. The fairness of investigating matters of great interest to a few when many are deprived of the means of meeting their basic needs must always be justified. Temptations to excess or deficiency in all these matters are ever present; the ambiguity of every social choice must be faced; tragic outcomes of social choices are sometimes inevitable. There is no automatic harmony between the pursuit of resources by institutions and communities that enable them to meet their wider worthy ends on the one hand, and the capacity to meet the needs and interests of all with whom they are interdependent on the other. But there is no avoiding the requirement of institutions to develop the conditions needed for their participation. To be participants, institutions, like individual persons, have duties to themselves.

I have stressed the unavoidable moral ambiguities that are inherent in the implications of the concept of participation. "So little knows/Any, *but God alone*, to value right/The good before him. . . . " The ambiguity is inherent in the dual conditions of finitude and responsibility. To be sure, there are limitations to our moral accountability because of the limitations of our causal accountability.[9] As an individual citizen my causal accountability for the Vietnam War was at most ultramicroscopic, and thus I as an individual had limited moral accountability for that event. I cannot be held morally accountable for the drowning of a person if that occurred beyond the range of my ability to swim. There are also expansions of collective moral accountability that ensue from those choices and actions in modern culture that have deep and far-reaching consequences. We know the importance of pure water for health, and thus we have a moral responsibility to attempt to ensure safe water for those persons with whom we share the earth. We know the disastrous consequences of a nuclear war, and therefore we have the moral responsibility to do all in our powers to keep one from occurring.

The recognition of ambiguity does not imply that it cannot be reduced through ethical reflection. Nor does it imply that in all circumstances we are denied certainty about what is required of us. But the recognition tempers our assessment of ourselves. To see ourselves from a theocentric perspective

9. See H. L. A. Hart, *Punishment and Responsibility* (New York: Oxford University Press, 1968), pp. 211–37.

is to see and feel ourselves in a condition of ambiguity. This condition cannot be totally relieved, from such a perspective, by the construction of an ideal ethical theory that provides almost absolute certainty about ourselves and our actions, even though we do our best rationally to direct our individual and collective capacities in the light of a theocentric construal of the world. Nor can it be totally relieved by a bland assurance that in the end all things work together for good for us and others, even though we see indications of some forms of "good" occurring as an outcome of events and affairs we judge to be evil. We need life together in human communities: some of its components are shared moral discourse, the ability to forgive and exercise mercy, and the provision of opportunities to renew and reorder life.

Another implication for our being is a readiness to restrain, deny, and even sacrifice justifiable interests of our own for the sake of others. We are enabled and required to be ready to give of ourselves for the well-being of other persons; to give of our collective assets (of many sorts) for the sake of the well-being of other communities; to restrain some of our activities for the sake of the generations that are to follow; to train, discipline, and exert ourselves so that we can benefit others. To see and feel ourselves (individuals, communities, and institutions) as parts of larger wholes whose common good cannot be realized apart from our restraints and our interventions is to be in a state of readiness to deny ourselves. Our participation in the patterns and processes of interdependence enables and requires us for the sake of worthy wider ends and purposes to be self-giving. Satisfactions may follow, but they are not guaranteed. In this way we participate in what is ultimately the divine ordering of life in the world, in the service of God.

More could be written about our being before God, and about the characteristics of it in the light of both the theology and the ethics I have delineated. To be such persons, communities, and institutions, however, requires our participation in communities that interpret or construe the world as ultimately brought into being, sustained, borne down upon, and provided with conditions of possibility by the ultimate power and orderer of all life. Herein lies the significance of what was written in volume 1 about life in the Christian community with its symbols and concepts, its liturgies and communal life, and with its distinctive determination by the accounts given in the Bible and particularly, for it, those given in the New Testament.

The characteristics of persons and communities are shaped and nourished by the symbols, myths, rites, and stories that they share, and by the education they receive. Piety, which I have indicated is an aspect of our being before God, is evoked, nourished, and sustained not only by reflections on common experience, but also by the symbols that interpret that experience. The sense of calling, to which I have referred, comes not simply from seeing how one's life and work function in the patterns of life, but also from an interpretation of life and work in relation to the divine ordering of life. Worship, as I indicated in volume 1, directs ourselves—our intellects and our feelings—toward God.[10] It focuses our attention and our affections on the ultimate power on which all things depend. Both our seeing and our sensing the place of being human are affected by being open to the powers of religious symbols. Not only do we see and sense the relative insignificance of ourselves and of the human venture in the light of the power and the majesty of God; we also see and sense our own possibilities and accountabilities, individual and communal, in the light of what the sustaining powers enable and require.

I shall not repeat here what I developed in volume 1, but only remind the reader of what was said there about the practical importance of primary religious language and of prayer. I claimed that the practical significance of life in religious communities, and for Christians in the church, was a matter of great importance. It is a necessary instrument, not in service of our self-interest as individuals, or in the narrow interests of our communities and species. It is instrumental in directing our consciousness of our lives and of the human venture toward God, the ultimate power and orderer of all things. A theocentric perspective is hardly possible without the symbols, myths, rites, and stories that move us to an awareness of God; the proper assessment of ourselves is hardly possible without a perceived, conceived, and deeply felt relationship to God.

To be sure, the theology of volume 1 is developed with conscious deviation from certain traditional Christian doctrines, symbols, and assurances. The piety that it sustains is, in some respects, different from some aspects of traditional Christian piety, and the self-understanding that follows is also in some respects different. This is, in part, because there are in our culture various ways of construing the world, various "myths" which point to what the powers that order the world are, and what human life is. The symbols of the Christian community are not the only ones to which even the most zealous church members are exposed. It cannot be assumed that the participants in the life of the Christian community are not also exposed to other ways of construing the world, some of which carry a considerable weight of evidence supporting their serious consideration. Few middle-class Christian congregants in the Western world, at least, are ignorant of the general lines of scientific accounts of how the planets, life, and human life came to be. If only by exposure to these ideas from television the thoughtful ones must make choices: split their lives into two ways of interpretation without relating each to the other, retreat into a narrow version of the Christian tradition and ignore others, be converted to another version to seek in it a sufficient view of life, or somehow to reconstruct a view of God, and thus of being human before God, that is at least not radically incon-

10. Gustafson, *Ethics*, 1:318.

gruous with evidences and theories from the sciences.[11] The symbols, like the concepts of the theologian, are modified in their references and in their articulation, but they continue to evoke and sustain theocentric piety.

The common life of the Christian community must continue to be formed in great measure by the biblical literature. The varieties of the biblical literature (myths, legends, sagas, laws and casuistry, narrative history, prophetic indictments, poetry, aphorisms, parables, theological reflection, apocalyptic visions, historical analogies, etc.) bear meanings of human life before God as they have come out of communities' conscientious participation in nature, history, society, and culture, felt and seen as ultimately under the governance of God. The gospels powerfully portray Jesus as one who incarnates in his teachings, his manner, and his actions theocentric piety and fidelity. History and teachings powerfully form human life.

This characterization of human life, the kind of persons and communities we are enabled and required to be, is congruous with many strands of the biblical material from both Testaments, and is deeply informed by them. The community that bears that tradition must continue to bear it; the same community that throughout its history has selected from it, reinterpreted aspects of it, and abandoned some of it, will continue to select, reinterpret, and abandon. With its continuity and its changes, it will continue to function as a necessary instrument that enables and requires human beings to be: to form and sustain those characteristics of life which are appropriate to us as participants in the divine ordering through the patterns and processes of interdependence of life.

Man's Doing

The central concept of man as a participant in the patterns and processes of interdependence of life framed the ways in which I wrote about marriage and family, suicide, population and nutrition, and the allocation of biomedical research funding. Those chapters have illustrated the way in which one proceeds to discern what God is enabling and requiring us, as participants, to do in particular spheres of human life and choices. In this section I shall draw general conclusions about three topics: the relations between the beliefs about God delineated in volume 1, the patterns and processes of interdependence, and various values and moral principles;

11. Ibid., pp. 251–59. For theologians and pastors, in large numbers, to continue their work as if the Christian tradition could be separated from scientific interpretations of life, as if the theological school transmits the tradition and the university the secular culture, and as if lives of the laity were isolated from other ways of construing the world is at least shortsighted. To assure people that the reason that bad things happen to good people is because there is chance in the world, and in the next breath to assure them once again that God is ultimately concerned for their own individual well-being, or is "just," strikes me as an incongruity.

some of the values and principles and their ordering; and how the values and principles function in the process of moral discernment.

Theology, Patterns and Processes, Values and Principles

God is the ultimate power that brings all things into being; sustaining, ordering, and bearing down upon them; and creating the conditions for possibility of change and development in them. God is the determiner of the ultimate destiny of all things. In piety the patterns and processes of interdependence that we perceive and conceptualize are indicators, signals, or signs of the divine governing and ordering of life. Through these patterns and processes man can know some things about the ultimate ordering power that determines the destiny of all things.[12] But these patterns and processes are indicators or signs only: they are not evidences or proofs of an immutable divine order to which all relationships of persons and things must necessarily be conformed. They inform and give direction to what persons, institutions, and communities are to do to relate things in a manner appropriate to their relations to God. They are not, however, a clear and infallible guide in and of themselves of God's moral will. They do not, in themselves, determine the morality of particular acts. There are two principal reasons why it is not possible to read off of these patterns and processes of interdependence an eternal or ideal moral order from which particular values and moral principles can be directly and simply deduced.

One is that God is *ordering* all things; God has not established an immutable order of all things. The patterns and processes undergo change and development over time. Nature itself changes and develops; it is subject to change without human intervention. Genetic change, in the interpretation of many evolutionists, is random and not purposive; adaptation occurs after genetic mutations occur. The physical universe is "in process," though the process is in the main orderly. In addition, nature's ordering is altered by human interventions. By intervening into nature we manipulate it or in other ways affect natural processes. Man intervenes into plant life, for example, developing new hybrids, fertilizing and irrigating, eliminating weeds through the use of chemicals. In human relationships the patterns of interdependence are even more malleable. Certain necessary conditions have to be met for human society to function: for some of them we are naturally programmed, such as caring for the very young. Survival conditions must be met universally; ordering of life among human beings leads to divisions of labor and patterns of authority; the lore of a culture has to be transmitted. But how these conditions are met is culturally varied, not only between rural and agricultural societies and more urbanized and industrial-

12. For a fuller development of this, see Gustafson, *Ethics*, 1:251 ff., especially p. 257, p. 264, and p. 270.

ized ones but also between those historically dominated by different religions. Utopian visions constructed from some idealized natural or social order falter on existing orderings of nature and societies that are always undergoing (to be sure at different rates) some changes. The discernible patterns and processes of interdependence, thus, are indicators or signs, of the divine ordering; they are not proofs of an immutable order from which values and principles can be deduced in a simple unilinear way. They are not a sufficient basis for ethics.

The second reason one cannot read a moral order of nature from these patterns and processes is that we are not simply reactors but participants in the patterns and processes of interdependence. Human participation is obviously very different from the participation of plants, insects, and animals. We are not as determined by the laws of natural ordering as they are; within the limits of our bodies, our institutions, our technology, and our occasions in history we have capacities for self-determination, and for deciding how to exercise powers that affect others both in space and through future time. We have capacities for analysis, explanation, and understanding that enable us to construe why events have taken their courses, and why states of affairs exist as they are. We make judgments about what is to be valued, what ends are to be sought, what principles and rules should guide the exercise of our various powers. We can exercise powers in the light of ideals, ends, values, and principles of conduct. While, in the light of the present work, this "freedom" is not as broad and deep relative to the nexus in which it is exercised as others argue, it marks our distinctiveness relative to the rest of nature.

Man has, still relying on the ordering of nature, the capacities to alter the patterns in the light of human intentions and ends. Animals also participate in nature; they feed on plants and often other animals for the sake of their survival; they construct dwelling places. But human capacities for participation are inestimably greater, and thus our aspirations, values, and principles of conduct are of great significance in determining the course of nature and social order and processes. To relate to persons in a manner appropriate to their relations to God requires the honoring of their capacities for self-determination. These capacities are part of the nature of human life. The question, What ought we to do? is vital since we can and do respond to the limits and possibilities that the ordering of life has established, and by virtue of our choices and actions we affect the present and the future. Some patterns and processes are alterable; we can change them in the light of intentions and ends. We are never totally emancipated, however, from nature or from the social arrangements in which we find ourselves at particular junctures of history or in particular societies. But we are not simply to resign ourselves to existing orders; we are responsible for choosing purposes and acting in accord with them. While we do not derive our ends and "oughts" by simple deduction from an existing set of processes and patterns, they nonetheless function as signs or indicators of what is necessary, what is possible, and to some extent what is to be desired.

The patterns and processes of interdependence of life in the world are *a basis*, *foundation*, or *ground* upon which ethical reflection is further developed, and which must be taken into account in determining the values and principles that are to guide human ends and action. From this basis, foundation, or ground, further considerations are developed; the patterns are not sufficient to determine what we are enabled and required to do. They are *necessary conditions* for human action, and they are necessary conditions for what human beings value. One adduces them to support and justify values, ends, and principles, but in and of themselves they are not sufficient justifications. They are the "is" on which "oughts" depend, though the oughts are not deduced simply from an "isness." They are "facts" which ground values, though what is valued is not derived simply from their facticity. They indicate necessary conditions that have to be met for the realization of human purposes. They back, or support, the reasons given for human ends and values, and for moral principles. Thus, as signs or indicators of the divine ordering they become a basis, foundation, or ground for discerning how we are to relate to nature, persons, and things in a manner appropriate to their relations to God.[13]

The patterns and processes of interdependence in which we participate provide the conditions for specific individual and corporate actions, and back specific ends and values. Our actions are directed by our purposes, and different conditions are necessary for different purposes. The importance of the conditions varies according to the purposes we have; some are more central and others more peripheral. We normally and naturally seek to preserve our lives; our dependence upon the rest of nature is quite immediate and direct in this regard. Survival requires that we ingest nutrients,

13. The issue of the relations of "is" to "ought," or of "fact" to "value" has generated a vast body of literature in the modern period. The various resolutions offered by moral philosophers are known to students of ethical theory, and I shall not rehearse the alternatives here. Apparent to everyone is the importance of some distinction, for it is necessary for morality itself. My impression is that much of the discussion was in focus on a problem of logic more than on a problem of morality. The question was whether one can logically derive language in the imperative mood (ethical language being imperative language) from statements in the indicative mood. If one can logically derive imperatives from indicatives, how? And if not, what follows for ethical theory? Facts do not yield value without remainder; the is does not yield an ought without remainder. Nor can the is, or the "ought to be," be completely derived only from the ought. The relations are always reciprocal.

I shall not defend a philosophical position on these issues here. If I were to do so I would take my principal cues from Morton White, *What Is and What Ought To Be Done: An Essay on Ethics and Epistemology* (New York: Oxford University Press, 1981). White develops a position he calls "limited corporatism" in the course of his analysis both of scientific and ethical thought. I believe a position implied in my work could be largely defended on the basis of White's argument.

protect ourselves from extreme weather conditions, have a certain combination of elements present in the air we breathe. This is part of our biological nature. While this is so obvious as to be deemed relatively unimportant with reference to some other purposes we have, under threatening circumstances its priority rises. The interdependence with nature that we share with all living things backs our proper concern for survival; any other participation we might choose to undertake makes attention to it the requisite of greatest value. Our capacities to be participants depend upon our valuing of patterns and processes of interdependence of life. What nutrients we ingest, and how we contend with the cold or the heat are not determined by the most general patterns of interdependence with nature. Our interdependence requires that certain conditions be met for the sake of our participation; an "ought" is based upon those conditions; we fail to meet them at peril to our being. Our activities on behalf of survival and health, i.e., our valuation of them, are grounded in nature. While from one perspective this seems trivial, from another it can be judged to be of greatest importance. The preservation and development of these primal requisites for life is important because all other possibilities depend upon them. These requisites are a basis for all other human values.

The importance of conditions varies according to purposes. The value of the preservation of human life and of other varieties of life issues in caring for the fundamental natural conditions on which life is dependent. In a sense this is the "bottom line"; it is the juncture at which the most determined patterns and processes on which we depend yield the most immediate and direct values and imperatives. While the enjoyment of the arts requires that other conditions be valued, the bottom line is fundamental even to all such values. To say it is "instrumental" is not to denigrate its significance; since it is instrumental to everything else, it is worthy of fundamental concern.[14] The patterns and processes of interdependence on this basic level are signs of the divine ordering of life; while precise forms of human compliance with their requirements are not determined by them, some forms are absolutely necessary. God will be God; God will not be denied.

The conditions that have to be met for human society are grounded in nature, but the precise ways in which they are met are not naturally determined. Some form of family life is necessary for the raising of the young; patterns of natural dependence require this. But the natural ends of family life are not confined to meeting biological survival needs. There are also needs for mutual affection, for some stability in human relationships, for trust and trustworthiness, and for patterns of relationships that sustain not only individual members but a family as a whole. These needs are the sorts

14. Why have we come to assume that intrinsic values are "higher" or more worthy than instrumental values? The assumption is ancient in Western ethics but is subject to query.

of things that some social theorists have in mind when they list the "functional requisites" for human society. The "purposes" of family life are many: biological, spiritual, economic, recreational, educational, and so forth.

As these various purposes are pursued, implicitly or explicitly, further specific conditions have to be met. The varied purposes are the basis on which different "things" are valued and thus sought, and different patterns of relationships developed. There are culturally conditioned differences in the ordering of purposes, but choices can be made about how various purposes will be pursued and which (at least above a minimum level) will have priority. The precise patterns of family life take very different forms both as a result of the wider society and culture of which they are a part and of the aspirations and values that given families come to share. Interrelationships between family and more extensive processes in society become critical in times of social change; multigenerational extended families are broken, for example, as societies become industrialized and urbanized. If family life is sustained, the conditions for it alter; its "functions" change, the form of responsible relationships change, and different "values" come to the fore. The patterns and processes of family life are thus conditioned by the family's interdependence with its wider society, by the characteristics of its individual members, and by choices that are made about the values it ought to realize.

Each nation-state has to fulfill certain functions for the sake of its common good, and for the sake of its citizens. Powers are exercised to maintain and facilitate the necessary conditions for a modicum of internal social order, for example. Needs grounded in the "nature" of human societies necessarily have to be met. But the ways in which they are met, and what needs are deemed to be the responsibility of the state to meet are varied. Mass urban life creates conditions which are very different from dispersed rural and village life. And the ways in which the needs of urban society are met differ to some extent in relation to various cultures and economies. Not all nation-states agree upon what conditions ought to be met by government; different ones have different priorities of values. The advanced welfare states of Northern Europe clearly believe that the provision of health care, care of the aged, and even care of the very young are matters of state responsibility. In the name of distributive justice, high taxation rates have been tolerated so that the state can fulfill needs which in other nations have been left to the family and private initiatives. The collective choice of certain ends as the responsibility of the state "demands" alteration in economic and social arrangements among its citizens. Reasons are given for those choices; they follow from respect for persons which accents their living conditions as much as it accents their liberty; they issue from a commitment to a greater degree of egalitaranism in the distribution of benefits; they issue from an understanding that love of neighbor requires a degree of social paternalism.

My general point here is that the patterns and processes of interdependence in social life, e.g., in family or state, are the ground of certain values and purposes which in turn support certain imperatives. They "demand" that certain conditions be met not only for human survival but for any other ends. Moral and practical imperatives are backed by ends and values that are provided in patterns and processes of interdependence. Patterns of division of labor and authority are required; the forms these take are not only relative to particular cultures and economic conditions but also to certain assumed or chosen values. The "democratic" family idealized in much of American middle-class culture, with its division of responsibilities and its attention to participation of all members in decisions that affect it, has been the result of the ascendance of values quite different from those that sustained the father-dominated authoritarian family that in many cases preceded it. Changes occur as a result of higher valuation placed on respect for individuals regardless of sex or age, on consensus as both an outgrowth of this respect and as a condition for it, and on other factors. If certain "moral" conditions, e.g., increased respect for the individuality and autonomy of individuals are to be met, the social arrangements or conditions of the family must also be changed.

In sum, God orders the life of the world through the patterns and porocesses of interdependence in which human persons, institutions, communities, and the species participate. These patterns and processes are a basis, foundation, or ground for human ends and values and for moral principles. They are fundamentally necessary conditions which have to be met for other values and ends to be fulfilled. They are not a sufficient basis of ethics; specific ends and moral principles are not simply deduced from them. But they are a necessary basis for ethics; the oughtness of ends and principles is grounded in, or based upon, their isness. To relate things in a manner appropriate to their relations to God requires that these patterns and processes be perceived and conceptualized as accurately as possible, and that their conditions be met.

Ends, Values, and Principles: The Problem of Ordering

"So little knows/Any, *but God alone*, to value right/The good before him. . . ."

On the basis of some ethical theories it is possible to propose a fixed heirarchy of ends, values, or moral principles. The theology of this book and the ethics that follow from it do not warrant the formation of an immutable rank order of ends, values, and principles. The four previous chapters show, I believe, how alterations in presumptive and traditional orderings of ends and principles can be justified. There is no automatic harmony of ideal ends and values; more than one moral principle can make proper claims on conduct, and conflicts between them cannot be resolved in all circumstances. The only completely consistent ethics, from a logical point of view, would be characterized by a single value which is to be adhered to in all possible circumstances, or a single substantive moral principle which always overrides all others.

For example, if human physical life were of absolute value there would be no circumstances in which taking it would be justified, and positively all resources available would have to be used to save or extend it under every circumstance. Or, if individualistic libertarianism were carried to its logical extreme there would be no circumstances in which the imposition of the authority of the state could be justified for the sake of a common good. Different ethical systems have different centers of gravity, i.e., those values and principles that are most treasured and adhered to, but under certain circumstances each finds ways of qualifying a logically consistent application of a single dominant value or substantive principle in the light of other considerations. Those for which the common good of a society is the center of gravity cannot and do not adhere to it without attention to some range of liberty of choice for individuals even if those choices do not serve a particular conception of the common good. Those for which individual liberty is the center of gravity define some areas in which state or common interest rightly qualifies its exercise.

Thus the fact that ethics from a theocentric perspective cannot yield a single value or principle which always overrides all others, or an immutable hierarchy of values and principles, does not make it unique. Nor does it issue in absolute relativism or warrant irrational intuitions of what seems or feels right to do. It does, however, force forthrightness about recognizing serious moral conflicts, and requires the acknowledgment of human and other costs of morally justifiable actions. In the final part of this section I shall delineate four patterns of practical reflection that can direct moral discernment, all of which are compatible with the present work. At this point, however, I wish to draw some conclusions about why the present work cannot provide what many persons would find highly desirable, an ethical theory that would give absolute certainty in the resolution of all, or at least almost all, apparent moral conflicts.

The most basic reason why that cannot be done is theological. "The purposes of the Almighty are His own," Abraham Lincoln wisely said in his Second Inaugural Address. While we receive signals of these purposes, we cannot know them indubitably. The theology delineated in volume 1 and the construal of the world in its light show that the well-being of man is not the ultimate purpose of the power that orders the world and determines its destiny. God created and orders life so that its aspects are functionally interdependent with each other; this is the case not only in nature but in human society as well. In the conditions of finitude the special valuing of one aspect of the creation, even when it is warranted, has both beneficial and deleterious consequences for other aspects. The same is true within the strictly human sphere.

More traditional or orthodox theologies are not fully successful in providing the grounds for an immutable hierarchy of values or moral principles. Those that justify the assertion that all things were created for the sake of man have to account for the various values of human life, and find that they are not in a state of automatic harmony. Violence to others has been justified in the pursuit of a theologically backed vision of human liberation. The establishment of more egalitarian societies in the name of a theologically backed conception of distributive justice requires the infringement of liberties of certain persons and groups. If a revealed moral norm of *agape*, Christian love, is theologically authorized, that norm requires application to complex human conditions and, as we have seen, can be used as the ultimately justifying principle for certain wars. Those who adhere to a strict principle of pacifism as the morally right course of life for Christians bear accountability for possible dire outcomes of their moral stance to the victims of evil. And when the preoccupation with what is good for man has led to exploitation of nature with bad outcomes for man and other aspects of nature, qualifications of anthropocentric theological ethics are undertaken.

The concept of man as a participant in the patterns and processes of interdependence of life requires that the interpretation of life take very high priority in ethical reflection. The existing and developing order of life requires moral choices that are necessarily related to particular contexts. Moral and value choices give direction to the existing ordering; they issue in actions which either restrain changes or rearrange and alter patterns and processes inherited from the past in the light of different values and principles. Actions seldom flow from the imposition of the conclusions of an ideal or rationalistic moral theory on the relations of persons to each other, or of human activity to nature. Rather they are generally corrective responses to perceived errors in the ordering of life that is inherited from the past or is evolving. I have shown this to be the case in the illustrative chapters. Recall, for example, how perceptions of adverse consequences of authoritarian family relationships (at least in some societies) yield a reordering of values and motivate increased respect for individual members of families. Respect for persons ascends in importance over a certain pattern of authority and order; presumably it leads to better outcomes for individuals and for the family as a whole.

The customary morality that has developed through human reflection and experience has a measure of reliability; this has been supported even by arguments of moral philosophers. As I noted in chapter 1, Alan Donagan's theory of morality is a rational defense of what he conceives to be the morality of the Jewish and Christian traditions. I noted that Sidgwick argued that utilitarianism as an ethical system does not necessarily require radical changes in commonsense morality that developed in the course of human experience. Indeed, in his view, it gives good reasons to support much of existing morality.

Karl Rahner wrote about self-corrective processes that occur in the development of moral experience, though he was careful to indicate that they are not automatic. I believe he is basically correct in the general observation. Excesses in the ordering of life that result from the purusit of certain ends or values evoke the attention of persons and institutions to the need for reconsideration of the existing order of preferences. Indeed, historically, groups whose justifiable interests and needs are being neglected rise to the occasion to insist that their rights and needs be addressed. There is a sense in which the notion of a *kairos*, a time to be fulfilled, is correct; new possibilities for justifiable changes occur. New patterns of relationships take shape as civil rights are extended to persons and groups that had been deprived of them; threats to human health and to the vitality of the environment raise human awareness of the necessity of a new respect for nature. Interest groups collect around such matters and marshall various forms of power to redress grievances or to protect newly appreciated values. Conditions must be altered to extend the effectiveness of liberty or justice, or to preserve places of natural beauty.

The functional interdependence of human activity, persons, communities, and institutions each with others, and human life with the natural world, simply requires that certain conditions be met, and that certain values and principles that they back be followed. In this respect the present work has affinity with the classic natural-law tradition. This does not license an imprimatur for existing relationships or existing customary morality in all of their respects. There is a dynamic relationship among various values, and it does not take a moral theorist to call attention to the occasions when particular values are pursued disproportionately to others. It does not take a theory to call attention to the disorder of life that occurs when for the sake of social stability the repression of individuals becomes unbearable and is morally wrong, or when for the sake of maximizing individual liberty there are evil consequences to others. Ethical reflection lifts out the conflicts of values and principles that are implied in human experience, and seeks to revise and correct their ordering so that actions can be directed more properly. That correction might well require drastic changes in an existing order of life, as in the case of justifiable revolutions; or it may require more gradual and meliorative corrections.

In functional interdependence any equilibrium of values is dynamic and has aspects of instability simply because of the absence of an immutable ordering of life and of an automatic harmony of values. An oversimple illustration will show what I mean. Any human society requires attention to the value of social order and stability, fairness or distributive justice, and individual liberty of some scope. In totalitarian and oligarchic societies concentrations of power are often justified in the name of social stability. But to maintain social stability vast numbers of persons are deprived of political and economic power, and the range of their liberties is severely limited both by coercion and by lack of resources. The principle of distributive justice ascends in importance, as well as the value of individual liberty. The reordering of social life in accord with a more egalitarian concept of justice leads to social instability, and may require the infringement of the liberties of persons. Any actual equilbrium among stability, justice, and liberty is dynamic; any ethically and politically justified reordering of social life to pursue one of the three has outcomes for the other two.

The crucial bases which make it impossible to establish an immutable hierarchy of ends, values, and principles, are by now clear. The theology is based on part upon a description of the interdependence of things in life, and in turn backs a construal of life in the world that highlights this feature. The well-being of any single entity is interdependent with others; all are parts of wholes. No individual thing or persons is simply an end in itself; what constitutes its well-being is dependent upon its relations to others. Things mutually serve one another, and there is no guarantee that the service of one another issues in a desired outcome of each, or in the well-being of each. Relations are reciprocal but not necessarily harmonious. The common good of a whole is never in perfect harmony with justifiable goods of its parts. To be sure, there are constellations of values that are more fundamental than others; survival conditions must be met to insure the possibilities of development of persons and even of nature. Certain values are "almost absolute," certain principles and rules guide actions in such a way that their application leads to few exceptions. But the ethics of this work cannot provide risk or cost-proof morality. "So little knows/Any, but God alone, to value right/ The good before him. . . . "

Patterns of Discernment

Nonetheless, the human task is to decide what is the morally best possible course of events and state of affairs. As participants we are always faced with this task in a particular set of circumstances; it is context-bound, though the delineation of the context to be taken into account is a matter of human choice. The desired and desirable certainty of being absolutely right in our choices often is not achievable from the perspective of the present work, though ethical reflection reduces the uncertainty, limits (and in some instances completely forecloses) the range of responsible options, and guides our actions.

I described and defended in the last chapter of volume 1 a process of discernment by which persons and communities come to particular moral choices. There is no need to go over that again here, but I wish to show how the values and principles that can be backed by, or grounded in, the patterns and processes of interdependence function within the process of discernment. Discernment involves "points to be considered" (a term from Karl Barth's special ethics); boundary conditions; presumptions in favor of certain values and principles; and general rules.

Barth's language of "points to be considered" has some merit, even when one prescinds from his theological and religious assumption that such points prepare one to hear the particular command of God. There are points to be considered in the process of determining what we ought to do to relate things in a manner appropriate to their relations to God. From the theocentric perspective developed here the points to be considered are enlarged in comparison with some other ethics, both theological and philosophical.

A question of morality or of human valuation comes to consciousness in the course of our participation when there are reasons and feelings that signal some uncertainty or conflict, i.e., when common sense or customary responses are challenged. The availability of high technology in medical care, for example, creates opportunities to extend life that did not exist decades ago; a provoking uncertainty is whether such a possibility ought to be used for a particular patient. What points are deemed relevant, as I have previously argued, are determined to some extent by the moral views of the agents involved: in this example by a judgment of whether others than the primary patient should be considered, whether the physician has an obligation to sustain biological life as long as it is technically possible, and, if not, whether the probable qualities of the life of the patient are sufficiently limited to merit not taking aggressive action. What I have called the time and space boundaries of the circumstances are restricted, and how they are evaluatively described is a function in part of the moral orientation of those making a choice.

Ethics from a theocentric perspective calls attention to these restrictions, and requires that even if the limited view is finally deemed appropriate, other relationships must be considered: the consequences of a choice to use various scarce technical and human resources for the family and institutions that are involved, no matter what choice is made, and so forth. What is deemed a relevant whole has to be set in a larger context; either to retain or extend the limits requires moral justification. Certain "causal" or interdependent relations have to be judged either morally relevant or irrelevant. The weight given to the points to be considered will depend upon the values or principles that the persons making a choice adhere to.

The expansion of the points to be considered inevitably makes a choice more difficult. The difficulty necessarily follows from the concept of man as participating in patterns and processes of interdependence in life. As I have indicated, this descriptive concept requires, first, that the whole we attend to be set in the patterns and processes of which it is a part, and, second, that the agents involved conscientiously determine the grounds on which persons and "things" that are involved in the interdependence are of greater or lesser moral relevance. The expansion does not necessarily imply that a choice of action based on a limited description is morally wrong. But it presses for self-consciousness in moral choice, for justification of why certain features of an expanded description are or are not significant, why the boundaries chosen are appropriate. Taking account of the relationships which a focus of attention has to other aspects of a larger whole also disposes one to qualify the propriety of a more limited account, and give reasons for overriding presumptive values implied in it.

Different cultures tend to sustain different implied orderings of points to be considered in their public life. So also various professions and persons have either implied or articulated rank orderings of the weight that various points ought to have. With reference to institutions and professions these are contractually determined, or determined by a customary definition of social roles. These, however, change by enlarging the whole to be considered. It is worth noting that in recent American history there have been extension of items to be ranked, and pressure to revise customary priorities.

An example of this can be taken from the policies of business corporations. The traditional boundaries were that the officers were responsible only to the stockholders, and for achieving the greatest possible net return on investments. We have seen in the past two decades that when the activities of corporations are set in the context of larger wholes the corporations are causally responsible for consequences to which they are increasingly held legally and morally responsible. Their activities affect the consumers, the social and natural environment, the labor force with its relative immobility, and so forth. These more extensive patterns of interdependence become the basis upon which new weight is being given to various points to be considered in corporate policies. From the ethics being developed here such extension and revision of priorities is most appropriate. It can be defended on the basis of different ethical theories; a defense by a Kantian would be different from one by a utilitarian. But underlying any defense, I believe, is an enlargement of the range of what a corporation is held accountable for based on an explanation and interpretation of more extensive patterns and processes of interdependence. The larger whole requires that more "participants" be taken into account and that the "common" whose good is to be considered be enlarged. The traditional limits on corporate responsibility—on what a corporation is responsible for and to whom—are altered, and with this the aims or values that determine policy are to some extent rearranged; attention to environmental impact can affect profits, for example. The points to be considered are expanded.

A second way to consider the function of various values and principles is that they set boundary conditions that no course of action is permitted to violate. The boundaries are established in part by the values or aims of the agent.

I shall use this metaphor to interpret one of the most interesting casuistic passages in the New Testament; both its strengths and weaknesses become apparent. The Apostle Paul had proclaimed the freedom of Christians to the church in Corinth. He had, however, received questions about the use of that freedom. With regard to a relatively trivial question (from a moral perspective), whether to eat meat from animals that had been offered as sacrifices to the pagan gods, he is unwilling to counsel that freedom be given up. "All things are lawful," he writes. The remainder of the passage sets certain boundary conditions to be taken into account in choices on this particular matter. One ought not to do anything that is unhelpful, that does not build up the community, that seeks one's own good in preference to the good of the neighbor, that violates the liberty of one's own conscience, that violates the consciences of others, that is deliberately offensive to other groups, and that is not worthy of the imitation of Paul, who is an imitator of Christ.[15] Of course there was a particular historical context to this passage. Paul's preaching was directed to freeing the early Christians from obligations to adhere to the ritual laws of contemporary Judaism. He also had an instrumental reason for some of the boundary conditions; he did not wish to offend groups whose "advantage" he was seeking by saving them. The net effect, however, was, "Do not give up your freedom, but exercise it within boundary conditions." The boundary conditions are determined by Paul's ends—the preservation of Christian freedom and the conversion of Jews and Greeks.

On other issues Paul was more prescriptive, but in this passage it is clear that some of the boundary conditions are inconsistent with each other. One ought not to violate one's own conscience, yet if acting according to conscience offends some other person's conscience one ought to violate one's own for the sake of the other's. The setting of boundary conditions leaves more open to an intuitive choice than is necessary. But one can use the metaphor and supplement it with other considerations in ethical reflection. If one first establishes ends, then boundary conditions are indications of limits within which the ends ought to be pursued.

The application of the metaphor of boundary conditions to statements of values that cannot be violated is particularly apt; the idea of boundary suggests limitations. As I noted, the choice of ends is crucial to the determination of what values become boundaries, and of some rank ordering of the conditions necessary to achieve those ends. Many moral disputes take

15. 1 Corinthians 10:23–11:1.

place precisely about this ordering. It may also be the case, however, that parties to a moral dispute can agree at least on boundary conditions and thus move toward possible resolution.

The metaphor of boundary conditions is a way of phrasing certain proscriptions of conduct. For example, in the just-war tradition the principle of non-combatant immunity is a boundary condition. Wars can be justified if there is a just cause and if certain other conditions are met. Thus the taking of human life is warranted. What has been traditionally proscribed is intentionally killing or injuring persons who are not officially involved in combat. The boundary is to be kept regardless of the consequences for the conduct of the war.

There are many other examples of where and how the question of boundaries emerges. In the pursuit of social justice is the use of violence ever permitted? Or is it permitted only when all possible nonviolent means of change have been exhausted? I have already noted another example, namely, from Kant's discussion of whether it is ever permissible to lie from an altruistic motive. Or, there are those who argue that it is immoral to experiment on aborted fetuses no matter what benefits might accrue from such work.

Some ethicians tend to begin by defining the morally permissible boundaries within which any activity can take place. In effect, most deontic ethics are of this sort. The moral and immoral are determined precisely by whether an action is in compliance with an established proscription of conduct. The ethics of the present work is closer to the classic type of teleological ethics; values and ends are chosen, and conditions needed to achieve or approximate them are developed. But there are boundaries within which particular ends ought to be pursued. Examples of this approach were noted in some of the illustrative chapters.

What is valued, or the ends being sought, affect what conditions become boundaries and how they are drawn. An example of this process is furnished by developments in law and public life that occurred during the civil rights movement of the 1960s. Prior to that time the owners and operators of public facilities such as restaurants, on the basis of the right to determine who should have access to and use of their property, were legally able to refuse service to certain groups of people. The civil rights movement was oriented toward the extension of the rights of individuals, regardless of race, and toward social justice. When these ends were legally supported certain boundary conditions which had held for a long time were altered; in the case of facilities available to the public, ownership no longer authorized discrimination. Boundary conditions change; they are accepted, set, altered, or even rejected in the pursuit of a particular end in the context of a relevant whole. Moral and legal reasons are given to support the alterations.

The third way in which to consider the use of values and principles in the process of discernment is that presumptions are made in favor of certain ones; they cannot be overridden or violated without strong justification.[16] The description of man as a participant in the patterns and processes of interdependence of life is the basis for raising questions about some customary and traditional presumptions in our culture; inferences can be drawn from the description about the order of presumptions both in general and in specific contexts of human activity. What we ought to do is affected by the evaluative descriptions that are given of the place of man in the world. How the relations of parts to wholes is interpreted is particularly critical in grounding presumptions of values and principles: man as a part of an interdependent ordering of nature, groups with legitimate interests as parts of larger societies, individual persons as parts of communities and institutions.

I have argued that in our culture there has been a dominant presumption that all things exist for the sake of man, and that this has been backed by Christian theology as well as other beliefs. On the basis of this presumption all that is "below" man can be put to the service of man; it can be used for human ends regardless of the consequences for other aspects of life in the world. What is good for human beings has determined the evaluation of all other things. This has provided a general rank ordering of values. It has not resolved all particular orderings, since there is no unanimity about what ends are proper for human activity or what the ordering of values for human life ought to be. Ethics from a theocentric perspective raises a serious question about this traditional presumption.

The proper inference to be drawn is not that the value of plants, snail darters, and Hereford steers is the same as the value of human life. Rather, because man is interpreted to be interdependent with the rest of nature, the parts of which have "purposes" relative to others in patterns of functional interdependence in larger wholes, restraints of purely human ends can be more readily established. For the sake of the common good of life on this planet in the future, a restraint on human population growth, for example, is warranted. Necessary conditions for sustaining future human populations and for possibilities of future developments of other aspects of life might be threatened by overpopulation. As I indicated in the chapter on "Population and Nutrition," there is no immutable ratio on the basis of which a proper proportion of human beings relative to other aspects of life can be determined to prescribe specific limits. Any equilibrium will be dynamic, and relative to many factors including the capacities to enlarge and improve the production of nutrients. The traditional presumption that all things exist for the sake of man is, however, qualified, and other values have to be taken into account in human activity.

16. Philip Wogaman has made the notion of presumption central to his discussion in *A Christian Method of Moral Judgment* (Philadelphia: Westminster Press, 1976).

There is a presumption in radically libertarian conceptions of human society that the good of the whole is best served by particular groups striving to fulfill their particular interests. Thus corporations should be relatively unfettered to pursue the maximization of profits; in the long run the economic and social well-being of a society will be served by the operations of some invisible hand. In the previous discussion of boundary conditions I noted an example relevant here, namely, how the setting of the activities of corporations in the context of large wholes expands the range of consequences for which they are causally and therefore morally and legally accountable. The presumption that the good of the society is served by a narrow definition of the purposes of a corporation is questioned. For the sake of a larger common good, the ordering of the values that determine corporate policy is modified even at economic cost to corporations.

The presumption in favor of the individual that is deep within our culture is also brought under criticism by the description of human life in patterns of interdependence. There are clearly significant cultural differences in the perceptions of the relations of individuals to "society." Traditional social arrangements in India, for example, backed by religious and customary beliefs, do not pit individual and society over against each other in a way that is often the case in American society. The descriptive premises of the present work support an earlier overriding of a presumption that communities exist for the sake of the benefit of their individual members, or that moral claims for restraint upon individual activity are wrong for the sake of the well-being of other persons or a common good. This does not mean that a definition of a collective good always overrides the claims of individuals, or that totalitarian concentrations of power are justified because they can coerce persons to serve what those in power claim to be the national interest. To relate to persons in a manner appropriate to their relations to God requires the honoring of their capacities for self-determination. Equitable distribution of benefits and of costs for the sake of a justifiable common good always needs to be adhered to. Realms of personal discretion and self-determination are required, it appears, by human nature; historically tyrannies tend always to provoke dissent.

There are specific occasions and events which bring conflicts with a traditional order of presumptions to the fore.[17] In medical research, for

17. Examples of this can be drawn from many realms of life. In current discussions of the ethics of the legal profession, for example, the long-honored right of confidentiality in lawyer-client relations has been questioned when the lawyer knows that the client is engaged in fraudulent activities. Ought an absolute become only a presumption? The reasons for sustaining absolute confidentiality are clear: the client must be able to trust the lawyer to protect his or her interests; if the client doubted the confidentiality, he or she would not feel free to disclose all relevant information. The argument for modification of the privilege is that where evidence of fraud of other parties exists laws are being broken and other parties are its victims; the lawyer's responsibility is to more than the client.

example, the requirement of the principle of informed consent rests on the very high value given to individual liberty, to the rights of an individual not to have his or her life intervened into without consent and without the best and most comprehensible knowledge of the prospective risks and benefits. Only on a voluntary basis (also honoring individual liberty) can an individual be expected to risk his or her health for the sake of possible benefits to large numbers of others or for the sake of some future "good." A common conflict occurs when the verification of the efficacy of certain medical interventions requires randomized clinical trials in which it is conceivable that certain individuals will not receive what is the best therapy for their conditions. This is a particular problem when the subjects are minors. Both in policy and in practice ways have been devised to honor the presumption in favor of individual liberty while at the same time attempting to gain the knowledge that will be beneficial to others, including future generations. Compensation is offered to those put at risk which is presumably proportionate to the inconvenience or risk involved in their participation. The question is debated whether a parent has a right to give "proxy consent" for an infant to become the subject of experimentation if there is risk but no therapeutic benefit to the infant. Criteria are developed to grade risks and benefits. All of these procedures are proper in the light of the presumption in favor of the individual that informed consent protects. If the alternative to them is that the research community could coerce persons to be experimental subjects, clearly that would open the moral door to a form of tyranny.

From the perspective of the present work, however, it is fair at least to call attention to the possibility that there might be occasions when the health-preserving benefits from experimentation for future generations and for large numbers of others are unfulfilled by virtue of a stringent adherence to the principle of individual autonomy. Adherence to it might possibly lead to moral and legal restraints that would inhibit genuine progress in clinical medicine. Some risks are required of some persons for the sake of benefits to others. From the perspective of the present work, stronger, though perhaps not conclusive, arguments can be made for overriding the protection of individual liberty for the sake of benefits to others or to a justifiable common good if all possible alternatives have been exhausted. I continue to cite the example of military conscription during wartime as a precedent. In wartime presumably the enemy is an "unjust aggressor" against one's own nation; by weak analogy a preventable disease is an aggressor against the health of the community. It is arguable, at least, that where the risk of death is not as high as it is during combat, or where the maximum harm falls short of the risk of death, there are grounds for putting some persons at risk for the sake of prospective benefits to others. If such a possibility would be deemed morally approvable, the ways in which persons would be chosen, of course, introduce other ethical problems; for example, can the risks entailed be fairly (i.e., justly) distributed across a relevant population?[18] Is casting lots the fairest way to achieve equity?

The ordering of life in the world through the patterns and processes of interdependence, and the interactive view of human participation ground a bias in the order of presumptions. I have indicated throughout this work that this bias does not warrant some ideal vision of a common good of all things, or even of particular human communities as intimate as the family, from which deductions could be drawn about the range of activities proper to all individual things. The well-being or common good of a whole is not the single end of the participation of individuals, any more than the well-being of individuals is the single end of the patterns of interdependence. Presumptions in practice are related to contexts; correctives are required under particular circumstances. But, to make a very general judgment, the theology and ethics developed here run counter to the anthropocentrism and the individualism of much of our culture. The basic reasons for this are theological; the basic argument is against either overtly theological arguments that support anthropocentrism and individualism, or against the "functional equivalents" of theology imbedded in secular beliefs. To discern how things are to be appropriately related to their relations to God requires serious consideration of larger contexts of which foci of attention are a part, i.e., how the parts are related to larger wholes and thus the consequences of action for wider, long-range consequences.

The fourth way to consider how various values and principles function in discernment is the idea of general rules. Values ground general rules. General rules are not unexceptionable rules; various grounds can be established for exceptions to their application in certain circumstances, and the application itself requires that specific circumstances be taken into account. The use of general rules is backed not only by the wider and deeper patterns and processes of interdependence but also by the arguments developed through the history of ethical thought and by human experience. General rules, like implied orders of presumptions, become culturally imbedded;

18. A good example of the unfairness of distribution of risk from recent American history is the way in which conscription was administered during the Vietnam War. Presumably the "national interest," a version of the common good, was threatened. The threat was sufficient to require conscription. But the injustice of the procedures is, in my judgment, a major blot on the history of public morality in the United States. The deferment of college students meant that those who could not afford to attend college, or who were socially and culturally disadvantaged, or who simply chose not to attend, were put at far greater risk. Equals, in this case young men of the draftable age group, were not exposed equally to threats to life and limb. Justification for preferential treatment could not be made on the grounds that the deferred made their own distinctive contributions to the larger common good. Even more unjust was the total exemption of students enrolled in schools that train persons for the clergy. If the war was deemed justifiable because of a threat to the national interest, justice ought to have been adhered to in the conscription procedures.

they have become parts of customary relationships and patterns of action. General rules, backed by values and principles, foreclose the range of acceptable choices in any particular set of circumstances. There is always a strong presumption that they ought to be obeyed, or at least that they ought to guide deliberation about the right course of action almost to the point of the particular choice. Yet at some point they become "action guides" that direct human discretion or discernment, rather than prescriptions to be complied with in a rigorous way.

How various moralists, philosophical or theological, deal with the authority of rules is, in my judgment, related to aspects of their perspectives. For example, in a pattern of morality that has the intention of restraining persons from commiting sinful acts, i.e., one oriented toward maintaining the moral purity of agents, rules have been developed to cover very specific and detailed circumstances. The manuals of moral theology developed by Roman Catholic rigorists and the writings of orthodox Jewish Halakhists are cases in point. Casuistry, a necessary and valuable procedure, is developed to cover as many conceivable circumstances as possible, and in extreme uses the effort is made to show that the prescribed conclusion is the only logically possible, and therefore morally right, choice. Distinctions are made with reference to the intentions of agents or to the descriptions of circumstances which, from another point of view, keep actions within the realm of the permissible. In discussions of the requirement to tell the truth, failure to disclose relevant information becomes a licit "mental reservation" when disclosure could cause grave harm to another person. Or, the rule against murder does not cover occasions of self-defense since the intent is to save one's own life rather than to take the life of another. Application procedures are refined in such a way that the range of discretion of the agent, a discretion which might lead to something sinful or immoral, is eliminated. It is not only religious moralists who can be primarily concerned with the purity of agents; as we have seen, this is the major intention of Kant's ethics as well.

Another impulse behind the development of detailed rules and demands for rigorous compliance is the fear of consequences if such a pattern is revised. The charge is that if one permits a general rule to be applied in a way that is deemed to be lax, or if one permits an exception in a particular class of cases, the door has been opened to even laxer applications or to more exceptions. Kant was rigorous on truth-telling in part because to slacken adherence to that maxim would be to raise doubts about the trustworthiness of speech in general. Some medical moralists fear that a moral justification for not intervening to save the lives of one class of defective newborn children will lead to neglect of others whose defects are not as grave. Not only "moral conservatives" argue this way; defenders of the right to publish and sell pornographic literature argue that if one permits censorship of pornography one has opened the door to censorship of other thoughts and ideas. In the metaphors of some writers, the camel gets its nose under the tent, and thus the stability of the whole tent is in jeopardy; or, one has gotten on a slippery slope, and once on it there is nothing fixed to keep one from sliding into laxer applications or exceptions. Morality is fragile, and any procedures that appear to threaten it are to be avoided.

Deep suspicion of other persons' motives also leads to detailed proscriptions of actions. This is not uncommon in the discussions of biological and medical experimentation. The process of in vitro fertilization has been criticized for a number of reasons, but one is the suspicion that those who developed it were motivated more by scientific curiosity, that is, to see whether it could be done, than by the desire to enable women to bear their own children. Similar suspicions have been articulated, and with propriety, in regard to the development of an artificial heart, and especially in regard to the use of one by Dr. Denton Cooley in 1969.[19] Of course, suspicion of motives cuts every way, and can be raised with reference to those who raise it about others. And usually one is more suspect of the motives of others than of one's own.[20]

There is some merit to each of these grounds for supporting a stringent rule-morality. Whatever its source, an undue burden of guilt can result from uncertainty about the moral rectitude of one's actions; detailed rules that are complied with can limit the occasions for guilt. They also have the effect, however, of transferring the sense of moral accountability from the agent and his or her self-determination to the authority that prescribes the rules. Morality is fragile, and it is fitting to be concerned about getting onto a

19. For a discussion of this, see Renée C. Fox and Judith P. Swazey, *The Courage to Fail: A Social View of Organ Transplants and Dialysis*, 2d ed., pp. 134–97.

20. The relationship between "motives" and "reasons" for action is a matter that is much discussed in the literature on human action. Motives refer to what moves us to act in a specific way; reasons can have the power to move, but many persons are sufficiently wary that they suspect their reasons to be rationalizations for other impulses. Of introspection about "real" motives there is no end, and one impact of modern psychological sciences is to expose the complexity of those powers that move us. Novelists are sometimes better than scholars in exposing this complexity. For example, the Japanese novelist Shusaku Endo, in his very powerful *Silence* (New York: Taplinger Publishing Co., 1979), portrays the process by which a Portuguese missionary priest in Japan comes to apostatize during the suppression of Christianity in the seventeenth century. As long as he remains faithful to his vows Japanese Christians are tortured and martyred. Is his apostasy motivated by love, and thus in keeping with a deeper fidelity to Christ? Is his resistance to apostasy finally self-referential so that he would maintain his purity even though it costs suffering and death to others? Is his apostasy finally a matter of moral weakness? A rigoristic response might be that his vows were unconditional, and should provide the reasons as well as the strength of will to maintain fidelity to them regardless of the consequences to others. That would seem to me, however, to be a curious way of loving one's neighbor, and particularly those who are of the household of faith. It does not follow from this case, however, that vows, contracts, promises, and other time-binding commitments are without motivating force, or that they always can be ignored because they can in this extreme case.

slippery slope, not only with reference to one's individual actions but with reference to the effects on the ethos of a particular community. Practices which deny lifesaving procedures to those judged to be defective can lead to a hardening of the heart toward all persons judged to be defective in society. But to adhere rigorously to certain rules is often not without deleterious consequences for other persons and for societies. For example, while the impulse to self-glorification can lead to moral carelessness and the premature use of experimental procedures in medicine, at some point risks are required to achieve worthy ends even though the motives of agents are mixed.

The support of general rules, rather than of unexceptionable ones, is also related to the perspective of the moralist, and in my case follows from both the theology and ethics that have been developed. It would be tedious once again to develop fully why this is the case. The use of general rules follows from several features of the profile given in chapter 1: the enlargement of the time and space dimensions in the description of the place of man in the universe; the inclusion of the wider patterns and processes of interdependence within the morally relevant features of our circumstances; the relationships of parts to wholes and thus the required attention to consequences of actions; and the absence of an immutable hierarchy of ends and values. General rules narrow the scope of moral ambiguity, but they allow room for discretionary judgments, i.e., for the virtue of equity and the practice of discernment.

To affirm the use of general rules, however, requires attention to the different settings and circumstances of life in which actions take place. Different circumstances do make a difference. The rule of truth-telling is absolute in conducting scientific research; the disclosure of several instances in American science in recent years in which data have not only been "fudged" but falsified is rightly perceived to be a scandal, and damaging to the integrity of the profession. The conclusions of an experiment are not valid if honesty is not adhered to by the investigator. But such circumstances are quite different from the narrative involved in Kant's essay on lying.[21] In various negotiations, whether between labor and management or between nation-states, there is a justification for withholding information that could not be made in the conduct of scientific research.

The emphasis of the present work goes against extreme rigorism in morality; all four procedures I have delineated carry this emphasis. It does not go against providing good reasons for the choices that are made; it is, in my judgment, an error to assume that only the rigorists are rational. Nor

21. For a recent discussion of the ethics of truth-telling see Sissela Bok, *Lying: Moral Choice in Public and Private Life* (New York: Pantheon Books, 1978).

does the weight of the present work deny the importance of very refined distinctions that are made in various moral theories; I do not believe, however, that they have the decisive significance that on some occasions they are given.

I wish to illustrate this position from an area in medical morality, namely, the decisions required when a radically defective infant is born. There are ongoing debates about what extent of defectiveness is sufficient for the withholding of aggressive medical and technological interventions to save the life of the child; these debates are themselves context-bound since the development of new technologies creates new possibilities to save lives. Those who argue that it is not morally obligatory to save every radically defective newborn whose physical life might be prolonged usually argue, interestingly, that it is morally wrong to intervene actively to hasten the infant's death. The distinction is between a more justifiable act of omission and a less justifiable act of commission. Thus, there are reports of infants who are consigned to die but whose death occurs as a result of the withholding of the kind of care other infants get. The distinction between omission and commission is justified on various grounds, including that of slipping down the slope if it is not made.

I have long asked in such a case, for whose advantage is the distinction made? It is to the moral advantage of those agents who make the choice; it is not to the advantage of the defective infant. The infant dies of neglect; surely there is some human suffering caused for the sake of avoiding a certain culpability for the medical staff. An alleged slippery slope is also invoked; if one permits aggressive action to hasten death in such a case, what is there to keep it from being done in cases that are dissimilar? The rigorist can make a case only by ignoring the adverse consequences to the infant. The intention is for the infant to die; the intended consequence is its death. It can be argued that even for the rigorist consequences count; the relevant consequences are for the agent and not the recipient. The agent avoids a kind of moral culpability at the cost of the suffering of another. From the perspective of the present work the dependence of the infant on the care of others implies that *if* the intention to have it die is morally justifiable, then, for the sake not of the agent but of the recipient, it would be morally permissible to intervene actively to hasten its death. Whatever choice is made, the first choice not to save the life of the newborn, and the subsequent one about how the infant will die, is tragic.

A counterargument can be made from within the perspective of this work. It can be argued that the community must take into account long-range consequences of such a choice for a larger whole. To permit an act of commission rather than omission could have adverse consequences for the confidence that patients have in physicians and for the general respect for human life in the society. The point is arguable; the toleration of approximately 50,000 deaths by automobile accidents per year in the United States has not adversely affected respect for life in other circumstances, and the confidence that patients have in physicians has many grounds and thus would not necessarily be affected adversely. My basic point, however, is that a rigoristic adherence to the distinction involved has mixed consequences, that ambiguity should be faced in making the choice, and that agents should be required to give their reasons for whatever choice is made.

General rules function to focus discernment of what one is enabled and required to do in specific circumstances. The presumption in their favor requires that good reasons be given for the particular application of them and for any outright exceptions that might be made. Like the other procedures I have indicated, they do not heteronomously foreclose courses of action in most circumstances. Rather they direct discernment; the agent (an individual, a community, or an institution) relies on the virtue of equity and on other human capacities to make the particular choice. This does not imply that there are no actions which are prohibited; to take human life without moral justification is always wrong, for example. But in most courses of events in which choices are made a discriminating judgment, directed but not fully determined by general rules, is required to decide what ought to occur.

All four of these procedures (points to be considered, boundary conditions, presumptions, and general rules) honor the capacity for self-determination by moral agents in ways that some theorists who make autonomy, i.e. self-legislation, supreme do not. To respect the capacities for self-determination in others is, in my judgment, not only to restrain them from being coerced or unduly influenced but also to acknowledge their rights to make conscientious moral choices as they see fit and to accept the responsibility for them. The practical procedures of ethics from a theocentric perspective inform the moral conscientiousness of agents; they do not assume the position of moral infallibility so that the ethician always has a right to determine for other agents what is the morally proper course of action to be taken. The practical function of the ethician is not primarily to prescribe and proscribe the conduct of others, but to enable them to make informed choices. Agents who have responsibility for particular spheres of interdependence and action must be accountable for the choices that they make. Their roles, technical competence, experience, and character also enter into the decisions. The function of the ethician is to broaden and deepen the capacities of others to make morally responsible choices.

There are two important practical conditions which require attention if this function is to be effective. One is the existence of communities of moral formation, that is, of outlook, of development of virtue and character. I attended to this at the end of the section on "Man's Being." The other condition is the existence of communities of moral discourse.

Communities of Moral Discourse

To some extent moral discourse does take place in communities and it ought to do so to a greater extent. From the perspective of the present work the importance of such communities cannot be overstressed. Even significant choices made by individuals in problematic circumstances are more likely to "value right" the good or evil before them if opportunities for reflection and consultation occur in the presence of another person. When more complex matters of public policy such as reduction of poverty, disarmament negotiations, and environmental programs are under consideration a communtiy is indispensable. The ethics developed here strongly back the formation and utilization of what I have elsewhere called "communities of moral discourse."[22] No single person has the capabilities to be sufficiently informed about factual matters, analyses of processes and patterns of interdependence, and projection of possible consequences of alternative courses of action to be absolutely self-reliant. Insofar as an individual seeks to make recommendations about complex matters, he or she is intellectually obligated to become as well informed as possible about the relevant data and analyses. Discernment ought to be a social as well as individual process.

To be sure, there is often no consensus among those who are experts on precisely what circumstances are relevant, what information is most important, what analysis of the situation is correct, and what consequences are most likely to occur. Accuracy and possible consensus on these items occur more frequently where the matter under consideration (for example, a routine medical problem) is governed by "laws" that determine both analysis and predictions of consequences. In matters of complex public policy greater divergence of judgment occurs.

The moralist or the moral community is likely to be tempted to grasp the interpretation that most fits its moral predispositions; it is incumbent upon all agents to examine alternatives. In previous allusions to the abortion debates I have noted how, for example, the choice about when fetal or embryonic life is judged to be a human person can be made in such a way that it gives support to either the most conservative or the most liberal positions on the question. There is no simple answer to the question of which analysis ought to be given the most weight in complex circumstances, but there is an obligation to take into account those analyses that bear respectable authority. Judgments about their adequacy have to be made not primarily on the grounds of whether they fit a moral predisposition, but on the grounds of their sufficiency to explain the problem under discussion. It is

22. See James M. Gustafson, "The Church: A Community of Moral Discourse," in *The Church as Moral Decision Maker* (Philadelphia: Pilgrim Press, 1970), pp. 83–95; idem, "The University as a Community of Moral Discourse," *The Journal of Religion* 53 (1973):397–409. See also John H. Yoder, "The Hermeneutics of Peoplehood: A Protestant Perspective on Practical Moral Reasoning," *Journal of Religious Ethics* 10 (1982):40–67.

also the case that moral dispositions and perspectives affect analysis made presumptively on purely scientific or technical grounds; this further complicates the work of the moralist or moral community.

A community of moral discourse is important also because differences in moral points of view are exposed. Mutual understanding of why different persons and groups hold different moral opinions, have different perceptions of what is to be valued, and have different procedures for coming to judgments is made possible, But understanding and toleration, much needed in moral discussions, are not the only possible benefits. Persons can and do change their minds, consensus can sometimes be achieved as a result, and in this way the quality of corporate and public discussion can be improved.

The participation of persons whose roles put them in particular positions of responsibility, and thus whose choices will actually affect the course of events and state of affairs, is necessary in such communities. Such persons bring to bear perspectives and interpretations that are grounded in experiences that academicians and members of the clergy do not have; they also have access to arenas of action.

The purpose of moral discourse in communities is not in most cases to come to a unanimous conclusion, though there are occasions when this is proper. It is to help form the "consciences" of persons, to educate their rational activity, to enable them to think more clearly and thoroughly about the moral dimensions of aspects of life in the world. It is to hone more sharply their moral thinking from which choices and actions in part flow.

The individual ethician who writes about particular matters has an obligation to become as informed as he or she can about all the dimensions that are required for an effective community of moral discourse. The ethician, to be sure, has a particular angle of vision and a particular competence; one expects this to be his or her particular strength. But from the perspective of the present work that competence cannot be appropriately used apart from some grounding in the particularities of the problems addressed.

Religious communities have distinctive opportunities to foster serious moral discourse. Indeed, since both the communities and their members are prone to make strong moral judgments, they have an obligation to take more seriously than they have the requirements of sound moral discourse. It is appropriate for them to work from their traditions, though it is also important for them to recognize the historically particular features of those traditions. Although their effectiveness as communities of moral formation may be eroding in modern Western societies they nonetheless remain identifiable social units with beliefs and traditions that give shape both to the choices of individuals and to the ethos of our culture. The morality that they foster is generally not unique, though they may have distinctive religious and theological backings for it. And where their moral judgments are distinctive and defended they ought to be taken seriously in the public arena.

The distinctiveness is generally shaped by the loyalty of the members to their traditions, and to aspects of their traditions which bias them in particular ways. This, in my judgment, is quite legitimate. For example, as many authors are currently stressing, one cannot read the biblical materials without recognizing a bias in favor of the poor and the oppressed. Such a bias sustains an attitude of compassion and motivates "charitable" activity, but it also signals a preference that must be taken in account in matters of public policy. The historical particularity leads to an emphasis on a particular concern, and though this does not in itself determine precisely what ought to be done, it lends weight to a more egalitarian understanding of what distributive justice requires. This issues not only in voluntary "charitable" activity but also in arguments in favor of particular social policies.

What is reprehensible about a great deal of ecclesiastical moralizing about policy issues is the intellectual and academic flabbiness of most of the "pronouncements," whether by church agencies or by individuals. There is a prophetic role, backed by ancient tradition in biblical religion, namely, to speak out passionately in indicting the evils of life in the world. But the prophet is not an ethician. To many persons, what I understand the function of ethics to be does not seem to be sufficiently "prophetic." To call attention to changes that need to be made on the grounds of human values and moral principles, however, carries with it an obligation to "follow through," that is, to be informed about particular and achievable alterations that need to be made and can be made, to know as well as possible the technical data that pertain to the issues at hand, to be in communication with those who have actual responsibilities for exercising power in the areas under consideration, and to make sound ethical arguments in support not only of particular indictments but also recommended courses of action. The simpleminded moralism that Protestant churches (more than the Roman Catholic Church) engage in is morally irresponsible, in my judgment; it is often more the expression of moral passion than of careful research and rigorous theological and ethical argumentation.[23] The moral certitude of many church bodies and of individual Christian leaders is often more dogmatic than the opinions and policies of those they passionately oppose. Churches will have little

23. The 1983 Pastoral Letter on war and peace by the United States Conference of Catholic Bishops has received a great deal of public attention. This is not simply because it is a statement from leaders of a visible community in the United States, but also because of the thoroughness of the research, the openness to critical comment, the care of argumentation, and the recognition of areas of ambiguity that it manifests. Whether or not one agrees with its theology, appeals to papal authority, and its ethical conclusions, it can well serve as a model of intellectually responsible ethical reflection for all churches and other communities. See "The Challenge of Peace: God's Promise and Our Response," *Origins* (National Catholic Documentary Service) 13(1983), no. 1:1–32.

impact on social policy until they are more committed to difficult and serious academic work: becoming thoroughly informed about the complexities of the matters they address and developing sound theological and ethical arguments to support their proposals. They also need to recognize the probability of reasonable dissent from positions held, and to permit well-developed minority arguments to be heard.

It is also justifiable, as I have previously argued, for particular religious communities to have particular ways of life, ideals of conduct, and expectations of behavior that are consonant with their particular religious beliefs. In the example of classical sectarianism, the beliefs lead to a separation of the community from areas of public life and responsibility. That sort of theology and ethics cannot be defended on the basis of the present work. Within the bounds of the present work, however, there are claims upon persons who participate in the Christian community that are distinctive. One that I have often remarked on is that of the expectation, or indeed obligation, that Christians be ready voluntarily to deny their own individual and collective interests for the sake of the well-being of other persons, communities, and even of the natural world. This obligation is also borne out by general human experience. For Christians, however, this claim is very strong, for in the person and accounts of Jesus, who marks the particular historic identity of this community, there are poignant exemplifications in his life, activity, teachings, and death of what theocentric piety and fidelity call upon us to do.

We are participants in the patterns and processes of the interdependence of life. What are we to do? We are to relate ourselves and all things in a manner appropriate to their relations to God. From my theocentric perspective this is not achieved simply by looking to the biblical material to see what it claims God has commanded, though that is an ingredient. It requires attention to the divine ordering of life, and to the ends and values that are backed by the power and powers that bring life into being, sustain it, bear down upon it, and create conditions of possibility within it. It requires attention to the particular relationships and events, the patterns and processes of interdependence of life in which we are participants. "So little knows/Any, but God alone, to value right/The good before him. . . . " But we are agents who can judge what ought to be valued and how, what principles ought to guide conduct, what ends ought to be sought.

A Coda: God Will Be God

The history of religion is the history of human attempts to manage and manipulate the awesome power of God, who finally is beyond our capacities to know fully, to capture in human thoughts and words. It is the history of human efforts to nail down God's power and goodness, to avoid God's wrath and judgment. It is the history of efforts to control the times and places of God's presence, to create devices by which to make God serve our interests, to give God form and shape so that we can caress "him." Indeed, it is the history of human efforts to exercise sovereignty over God.

Much of religious life is a trivial and misguided effort to manage a sovereign power and will whose defining character is that it is beyond our manipulative control. Much of religion is practiced for its utility value to us. Much of worship attempts to make us feel good; many of our prayers are made without the qualification of "thy will be done." Much of contemporary life in the churches is an effort to determine our relation to God on our terms; to enlist God's support for our causes rather than to seek what is God's cause; to seek God's presence in what turns out to be in our favor and to forget or deny it in what turns out against us; to beg God's intervention in affairs in the hope that the inexorable limitations of our humanity can be overcome when it is by God's determination that we are bound to the limits of our finitude: of our capacities, of our bodies fated to rot. We want a God we can manage, a God who comes when beckoned, a God who permits us to say that "he" is here but not there; a God who supports our moral causes and destroys the forces we judge to be evil; a household God and a kitchen God who cares more for us and ours than "he" cares for others who suffer like we suffer, who fear like we fear. We desire to manage and manipulate the ultimate power that has brought the worlds into being, sustains them, bears down upon them, and determines their ultimate destiny. We want to shape God to look like us, to change "his" mind so it is in accord with ours. But such a god is not God.

We curse God when our desires are not fulfilled, when unbearable anguish comes upon us, when the forces we think are good are defeated by the forces we think are evil, when we grieve and are in the depths of despair. And well we might curse God, for "he" might be "speaking" to us. God might be signalling that "he" is the sovereign power and that our destiny and the destiny of the worlds are not in our hands. God might be signalling us that "he" is beyond manipulation by religious practices, that finally we must consent to God being God, that a god who is God cannot be manipulated by mortal human beings.

The desire to manipulate God is the temptation of religious persons.

But God will not be manipulated.
God will be God.

The history of our culture is largely the history of efforts to overcome the uncertainties of being merely human. It is the history of devising ways through politics and science, through military technology and medicine, through therapies and education to assure ourselves that we are sufficient unto ourselves, that we are the masters of our fate, that we can control the destiny of the world. It is the history of human efforts to overcome human limitations: the limits of bodies that waste away and die, of a planet that is exhaustible, of a species that has come only very lately in the development of creation and that will ultimately suffer extinction. It is the history of human efforts to become self-sufficient, to deny our boundedness and the limitations of our power. It is the history of suppressing the ambiguities and limits of human activity while basking in the glories of its capacities and achievements. It is the history of denying man's ultimate dependence on a power we cannot control, a source of goodness we did not and cannot create. It is the history of the denial of God by ignoring "him."

But culture is also the history of great human achievements. We can tap nuclear energy when oil seems to be depleting; we can build machines to keep hearts and lungs going when unassisted they would stop; we can devise systems by which the aged are pensioned and the young are educated. In many ways we do use our human capacities to control finite human destinies. We know how to control births; what man used to think was in God's plan or was accidental is now a matter of human choice. We know how to use words and pictures so that human desires and aspirations can be shaped. We can control our moods with wine and roses and with pills and electrical impulses into our brains. We can travel in hours distances that once took months, we can converse from the privacy of our homes to the privacy of homes in many parts of the world. We can put a human being on the moon, and we can learn the chemical components of the surface of Mars. We can blanket space with signals so that somewhere, sometime, someone might hear that we are on this little planet, and that we have evolved to find out if anyone is out there. We create varieties of music: folk and rock, chants and symphonies, ragas and dirges. Poetry, drama, novels, sculpture, and paintings enlarge our sensibilities and stimulate our imaginations.

No other living thing on earth has ever achieved such mastery over forces before which our ancestors stood in fear, in awe, and in a sense of helplessness and hopelessness. No other living thing on earth has enriched its existence with created beauty. Our achievements are glorious, and they are human achievements. Without human intelligence, intentions, efforts, ambition, these things would not be.

The desire to ignore God is the temptation of culture: the desire to deny ultimate dependence on power and powers man did not and cannot create, powers that sustain and bear down on us as well as create possibilities for human achievement.

But God will not be ignored or denied.
God will be God.

The human capacity to be participants in the patterns and processes of interdependence of life grounds our vocation to discern what God is enabling and requiring us to be and to do. The task of ethics is to use knowledge and intelligence to discern, under the inexorable conditions of finitude, how we are to relate ourselves and all things in a manner appropriate to our and their relations to God. It is to seek how to participate in nature and society, in history and culture, and in the ordering of ourselves so that human life is in the service of God, the power that brings all things into being, sustains them and bears down on them, and creates the conditions of possibility for newness and renewal. We are fated never to have the certainty we desire in the human venture. As Lincoln observed, "The ways of the Almighty are His own." God does not exist simply for the service of human beings. Human beings exist for the service of God.

God will not be manipulated.
God will not be ignored or denied.
God will be God.

Index